THE RULE OF LAW'S ANATOMY IN THE EU

This study, with its approach rooted in EU law and its clear focus on conceptual underpinnings, grapples with one of the most challenging questions facing constitutional lawyers today; namely, the rule of law. Drawing on the expertise of leading scholars and judges at the forefront of the question, it takes a dual approach. It opens by setting out the foundations of the rule of law, including legal certainty, democratic principles and judicial independence. It goes on to explore the protections that can be relied upon, from policy developments to human rights sanctions, and infringement actions. This is a rapidly developing question in EU constitutional law, so this masterful collection will be welcomed by both scholars and policy-makers in the field.

The Rule of Law's Anatomy in the EU

Foundations and Protections

Edited by
Allan Rosas
Juha Raitio
and
Pekka Pohjankoski

•HART•
OXFORD • LONDON • NEW YORK • NEW DELHI • SYDNEY

HART PUBLISHING
Bloomsbury Publishing Plc
Kemp House, Chawley Park, Cumnor Hill, Oxford, OX2 9PH, UK
1385 Broadway, New York, NY 10018, USA
29 Earlsfort Terrace, Dublin 2, Ireland

HART PUBLISHING, the Hart/Stag logo, BLOOMSBURY and the Diana logo are trademarks of Bloomsbury Publishing Plc

First published in Great Britain 2023

A catalogue record for this book is available from the British Library.

Library of Congress Cataloging-in-Publication data

Names: Rosas, Allan, editor. | Raitio, Juha, editor. | Pohjankoski, Pekka, editor.

Title: The rule of law's anatomy in the EU : foundations and protections / edited by Allan Rosas, Juha Raitio, and Pekka Pohjankoski.

Description: OXford, UK ; New York : Hart Publishing, An Imprint of Bloomsbury Publishing, 2023. | Includes bibliographical references and index. | Summary: "This masterful collection draws on the expertise of scholars and jurists on the place of the rule of law in the EU's constitutional order"—Provided by publisher.

Identifiers: LCCN 2023005473 | ISBN 9781509955077 (hardback) | ISBN 9781509955114 (paperback) | ISBN 9781509955091 (pdf) | ISBN 9781509955084 (Epub)

Subjects: LCSH: Rule of law—European Union countries.

Classification: LCC KJE5037 .R87 2023 | DDC 340.11—dc23/eng/20230403

LC record available at https://lccn.loc.gov/2023005473

ISBN: HB: 978-1-50995-507-7
ePDF: 978-1-50995-509-1
ePub: 978-1-50995-508-4

Typeset by Compuscript Ltd, Shannon

Acknowledgements

THE RULE OF law is a complex topic, not least in the context of the European Union (EU). Early on in the process of preparing this volume, we realised that approaching its theme benefits from adopting a broad view. To that end, we established the Helsinki Rule of Law Forum (HROLF), a group of experts – academics, judges, and other EU professionals – to discuss and analyse the existing rule-of-law challenges in today's Europe.

The origins of this book are in the collective reflections of the HROLF. Our heartfelt gratitude is to its esteemed members, including but not limited to all the contributors of this volume, who agreed to share their expertise with us. Similarly, the other speakers and panelists who participated in our seminars in 2021–22 provided invaluable insights on what the rule of law means in the legal order of the EU and beyond, contributing to the groundwork of this volume as well as to the 'Declaration on the Rule of Law in the European Union', annexed to this book.

The Government of Finland has consistently shown vision in defending the rule of law both at home and at the European level, particularly during the Presidency of the Council of the EU in 2019. The specific funding for the project 'The Rule of Law, Finland, and the European Union', provided from the Government's Analysis, Assessment and Research Activities (VNTEAS) enabled the work of the HROLF from February 2021 through June 2022.

While that funding cycle is over, the work on the rule of law is not finished. In this regard, our sincere thanks are extended to the Rule of Law Centre (*Oikeusvaltiokeskus*), hosted by the University of Helsinki, under whose auspices the work of the HROLF may continue.

Finally, it has been a pleasure to collaborate with Hart Publishing whose skilled professionals have ensured a swift and attentive production process.

Helsinki, 17 February 2023
The Editors

Contents

List of Contributors

Leonard F. M. Besselink is Emeritus Professor of Constitutional Law, University of Amsterdam

Steven Blockmans is Director of CEPS, the Brussels-based think tank, Visiting Professor at the College of Europe (Bruges and Natolin), Senior Fellow at ICDS (Tallinn) and Editor-in-Chief of the European Foreign Affairs Review

Sanja Bogojević is Fellow and Professor of Law at Lady Margaret Hall and the Faculty of Law, University of Oxford

Paul Craig is Emeritus Professor of English Law at St John's College and the Faculty of Law, University of Oxford

Xavier Groussot is Professor of EU Law at the Faculty of Law, Lund University

Inge Govaere is Professor of EU Law and Director of the Ghent European Law Institute (G.E.L.I.) at Ghent University, and Director of the European Legal Studies Department, College of Europe (Bruges)

Joni Heliskoski is Justice at the Supreme Administrative Court of Finland

Niilo Jääskinen is Judge at the Court of Justice of the European Union

Katalin Miklóssy is Head of Eastern European Studies at the Faculty of Humanities, University of Helsinki

Paul Nemitz is Principal Adviser on Justice Policy at the European Commission, and Visiting Professor, College of Europe (Bruges)

Pekka Pohjankoski is Researcher at the Faculty of Law, University of Helsinki

Juha Raitio is Professor of European Law at the Faculty of Law, University of Helsinki

Allan Rosas is former Armfelt Professor of Law, Åbo Akademi University, former Judge at the Court of Justice of the European Union, and former Deputy Director-General at the European Commission

Werner Schroeder is Professor and Director of the Department for European Law and Public International Law, University of Innsbruck

1

Introduction: The Rule of Law's Anatomy in the EU

ALLAN ROSAS, JUHA RAITIO AND PEKKA POHJANKOSKI

I. THE COMING OF AGE OF THE RULE OF LAW IN EU LAW

THE RULE OF law is foundational for the legal order of the European Union (EU). From very early on, legality, judicial protection, and fundamental rights have ranked among the building-blocks of European legal integration. However, it is only more recently that the EU has found itself thoroughly engaging with the concept of the rule of law, and its defence. The erosion of judicial independence, constraints on media pluralism, and the dismantlement of the checks and balances regarding constitutional democracy have become concerns in various Member States. In consequence, the Union has been forced to transform itself from an observer into a genuine rule of law actor. This transformation has not been easy, and it remains unfinished. It is complicated by the EU's limited constitutional powers to directly engage with matters related to the rule of law in Member States. Moreover, the different national traditions and ideas on how the rule of law is articulated, and understood, complicate discussions at the Union level. Against this backdrop, two questions continually arise. What does the rule of law mean in EU law? And how can the EU safeguard it within its constituent Member States?

This twin enquiry is at the heart of the present collection. It is the editors' view that, from the perspective of EU law, the concept of the rule of law as well as the methods to safeguard it within Member States are among the most consequential topics in the field of 'EU rule of law'. Under their umbrella, many of the thorny enquiries surrounding the rule of law in the EU legal order can be addressed. On the one hand, these include the conceptual interrelationship of the rule of law, democracy, and fundamental rights; the reconciliation of primacy of EU law and national constitutional identity; and the substantive dimension of the rule of law with links to 'illiberal' democracy, legal certainty, and judicial independence. On the other hand, protection of the rule of law covers the EU's policy on the rule of law, including not only mainstreaming it within substantive policies but also the active promotion of democracy; the infringement procedure and financial conditionality as tools for remedying backsliding in Member States, as well as reflecting on how the rule of law within the EU differs from its worldwide application in the Union's external relations, including within its foreign policy.

The rule of law as an EU law phenomenon has come of age. A former classic of legal philosophers, the rule of law is now a dynamic topic of EU law in its own right. It features in law school curricula, and much ink has been spilled on its analysis by scholars. It is no longer an obscure topic for EU lawyers, but part of the Union's constitutional landscape. The EU's approach to it has in recent years been the focus of monographs, collected volumes, as well as thematic journals.[1] The proliferation of rule-of-law literature and coverage on related issues means that the topic can hardly be covered in a single article, or by a single author. In the light of this development, the present work aims to bring together scholars and legal practitioners to engage in a collective reflection, albeit through their individual chapters, on the foundations and protections of the rule of law in the EU legal order. Besides their individual scholarly or practitioner's interest in the rule of law, the authors, as well as the editors, are members of the Helsinki Rule of Law Forum (HROLF), a community of researchers of EU law, whose work focuses particularly on issues related to the rule of law from an EU law perspective.[2]

A clearer idea of what the rule of law means in EU law is emerging. As it is consistently expressed in EU law, the rule of law presents substantive rather than purely formal characteristics. As such, it sets concrete obligations for the Member States, the content of which is being filled in by legislation and judicial practice, but the conceptual understanding of the rule of law in EU law is not settled yet. Until now, judicial independence has received the most attention in the practice of the European Court of Justice (ECJ) and, consequently, in scholarly commentary. However, equally relevant for the EU legal order are other aspects of the rule of law, which include, among many other components, the separation of powers and legal certainty. The ECJ has noted the constitutional significance of the rule of law as part of the Union's 'very identity'.[3] While the rule of law has reached a certain level of maturity as a subfield of EU law, arguably that field still remains relatively unsystematised, not least because of its constant evolution. To enhance our understanding of the nature of these legal phenomena, the present work's consecutive chapters explore the various parts of the rule of law's anatomy in the EU.

[1] See, for monographs, eg T Konstantinidis, *The Rule of Law in the European Union: The Internal Dimension* (Oxford, Hart Publishing, 2017), and M Kmezić, *EU Rule of Law Promotion: Judiciary Reform in the Western Balkans* (London and New York, Routledge, 2017). For edited collections, see eg W Schroeder (ed), *Strengthening the Rule of Law in Europe: From a Common Concept to Methods of Implementation* (Oxford, Hart Publishing, 2016); S Garben, I Govaere and P Nemitz (eds), *Critical Reflections on Constitutional Democracy in the European Union* (Oxford, Hart Publishing, 2019), U Belavusau and A Gliszczyńska-Grabias (eds), *Constitutionalism under Stress: Essays in Honour of Wojciech Sadurski* (Oxford, Oxford University Press, 2020), F Bignami (ed), *EU Law in Populist Times: Crises and Prospects* (Cambridge, Cambridge University Press, 2020). For thematic journals, see esp the *Hague Journal on the Rule of Law*, published by Springer.

[2] For more on the HROLF, see: helsinki.fi/rule-of-law. Annexed to this volume, readers will find the Helsinki Rule of Law Forum's 'A Declaration on the Rule of Law in the European Union', a consensus document drafted by a number of the forum's members.

[3] See eg Case C-156/21 *Hungary v Parliament and Council* ECLI:EU:C:2022:97, para 127.

II. SOMETHING BORROWED, SOMETHING NEW? THE CONCEPT OF THE RULE OF LAW FOR THE EU

The rule of law is a classic explanatory tool to describe the role, function, and limits of law in society. It is used to articulate the conditions for the existence and the 'flourishing of the legal order'[4] by jurisprudence and political theory alike. The concept is as old as it is contested. With its roots conventionally located deep in antiquity, its present-day meaning is the product of diverse developments, and attributing any precise meaning to the rule of law is bound to be contested.[5] Today, the rule of law is habitually approached from myriad perspectives including, besides history, its morality, the critique of the existing rule-of-law theories, or as part of a global rule of law.[6] The field of rule-of-law studies within EU law has mostly, so far, striven to keep pace with the fast emerging new legislative material and the ECJ's case law. As the dust is settling, EU law scholarship is taking stock of the rule of law in EU law from broader perspectives, even if much of the writing is still concerned with placing the new field within the existing discipline, including the major jurisprudential features of the EU legal order.

Aside from attempts to frame the rule of law as a global phenomenon, most scholarly literature is focused on the rule of law as a feature of the legal system of the nation state. This is where the rule of law in the EU parts ways with the conventional discussion. The EU is, notoriously, not a state, but a union of states. This renders the enquiry into the nature of the rule of law within the constitutional framework of such a union distinct from the traditional literature, which focuses on the national constitutional setting. The EU is structurally different from many states in that it is a federative union with only conferred powers, the impact of which is most visible in the limited powers of enforcement that the Union has over its constituent members. The composite nature of the EU's legal order, being autonomous but also inspired by the national legal orders of the 27 Member States, is equally significant for the formulation of the concept of the rule of law. Should there be a common minimum understanding of the rule of law? Is it an autonomous concept of EU law? From what elements does the EU's conceptual understanding of the rule of law stem?

Examining the anatomy of the rule of law in the EU requires detailed study. The present work invites the readers to join the metaphorical amphitheatre where this occurs, as the cover illustration with Padua's *teatro anatomico* suggests. The rule of law has received a statutory articulation, namely in Regulation 2020/2092.[7] But what is this 'definition' worth? It builds on the European Commission's work which,

[4] NW Barber, *The Principles of Constitutionalism* (Oxford, Oxford University Press, 2018) 85.

[5] J Waldron, 'The Rule of Law as an Essentially Contested Concept' in J Meierhenrich and M Loughlin (eds), *The Cambridge Companion to the Rule of Law* (Cambridge, Cambridge University Press, 2021).

[6] See, for a range of approaches, eg J Meierhenrich and M Loughlin (eds), *The Cambridge Companion to the Rule of Law* (Cambridge, Cambridge University Press, 2021).

[7] Regulation (EU, Euratom) 2020/2092 of the European Parliament and of the Council of 16 December 2020 on a general regime of conditionality for the protection of the Union budget [2020] OJ L433I/1.

in turn, is inspired by the case law of the ECJ. Although that case law is informed not only by the EU Treaties, but also the legal traditions of the Member States, the rule of law at the EU level struggles with the common dilemma in EU law: how to reconcile diversity with uniformity. The quest for a common understanding for the rule of law is entangled with basic issues such as the primacy of EU law, the fundamental political and constitutional structures of Member States which reflect their national identity, the division of powers between the Union and its members, as well as the justiciability of the Union's values. While a written articulation of the concept of the rule of law is useful to dissect its elements, the implications of providing a definition of the rule of law, and navigating its practical application, require further analysis.

III. SAFEGUARDING THE RULE OF LAW: PROACTIVE AND REACTIVE TOOLS

As a value common to the Member States, the rule of law is presumed to be shared throughout the EU. But if that presumption proves incorrect, what can the EU do? The rule of law is operationalised within EU law in many ways. To the extent that its foundational elements are governed by concrete instruments of EU law, upholding the value basis can occur through use of the constitutional procedures provided by the EU Treaties. Most obviously, breaches of the Union's values can be addressed under Article 7 of the Treaty on the European Union (TEU) and failures to fulfil membership obligations can be tackled in accordance with Articles 258 to 260 of the Treaty on the Functioning of the European Union (TFEU). Breaches of the rule of law may, however, reach deep into the constitutional structures at the national level, which can reveal tension between the conferred powers of the EU and those retained by the Member States. The legislation on the financial 'rule of law' conditionality of EU spending strives to provide a solution which is both legitimate and effective, but the practical operation of this new tool remains a testing ground.

While the Union has various legal instruments at its disposal to take corrective action if Member States disregard principles of the rule of law, each instrument comes with inconveniences. These instruments, aimed at conflict resolution, can in reality lead to heightened political tension. A further common difficulty with all the instruments in the Union's 'enforcement' toolkit is that they are used to effect structural changes after the troublesome developments have already taken place. Therefore, not only do they bring the Union and the Member State in question into conflict, but they are also fundamentally reactive. However, to build or rebuild sustainable rule-of-law environments within Member States, systemic change is needed from within. It is with this aim as its lodestar that the Union has recently increased its spending on programmes which proactively support the rule of law in Member States. The paradigm shift, which nevertheless should not detract from the Union's effective enforcement of EU law, is to be welcomed as a complementary remedy. Considering the magnitude of the issues at stake, namely the foundations of the rule of law in the Union's constituent states, the proactive approach to building the conditions for the legal orders to prosper nationally may have to intensify in the future.

IV. STRUCTURE OF THE WORK

The present work is divided into two parts. The first part concerns the conceptual foundations of the rule of law in the EU, with Chapters two to seven. In this part, the authors examine themes such as the rule of law's relationship, and overlap, with democracy and fundamental rights, illiberal democracy, legal certainty, national constitutional identity, as well as judicial independence. The second part, Chapters eight to fourteen, is on the protections that the rule of law enjoys in the EU, both proactive and reactive. These chapters explore, besides the EU's rule of law policy and methods of enforcement, the challenges in rule-of-law policing as regards authoritarian governments, as well as the external dimension of the rule of law.

The opening chapter by Allan Rosas examines the conceptual relationship between democracy and the rule of law. Arguing that they are rather to be seen as 'Siamese twins' than 'odd bedfellows', Rosas concludes that the two concepts overlap, and even when no direct overlap exists, they are nonetheless interdependent. Following the conceptual overview, the chapter furthermore assesses the significance of political rights enshrined in the European human rights instruments, in particular the European Convention on Human Rights (ECHR), for the rule of law and democracy.

Paul Craig's chapter looks at the rule of law discussion in EU law from the perspectives of responsibility, independence, and rights. He first discusses what can be expected of the EU as a rule-of-law actor, considering its objectives and powers. He then considers why judicial independence is central for the rule of law both as a general matter and specifically in the EU. He finally reflects on the issue of fundamental rights as an ingredient of various conceptions of the rule of law, and on how the EU's legal system fits these conceptions.

In their chapter, Sanja Bogojević and Xavier Groussot analyse the issues of illiberalism and 'rule by law' from the perspective of the EU legal order. They present the 'people' and 'legalism' as the two canons of illiberal democracy to which recourse is typically had by populists. Following an analysis of these concepts, the chapter looks at the EU's response to the crises in Poland and Hungary and assesses the effectiveness of that response in relation to the challenge that illiberalism poses for the EU.

Juha Raitio looks in his chapter at the related concepts of the rule of law and legal certainty. Positing first legal certainty as a component of the rule of law, he then analyses the content of the two concepts in EU law. The presentation is followed by a theoretical enquiry into whether both the rule of law and legal certainty can be approached as 'thick' concepts with material content. The author argues that both concepts can indeed be understood as having both formal and substantive elements. As far as legal certainty in concerned, Raitio concludes that the 'thick' version of legal certainty can be related to the conceptual scale for weighing up and balancing between predictability and acceptability, between formal justice and material fairness, in legal decision-making.

In his chapter Leonard Besselink reflects on the relationship of the primacy of EU law, national constitutional identity, and the rule of law. Describing various forms of constitutional review directed at EU law, he analyses how the respective rules of conflict resolution in the EU and the Member States should be applied together. Besselink also relates the well-known 'thin'–'thick' dichotomy on the rule of law to his analysis of primacy, arguing that the latter concept cannot be simply based on a formal hierarchy which disregards constitutional values.

Niilo Jääskinen provides an overview of the minimum requirements of judicial independence and impartiality as they result from the case law of the ECJ. Presenting first the primary law bases for the independence of justice, he then proceeds to identify such requirements in the case law, particularly as regards the irremovability of judges, their appointment procedures, and their disciplinary and civil liability regimes. On this basis, Jääskinen reflects on the cumulative impact of the ECJ's case law with particular reference to an emerging EU law notion of 'judgeship under the rule of law'.

Werner Schroeder argues in his chapter that the EU needs an 'active rule of law policy'. He reasons that whereas the rule of law and the other values contained in Article 2 TEU define the EU's constitutional identity, Article 3(1) and (6) TEU, in conjunction with Article 2 TEU, indicate that the rule of law is not only a constitutional principle but gives the Union a mandate to shape its policies accordingly. Thus, the Union should actively promote and pursue the rule of law as one of its core values. He then explains how the Union can and should take positive steps to strengthen and consolidate the rule of law in the Member States by making use of its sectoral law-making competences.

In his chapter, Paul Nemitz discusses how to proactively safeguard the rule of law in the EU. For him, the rule of law and the independence of the judiciary can only be secured in a democracy. As remedies, he proposes that the EU should invest more resources in protecting and strengthening democracy in Member States, and that the Commission should adopt a 'democracy mainstreaming' strategy to systematically seek to insert space for participatory democracy in the implementation of EU law by Member States, including an evaluation of the effects on democracy in impact assessments. Finally, he argues that, as a follow up to the Conference on the Future of Europe, the Union should work on a European Charter for Democracy which would strengthen the role of democracy in the EU.

Joni Heliskoski's chapter critically examines the feasibility of using the infringement procedure as a tool for enforcing the rule of law against Member States. To that end, he assesses, first, the Commission's policy of deploying the infringement procedure in the context of 'rule of law' violations, and evaluates the coherence of this practice. He then presents and reviews the scholarly literature advocating a greater role for the Commission and the use of the infringement procedure in this regard. As Heliskoski finds some of the scholarly propositions unhelpful, his chapter sheds light on how to reconcile the law and the institutional practice with some of the suggestions made by scholars.

Pekka Pohjankoski's chapter discusses the constitutional limits to 'rule-of-law conditionality' in EU law. After outlining the EU's rule-of-law conditionality tools, his chapter enquires whether the Conditionality Regulation 2020/2092 provides a carrot or a stick; that is, a constitutionally permissible mechanism to support the rule of law, or a punitive sanctioning tool. The chapter examines the concept of a 'sufficiently direct' link between alleged breaches of rule-of-law principles and the EU's financial interests which are affected in consequence. Based on an analysis of prior ECJ case law at the origin of the notion, he argues that the 'breach–money link' is an essential factor in assessing the constitutional propriety of rule-of-law conditionality in the framework of the Conditionality Regulation.

Katalin Miklóssy's chapter problematises the EU's conditionality policy from the perspective of Hungary. She argues that the Hungarian administration displays legal flexibility and fluid administrative practices which have served the powerholders in their conflicts with the EU. Her analysis concentrates on three central aspects of this practice, namely the institutional re-arrangements regarding the use of EU funds, competition regulations for EU tendering procedures, and the restrictions on the 'elbow-room' of regional and local self-government bodies, which are the end-users of EU funds. The chapter, moreover, highlights how the Hungarian case has profoundly influenced the evolution of the EU's rule-of-law instruments ever since 2011, and discusses the effects of the Covid-19 pandemic on the rule of law.

Inge Govaere's chapter enquires to what extent the rule of law is commensurate in the EU's internal and external legal spheres. Taking account of differences in treaty language, as well as the different situations around the globe, she presents a frame of reference with which to assess the EU's external action regarding third states which do not share the EU's value basis regarding a thick understanding of the rule of law, democracy, and fundamental rights. She argues that one size does not necessarily fit all situations in the EU's external sphere, but that the EU should nonetheless be consistent, albeit pragmatic, in its role as an international rule of law actor.

Finally, in his chapter, Steven Blockmans takes stock of the EU's still-recent 'Magnitsky Act', the Global Human Rights Sanctions Regime (GHRSR). He assesses the practical operation of the sanctioning instrument and how it may contribute to uphold the rule of law in serious cases of human rights violations in third countries. Besides outlining and analysing the content and features of the GHRSR as an international rule-of-law device for the EU, his contribution also enquires into how well the sanctioning mechanism responds to the rule-of-law concerns which could be raised regarding its own operation.

V. THE RULE OF LAW, THE EU, AND THE WIDER WORLD

This work is about the rule of law in the EU legal order. That order encompasses, besides the internal operation of the EU's legal system, also its external relations. The world outside the EU is less secure than before. Russia's war of aggression against Ukraine has cast the foundations of the rule-based international order into sharp relief, both within Europe and outside it. Being itself constructed upon treaties, the EU's existence and its interests are fundamentally premised on the respect of the rule-based international order. While the impact of the war at the Union's doorstep has overshadowed some of the internal rule-of-law issues within the EU, it is the view of the editors of this volume that, in the end, the EU's concern with the rule of law should remain unwavering, whether its immediate object be outside the Union or within it. At its core, the rule of law is black and white.

Yet, many times the exact meaning of the rule of law is murky, especially outside the EU. The Union's external action is guided by the EU's values, including the rule of law. That said, the practical operation of the rule of law in the EU's external action at times differs from the internal sphere. It is worthwhile to enquire to what extent the conceptual understanding of the rule of law can be the same inside the EU and in the work of the Union in the wider world. And what room is there for the rule of law in all areas of the EU's Common Foreign and Security Policy (CFSP)? In its external relations, the EU is caught between its familiar challenge of living up to its values and standards and its need to be an effective actor internationally. Outside its own jurisdiction, the EU is engaged in a rule-of-law dialogue which is fundamentally different from its internal discussions.

What is clear, though, is that to understand the rule of law both within and outside the EU, one cannot regard it solely through the prism of the old doctrines developed within the nation state. Whether it be within the EU's internal constitutional order or as part of its external relations, gaining that understanding requires investigating the Union's particular anatomy. The multilayered legal order which governs today's Europe is complex, and so are the basic questions regarding the rule of law within it. Analytical approaches are needed to clarify its intricacies. That being the case, it is the hope of the editors that this work may contribute, however modestly, to shining light on that complexity. By so doing, it is the aim of this volume to enhance our understanding of the EU legal order and thereby help find ways forward to preserve a Union based on the rule of law.

Part I

Foundations

2

Democracy and the Rule of Law: Odd Bedfellows or Siamese Twins?

ALLAN ROSAS

I. DEMOCRACY, HUMAN RIGHTS AND THE RULE OF LAW: A EUROPEAN TRINITY

EVEN A CURSORY look especially at European legal texts and pronouncements will reveal that the concepts of democracy, human rights (or fundamental rights[1]) and the rule of law often go together. A well-known example is to be found in Article 2 of the Treaty on European Union (TEU), according to which the Union is founded on the values of respect for, inter alia, 'democracy', 'the rule of law' and 'respect for human rights'.[2] A comparison with the Treaty establishing the European Economic Community (Treaty of Rome) of 1957 demonstrates a marked difference between the two texts: The Treaty of Rome contains no comparable values list, only a short assertion in its Preamble that the founding States were '[r]esolved to strengthen the safeguards of peace and liberty by establishing this combination of forces'.

In the aftermath of the Second World War, it was largely left to the Council of Europe, established in 1949, to focus on the value foundations of European cooperation and integration. The horrors of the 1930s and the ensuing war called for resolute language and action to herald a new era. That there is a link between democracy, human rights and the rule of law was made explicit in both the Statute of the Council of Europe and the European Convention on Human Rights (ECHR).[3] Article 3 of the

[1] The concept of human rights appears predominantly in the context of international conventions, while fundamental rights is the preferred concept in constitutional settings such as national constitutional bills of rights and the EU Charter of Fundamental Rights: see, eg A Rosas and L Armati, *EU Constitutional Law: An Introduction*, 3rd edn (Oxford, Hart Publishing, 2018) 160.

[2] Consolidated Version of the Treaty on European Union [2016] OJ C202/13. Article 2 TEU also refers to' human dignity', 'freedom' and 'equality'. It is here assumed that these concepts can be grouped under the heading of human rights (or fundamental rights). In this vein, the EU Charter of Fundamental Rights covers both 'human dignity' (art 1) as well as several rights appearing under the headings of 'freedoms' (Title II, arts 6 to 19) and 'equality' (Title III, arts 20 to 26).

[3] Statute of the Council of Europe, ETS 1 (adopted 5 May 1949, entry into force 3 August 1949); Convention for the Protection of Human Rights and Fundamental Freedoms (adopted 4 November 1950, entry into force 3 September 1953).

Statute provides that every Member State 'must accept the principles of the rule of law and of the enjoyment by all persons within its jurisdiction of human rights and fundamental freedoms'. The Preamble of the Statute also refers to democracy, stating that 'individual freedom, political liberty and the rule of law' are 'principles which form the basis of genuine democracy'.

As to the ECHR, its Preamble reaffirms the conviction of the signatory governments to the effect that fundamental freedoms are best maintained 'on the one hand by an effective political democracy and on the other by a common understanding and observance of the Human Rights upon which they depend'. In the following preambular paragraph, the signatories recall that they are European governments which are 'like-minded and have a common heritage of political traditions, ideals, freedom and the rule of law'. The case law of the European Court of Human Rights (ECtHR) brings out the interdependence of the concepts of democracy and the rule of law,[4] seen through the lens of human rights. That the ECHR, together with many other human rights conventions, also contains several substantive provisions of direct relevance for democracy and the rule of law will be elaborated on later, in the context of a discussion of overlap between the three concepts.

It is beginning with the Treaty of Maastricht (1992) that the value foundations of the European Union (EU) have found more explicit expression in amendments to the basic Treaties, particularly those introduced by the Treaty of Lisbon (2007). Apart from Article 2 TEU already mentioned above, the Preamble to the EU Charter of Fundamental Rights recognises that the Union 'is based on the principles of democracy and the rule of law'. The 2020 Commission report on the rule-of-law situation in the EU states that '[t]he European Union is based on a set of shared values, including fundamental rights, democracy and the rule of law'[5] and this is seconded by a similar statement in the Commission's Democracy Action Plan of the same year.[6] The new 'Conditionality Regulation' relating to respect for the rule of law with a view to protecting the Union budget[7] – the legality of which was upheld by the European Court of Justice (ECJ) in two judgments of 16 February 2022[8] – contains several references not only to the rule of law as such but also to the links which exist between

[4] E Steiner, 'The Rule of Law in the Jurisprudence of the European Court of Human Rights' in W Schroeder (ed), *Strengthening the Rule of Law in Europe* (Oxford, Hart Publishing, 2016) 135 at 140. To mention but one classic example from case law, in its judgment in *Klass and Others v Germany*, judgment of 8 September 1978, Application no 5029/71, para 55, the ECtHR observed that the rule of law is 'one of the fundamental principles of a democratic society'.

[5] Communication from the Commission to the European Parliament, the Council, the European Economic and Social Committee and the Committee of the Regions, *The rule of law situation in the European Union*, COM(2020) 580 final of 30 September 2020 (*2020 Rule of Law Report*).

[6] Communication from the Commission to the European Parliament, the Council, the European Economic and Social Committee and the Committee of the Regions, COM(2020) 790 final of 3 December 2020 (*European Democracy Action Plan*), where it is observed that '[d]emocracy, the rule of law and fundamental rights are the foundations on which the European Union is based'.

[7] Regulation (EU, Euratom) 2020/2092 of the European Parliament and of the Council of 16 December 2020 on a general regime of conditionality for the protection of the Union budget [2020] OJ LI 433/1 (*Regulation 2020/2092*).

[8] Cases C-156/21 *Hungary v Parliament and Council* ECLI:EU:C:2022:97 and C-157/21 *Poland v Parliament and Council* ECLI:EU:C:2022:98.

the rule of law, democracy and fundamental rights. In its definition of the rule of law, the Regulation (Article 2) states that the rule of law 'shall be understood having regard to the other Union values and principles enshrined in Article 2 TEU'. In a recital (3), it is observed that the rule of law requires that all political powers act within the constraints set out by law, 'in accordance with the values of democracy and the respect for fundamental rights', while another recital (6) states that respect for the rule of law 'is intrinsically linked to respect for democracy and for fundamental rights'.

The fundamental nature of these values is also evident from the case law of the ECJ, which refers to one or the other of the said values as forming part of the very foundations of the European Union legal order.[9] True, while fundamental rights and, since the judgment in *Les Verts*,[10] the rule of law are often referred to by the Court, the concept of democracy has figured less in its case law. But the situation may be changing.[11] The Court has also recognised not only that the fundamental right to a fair trial is of cardinal importance as a guarantee that the rights which individuals derive from EU law will be protected but also 'that the values common to the Member States set out in Article 2 TEU, in particular the value of the rule of law, will be safeguarded'.[12]

As shown by the above citations from some basic European instruments as well as ECtHR and ECJ case law, it is widely recognised that there is a close link between democracy, human rights and the rule of law. Given that there is overlap between these three values (concrete examples will be given below) and it is also arguable that safeguarding any one of the three presupposes respect for the two others as well, one can speak of a 'tripod', or preferably 'trinity', formed by them.[13] Such a 'trinity' is characteristic for what has been called 'constitutional', 'liberal' or 'pluralist' democracy, or, to cite the Preamble of the Statute of the Council of Europe referred to above, 'genuine' democracy.[14] One can also refer to the degree of 'competitiveness' of a democratic system, as a complement to its degree of 'inclusiveness' (the extent

[9] See, eg Case C-621/18 *Wightman and Others v Secretary of State for Exiting the European Union* ECLI:EU:C:2018:999, 62 (referring mainly to 'liberty' and 'democracy'). See also Joined Cases C-402/05 P and C-415/05 P *Kadi and Al Barakaat International Foundation v Council and Commission* ECLI:EU:C:2008:461, paras 303 and 304 (referring to 'liberty', 'democracy' and 'respect for human rights and fundamental freedoms').

[10] In Case 294/83 *Parti écologiste 'Les Verts' v European Parliament* ECLI:EU:C:1986:166, para 23, the Court famously referred to the European Economic Community as a 'community based on the rule of law'.

[11] See, eg Joined Cases C-39/05 and C-52/05 *Sweden and Turco v Council* ECLI:EU:C:2008:374, paras 45–46, 67; Case C-621/18 *Wightman* (above n 9), para 62; C-418/18 *Puppinck and Others v Commission* ECLI:EU:C:2019:1113, 64–65; C-502/19 *Junqueras Vies* ECLI:EU:C:2019:1115, paras 63–64, 86.

[12] See, eg, Case C-216/18 *Minister for Justice and Equality v L.M.* ECLI:EU:C:2018:586, para 48; Case C-824/18 *A.B and Others v Krajowa Rada Sądownictwa and Others* ECLI:EU:C:2021:153, para 116; Case C-896/19 *Repubblika v Il-Prim Ministru* ECLI:EU:C:2021:311, para 51.

[13] A Rosas, 'The EU and the Rule of Law: A View from the European Court of Justice' in Tribunal constitucional, *Estudos em homenagem au Conselheiro Presidente Joaquim Sousa Ribeiro*, Vol II (Lisbon, Almenida, 2019) 1312. I prefer to see the relation between the three concepts as a 'trinity' rather than 'tripod', to capture the dynamic and to some extent even dialectic nature of the relationship. The word 'tripod' seems to suggest a more static relationship between three legs.

[14] On the concept of constitutional democracy see S Garben, I Govaere and P Nemitz (eds), *Critical Reflections on Constitutional Democracy in the European Union* (Oxford, Hart Publishing, 2019).

to which the principle of political equality of citizens is respected).[15] In the following, I shall use the concept of *liberal* democracy to denote systems that are both inclusive and competitive.

Nor has the close link which exists between democracy, human rights and the rule of law gone unnoticed at the universal level: the Preamble to the Universal Declaration of Human Rights of 1948 states that 'it is essential, if man is not to be compelled to have recourse, as a last resort, to rebellion against tyranny and oppression, that human rights should be protected by the rule of law'.[16] The concept of human rights here includes some fundamental guarantees of democracy, as the Declaration refers both to political rights, such as the right to vote (Article 21), and political freedoms, such as freedom of opinion and expression (Article 19) and freedom of assembly and association (Article 20).[17] And according to a preambular paragraph appearing in several United Nations (UN) General Assembly resolutions since 2006, the Assembly has reaffirmed 'that human rights, the rule of law and democracy are interlinked and mutually reinforcing and that they belong to the universal and indivisible core values and principles of the United Nations'.[18] These resolutions have been adopted without a vote.

That said, especially at the universal level, the idea that democracy, human rights and the rule of law presuppose each other is not accepted by everybody, or at least not without reservations. In a report of the UN Secretary-General of 2004, the rule of law was characterised as a 'principle of governance', in which all persons, institutions and entities, including the State itself, are accountable to laws which, inter alia, 'are consistent with international human rights norms and standards', and which also require, inter alia, the 'separation of powers', 'participation in decision-making' and 'procedural and legal transparency'.[19] However, a declaration of a high-level meeting of the General Assembly on the rule of law at the national and international levels, held in September 2012,[20] does not contain the same broad definition of the rule of law, and the references in the 2004 report to the separation of powers and the participation in decision-making, in particular, have been omitted.[21] True, the Declaration *does* reproduce the general passage appearing in the annual rule-of-law resolutions

[15] The notions of inclusiveness and competitiveness are borrowed from Robert Dahl: see A Rosas, 'Democracy and Human Rights' in A Rosas and J Helgesen (eds), *Human Rights in a Changing East-West Perspective* (London, Pinter Publishers, 1990) 17, at 25, 38–47.

[16] UN General Assembly resolution 217 A (1948).

[17] For commentaries on these and other provisions, see G Alfredsson and A Eide (eds), *The Universal Declaration of Human Rights: A Common Standard of Achievement* (The Hague, Martinus Nijhoff Publishers, 1999).

[18] See the third preambular paragraph of UN General Assembly resolution 61/39 on 'The rule of law at the national and international levels' (4 December 2006). See also, eg UN General Assembly resolution 75/141 (15 December 2020) on the same subject, and the first preambular paragraph of UN General Assembly resolution 75/199 on 'Education for democracy' (21 December 2020).

[19] Report of the Secretary-General, 'The rule of law and transitional justice in conflict and post-conflict societies', 23 August 2004, UN doc S/2004/616, 6.

[20] Declaration of the High-level Meeting of the General Assembly on the Rule of Law at the National and International Levels, adopted by UN General Assembly resolution 67/1 (24 September 2012).

[21] See N Arajärvi, 'The Core Requirements of the International Rule of Law in the Practice of States' (2021) 13 *Hague Journal on the Rule of Law* 173, 180.

referred to above, namely that human rights, the rule of law and democracy are interlinked and mutually reinforcing and that they belong to the universal and indivisible core values and principles of the United Nations.[22] Being 'interlinked' and 'mutually reinforcing', however, does not necessarily imply outright interdependence.

The idea that the three concepts are interlinked has developed only gradually, with many ups and downs. While it can be traced back, inter alia, to the constitutional, 'liberal' strands discernible in French revolutionary thought of the late eighteenth century, the so-called Montagnard strand which coalesced around *Robespierre* (1758–93) put emphasis on the 'will of the people' (as defined by its proponents), at the expense of fundamental rights and the rule of law. This led to the sidestepping of a new constitution based on the idea of constitutional democracy and instead to a reign of terror, directed against real or perceived political opponents branded as 'enemies of the people'.[23] It goes without saying that the idea of liberal democracy was flagrantly absent also from fascist and Soviet-style communist thought and practice of the twentieth century.

As demonstrated throughout this book, we are today witnessing a reluctance even among some EU Member States' governments and political movements to accept that democracy and the rule of law are interdependent. The notions of 'populism' and/or 'illiberal' democracy are often used to depict such tendencies.[24] They seem to be based on the idea that there is tension, to say the least, between the requirements of human rights/fundamental rights and the rule of law, on the one hand, and democracy as majority rule, on the other. Human rights/fundamental rights and the rule of law are then seen rather as 'odd bedfellows' to democracy, as they may constitute impediments to the articulation and realisation of the 'will of the people' and/or the 'interests of the nation' (whether the 'will of the people' or the 'interests of the nation' correspond to a genuine majority opinion may, as will be elaborated below, depend, inter alia, on the electoral system). To give an example of an overt explication of 'illiberal' democracy, the Hungarian Prime Minister, Viktor Orbán, has heralded a 'reorganisation' of the Hungarian state, 'in contrast to the liberal state organisation logic'. The illiberal state 'does not reject the fundamental principles of liberalism such as freedom … but it does not make this ideology the central element of state organisation, but instead includes a different, special, national approach'.[25]

[22] UN General Assembly resolution 67/1 (above n 20), 5.

[23] See, in particular, J Israel, *Revolutionary Ideas: An Intellectual History of the French Revolution from the Rights of Man to Robespierre* (Princeton NJ, Princeton University Press, 2014), *passim*. See also A Rosas, 'Democracy, Fundamental Rights and the Rule of Law: Some Historical Observations' in K Szczepanowska-Kozłowska (ed), *Professor Marek Safjan Znany I nieznany: Ksiega jubileuszowa z okazji sidemdziesiatych urodzin* (Warszawa, CH Beck, 2020), 383.

[24] See, eg C Pinelli, 'The Rise of Populism and the Malaise of Democracy' in Garben, Govaere and Nemitz (above n 14), 28 at 40–41; U Belavusau and A Gliszczynska-Grabias (eds), *Constitutionalism under Stress* (Oxford, Oxford University Press, 2020). See also S Levitsky and D Ziblatt, *How Democracies Die: What History Reveals About Our Future* (London, Penguin Books, 2019), 22.

[25] C Toth, *Budapest Beacon*, 29 July 2014, Speech of 26 July 2014 at the XXV Bálványos Free Summer University and Youth Camp, Baile Tusnad, budapestbeacon.com/full-text-of-viktor-orbans-speech-at-baile-tusnad-tusnadfurdo-of-26-july-2014/.

In any case, and independently of the question of 'illiberal' democracy, it is incontestable that the precise way the three concepts are interlinked and interact, and the degree to which they presuppose each other, merit further reflection and discussion. The following discussion will focus on the relationship between the rule of law and democracy. At the same time, the overlap which exists between human rights/fundamental rights and the rule of law, and between them and democracy, implies that human rights/fundamental rights cannot be left out of the equation.[26]

II. DISTINGUISHING THE THREE CONCEPTS AND CONCEPTUAL OVERLAP

Determining the extent to which democracy, human rights/fundamental rights and the rule of law overlap conceptually requires an idea of how each of these concepts should be defined, seen separately. To take an example, in a 2011 report on the rule of law issued by the European Commission for Democracy through Law (Venice Commission),[27] the 'core elements' of the rule of law are said to include not only such notions as legality, legal certainty, prohibition of arbitrariness and access to justice before independent and impartial courts but also '[r]espect for human rights' and '[n]on-discrimination and equality before the law'. The principle of legality again is said to include 'a transparent, accountable and democratic process of enacting law'.[28] It is evident that if respect for the rule of law requires full respect for all human rights, the overlap between the two concepts would be significant, and if respect for human rights requires respect for all elements of the rule of law, they would converge entirely. Likewise, if respect for the rule of law requires 'a transparent, accountable and democratic process of law', it would be arguable that a chunk of the principle of democracy would be covered by the need to respect the rule of law.

It is assumed in the following that each of the three concepts has their own substance or at least a core substance which makes it unique as a distinct concept. It is interesting to note that in a Rule of Law Checklist, adopted by the Venice Commission in March 2016,[29] the main benchmarks that are listed are 'legality', 'legal certainty', 'prevention of abuse of powers', 'equality before the law and non-discrimination' and 'access to justice', without separate reference to respect for human rights in general. On the other hand, the link between the rule of law and the democratic nature of the legislative process made in the 2011 report has been maintained: in the context of the main benchmark of 'legality', it is recommended, inter alia, that the law-making powers of the executive be restrained in favour of the supremacy of the legislature and

[26] On the relationship between human rights and democracy see also Chapter 3 by Paul Craig in this book.

[27] 'Report on the Rule of Law', adopted by the Venice Commission at its 86th plenary session (Venice, 25–26 March 2011), CDL-AD(2011)003rev. The Commission is the Council of Europe's advisory body on constitutional matters, consisting of experts designated by the Member States but acting in their individual capacity.

[28] ibid 41.

[29] Rule of Law Checklist, adopted by the Venice Commission at its 106th Plenary Session (Venice, 11–12 March 2016), endorsed by the Ministers' Deputies at the 1263rd Meeting (6–7 September 2016), Council of Europe, Study No 711/2013, CDL-AD(2016)007rev.

that the process for enacting laws be 'transparent, accountable, inclusive and democratic'.[30] This reference to the importance of the legislative process seems directly relevant for the principle of legality, a core element of the rule of law, and does not amount to merging the concepts of democracy and the rule of law more generally.

While the Rule of Law Reports of the European Commission, too, recognise that there are links between the rule of law, democracy and fundamental rights, they do tend to avoid a complete overlap. A Communication relating to a new framework to strengthen the rule of law of 2014, while drawing upon the Venice Commission's earlier definitions, does not mention respect for human rights as such.[31] The European Commission's first annual Rule of Law Report of 2020 makes an effort to describe, if not veritably define, the rule of law by stating, inter alia, that it 'includes principles such as legality, implying a transparent, accountable, democratic and pluralistic process for enacting laws'.[32] The reference to a democratic legislative process is similar to the one contained in the Venice Commission documents mentioned above.

The 2021 report, in listing the 'key principles of the rule of law', is largely based on a similar understanding of the rule of law: there are obvious links between this concept and those of democracy and fundamental rights, but there is no complete overlap between them; the rule of law, then, relates above all to the principle of legality and certain requirements for enacting, applying, interpreting and enforcing the law.[33] Democracy as a concept in itself is addressed in another Commission document, namely the above-mentioned European Democracy Action Plan, launched in 2020.[34]

It is in this stricter sense that the concept of the rule of law will be understood here. Not all elements of the concepts of democracy or human rights/fundamental rights will be seen as part of the concept of the rule of law.[35] That said, it is not possible or indeed desirable to establish watertight barriers between the three concepts. The rule of law is not understood as a purely formal concept but is viewed as containing some substantive elements, too (not to mention the fact that the borderline between formal and substantive requirements is not clear-cut).[36]

Democracy, as such, is about political participation by citizens in public decision-making, notably participation in elections, based on the principle of equal rights of all members of the adult population. According to the EU Democracy Action Plan, democracy 'allows citizens to shape laws and public policies at European, national,

[30] ibid 13.

[31] Communication from the Commission to the European Parliament and the Council, A new EU framework to strengthen the Rule of Law, COM(2014) 158 final of 11 March 2014, 4. See also J Polakiewicz and J Sandvig, 'The Council of Europe and the Rule of Law' in Schroeder (above n 4), 115, 120–121.

[32] *2020 Rule of Law Report* (above n 5), 1.

[33] Communication from the Commission to the European Parliament, the Council, the European Economic and Social Committee and the Committee of the Regions, *The rule of law situation in the European Union*, COM(2021) 700 final of 20 July 2021 (*2021 Rule of Law Report*), 1.

[34] *European Democracy Action Plan* (above n 6).

[35] For a discussion on different conceptions of the rule of law and the relationship between the rule of law and democracy see eg D Wohlwend, *The International Rule of Law: Scope, Subjects, Requirements* (Cheltenham, Edward Elgar, 2021), 2, 19, 25–26, who also advocates the separation of the two concepts.

[36] On the distinction between formal and substantive requirements, see eg Wohlwend (above n 35).

regional and local levels' and 'requires safeguards, checks and balances, and institutions that fulfil their roles and uphold the rules of pluralistic democratic debate'.[37] The EU Treaty contains a whole title (Title II) on 'Provisions on Democratic Principles'. These include provisions on the principle of equality of citizens (Article 9), a reference to 'representative democracy' and the direct representation of citizens in the European Parliament and indirect representation through the governments of the Member States (the latter being 'democratically accountable to their national Parliaments or to their citizens') and the right of every citizen to participate in the democratic life of the Union (Article 10). There are, furthermore, some specific provisions relating to participatory and deliberate democracy (Article 11) as well as the role of national parliaments (Article 12).[38]

As far as human rights/fundamental rights are concerned, it suffices to note that the main components of internationally recognised human rights are listed in universal (such as the Universal Declaration of Human Rights of 1948 and the International Covenants of 1966) and regional human rights instruments (such as the ECHR) while the main sources of fundamental rights are to be found in the EU Charter of Fundamental Rights as well as in national constitutional bills of rights.

Our three main concepts having been described each in their own right, an overview can be provided of the areas where they clearly overlap. It should be asked, first, to what extent there may be direct conceptual overlap between democracy and the rule of law. As was noted above, both the Venice Commission and European Commission reports bring out the idea that the principle of legality, which is a core element of the rule of law, requires a 'transparent, accountable, democratic and pluralistic process for enacting laws'.[39] It is proposed here to accept this meaning of the principle of legality, given that the requirement of abidance by the law rests on the assumption that the law is legitimate. Enforcing rules enacted by a tyrant is not applying the principle of the rule of law but that of 'rule by the law'. That said, the concept of the rule of law does not in itself seem to contain elaborate and detailed requirements of a democratic process but only a bare minimum. More far-reaching requirements follow from the concepts of democracy and political rights as human/fundamental rights.

While the direct conceptual overlap between democracy and the rule of law thus seems rather limited, the situation is different with respect to the relationship between democracy and human rights/fundamental rights. This is because a modern concept of human rights includes the right of political participation (political rights), including the right to vote and to be elected, which at the same time is an essential ingredient of democracy. Relevant international human rights provisions include Article 21 of the Universal Declaration of Human Rights of 1948, Article 25 of the International Covenant on Civil and Political Rights and Article 3 of the Protocol to the ECHR of 1952 (Protocol No 1).[40] Although the EU is not a contracting party

[37] *2020 Rule of Law Report* (above n 5), 1.

[38] See Rosas and Armati (above n 1), ch 9.

[39] The quotation is from the *2020 Rule of Law Report* of the European Commission (above n 5).

[40] Rosas (above n 15) 23–30. See also A Rosas, 'Article 21' in Alfredsson and Eide (eds), *The Universal Declaration of Human Rights: A Common Standard of Achievement* (The Hague, Martinus Nijhoff Publishers, 1999), 431.

to these instruments[41] they are of EU relevance as guidelines for determining and interpreting general principles of Union law.[42] The ECtHR has ruled that an EU Member State may be held responsible for violations of Article 3 of Protocol No 1 concerning elections to the European Parliament.[43]

It follows from these and other similar provisions, taken together, that (1) there should be regular, free and fair elections and that (2) in principle every citizen should have the right of political participation (universal suffrage). In the European context, Article 3 of Protocol No 1 obliges the High Contracting Parties 'to hold free elections at reasonable intervals by secret ballot, under conditions which will secure the free expression of the opinion of the people in the choice of the legislature' while Article 39(2) of the EU Charter provides that the members of the European Parliament 'shall be elected by direct universal suffrage in a free and secret ballot'. The ECtHR has held that Article 3 of Protocol No 1 not only imposes an obligation of the contracting state but also entails an individual right to vote and be elected.[44] To what extent do freedom of expression and other political freedoms overlap with the principle of democracy? It is here suggested that in its narrow sense, this principle does not completely overlap with the political freedoms, although some requirements concerning freedom of expression, freedom of assembly and freedom of association do follow from the requirement of free and fair elections.[45] The remainder of these freedoms, while they do not completely overlap with democracy, constitute necessary ingredients of a democratic system classified as a liberal democracy.[46]

Another essential ingredient of a constitutional democracy is that there are legal rules concerning elections and other forms of political participation which are transparent and predictable and contain guarantees for their application and enforcement – in short, some of the essential features of the rule of law. There is even more of a direct overlap between the rule of law and certain human rights/fundamental rights, namely the right to legal remedies and effective judicial protection, including access to court and the right to a fair trial. The close relation which exists between the value of the rule of law, mentioned in Article 2 TEU, the principle of effective judicial protection referred to in Article 19(1) TEU and the rights enshrined in Article 47 of the Charter of Fundamental Rights is underlined in recent ECJ case law.[47] In the ECHR, Articles 6 (access to court and right to a fair trial) and 13 (right to effective remedies) are particularly important as key ingredients of the rule of law.

[41] The Universal Declaration was adopted as a non-binding resolution of the UN General Assembly (above n 16) and thus cannot have any contracting parties. On its relevance for the EU see A Rosas, 'The European Union: In Search of Legitimacy' in V Jaichand and M Suksi (eds), *60 Years of the Universal Declaration of Human Rights in Europe* (Antwerp, Intersentia, 2009) 415.

[42] On the relevance of international human rights instruments for EU law purposes see, eg Rosas and Armati (above n 1) 157–61.

[43] *Matthews v United Kingdom*, judgment of 18 February 1999, Application no 24833/94.

[44] See eg P van Dijk et al (eds), *Theory and Practice of the European Convention on Human Rights*, 5th edn (Cambridge, Intersentia, 2018) 911–13.

[45] See van Dijk et al (above n 44) 912, observing that the right to express political opposition does not follow from Article 3 of the Protocol but rather from Articles 10 and 11 ECHR.

[46] See Rosas (above n 15) 38.

[47] See eg Case C-896/19 *Repubblika v Il-Prim Ministru* (above n 12) 48–54.

III. INTERDEPENDENCE OF DEMOCRACY AND THE RULE OF LAW

It is argued in the following that while an outright conceptual overlap between democracy and the rule of law is limited, these two concepts are interdependent and mutually reinforcing. In a recital (6) of the above-mentioned EU Conditionality Regulation of 2020 it is stated that '[t]here can be no democracy and respect for fundamental rights without respect for the rule of law and vice versa'.[48] While a system based on the rule of law which is not democratic may be unsustainable at least in the long run, it is democracy that seems to be particularly dependent on the rule of law and it is to this dependence that I shall now turn. While democratic systems of government depend on a multitude of factors, the following observations will be centred around *elections* (in the broad sense, including, as the case may be, referendums and plebiscites). Some system of elections seems indispensable for safeguarding the possibility to change the government in power, in accordance with the popular will, and that possibility, again, seems indispensable for democracy.

At least the following factors are arguably important in devising a system of democratic elections which is both inclusive and competitive:[49]

(1) defining the categories of people having the right to vote and be elected;
(2) construing the system of fielding and rejecting candidates to stand for election, including the role of political parties and groups;
(3) devising the electoral system (proportional or majority voting, size and significance of electoral districts, possible weighted voting and minority quotas, etc);
(4) ensuring the existence and accessibility of accurate information about the election and respect for an equal enjoyment of political freedoms (freedom of expression and information, freedom of assembly and association), including the question of campaign finance;
(5) organising actual elections with a view to guaranteeing an equal right and opportunity to vote and be elected; and
(6) devising a system of counting and verification of votes which guarantees that the result corresponds to the number of votes cast.

In this section, an attempt will be made to illustrate the relevance of judicial review for assessing compliance with democratic standards, including preventing electoral fraud and abusive manipulation of electoral systems and elections, relating to the six factors listed above. This will be done primarily by considering the relevant case law of the ECtHR relating to Article 3 of Protocol No 1. This case law arguably provides a picture of some European-wide minimum standards concerning electoral systems

[48] See *Regulation 2020/2092* (above n 7).

[49] On the notions of inclusivity and competitiveness, see above n 15. For a detailed discussion of the various factors that govern elections and the electoral systems in Europe see Code of Good Practice in Electoral Matters, adopted by the Venice Commission at its 52nd session, Venice, 18–19 October 2002 (*Venice Commission Code of Good Practice in Electoral Matters*), and for the United States, see S Issacharoff et al (eds), *The Law of Democracy: Legal Structure of the Political Process*, 5th edn (St Paul MN, Foundation Press, 2016).

and elections as viewed by this Court.[50] While it is true that the jurisdiction of the ECtHR does not include the power to annul, and certainly not to amend, national decisions and measures relating to elections, the case law of this Court nevertheless shows the type of problems that will often arise in national contexts. Some references will also be made to ECJ case law as well as to recent debates concerning the United States (US) and case law with regard to the presidential elections of November 2020. The aim is simply to illustrate the types of issues which may call for independent judicial review, without analysing in depth the actual outcome of the cases referred to or investigating the actual consequences on the ground of the relevant litigation.

As for the subject population entitled to vote and to be elected (factor 1 above), it is important to note that the idea of political rights as human rights, and in particular the principle of equal voting rights for all adult citizens, was not free from discussion and even controversy in the preparatory works of the Universal Declaration of Human Rights, the International Covenant on Civil and Political Rights and the ECHR.[51] That doubts were expressed in this regard by some Western governments explains why it was not possible to insert the right to vote and be elected in the ECHR itself and why Article 3 of Protocol No 1 seems to be worded as an obligation for the state ('The High Contracting Parties undertake') rather than as an individual right. The European Commission on Human Rights (now defunct) and later the ECtHR have nevertheless ruled that Article 3 expresses a subjective right to vote and to stand for election and the Court has characterised Article 3 as a provision 'of prime importance in the Convention system'[52] enshrining 'a fundamental principle for effective political democracy'.[53]

That said, this right is far from absolute and the Court's case law admits of various restrictions of the right to vote and be elected.[54] Not only non-nationals but also non-residents, persons convicted of serious criminal offences, prisoners and incapacitated persons may find their right to vote curtailed. Arbitrary, unreasonable and disproportionate restrictions may, however, be disallowed by the Court. The Court found in the *Matthews* case that the exclusion of people living in Gibraltar from the right to vote in European elections, and in the *Aziz* case the exclusion of members of the Turkish community living in the government-controlled part of Cyprus, from the right to vote in national elections, constituted violations of the essence of the applicants' right to vote.[55] The decision of the United Kingdom to extend, for the implementation of the

[50] See also A Ruiz Robledo, 'The Construction of the Right to Free Elections by the European Court of Human Rights' (2018) 7 *Cambridge International Law Journal* 225.

[51] Rosas (above n 15), 18–28; Rosas (above n 40), 432–37.

[52] *W, X, Y and Z v Belgium*, decision of the Commission of Human Rights of 30 May 1975, Application nos 6745/74 and 6746/74; *Mathieu-Mohin and Clerfayt v Belgium*, judgment of 2 March 1987, Application no 9267/81, paras 47 and 51.

[53] *Melnychenko v Ukraine*, judgment of 19 October 2004, Application no 17707/02, 53.

[54] See Guide on Article 3 of Protocol No. 1 to the ECHR: Right to free elections (ECtHR, updated on 20 April 2021), www.echr.coe.int/Documents/Guide_Art_3_Protocol_1_ENG.pdf; ECHR Factsheet – Right to free elections (ECtHR May 2013), www.echr.coe.int/Documents/FS_Free_elections_ENG.pdf, and Factsheet – Right to vote (ECtHR May 2021), www.echr.coe.int/Documents/FS_Vote_ENG.pdf. See also Van Dijk et al (above n 44) 911–14, 919–28.

[55] *Matthews v United Kingdom* (above n 43); *Aziz v Cyprus*, judgment of 22 June 2004, Application no 69949/01.

Matthews judgment of the ECtHR, the right to vote in European elections to some persons living in Gibraltar who were not EU citizens was upheld by the ECJ, which nevertheless observed that the extension of the right to vote to other than own nationals or EU citizens should concern persons 'who have close links' to the Member State concerned.[56]

The case law of the ECtHR seems generally to have moved in the direction of a somewhat more robust review of voting restrictions. To take the example of prisoners, while earlier practice from the European Commission on Human Rights seems to have tolerated a general exclusion of the prisoner population, the ECtHR since *Hirst* has held that

> such a general, automatic and indiscriminate restriction on a vitally important Convention right must be seen as falling outside any acceptable margin of appreciation, however wide that margin may be, and as being incompatible with Article 3 of Protocol No 1.[57]

To take but one other example, the exclusion of minority groups from standing for election to the national parliament has been found to violate Article 14 (non-discrimination) taken together with Article 3 of Protocol No 1.[58]

While a person may in principle have the right to vote, and to stand as a candidate for election,[59] there may be an issue with the system of electoral registers and submitting and registering of candidates, including possible bans or restrictions on political parties or groups (factor 2 above). The ECtHR has in many cases found violations of Article 3 because of irregularities or arbitrariness in the procedures followed.[60] For instance, in *Petkov and Others v Bulgaria*, at issue was the failure of electoral authorities to reinstate the applicants on a list of candidates, in violation of a national court's final judgment. The ECtHR recalled that it had 'constantly stressed the need to avoid arbitrary decisions and abuse of power in the electoral context, especially as regards the registration of candidates' and that such procedures 'must be characterised by procedural fairness and legal certainty'.[61] The Court further recalled the importance of the rule of law and referred to the recommendations contained in the Venice Commission's *Code of Good Practice in Electoral Matters*.[62] While, for

[56] Case C-145/04 *Spain v United Kingdom* ECLI:EU:C:2006:543, para 78. Cf Case C-300/04 *Eman and Sevinger* ECLI:EU:C:2006:545 and *Sevinger and Eman v Netherlands*, judgment of 6 September 2007, Application no 17173/07, which concerned the right to vote in European elections of Dutch nationals living in Aruba.

[57] *Hirst v United Kingdom (No 2)*, judgment of 6 October 2005, Application no 74025/01, para 82. For an extensive survey of subsequent case law see ECHR Factsheet – Prisoners' right to vote (ECtHR April 2019), www.echr.coe.int/documents/fs_prisoners_vote_eng.pdf; Guide on the case-law of the ECHR – Prisoners' rights, (ECtHR, updated on 31 August 2021), 71–73, www.echr.coe.int/Documents/Guide_Prisoners_rights_ENG.pdf.

[58] *Sejdič and Finci v Bosnia and Herzegovina*, judgment of 22 December 2009, Application nos 27996/06 and 34836/06. See also *Zornič v Bosnia and Herzegovina*, judgment of 15 July 2015, Application no 3681/06.

[59] On possible restrictions in this regard (eg the exclusion of holders of public office), which may go further than restrictions on the right to vote, see, eg van Dijk et al (above n 44), 924–28.

[60] For a survey of relevant ECtHR case law see Guide on Article 3 of Protocol No. 1 (above n 54), 16–17, 20–22.

[61] *Petkov and Others v Bulgaria*, judgment of 11 June 2009, Application no 77568/01, para 61.

[62] ibid paras 62 and 63.

instance, the requirement of a deposit to be paid in advance by the candidate may pursue a legitimate aim, the amount must remain proportionate.[63] Likewise, various other formal requirements for the registration of candidates may be legitimate but arbitrariness in the rejection of candidates may constitute a violation.[64]

Electoral systems vary considerably between the Member States of the Council of Europe with regard to such questions as majority or proportional voting, voting for individual candidates or party lists, and the role and size of electoral districts (factor 3 above). In some countries it can happen that the political groupings represented in government can rely on a majority of seats in parliament although they received clearly less than 50 per cent of the popular vote.[65] The ECtHR has accepted that there is a very wide margin of appreciation and has not attempted to interpret the requirement in Article 3 that the elections be held under 'conditions which will ensure the free expression of the opinion of the people in the choice of the legislature' as requiring that all votes must necessarily have equal weight as regards the outcome of the election or that all candidates must have equal chances of victory.[66] There is thus no requirement of a system based on proportional representation[67] or on electoral constituencies of equal population.[68] On the other hand, the ECtHR *has* observed that the vote of each elector must have the possibility of affecting the composition of the legislature, albeit 'subject to compliance with the rules laid down in electoral legislation'.[69] These rules may, for instance, lay down an electoral threshold (namely the minimum share of the primary vote that a candidate or party must gain to obtain representation in a legislature) and the Court has accepted thresholds of five[70] and six[71] per cent. In *Yumak and Sadak v Turkey*, the Court, after having examined in detail various national systems and Council of Europe and other statements, concluded that 'in general a 10% electoral threshold appears excessive', although it was not persuaded that in the case at issue the threshold had had the effect of essentially impairing the rights secured by Article 3.[72] In this case, the Court also recalled that in examining compliance with Article 3, it had 'focused mainly on two criteria: whether there has been arbitrariness or a lack of proportionality and whether the restriction has interfered with the free expression of the opinion of the people'.[73]

[63] Guide on Article 3 of Protocol No 1 (above n 54), 17.

[64] See eg *Tahirov v Azerbaijan*, judgment of 11 June 2015, Application no 31953/11.

[65] In Hungary, the ruling party has received less than 50 per cent of votes cast but more than two thirds of the seats in the parliament. In the United Kingdom, with its system of single-seat constituencies, a party may obtain a majority in the Parliament although it has obtained less than 40 per cent of the popular vote. See also Rosas and Armati (above n 1) 129.

[66] *Mathieu-Mohin and Clerfayt v Belgium* (above n 52), para 54.

[67] *Matthews v United Kingdom* (above n 43), 64. See also *X v United Kingdom, decision of the Commission of Human Rights of 6 October 1976*, Application no 7140/75. See further Guide on Article 3 of Protocol No 1 (above n 54), 6–7; van Dijk et al (above n 44) 916–917.

[68] *Bompard v France*, decision of 4 April 2006, Application no 44081/02.

[69] *Riza and Others v Bulgaria*, judgment of 13 October 2015, Application nos 48555/10 and 48377/10, 148.

[70] *Parija 'Jaunie Demokrāti' and Partija 'Mūsu Zerne' v Latvia*, decision of 29 November 2007, Application nos 10547/07 and 34049/07; *Partei Die Friesen v Germany*, judgment of 28 January 2016, Application no 65480/10.

[71] *Federación nacionalista Canaria v Spain*, decision of 7 June 2011, Application no 56618/00.

[72] *Yumak and Sadak v Turkey*, judgment of 8 July 2008, Application no 10226/03, para 147.

[73] *Yumak and Sadak v Turkey* (above n 72), 109(iii).

As to freedom of information, freedom of expression, freedom of association and freedom of assembly (factor 4 above), there is an obvious overlap between Article 3 of Protocol No 1 and its requirement of 'free' elections, and other provisions of the ECHR. In some cases which have been considered under Article 10 (freedom of expression) or Article 11 (freedom of association) rather than Article 3 of Protocol No 1, the ECtHR has stressed the importance of freedom of expression for the right to free elections, observing that the two rights 'are inter-related and operate to reinforce each other'.[74] If the case has related more concretely to the election campaign it has been considered under Article 3, although in many cases the application has been declared inadmissible or no violation has been found. Even so, the Court has stressed that states are under a positive obligation to adopt measures to organise elections which will ensure the free expression of the opinion of the people and that even if states enjoy considerable latitude in this regard, it is for the Court ultimately to determine whether the requirements of Article 3 have been complied with.[75]

Even if there are free and periodic elections with universal suffrage, the actual participation in elections may be hampered in various ways (for instance, by reducing the number of polling stations or their opening hours) (factor 5 above).[76] Issues arising in ECtHR case law include the availability of appropriate ballot paper,[77] the organisation of polling stations, special assistance to disabled persons,[78] and the possibility to vote abroad in the elections in one's country of residence. Two cases deserve to be singled out: In *Karimov v Azerbaijan*, the use of special polling stations for the military in breach of domestic law and in a manner which did not guarantee a free and transparent electoral process was found to be in violation of Article 3.[79] In arriving at this conclusion, the ECtHR stressed the importance of the rule of law, 'one of the fundamental principles of a democratic society', which entails a duty on the part of the state to put in place a legislative framework for securing compliance with Article 3 and 'to ensure that its officials charged with executing those obligations do not act outside the law'.[80] In *Sitaropoulos and Giakoumopoulos v Greece* the issue was the lack of national legislation enabling nationals living abroad to vote in their country of residence.[81] The Court, referring, inter alia, to the fact that the applicants were not deprived of their right to vote, held that the fact that voting was more cumbersome (as they had to travel to Greece in order to cast their ballot) did

[74] *Mathieu-Mohin and Clerfayt v Belgium* (above n 53), para 54; *Bowman v United Kingdom*, judgment of 19 February 1998, Application no 141/1996, para 42. See also Guide on Article 3 of Protocol No 1 (above n 54), 22, and *Venice Commission Code of Good Practices in Electoral Matters* (above n 49), 8. For a case considered under art 11, see *Parti nationaliste basque – Organisation régionale d'Iparralde v France*, judgment of 7 June 2006, Application no 71251/01.

[75] *Communist Party of Russia and Others v Russia*, judgment of 19 June 2012, Application no 29400/05, paras 107–110.

[76] See *Venice Commission Code of Good Practice in Electoral Matters* (above n 49), 8–11. In the US, many States are in the process of enacting rules labelled by many critics as 'voter suppression', see below.

[77] *IZ v Greece*, decision of the Commission on Human Rights of 28 February 1994, Application no 18997/91.

[78] *Mólka v Poland*, judgment of 11 April 2006, Application no 56550/00 (but the application concerned local elections and fell thus outside Article 3 of Protocol No 1).

[79] *Karimov v Azerbaijan*, judgment of 25 September 2014, Application no 12535/06.

[80] ibid para 42.

[81] *Sitaropoulos and Giakoumopoulos v Greece*, judgment of 15 March 2012, Applicant no 42202/07.

not, taking into account also the state's margin of appreciation with respect to non-resident nationals' right to vote, amount to a violation of Article 3.

Impediments may be introduced not only to the right to vote but also to the right to stand for election and be elected, by preventing electoral candidates from campaigning, or successful candidates from taking up their seats. *Uspaskich v Lithuania* concerned a house arrest imposed on a candidate during the electoral campaign.[82] In *Junqueras*, the ECJ held that the Members of the European Parliament, after the official declaration of the election results, must have the ability to travel unimpeded to the first sitting of a new term, in order to comply with the procedural requirements in force.[83]

Finally, there need to be guarantees to ensure that the declared result corresponds to the votes cast and that the procedures for counting, verifying and validation of votes conform with the requirements of legal security and transparency (factor 6 above). The existence of adequate remedies and appeals is particularly relevant in this context.[84] In many cases, the ECtHR has found a violation of Article 3 of Protocol No 1 mainly in view of the fact that the system for examining alleged irregularities has been inadequate.[85] The case of *Mugemangango v Belgium* is particularly interesting: the ECtHR found that a Belgian regional system for dealing with complaints calling for a recount of votes – according to which the complaint was dealt with by the regional parliament (the newly-elected members of which had, by definition, an interest in the final result) – was in violation of Article 3.[86] The Court observed, inter alia, that the discretion enjoyed by the national authorities 'should nevertheless be compatible with the concepts of "effective political democracy" and "the rule of law" to which the preamble of the Convention refers'.[87] Thus, while credible allegations of irregularities deserve to be examined, there must also be sufficient grounds for invalidating election results in whole or in part, to prevent an arbitrary deprivation of the right to vote or the right to be elected.[88]

The risk of an arbitrary invalidation of votes cast has received a vivid illustration in the aftermath of the latest US presidential elections. President Trump and his supporters, dissatisfied with the victory of former Vice-President Biden, initiated a string of cases in federal and State courts attempting to invalidate votes and overturn the result especially in four States.[89] As there was no evidence of systemic

[82] *Uspaskich v Lithuania*, judgment of 20 December 2016, Applicant no 14737/08 (no violation; the applicant, albeit under house arrest, was not barred from standing for election).

[83] Case C-502/19 *Junqueras Vies* (above n 11).

[84] *Venice Commission Code of Good Practice in Electoral Matters* (above n 49), 10–11.

[85] See eg *Namat Aliyev v Azerbaijan*, judgment of 8 April 2010, Application no 18705/06; *Gahramanli and Others v Azerbaijan*, judgment of 8 October 2015, Application no 36503/11; *Davydov and Others v Russia*, judgment of 16 June 2017, Application no 75947/11. See also Guide on Article 3 of Protocol No 1 (above n 54), 26–28.

[86] *Mugemangango v Belgium*, judgment of 10 July 2020, Application no 310/15.

[87] ibid para 88.

[88] See eg *Kovach v Ukraine*, judgment of 7 February 2008, Application no 39424/02;*Kerimova v Azerbaijan*, judgment of 20 September 2009, Application no 20799/06; *Kerimli and Alibeyli v Azerbaijan*, judgment of 10 January 2010, Application nos 18475/06 and 22444/06; *Riza and Others v Bulgaria*, judgment of 13 October 2015, Application nos 48555/10 and 48377/10.

[89] B Williams, 'Did President Trump's 2020 Election litigation Kill Rule 11?' (2021) 30(2) *Boston University Public Interest Law Journal* 181.

irregularities, none of these cases had a tangible consequence for the outcome. Also, judges of the same political affiliation as President Trump, including federal judges appointed by him, either declared the claims inadmissible or dismissed them. The overt politisation of the election of US judges thus does not seem to have had tangible consequences for the 2020 election results. That said, if elections are very close, as in the 2000 presidential election, the situation may be different, as demonstrated by the US Supreme Court voting patterns in *Bush v Gore*.[90] Limited judicial control of the manipulation of electoral districts ('gerrymandering')[91] or of State efforts to limit access to the ballot ('voter suppression')[92] or the ongoing tendency to increase the powers of State political bodies in the resolution of contested elections casts doubts on the future viability of US electoral systems.[93]

IV. CONCLUSIONS

The conclusions to be drawn from the above discussion can be condensed into the following brief observations:

(1) There is an abundance of legally binding and 'soft law' European and universal instruments which bring out the close interrelation which exists between democracy, human rights/fundamental rights and the rule of law. This interrelation can be described as a 'trinity', implying that the three concepts are distinct but at the same time interrelated and interdependent. An 'illiberal' democracy, which means a system based on a perceived 'will of the people' but lacking checks and balances to secure that this 'will' is formed in an open and informed debate and corresponds to a genuine majority opinion of the population, and that minority rights are respected, is not in line with authoritative normative texts. Democracy and the rule of law are not strange bedfellows but rather Siamese twins.

(2) While the concepts of democracy, human rights/fundamental rights and the rule of law each have their own core substance, there is also conceptual overlap between them. The overlap between democracy and the rule of law is partly to be seen through the intermediary of human rights/fundamental rights (political rights and freedoms). Where there is no direct conceptual overlap, there is interdependence.

(3) While it is difficult to envisage a system guaranteeing fully the rule of law which is not democratic, it is even harder to imagine that a democratic system could

[90] *Bush v Gore*, 531 US 98 (2000). The decision, which had the effect of preventing a recount of votes in some electoral districts, was partly subject to a 5–4 vote along party political lines.

[91] See *Rucho v Common Cause*, 588 US — (2019). Gerrymandering claims present political questions beyond the reach of federal courts. The decision was again split (5–4), along party political lines.

[92] See eg L Hardy, 'Voter Suppression Post-*Shelby*: Impacts and Issues of Voter Purge and Voter ID Laws' (2020) 71(3) *Mercer Law Review* 857.

[93] In its annual Global State of Democracy Report 2021, International IDEA (International Institute for Democracy and Electoral Assistance) has included the United States in the category of 'backsliding democracies', *The Global State of Democracy Report 2021: Building Resilience in the Pandemic Era* (Stockholm, 2021), www.idea.int/gsod/global-report, chapter 2. See also, eg 'The Future of Voting', *Yale Alumni Magazine*, September/October 2021, yalealumnimagazine.com/articles/5379-the-future-of-voting.

survive without the rule of law. The case law of the ECtHR illustrates the various issues that may arise in devising, organising and verifying electoral systems and which require judicial and other legal oversight. While that Court does recognise a wide margin of appreciation, the case law also demonstrates that judicial control is both possible and necessary for ensuring a sustainable constitutional democracy. If there is no or weak judicial control, or if the judiciary is not independent and impartial, the door is open for electoral fraud and manipulation. Unless national judiciaries are allowed to function as they should, democracy will be under stress both in Europe and the US.

3

The Rule of Law and the EU: Responsibility, Independence and Rights

PAUL CRAIG*

THERE IS A very considerable literature on the rule of law and the EU, the principal focus of which is on rule-of-law backsliding by certain Member States, and the EU's response. This chapter does not seek to replicate this analysis, but to complement it in three different ways.

The discussion begins with responsibility, more specifically the conjunction of power and responsibility for the current situation. There are three levels at which the rule of law can be protected: statal, international and regional. The initial focus is on the state itself. Insofar as there are deficiencies, we need to understand not only the immediate consequence – whether incursions into judicial independence or limits of free speech – but also the deeper malaise driving the negative policies. There is then analysis of the potential and limits of international and regional action to combat rule-of-law problems.

The second part of the chapter addresses judicial independence and its centrality to the rule of law. It explicates the ways in which such independence lies at the core of three prominent versions of the rule of law. The rationale for judicial independence is explored for the rule of law and lawful authority, the rule of law and guiding conduct, and the rule of law and rights. This is followed by discussion of why such considerations are especially pertinent in the EU.

The final section of the chapter is concerned with the relationship between the rule of law and rights. It is acknowledged that there are different conceptions of the rule of law, and the principal fault line between formal and substantive conceptions of the rule of law relates to the issue of whether rights are regarded as *part of* the rule of law. The proximate rationale for this disagreement is explained, and so too is the deeper reason for the divide, which concerns the very theory of law and adjudication espoused by the protagonists in the debate. This theoretical discussion is followed by

* Emeritus Professor of English Law, St John's College, Oxford.

consideration of the relationship between the rule of law and rights within the EU, and the implications that this has for the current challenges facing the EU.

I. THE RULE OF LAW, POWER AND RESPONSIBILITY: STATAL, INTERNATIONAL AND REGIONAL

The rule of law is a central constitutional precept. There are three levels at which the rule of law can be protected: statal, international and regional.

A. Statal

It is axiomatic that the initial and primary focus for protection of the rule of law is the state itself. The state has the responsibility for securing the rule of law within its borders, and the duty falls on all organs of the state, legislative, executive and judicial. The state may receive advice or admonition in equal measure from outside, but this does not alter the fact that we expect the state to keep its own rule-of-law house in good order and lament the fact when it does not do so. Reflect on the assumptions underlying this sentiment. They are grounded on an admixture of power and responsibility. It is the state that has plenary authority within its borders, which carries the commensurate responsibility for ensuring that the rule of law is adhered to. This is foundational and too easily lost sight of in current discourse.

It is especially important when considering the rule of law and the EU. There may well be problems concerning the rule of law and its application to the EU's own institutional ordering. This does not alter the fact that the principal focus is on rule-of-law problems that emanate from Member States. Membership of an international or regional organisation does not obviate the state's primary responsibility for compliance with the rule of law within its borders. Indeed, such membership increases this responsibility, since failure to comply with the rule of law can have negative spill-over effects on an organisation to which the state has duties flowing from its EU membership.

B. International

If there are failings in this respect, then the traditional recourse has been to international law. The errant state may be condemned by international organisations such as the United Nations or the International Labour Organization for failure to comply with the rule of law. Such missives are important, but are bounded, both formally and substantively.

The formal powers of such organisations are circumscribed, and so too are their substantive powers. The bottom line is that while we might expect international condemnation, we do not have high hopes for causal impact on the situation on the ground. We 'discount' in advance the extent to which such intervention can really change matters.

These considerations should, nonetheless, not mask the potential of international law. Consider in this respect the Vienna Convention on the Law of Treaties (VCLT),[1] which contains several provisions pertinent to rule-of-law violations by contracting parties. Thus, Article 19 VCLT stipulates that contracting parties have duties not to defeat the object of the Treaty prior to its entry into force. Article 26 VCLT, further amplified by Article 31 VCLT, embodies the principle of *pacta sunt servanda*, with the correlative obligation of good faith performance of the Treaty. This is complemented by Article 27 VCLT, which provides that a state cannot invoke its internal law as a reason for non-compliance with Treaty obligations.

Article 60 VCLT deals with the effect of material breach by one of the contracting parties. A material breach of a multilateral treaty by one party entitles the other parties by unanimous agreement to suspend the operation of the Treaty, or to terminate it, either in the relations between themselves and the defaulting State, or as between all the parties. Article 60(3) VCLT defines a material breach in terms of a repudiation of the Treaty not sanctioned by the Vienna Convention, or violation of a provision essential to the accomplishment of the object or purpose of the Treaty. Not every breach of the rule of law would necessarily constitute a material breach as defined in Article 60(3), but serious violations would do so.

C. Regional: Council of Europe

We now consider the regional level. In Europe the two principal regional organisations are the Council of Europe and the European Union. They are very different in terms of their powers, which affects our expectations of what they can achieve. The Council of Europe has made significant contributions to preservation of the rule of law through the European Court of Human Rights (ECtHR) and the Venice Commission for Democracy through Law. They have done broadly what is expected of them, but this expectation is framed by the nature of their powers.

The European Court of Human Rights is, precisely by its judicial nature, triggered when a case comes before it. The Strasbourg Court has made significant contributions to preservation of the rule of law, as exemplified by *Baka v Hungary*,[2] which concerned Articles 6 and 10 of the European Convention on Human Rights (ECHR).[3] The applicant alleged that he had been denied access to a tribunal to contest the premature termination of his mandate as President of the Supreme Court in Hungary, and also that his mandate had been terminated in the first place because of views he had expressed publicly in his capacity as President of the Supreme Court, concerning legislative reforms affecting the judiciary.

The Strasbourg Court unanimously held that there had been a violation of Article 6(1). It acknowledged that there had to be a violation of a civil right for the

[1] Vienna Convention on the Law of Treaties, 1155 UNTS 331 (adopted 23 May 1969, entry into force 27 January 1980).

[2] *Baka v Hungary*, judgment of 17 May 2014, Application no 20261/12.

[3] Convention for the Protection of Human Rights and Fundamental Freedoms (adopted 4 November 1950, entry into force 3 September 1953).

purposes of Article 6(1),[4] but decided that the domestic legislative framework at the time of the applicant's election and during his mandate gave him an entitlement under Hungarian law to protection against removal from his office as President of the Supreme Court during that period.[5] The new legislation could not take away the pre-existing right, since its legality was the very object of the dispute in the present case.[6] National legislation excluding access to court had to be compatible with the rule of law, which meant that it could not be *ad hominen* and had to be based on a law of general application.[7] The right of access to court fell within Article 6(1), and the claimant's premature termination was not reviewable by any domestic court. There had, therefore, been a violation of Article 6(1).[8] The ECtHR also found a further violation. It agreed with the claimant that his termination was due to the fact that he had criticised the government's judicial reforms. There was, therefore, prima facie a violation of Article 10.[9]

The Venice Commission is the other Council of Europe body relevant for discussion of the rule of law. Its role is elaborated in Article 1.1 of the statute,[10] which mandates that it is: to strengthen the understanding of the legal systems of the participating states, with a view to bringing them closer; to promote the rule of law and democracy; and to examine the problems raised by the working of democratic institutions and their reinforcement and development. Article 1.2 instructs the Venice Commission to give priority to work concerning: (a) the constitutional, legislative and administrative principles and techniques which serve the efficiency of democratic institutions and their strengthening, as well as the rule of law; (b) fundamental rights and freedoms; and (c) the contribution of local and regional self-government to the enhancement of democracy. The reality is that the Venice Commission works in three broad areas:[11] democratic institutions and fundamental rights;[12] constitutional justice;[13] and elections,[14] including referendums and political parties.[15] The Venice Commission's work is an admixture of producing opinions concerning particular countries, and general studies that furnish more general guidance on particular fundamental rights or political parties.

This admixture of the general and the specific is apparent in the Venice Commission's important work on the rule of law. Thus, from a general perspective it published a 2011 Report on the Rule of Law,[16] which was complemented by

[4] ibid, paras 100–101.
[5] ibid, para 109.
[6] ibid, para 109.
[7] ibid, para 117.
[8] ibid, paras 120–21.
[9] ibid, para 151.
[10] Venice Commission, Resolution RES (2002) 3 Adopting the Revised Statute of the European Commission for Democracy through Law, CDL (2002) 27.
[11] P Craig, 'Transnational Constitution-Making: The Contribution of the Venice Commission on Law Democracy' (2017) 2 *UC Irvine Journal of International, Transnational, and Comparative Law* 57.
[12] 'Fundamental rights', venice.coe.int/WebForms/pages/?p=02_Rights&lang=EN.
[13] 'Constitutional justice – Cooperation between the Venice Commission and Constitutional Courts', www.venice.coe.int/WebForms/pages/?p=01_Constitutional_Justice&lang=EN, accessed 25 July 2022.
[14] 'Elections and referendums, political parties' www.venice.coe.int/WebForms/pages/?p=01_Elections_and_Referendums&lang=EN.
[15] 'Political Parties', www.venice.coe.int/WebForms/pages/?p=02_parties.
[16] Report on the Rule of Law, adopted by the Venice Commission at its 86th plenary session (Venice, 25–26 March 2011), CDL-AD(2011)003rev.

a more detailed Rule of Law Checklist in 2016.[17] The Venice Commission has, in addition, published numerous specific Opinions[18] on rule-of-law problems in EU Member States, such as Hungary[19] and Poland.[20] The Venice Commission does not have a formal enforcement mechanism. This is not as problematic as it might seem, given that in many instances it is the state itself that requests advice from the Commission. The issue is more problematic when the Venice Commission investigation is triggered in other ways, and/or where the state is resistant to suggestions for reform. The data on compliance is, moreover, incomplete and imperfect.[21]

D. Regional: European Union

We turn then to the other leading regional player in Europe, which is the European Union. There is a very large literature on the rule of law and the EU, more especially as concerns backsliding by certain EU Member States.[22] These problems relate principally, albeit not exclusively, to the independence of the judiciary in these countries. The present objective is not to repeat the measures taken by the EU to address rule-of-law backsliding. It is to reflect on what we expect from the EU, and how this affects commentary on what has or has not been achieved.

(i) The State: Objectives, Power and Responsibility

The EU is not a state, nor is it responsible for whatever reprehensible action was taken in relation to the judiciary. It is therefore important to consider, albeit briefly, the state's objectives, power and responsibility, before discussing those of the EU.

[17] Rule of Law Checklist, adopted by the Venice Commission at its 106th Plenary Session (Venice, 11–12 March 2016), endorsed by the Ministers' Deputies at the 1263rd Meeting (6–7 September 2016), Council of Europe, Study No 711/2013, CDL-AD(2016)007rev.

[18] 'Documents by opinions and studies', www.venice.coe.int/WebForms/documents/by_opinion.aspx?lang=EN.

[19] See eg Venice Commission, Opinion on the Law on Administrative Courts, CDL-AD(2019)004.

[20] See eg Poland – Urgent Joint Opinion of the Venice Commission and the Directorate General of Human Rights and Rule of Law (DGI) of the Council of Europe on amendments to the Law on the Common courts, the Law on the Supreme court and some other Laws, CDL-AD(2020)017.

[21] Craig (above n 11) 81–83.

[22] See eg A von Bogdandy, M Kottmann, C Antpöhler, J Dickschen, S Hentrei, and M Smrkolj, 'Reverse Solange – Protecting the essence of fundamental rights against EU Member States' (2012) 49 *CML Rev* 489; I Canor, 'My Brother's Keeper? Horizontal Solange: "An Ever Closer Distrust among the Peoples of Europe"' (2013) 50 *CML Rev* 383; A von Bogdandy and P Sonnevend (eds), *Constitutional Crisis in the European Constitutional Area: Theory, Law and Politics in Hungary and Romania* (Oxford, Hart Publishing, 2015); D Kochenov and L Pech, 'Monitoring and Enforcement of the Rule of Law in the EU: Rhetoric and Reality' (2015) 11 *EuConst* 512; J-W Müller, 'Should the European Union Protect Democracy and the Rule of Law in Its Member States' (2015) 21 *ELJ* 141; D Kochenov, 'EU Law without the Rule of Law: Is the Veneration of Autonomy Worth It?' (2015) 34(1) *YEL* 74; C Closa and D Kochenov (eds), *Reinforcing the Rule of Law Oversight in the European Union* (Cambridge, Cambridge University Press, 2016); D Kochenov and L Pech, 'Better late than never: On the European Commission's Rule of Law Framework and its first activation' (2016) 54 *Journal of Common Market Studies* 1062; A Jakab and D Kochenov (eds), *The Enforcement of EU Law and Values: Ensuring Member State Compliance* (Oxford, Oxford University Press, 2017); L Pech, 'The Rule of Law', in P Craig and G de Burca, *The Evolution of EU Law*, 3rd edn (Oxford, Oxford University Press, 2021).

We begin with the state's objectives. Discourse about rule-of-law backsliding focuses heavily on attacks on judicial independence, and their implications for the EU. This is, however, but part of a broader political strategy by the governing party to weaken constitutional constraints and to arrogate power. The constitutional meltdown thus precipitated has deeper roots in competitive authoritarianism and illiberal democracy.[23] Competitive authoritarianism connotes regimes where formal democratic institutions exist, but where incumbents' abuse of power places them at a significant advantage in relation to their opponents.[24] Illiberal democracy has a proximate connection to populism, the latter term encompassing the claim that populists alone represent the people – this being a moral, rather than an empirical claim–and that the people must be defended against a corrupt elite.[25] The salient point for present purposes is that the very existence of these deeper roots means that it is more difficult for any external actor to resolve the problem.

We then consider power and responsibility. The state, as noted above, has plenary authority, subject to obligations that flow from EU or international law. The corollary is that it has the commensurate responsibility for ensuring that the precepts of the rule of law are adhered to within its borders. The unacceptable action in question was taken by the Polish and Hungarian governments. It was not causally dependent on their EU membership. The challenge to judicial independence was but part of a broader assault on foundational elements of their respective constitutions.

(ii) The EU: Objectives, Power and Responsibility

The EU's response to the rule-of-law problems must be seen against the preceding backdrop. That response is framed by the EU's objectives, and delimited by its powers, which has consequences for its responsibility.

The EU's objectives are encapsulated in Articles 2 and 3 TEU. Article 2 TEU sets out the values underlying the EU, which include, inter alia, human dignity, freedom, democracy, equality, the rule of law and respect for human rights. Article 3 TEU then charts the EU's objectives, which include fulfilment of the values in Article 2.

This brings us to the EU's powers. Article 3(6) TEU is a neat fulcrum point for this shift, insofar as it provides that the 'Union shall pursue its objectives by appropriate means commensurate with the competences which are conferred upon it in the Treaties'. It thereby constitutes a bridge between the EU's objectives dealt with in Article 3(1)–(5) TEU and its competence, specified in Articles 4(1) and 5(1) TEU, and elaborated in more detail in Articles 2–6 TFEU. The injunction in Article 3(6) TEU is reflective of the legal reality as specified in Article 4(1) TEU, which is that competences

[23] S Levitsky and L Way, *Competitive Authoritarianism: Hybrid Regimes After the Cold War* (Cambridge, Cambridge University Press, 2010); N Bermeo, 'On Democratic Backsliding' (2016) 27(1) *Journal of Democracy* 5; D Adamski, 'The Social Contract of Democratic Backsliding in "the new" EU Countries' (2019) 56 *CML Rev* 62; K Lane Scheppele, 'Autocratic Legalism' (2018) 85 *University of Chicago Law Review* 545; S Levitsky and L Way, 'The New Competitive Authoritarianism' (2020) 31(1) *Journal of Democracy* 51; P Craig, 'The Politics of Constitutional Meltdown' in M Tushnet and D Kochenov (eds), *Research Handbook on The Politics of Constitutional Law* (Cheltenham, Edward Elgar, forthcoming).

[24] Levitsky and Way, *Competitive Authoritarianism* (above n 23) 5.

[25] W Galston, 'The Enduring Vulnerability of Liberal Democracy' (2020) 31(3) *Journal of Democracy* 8, 8.

not conferred on the EU remain with the Member States. This is further reinforced by Article 5(1) TEU, which makes clear that the limits of Union competence are governed by the principle of conferral. The EU therefore has attributed power; it does not have plenary authority. It must work within the parameters of what its founding treaties allow. There is a legal and a political dimension to the idea of attributed power.

In legal terms, the EU has, if truth be told, been pretty good at using a plethora of techniques to try to address the rule-of-law problem. These include invocation of Article 7 TEU; the Commission Justice Scoreboard; the Commission's Rule of Law Framework; the Council's Annual Rule of Law Dialogue; legal actions before the European Court of Justice (ECJ); the Rule of Law Cycle; and monetary incentives for compliance with the rule of law. It has deployed broad Treaty interpretation to good effect, as exemplified by judicial use of Article 19 TEU, and Article 258 TFEU. The Treaties nonetheless still limit the EU's powers. Thus, Article 7 TEU was devised implicitly on the assumption that there would only be one 'bad' state at any one point in time. The decisional rules reflect this. If there are two or more such states, the use of Article 7 TEU becomes a whole lot more difficult.

In political terms, the EU is bounded by rules for political decision-making grounded in Treaty provisions, which can be used by the defaulting states as shields to blunt the force of EU initiatives to deal with rule-of-law backsliding. This is regrettable but predictable. A 'rational' defaulting state will draw on legal rules to shape the political terrain when it can do so. This is exemplified by the passage of EU legislation to impose rule-of-law conditionality through cuts to the contributions from the EU budget that go to defaulting states.[26] The political deal-making on this was conducted under the shadow of threats from Hungary and Poland to veto approval of the general EU budget.[27] This constrained what could be achieved, but the legislation is still important. We should be wary of the best being the enemy of the good.

The discussion of objectives and power casts into sharp relief consideration of the EU's responsibility. The EU clearly has a responsibility to tackle rule-of-law problems within a Member State, since they undermine the values in Article 2 TEU and impede fulfilment of the EU's objectives in Article 3 TEU. It can, however, only do so within the legal limits of powers conferred on it, and within the political limits that shape their exercise. The EU's responsibility to deal with rule-of-law backsliding must, then, be judged against a twin backdrop. The initial malaise, in terms of lack of judicial independence, is the fault of the Member State and is but part of a larger problem concerning assault on the constitution at national level. The EU's responsibility is bounded by the legal limits on its power, the exercise of which is perforce shaped by political considerations; its responsibility is also circumscribed by the fact that there are limits as to what it can do to redress the problems associated with illiberal democracy and competitive authoritarianism. This does not mean that we should

[26] Regulation (EU/Euratom) 2020/2092 of the European Parliament and of the Council of 16 December 2020 on a general regime of conditionality to protect the Union budget [2020] OJ L433 I/1.

[27] J Shotter and V Hopkins, 'Hungary and Poland stand firm against EU rule of law conditions', *Financial Times* (18 November 2020), www.ft.com/content/6868477d-38a2-464e-b1c4-188fd0a62b1a; G Verhofstadt, 'We need to call Orbán's bluff by going ahead without him', *EUObserver* (18 November 2020) euobserver.com/opinion/150103?utm_source=euobs&utm_medium=email.

accept the status quo with equanimity. To the contrary, we should be fully mindful of the dangers that this presents for the EU.

II. THE RULE OF LAW AND JUDICIAL INDEPENDENCE: CONCEPTIONS, IMPORTANCE AND APPLICATION

Attacks on judicial independence lie at the heart of democratic backsliding by some EU Member States. The objective is not to analyse the CJEU's response to this malaise, which has been well documented in the literature. It is to consider why judicial independence is so central to many of the principal conceptions of the rule of law.

A. Rule of Law: Lawful Authority

A core feature of the rule of law is that the legislature and government must be able to point to some basis for its action that is regarded as valid by the relevant legal system. Thus, the EU only has the powers conferred on it by the Lisbon Treaty. The EU institutions must, therefore, be able to point to a Treaty foundation for legislative acts enumerated in Article 289 TFEU. This is equally true of other EU legal acts, which must fall within the legal parameters for the creation of delegated and implementing acts pursuant to Articles 290–291 TFEU.

This conception of the rule of law is narrow, but it is nonetheless central; any vision of the rule of law must embrace the requirement of lawful authority even if it goes beyond it. However, this conception tells one nothing as to the nature of the challenged governmental action. The government might be seeking to achieve some benign objective, or it might be attempting to do something that most would regard as undesirable. This is irrelevant for the purposes of the present inquiry. The measure would be equally contrary to the rule of law if the government could not point to some basis for its action that would be regarded as valid by that legal system.

Judicial independence is central to this conception of the rule of law. If the government or legislature exceeds the boundaries of its lawful authority, then its action will be null or invalid. There must be independent courts to assess whether the limits on lawful authority have been exceeded. If the courts lack such independence then there is a real danger that limits on the scope of political power will be ignored, or will be interpreted in a manner that is not objective and is too favourable to the government.

B. Rule of Law: Guiding Conduct

The preceding conception of the rule of law is important, but limited. Any law properly passed by the legislature would meet this precept. Thus, the fact that laws are enacted in the correct legal manner is a necessary facet of the rule of law, but it is not regarded as sufficient. A further important aspect of the rule of law is that laws should be capable of guiding one's conduct, in order that one can plan one's life, thereby facilitating legal certainty. It is from this general precept that Joseph Raz deduced a number of more specific attributes that laws should have to comply with in order to accord with the rule of law:[28] laws should be prospective, not retrospective; they should be relatively stable; particular laws should be guided by open, general and clear rules; there should be an independent judiciary; there should be access to the courts; and the discretion which law enforcement agencies possess should not be allowed to undermine the purposes of the relevant legal rules.

This conception of the rule of law is not concerned with the substantive content of the law, in the sense of whether the law is just or unjust, provided that the formal precepts of the rule of law are met. It is necessary to consider the content of the law to decide whether it complies with the preceding precepts of the rule of law. However, if it does so comply then that is the end of the inquiry. The corollary is that this conception of the rule of law could be met by regimes whose laws are morally objectionable, provided they comply with the formal precepts of the rule of law. It also follows that not all laws passed by a democratic regime will necessarily comply with the rule of law. However, the rule of law thus conceived minimises the danger created by law itself, by ensuring that whatever the content of the law, it should be open, clear, stable, general and applied by an impartial judiciary.

Judicial independence is central to this component of the rule of law; hence its inclusion on the preceding list. If the judiciary is not independent, people will not be able to plan their lives secure in the knowledge of the legal consequences of their actions. They will not be sure that the courts will faithfully apply the letter and spirit of the law to their situation. Judicial independence is also necessary to give effect to other facets of the rule of law. Thus, consider by way of example the rule of law precept to the effect that laws should not be retrospective. Independent courts have a number of juridical techniques at their disposal to deal with retrospective legislation. It might be annulled, because it offends the constitution. It might be invalidated pursuant to a statute that protects human rights. The retrospective legislation might be interpreted very narrowly. If, however, the courts are not independent then they may well not make use of these doctrinal precepts to control retrospective legislation.

C. Rule of Law: Rights, Justice and Accountable Government

There is a third conception of the rule of law that embraces the previous two, but goes beyond them, with the consequence that the rule of law is not purely formal, but substantive. On this view there is a rights-based component to the rule of law, such that certain rights are based on, or protected by, the rule of law, with the consequence that violation of these rights constitutes infringement of the rule of law. On this view the rule of law also provides the foundation for the controls exercised by courts over governmental action through judicial review, which commonly include principles such as legality, procedural propriety, participation, fundamental rights, openness, rationality, relevancy, propriety of purpose, reasonableness, equality, legitimate expectations, legal certainty and proportionality.

[28] J Raz, 'The Rule of Law and its Virtue' (1977) 93 *LQR* 195.

This vision has been espoused by a range of writers. It underpins the work of Ronald Dworkin,[29] who accepts the conception of the rule of law outlined in the previous section, labelling this the 'rule book' conception, since it would feature in any serious theory of justice. However, as Dworkin notes, this says little if anything about the content of the laws within a legal system. He argues for a rights-based understanding of the rule of law. Citizens have moral rights and duties with respect to one another, and political rights against the state. These moral and political rights should be recognised in positive law, and citizens should be able to enforce them through the courts. The rule of law in this sense is the ideal of rule by an accurate public conception of individual rights.[30] In a similar vein, Lord Bingham argued that the rule of law should include, but extend beyond, the formal precepts articulated by Raz. It should include adequate protection for fundamental rights.[31]

Judicial independence is central to fulfilment of this conception of the rule of law. Courts that lack independence cannot be trusted to enforce rights, and they cannot be trusted to apply the precepts of judicial review. Independent courts will enforce the rights-based component of the rule of law through the powers invested in the judiciary in that legal system. Independent courts will also develop and enforce the principles of judicial review. If courts lack independence the principles of judicial review will not be objectively enforced against the executive, and its discretionary power will not be properly controlled.

D. Rule of Law: Judicial Independence and Interlocking Legal Orders

The preceding discussion has considered the centrality of judicial independence to different conceptions of the rule of law. Judicial independence is of particular significance in interlocking legal orders such as the EU, which are reliant on both the EU courts and national courts to attain the objectives of the founding Treaties.

This is in part for horizontal reasons, in the sense that cooperation between national courts lies at the heart of the European Arrest Warrant regime that constitutes the core of the Area of Freedom, Security and Justice. This cooperation is predicated on mutual trust between national courts, which will no longer be forthcoming if the courts of the country to which a person is sent for trial are not trusted by other courts because they lack independence. It is in part for vertical reasons, since national courts are central to the regime of EU adjudication. They have the obligation to conform to, and apply, EU law within their jurisdiction and are therefore courts with general jurisdiction over EU law. They are also central to the flow of cases upwards to the ECJ, via the regime of preliminary references in Article 267 TFEU that lies at the core of the EU legal order. If national courts lack independence then the regime of EU adjudication will suffer in both respects. National courts that lack independence may not apply EU law correctly, and they may restrict the flow of

[29] R Dworkin, *Law's Empire* (London, Fontana, 1986).
[30] R Dworkin, *A Matter of Principle* (Cambridge MA, Harvard University Press, 1985) 11–12.
[31] T Bingham, *The Rule of Law* (London, Penguin, 2011).

preliminary references where there are challenges to national legislative or executive action that is contrary to EU law.

It is for these reasons that attacks on judicial independence in Hungary and Poland have assumed centre stage in discourse about rule-of-law backsliding. The tensions were cast into sharp relief by the decision of the Polish Constitutional Tribunal that challenged central tenets of the primacy of EU law.[32] This is not the place for detailed exegesis as to the consequences that should flow from this decision. My views can be found elsewhere.[33] Suffice it to say for the present that the decision by the Constitutional Tribunal reveals the importance of judicial independence and the consequences that follow when it is undermined. If you strip a court of its independence and pack it with government appointees with the intent that it will do the government's bidding, then sooner or later it will make a decision of this nature.

III. THE RULE OF LAW AND FUNDAMENTAL RIGHTS: CONCEPTIONS, IMPORTANCE AND APPLICATION

The difference of view as to whether the rule of law should encompass rights has been noted in the previous discussion. The present section considers how far this makes a legal difference. The discussion begins by clarifying the theoretical positions and then addressing the issue in the context of the EU.

A. Rule of Law and Rights: Theoretical Terrain

It is important to understand at the outset (a) why there is a difference of view concerning inclusion of rights within the rule of law; (b) the way in which this is dependent on divergent theories of adjudication that underpin the respective theories; and (c) the reasons why the gap between the two principal theories is less marked than might be thought at first sight.

The formal theory of the rule of law was espoused by Raz, who is also a leading exponent of legal positivism. He argued that the rule of law should not include consideration of rights for the following reason.[34] We may all agree that laws should be just, that their content should be morally sound and that rights should be protected within society. The problem is that if the rule of law is taken to encompass the necessity for 'good laws' then the concept ceases to have an independent function. There is a wealth of literature devoted to the meaning of a just society, the nature of the rights which should subsist therein, and the appropriate boundaries of governmental action. Political theory has tackled such questions from time immemorial. To bring these issues within the rubric of the rule of law would, therefore, rob the concept of an independent function. Laws would be condemned or upheld as being in conformity

[32] Constitutional Tribunal of Poland, Case K3/21, judgment of 7 October 2021.

[33] P Craig, 'The Rule of Law, Breach and Consequence', *EULawLive* (21 October 2021), eulawlive.com/op-ed-the-rule-of-law-breach-and-consequence-by-paul-craig/.

[34] Raz (above n 28) 196.

with, or contrary to, the rule of law when the condemnation or praise would simply be reflective of attachment to a particular conception of rights, democracy or the just society.

The message is, therefore, that if you wish to argue about the justness of society, do so by all means. If you wish to defend a particular type of individual right then present your argument. Draw upon the wealth of literature that addresses these matters directly. It is, however, not necessary or desirable to cloak this in the mantle of the rule of law, since it will merely reflect the conclusion that has already been arrived at through reliance on a particular theory of rights or the just society.

It is not fortuitous that Raz is a leading exponent of legal positivism, which is predicated, inter alia, on the twin assumptions that courts apply recognised sources of law, and that there is no necessary connection between the content of the existing law and moral precepts. Legal positivists who subscribe to a formal conception of the rule of law do not believe that the existing law is value neutral. They do maintain that there is a distinction between the existing rules and their normative justification. The formal conception of the rule of law follows, for exclusive legal positivists, from their belief that in determining what the law is, there is no necessary link between law and moral precepts.[35] Inclusive legal positivists maintain, by way of contrast, that there can be some instances where the determination of what the law is will entail moral considerations.[36]

Legal positivism does not, however, entail the exclusion of all moral considerations from public law discourse. Such considerations may, as inclusive legal positivists argue, be incorporated into the validity criteria of certain legal systems. There will, moreover, be many source-based norms, whether derived from statute, precedent or the constitution, which the courts must, on the positivist thesis, faithfully apply. These norms will, in liberal polities, commonly enshrine substantive rights to equality, speech and a plethora of other rights. There is, moreover, nothing in the positivist thesis to prevent the courts interpreting such norms so as to require substantive constraints on the way that power is exercised. It is also accepted by positivists that courts can have recourse to moral considerations in determining what the law ought to be, when the existing sources of law, whether based on statute or precedent, run out.[37]

Dworkin's substantive conception of the rule of law is grounded in his non-positivist theory of law and adjudication. He argued that subject to questions of 'fit', courts should decide legal questions according to the best theory of justice,

[35] J Raz, *The Authority of Law, Essays on Law and Morality* (Oxford, Oxford University Press, 1979) 49–50; J Raz, *Ethics in the Public Domain, Essays on the Morality of Law and Politics* (Oxford, Oxford University Press, 1994) ch 10, 13; A Marmor, 'Exclusive Legal Positivism' in J Coleman and S Shapiro (eds), *The Oxford Handbook of Jurisprudence and the Philosophy of Law* (Oxford, Oxford University Press, 2002) ch 3.

[36] J Coleman, 'Negative and Positive Positivism' (1982) 11 *Journal of Legal Studies* 139; P Soper, 'Legal Theory and the Obligation of the Judge: The Hart/Dworkin Dispute' (1977) 75 *Michigan Law Review* 511; Marmor (above n 35); K Himma, 'Inclusive Legal Positivism' in Coleman and Shapiro (above n 35) ch 4.

[37] Raz, *The Authority of Law* (n 35) 49–50, 181, 193–94; Raz, *Ethics in the Public Domain* (above n 35) ch 10, 13; Marmor (above n 35).

which is central to the resolution of what rights people currently possess.[38] On this view, 'propositions of law are true if they figure in or follow from the principles of justice, fairness and procedural due process that provide the best constructive interpretation of the community's legal practice'.[39] Subject to questions of fit, the court should choose between 'eligible interpretations by asking which shows the community's structure of institutions as a whole in a better light from the stand-point of political morality'.[40] An individual has a right to the legal answer that is forthcoming from the above test. These moral and political rights should be recognised in positive law, so that they can be enforced by citizens through the courts. The rule of law on this conception is the ideal of rule by an accurate public conception of individual rights.

It was then natural for Dworkin to advocate a rights-based conception of the rule of law, given his argument that citizens have moral rights and duties with respect to one another, and political rights against the state. This view of the rule of law

> does not distinguish, as the rule book conception does, between the rule of law and substantive justice; on the contrary it requires, as part of the ideal of law, that the rules in the book capture and enforce moral rights.[41]

It does not mean that this conception of the rule of law is consistent with only one theory of justice or freedom. It does mean that it is not independent of the particular theory of justice, or vision of freedom, which constitutes its content at any point in time.

The positivist and non-positivist accounts of law and adjudication are different, and this is reflected in the divergent interpretations of the rule of law. This can be acknowledged, while also accepting that the degree of difference may be less marked than initially thought. This is in part because, from the positivist perspective, courts will apply recognised sources that commonly include rights; the criteria of validity in a particular order may include moral considerations; and courts can have recourse to such matters when the law 'runs out'. It is in part because from a non-positivist perspective, the rights-based conception of law is framed by questions of fit that can circumscribe the options open to a court.

B. Rule of Law and Rights: Legal Terrain

The focus now shifts to consideration of the rule of law and rights viewed from the perspective of EU law, when read in the light of the preceding discussion.[42]

We begin at the beginning, which for this purpose is Article 2 TEU. It is framed in terms that distinguish between the rule of law and human rights, and this textual

[38] R Dworkin, *Law's Empire* (London, Fontana, 1986).
[39] ibid 225.
[40] Ibid 256.
[41] Dworkin (above n 30) 11–12.
[42] For discussion of the relationship between democracy and the rule of law, see A Rosas in Chapter 2 of this volume.

disjunction is further emphasised by the remainder of Article 2 TEU, insofar as it elaborates separately the *desiderata* of, inter alia, justice, non-discrimination and gender equality. This textual disjunction should not be pressed too far. The opening articles of the TEU should not be read in a manner akin to a biblical exegesis, more especially because they were almost certainly not drafted with a mind to the theoretical distinction concerning different conceptions of the rule of law adumbrated in the previous section. However, disaggregation between the rule of law and rights also characterised earlier versions of the Treaty, as exemplified by the Maastricht Treaty, the Preamble of which distinguished between respect for human rights and the rule of law. This distinction was reinforced by the language of Article F, with its focus on fundamental rights, and it was carried forward to Article J.1, which defined the objectives of the Common Foreign and Security Policy, and separated the rule of law and rights. This approach was retained in the revisions to Article F in the Amsterdam Treaty, wherein the EU's foundational values were said to include, inter alia, respect for fundamental rights and the rule of law, with the text edging closer to that in the current Article 2 TEU.

There is, however, another aspect of EU law that is suggestive of a more proximate relationship between the rule of law and rights. This relates to EU general principles of law, the history of which is imperfectly understood.[43] The salient point for present purposes is that the ECJ read them into the Treaty to ensure that the EEC had principles of judicial review that were fit for purpose. Fundamental rights were incorporated into the Treaty in the same manner, and in conceptual terms they were regarded no differently from the other general principles. Viewed from this perspective, the reasoning could be summarised thus: the rule of law demanded that the EU should have precepts of judicial review to control decision-making by the Commission and other EU bodies; these precepts were conceptualised as general principles of law; and fundamental rights were regarded as but one such principle, in line with the other principles that comprised the rule of law. Article 6(3) TEU is the enduring legacy of this pattern of thought, specifying as it does that fundamental rights shall constitute general principles of law.

This proximate connection between the rule of law and rights is also evident in Commission initiatives, as exemplified by its 2014 paper, which set out a new framework to strengthen the rule of law.[44] It acknowledged that the precise content of the rule of law could vary, depending on each Member State's constitutional system. The Commission nonetheless formulated a broad, substantive conception of the rule of law, drawing on case law from the ECJ, the Strasbourg Court, and documentation from the Venice Commission. For the EU Commission, the principles that comprised the rule of law included legality, which implied a transparent, accountable, democratic

[43] P Craig, 'General Principles of Law: Treaty, Historical and Normative Foundations' in K Ziegler, P Neuvonen, and V Moreno-Lax (eds), *Research Handbook on General Principles of EU Law* (Cheltenham, Edward Elgar Press, 2022).

[44] Commission Communication on a new EU Framework to strengthen the Rule of Law, COM(2014) 158 final of 19 March 2014, 2. See also, Commission Communication on Article 7 of the Treaty on European Union – Respect for and promotion of the values on which the Union is based, COM(2003) 606 final of 15 October 2003.

and pluralistic process for enacting laws; legal certainty; prohibition of arbitrariness of the executive powers; independent and impartial courts; effective judicial review, including respect for fundamental rights; and equality before the law. Respect for the rule of law was, therefore, intrinsically linked to respect for democracy and for fundamental rights: there could be no democracy and respect for fundamental rights without respect for the rule of law and vice versa. Fundamental rights were effective only if they were justiciable; democracy was protected only if the judiciary could ensure freedom of expression, freedom of assembly and respect of the rules governing the political and electoral process.[45] Compliance with the rule of law was, therefore, a prerequisite for the protection of all fundamental values listed in Article 2 TEU. It was also a prerequisite more generally for upholding all rights and obligations derived from the Treaties and from international law.[46]

The final point to make concerning the legal relationship between the rule of law and rights within the EU takes us back to the theoretical discussion. It was noted that the difference between the formal and substantive conceptions of the rule of law was less significant if a legal order protected fundamental rights as a recognised source of law. Fundamental rights would not be regarded as part of the rule of law if a legal system adhered to a formal conception of the rule of law, and the positivist theory of law and adjudication that underpinned it. However, insofar as such rights were enshrined in a recognised source of law, then positivism would dictate that they should be faithfully enforced in the same manner as any other source-based legal norm. This condition was met prior to the Lisbon Treaty, insofar as fundamental rights were regarded as general principles of law. It is further reinforced by the fact that the European Charter of Rights is, in accord with Article 6(1) TEU, treated as equivalent to the constituent Treaties.

IV. CONCLUSION

There will be no attempt to summarise the entirety of the preceding argument. Suffice it to say the following. We craft argument with the hope that it will shed light on a particular issue, whatsoever it might be. In doing so we might reason deductively, inductively or use an admixture of the two. We also have recourse to a combination of more abstract or theoretical arguments, and those that are more particular or grounded in positive law. The real world then generates facts against which to test such reasoning, as exemplified by the decision of the Polish Constitutional Tribunal.[47] This regrettable decision reveals the centrality of the issues discussed in this chapter.

It speaks directly to the concerns about power and responsibility and the statal, international and regional levels at which they can be addressed, revealing the way in which challenge to the independence of the courts is but part of the broader strategy

[45] COM(2014) 158 final (above n 44) 4.
[46] ibid 4–5.
[47] Case K3/21 (above n 32).

of illiberal democracy that pertains in such countries. It reveals in the most powerful manner the corrosive impact of lack of judicial independence and the way in which this undermines legal orders to which the country belongs. It demonstrates the proximate connection between the rule of law, democracy and the protection of rights, such that if independence is compromised and the courts are beholden to the executive, then rights, whether enshrined in the constitution or statute, will be but paper promises without substance.

4

Illiberal Democracy and Rule by *Law from an EU Perspective*

SANJA BOGOJEVIĆ AND XAVIER GROUSSOT

I. INTRODUCTION: 1989 AND THE 'ETERNAL VIGILANCE' OF CONSTITUTIONAL DEMOCRACY

To understand the present rule-of-law crisis in Europe, we need to go back to 1989. That was the year that saw the fall of the Berlin Wall, leading to the independence of those former states of the Soviet bloc which would later join the EU. It was also the year that the British scientist Tim Berners-Lee invented the world-wide web while working at CERN, the European Organization for Nuclear Research,[1] and that Professor Koen Lenaerts, today President of the Court of Justice of the European Union, became a judge at the General Court in Luxembourg. These events occurred independently of each other, but fast-forward to today, and the three appear intimately connected. The Court of Justice is the protagonist in the story about protection of the rule of law in the EU and the fight against illiberal democracies, which have emerged with the help of the internet[2] and predominantly, though not exclusively, in countries once part of the Soviet bloc.[3]

Conceptualising 'illiberal democracy' is not a straightforward exercise. Some argue that the concept is an oxymoron, as any liberal order demands protection of the rule of law, human rights and democracy, which then, in the opposite corner of the boxing ring, illiberal democracies seek to take down.[4] Others take a more fluid view, arguing that the rule of law and democracy 'have coexisted or lived separately' and that there

[1] See T Berners-Lee, *Weaving the Web: The Original Design and Ultimate Destiny of the World Wide Web* (New York, Harper Business, 2000).

[2] See eg P Pomerantsev, *This is Not Propaganda: Adventures in the War Against Reality* (New York, Public Affairs, 2019); F Fukuyama, 'Making the Internet Safe for Democracy' (2021) 32 *Journal of Democracy* 37.

[3] See eg MA Vachudova, *Europe Undivided: Democracy, Leverage, and Integration After Communism* (Oxford, Oxford University Press, 2005) ch 2.

[4] See eg J Weiler, 'The European Circumstance and the Politics of Meaning: Not on Bread Alone Doth Man Liveth (Deut. 8:3; Mat 4:4)' (2020) 21 *German Law Journal* 96, 96.

is 'no historical evidence as to the necessity of their simultaneous presence'.[5] Moving beyond the theoretical discussions, it is obvious that the rule of law and constitutional democracy, as the EU understands them, are being significantly undercut by multiple European governments. Here we will focus on Poland and Hungary. In the former, the ruling party has taken actions and introduced regulations to overhaul the judicial system in the party's favour.[6] In the latter, the government has made legislative moves reducing the independence of the judiciary, as well as the educational system and the media.[7] The aim successfully pursued by these elected political powers is, in short, to eschew the rule of law[8] through legally compliant changes and through processes whereby the checks and balances that the separate powers impose on each other are undone for the benefit of the government,[9] resulting in a meltdown of the separation of powers.[10]

How does, and how should, the EU respond to illiberal democracies? This chapter offers a tentative reply. It does so by first briefly examining some illiberal democracy concoctions, narrowing their core ingredients down to a reliance on the will of 'the people' (populist convictions) in insisting on sovereignty, followed by creation of rules in the spirit of legalism that dismantle constitutional democracy and its safeguards and, in this way, establishing a system of rule *by* law. We then turn to analyse what has, so far, been the EU's response, both in the legislative and the judicial arena, vis-à-vis illiberal democracies. We end with some reflections on what further steps are need to ensure the 'eternal vigilance'[11] of the rule *of* law, and indeed of the EU legal order.

II. ILLIBERAL DEMOCRACY AT A GLANCE

The year the Berlin Wall came down, Francis Fukuyama proclaimed that liberal democracy had finally triumphed.[12] With the end of fascism in the Second World War, and communism in the Cold War, free markets and representative government – that

[5] G Palombella, 'Illiberal, Democratic and Non-Arbitrary? Epicentre and Circumstances of a Rule of Law Crisis' (2018) 10 *Hague Journal of the Rule of Law* 5, 10.

[6] See eg M Wiącek, 'Constitutional Crisis in Poland 2015–2016 in the Light of the Rule of Law Principle' in A von Bogdandy, P Bogdanowicz, I Canor, C Grabenwarter, M Taborowski, and M Schmidt (eds), *Defending Checks and Balances in EU Member States: Taking Stock of Europe's Actions* (Berlin, Springer, 2021) 15.

[7] See eg B Bakó, 'Hungary's Latest Experience with Article 2 TEU: The Need for "informed" EU Sanctions' in A Bogdandy et al, ibid, 35. For an overview of the status of the rule-of-law protection across the Member States, see Communication from the Commission to the European Parliament, the Council, the European Economic and Social Committee and the Committee of the Regions, *The rule of law situation in the European Union*, COM(2022) 700 final (*2021 Rule of Law Report*).

[8] Similar point made in a more general context in S Bogojević, 'The Erosion of the Rule of Law: How Populism Threatens Environmental Protection' (2019) 31 *Journal of Environmental Law* 389.

[9] A Sajó and J Tuovinen, 'The Rule of Law and Legitimacy in Emerging Illiberal Democracies' (2018) 64 *OER Osteuropa Recht* 506, 522.

[10] P Craig, 'The Rule of Law, Breach and Consequence', *EU Law Live* (21 October 2021).

[11] Term borrowed from M Krygier, 'Democracy and the Rule of Law' in J Meierhenrich and M Loughlin (eds), *The Cambridge Companion to the Rule of Law* (Cambridge, Cambridge University Press, 2021) 406.

[12] F Fukuyama, 'The End of History?' (1989) 16 *The National Interest* 3, 15.

is, symbols of liberal democracies – had no ideological competitors left (even if he noted that religion and nationalism might still emerge as sources of conflict not easily resolvable in a liberal democracy).[13] This prediction gained traction, but the idea that liberal democracy and its associated institutions and values were safe would soon be proven wrong.[14] In 1997, Fareed Zakaria warned of the emerging threat posed by the global rise of democratically elected regimes which routinely ignored constitutional limits on their power and thereby deprived their citizens of their basic rights and freedoms. This practice and its associated problems, he pointed out, were widespread – from Peru to the Palestinian Authority, from Sierra Leone to Slovakia, from Pakistan to the Philippines – but had been difficult to recognise because

> for almost a century in the West, democracy has meant *liberal* democracy – a political system marked not only by free and fair elections, but also by the rule of law, a separation of powers, and the protection of basic liberties of speech, assembly, religion.[15]

This meant that the threat to liberal democracies came from within – not, as had been Fukuyama's focus, from outside. Today, the presence of illiberal democracies in the EU is obvious. Two Member States in particular – Hungary and Poland – are notorious examples,[16] with Viktor Orbán often seen as the poster boy.[17]

Hungary and Poland elected right-wing populist and national-conservative political parties to power in 1998 and 2005 respectively,[18] and have since held the dual status of democratic and authoritarian states. These governments' legitimacy, it is often argued, stems from the fact that they are 'reasonably democratic'.[19] Orbán, for example, calls his own illiberalism 'Christian democracy' so as to legitimise the authoritarian character of his government.[20]

This has sparked a debate in the EU about how to make sense of illiberal political parties that operate within the EU legal system. Are they a real threat to the liberal order upon which the EU is based, and if so, *how*? As mentioned earlier, the opinions on this are divided. Joseph Weiler, for instance, has argued that the notion of an illiberal democracy is an oxymoron, and that illiberal regimes and liberal democracies cannot coexist.[21] Allan Rosas seems to agree, explaining that, at least

[13] This was presented first as a talk, then as an article, see ibid, and finally as a book: F Fukuyama, *The End of History and the Last Man* (London, Penguin, 1992). For a contextual tracking of Fukuyama's work related to *The End of History*, see L Menand, 'Francis Fukuyama postpones the end of history', *The New Yorker* (27 August 2018).

[14] More recently, see L Ypi, *Free: Coming of Age at the End of History* (London, Penguin, 2021). Indeed, Fukuyama too recognises that liberal democracy, contrary to his earlier predictions, are fragile achievements, see F Fukuyama, *Identity: The Demand for Dignity and the Politics of Resentment* (New York, Farrar, Straus & Giroux, 2018).

[15] F Zakaria, 'The Rise of Illiberal Democracy' (1997) 76 *Foreign Affairs* 16, 22.

[16] See eg G Halmai, 'Illiberal Constitutionalism in East-central Europe' in A Bakardjieva-Engelbrekt, Andreas Moberg and Joakim Nergelius (eds), *Rule of Law in the EU: 30 Years After the Fall of the Berlin Wall* (Oxford, Hart Publishing, 2021) 51.

[17] F Plattner, 'Illiberal Democracy and the Struggle on the Right' (2019) 30 *Journal of Democracy* 5.

[18] See eg Halmai (above n 16).

[19] Zakaria (above n 15) 22.

[20] H Nyysönnen and J Metsäla, 'Liberal Democracy and Its Current Illiberal Critique: The emperor's new clothes?' (2021) 73 *Europe-Asia Studies* 273. Similar points are made in O Varol, 'Stealth Authoritarianism' (2015) 100 *Iowa Law Review* 1673.

[21] Weiler (above n 4).

in practice, it is impossible to establish 'watertight barriers' between democracy and rule of law,[22] while others, including András Sajó, reject the idea that illiberal democracies are based on a radical denial of the rule of law. The argument is that illiberal democracies are 'democracies of a troubling sort' in that they enable the totalitarian potential inherent in mass democracy and 'bring to light the authoritarian elements in liberal constitutions, which are historically unfinished and internally vulnerable'.[23]

Ultimately, this leads us back to a much older debate about the relationship between the rule of law and democracy.[24] What can be added is that the current ruling parties in both Hungary and Poland have become sources of inspiration for populists elsewhere in Europe. Take for example Marine Le Pen, the French right-wing front-woman. As part of her 2022 presidential bid, and following the delivery of the *K 3/21* judgment in which the Polish Constitutional Court sided with the ruling party in shooting down the supremacy of EU law, she went to Budapest to start her international political campaign. Having picked this particular right-wing hotspot as her destination, she made sure to applaud the Polish as well as the Hungarian governments for their insistence on national sovereignty and the will of 'the people' in rejecting rule-of-law-related demands by the EU.[25] In fact, the emphasis on sovereignty and 'the people' are the two canons of illiberal democracy.

III. TWO CANONS OF ILLIBERAL DEMOCRACY UNPACKED

The essence of illiberal democracy is difficult to pin down, as each such system is undoubtedly influenced by cultural factors.[26] Still, it is fair to say that it depends on two basic canons: emphasising the will of 'the people' and governance as 'rule *by* law' (legalism).[27] These two ingredients are fundamentally intertwined. As will be further explained below, in a typical illiberal democracy the will of 'the people' – through elections and/or general popular support – is used to demonstrate state sovereignty, which is then relied on to circumvent any rule-of-law demands by stipulating laws and procedures that evade these.

[22] See A Rosas' Chapter 2 of this book.

[23] A Sajó, *Ruling by Cheating: Governance in Illiberal Democracy* (Cambridge, Cambridge University Press, 2021) 25 and 32.

[24] See eg A Peczenik, *Vad är rätt? Om demokrati, rättssäkerhet, etik och juridisk argumentation* (Stockholm, Norstedts, 1995).

[25] 'Election présidentielle 2022: depuis la Hongrie, Marine Le Pen critique "la volonté d'asservissement de l'Union européenne"', *Le Monde* (26 October 2021).

[26] See eg *Green Wedge: The Report* (Counterpoint, 2020), counterpoint.uk.com/wp-content/uploads/2021/03/Green_Wedge_Counterpoint_OSEPI.pdf.

[27] This idea about legalism as a core component of populist regimes takes its inspiration from a rich range of scholarship, including J Corrales, 'The Authoritarian Resurgence: Authoritarian Legalism in Venezuela' (2015) 26 *Journal of Democracy* 37; and J-W Müller, *What is Populism?* (Philadelphia PA, University of Pennsylvania Press, 2016) and KL Scheppele, 'Autocratic legalism' (2018) 85 *The University of Chicago Law Review* 545.

A. 'The People' as per Populist Rhetoric

So, the first ingredient of any illiberal democracy is 'the people' (indeed, that is a crucial component of any populist rule). Although who exactly the people are is not always clear in populist rhetoric, it is not an inclusive concept,[28] but one that is 'anti-pluralist' and 'anti-elitist',[29] where 'the people' tend to be conceived as a moral entity with its claims rooted in moral precepts.[30] This is significant. If, as Benjamin Moffitt reconstructs the implicit logic, the leader represents or embodies 'the people's will', and 'the people' are always right, 'then the leader is also always right'.[31] As a consequence, any opposition, whether institutional or within civil society, poses a difficulty for populists, as it undermines their claim to being the sole representatives of the people.[32] This is why populist regimes go to such lengths to discredit their opponents, as can be observed in both Poland and Hungary in their governments' attacks on, for example, the independence of the judiciary and the media.

This is also to say that although reference to 'the people' promises to make good on democracy's highest ideals ('Let the people rule!)',[33] the concept of 'the people' creates the perfect circumstances for 'the tyranny of the majority'.[34] The business model of illiberal democratic regimes is thus simple: first pay allegiance to democracy; then use illiberal tactics to increase and perpetuate your own powers.[35] In this way, populism operates as 'the shadow of democracy'.[36]

Clearly, illiberal democracies have a complicated relationship with democracy, but when exactly do they pose a threat to it? Manuel Anselmi points out that once populist rule takes hold, it starts chipping away at democratic institutions.[37] Jan-Werner Müller further explains that populist rule will attempt to do three things once in power: colonise the state; engage in mass clientelism; and pass discriminatory laws.[38] This is done for the purpose of increasing populist domination over society, replacing the former reigning elite by an 'illiberal elite' and staying in power. This is the

[28] See I Berlin, 'To Define Populism' (1968) 3 *Government and Opposition* 137.

[29] See C Pinelli, 'The Rise of Populism and the Malaise of Democracy' in S Garben, I Govaere and P Nemitz (eds), *Critical Reflections on Constitutional Democracy in the European Union* (Oxford, Hart Publishing, 2019) 27.

[30] C Fieschi, *Populocracy: The Tyranny of Authenticity and the Rise of Populism* (Newcastle-upon-Tyne, Agenda, 2019) 27.

[31] B Moffitt, *The Global Rise of Populism: Performance, Political Style, and Representation* (Stanford CA, Stanford University Press, 2016) 148.

[32] J-W Müller, 'Populism and the People' (2019) 41(10) *London Review of Books* 35, 37.

[33] Müller (above n 27) 6.

[34] For an overview of the threat of executive power in particular, and how the barrier raised against tyranny sometimes itself becomes 'an insufferable tyranny', see B Constant, *The Liberty of the Ancient Compared with that of the Moderns* (1819, unknown), oll.libertyfund.org/title/constant-the-liberty-of-ancients-compared-with-that-of-moderns-1819.

[35] TS Pappas, 'The Specter Haunting Europe: Distinguishing Liberal Democracy's Challengers' (2016) 27 *Journal of Democracy* 22, 28.

[36] For a discussion on Margaret Canovan's idea of 'the shadow of democracy' in this context, see M Anselmi, *Populism: An Introduction* (New York, Routledge, 2018) ch 5.

[37] ibid 2.

[38] Müller (above n 27) 6.

reason why some scholars argue that populist governments should not be seen as corrupted democracies but quite simply as totalitarian,[39] and why some insist that 'illiberal democracy' is a misnomer.[40] From this point of view, populism is not simply a reaction to liberalism but an immediate threat to democracy itself.[41] It undermines the very essence of democracy by 'cheating the people'[42] of their legal and political safeguards through legislation and the rule *by* law.[43]

B. Rule *by* Law

Illiberal democracies favour a direct, unmediated relationship between the personal leader and the people. Yet this is not to say that they 'eschew constitutionalism'[44] altogether. As Catherine Fieschi has explained, institutions and procedures are needed in order to create those 'betrayal stories' upon which populist rule depends,[45] and ultimately, to undermine the rule of law. This is done by the principle of the rule *by* law, or *legalism*.[46]

In fact, legalism constitutes a key weapon of autocratic governance.[47] The concept is traceable at least as far back as to Thomas Hobbes's *Leviathan* wherein a sovereign ruler is envisaged as securing order through law.[48] This is not to say that legalism does not allow the possibility of an equilibrium of power in a democratic society. Legalism may help to establish a so-called 'lawyerdom' where law is separate from politics and morals, and rights and duties are determined by rules.[49]

This, however, is not the point of illiberal democracies. Rather, as Kim Lane Scheppele puts it, their aim is 'constitutional capture'; that is, to target 'the features of the constitutional order that will ultimately stand in the way of their domination of the political space'.[50] What populist leaders have understood is that they do not need to kill off their opponents to exercise unconstrained power – it will suffice to use

[39] See Scheppele (above n 27) and Pinelli (above n 29) 41.

[40] Pinelli (above n 29) 41.

[41] See eg Berlin (above n 28).

[42] See Sajó (above n 23).

[43] ibid, ch 7 and 8. See also N Bobbio, *The Future of Democracy* (Cambridge, Polity Press, 1987).

[44] N Lacey, 'Populism and the Rule of Law' (2019) 15 *Annual Review of Law and Social Sciences* 79.

[45] C Fieschi, *Populocracy* (Agenda 2019) 35.

[46] There has recently been an upsurge of scholarly treatments of rule *by* law, which have also inspired the present study. See in particular, G Palombella 'The Abuse of Rights and the Rule of Law' in A Sajó (ed), *The Dark Side of Fundamental Rights* (Eleven International Publishing 2006) 5, F Lovett, *A Republic of Law* (CUP 2016), A Barak, *The Judge in a Democracy* (Princeton NJ, Princeton University Press, 2008), M Tushnet, 'Rule by Law or Rule of Law' (2014) 22 *Asia Pacific Law Review* 79, J Meierhenrich, 'What the Rule of Law Is … and Is Not' in Meierhenrich and Loughlin (n 11) 569. Legalism, however, is not a new scholarly topic and was studied as part of the Weberian school of thought, see M Rheinstein (ed/tr), *Max Weber on Law in Economy and Society* (Cambridge MA, Harvard University Press, 1954).

[47] In the case of China, see Y Wang, *Tying the Autocrat's Hands: The Rise of the Rule of Law in China* (Cambridge, Cambridge University Press, 2015).

[48] For a comparator and discussion on this point and the tracing of rule of *laws* more generally, see F Pirie, *The Rule of Laws* (London, Profile, 2021) 326. See also Bobbio (above n 43) 143.

[49] See J Shklar, *Legalism: Law, Morals and Political Trials* (Cambridge MA, Harvard University Press, 1986) 17.

[50] See Scheppele (above n 27) 570.

the law.[51] This takes us to the distinction between 'thin' and 'thick' aspects of the rule of law.[52] As outlined by Brian Tamanaha, legalism is part of the 'thin', or 'formal', understanding of the rule of law, where the safeguards and checks are merely procedural and not substantive, or 'thick', requirements of the law.[53]

Why does this matter? As András Sajó and Juha Tuovinen explain, it makes responding to illiberal democracies hard, as they do not, at least not outright, reject the rule of law:

> To assume that the emerging illiberal regimes are based on a radical denial of the rule of law is wrong. We are confronted here with a borderline case, a mixture of an abused rule of law and rule by law; it is true that the rule of law is fatally compromised in matters crucial for the political power and related economic domination, but much less in everyday life. We can see how this legalism leads to a pattern where the rule of law is simultaneously followed and breached. There are two parts to the process: the first is a legally compliant change, the second is a replacement by a process that while on its face acceptable, works in the government's favour, or at least does not hinder it, ultimately – step by step – undoing the checks and balances of the constitutional system.[54]

In the end, illiberal regimes slowly break the so-called 'grammar of legality'[55] by pushing through constitutional reforms that change entirely the core structures, application and interpretation of the law, as in Hungary, where a new judiciary design as well as explicit principles and methods of constitutional interpretation have been introduced.[56] Poland has created its 'new grammar' by revising its laws on the retirement of judges, which has led to an overhaul of the judicial system.[57] This means that both Hungary and Poland insist on legalism. To these actors, respect for the rule *of* law is only a matter of form, not of substance. As Sajó explains, it is 'the unfaithfulness to the principles of constitutionalism and the narrowness in interpretation [that] disclose the importance of cheating with law as a central legal and social technique of illiberal democracy'.[58] These practices may not meet 'thick' or substantive rule-of-law checks, but they may well satisfy procedural or 'thin' rule-of-law safeguards.[59]

How, then, to respond to such actors? For a start, we must appreciate that illiberal democracies are chameleon democracies,[60] and be wary of their true intentions, which are often invisible or well hidden.[61] Unwrapping their abuse of the law – through

[51] ibid 577, the new autocrats aim to capture and exercise unconstrained power but they have realised that they don't need to annihilate their opponents to do so.

[52] For an overview of the debate, see J Waldron, 'The Rule of Law as an Essentially Contested Concept' in Meierhenrich and Loughlin (above n 11) 121.

[53] See B Tamanaha, *On The Rule of Law: History, Politic, History* (Cambridge, Cambridge University Press, 2004).

[54] Sajó and Tuovinen (above n 9) 522.

[55] See D Dyzenhaus, 'Thomas Hobbes and the Rule by Law Tradition' in Meierhenrich and Loughlin (eds), *Cambridge Companion to the Rule of Law* (above n 11) 261.

[56] For an overview and discussion on constitutional pluralism, see F Gárdos-Oroszorosz, 'The reference to constitutional traditions in populist constitutionalism – The case of Hungary' (2021) 61 *Hungarian Journal of Legal Studies* 23.

[57] This is discussed in section IV.

[58] Sajó (above n 23) ch 8.

[59] ibid.

[60] Scheppele (above n 27) 581.

[61] See Bobbio (above n 43) 79.

public reports, infringement actions or political sanctions – must thus be the first step in responding and counteracting rule-of-law abuses. This, indeed, is part of the EU's arsenal.

IV. TAKING STOCK: THE EU'S RESPONSE TO THE CURRENT RULE-OF-LAW CRISES

As the Treaty on the European Union (TEU) states, the Union 'is founded on the values of respect for … the rule of law'.[62] Although the scholarly debate as to what precisely this principle entails is ongoing,[63] the Commission offers a seemingly straightforward definition: 'The rule of law means that all members of society – governments and parliaments included – are equally subject to the law, under the control of independent courts irrespective of political majorities.'[64] Its website on 'Upholding the rule of law' provides a list of what appear to be simple lines of defence to secure that principle.[65] It includes the Article 7 TEU procedure which allows serious breaches of the rule of law to be identified and followed by sanctions; the 'rule of law framework', which is an early-warning tool adopted by the Commission aiming to prevent escalation of rule-of-law erosion, allowing it to enter into dialogue with a Member State to address systemic threats; as well as specific assistance to Bulgaria and Romania in areas of judicial reform and action on corruption and organised crime.[66] Not mentioned on the Commission's website, but of clear significance, are the national courts which generate preliminary references on matters pertaining to the rule of law, and which have allowed the Court to develop its jurisprudence on that topic.

The Commission's actions against Poland in the wake of its judicial reforms provide a useful illustration of the various avenues available to the Union.[67] In short, the current Polish government introduced a law subjecting judges of the ordinary courts to disciplinary investigations and potential sanctions on the basis of their judicial decisions. The Disciplinary Chamber of the Supreme Court, which is tasked with

[62] EU law scholars tend to see the rule of law as a 'common concept' of the EU Member States, see eg T Konstadinides, *The Rule of Law in the European Union* (Oxford, Hart Publishing, 2017); E Wennerström, *The Rule of Law and the European Union*' (Uppsala, Iustus, 2007); L Pech, 'The Rule of Law as a Constitutional Principle of the European Union', *Jean Monnet Working Paper 04/2009*. Cf M Loughlin, 'The Rule of Law in European Jurisprudence' (Venice Commission, Expert report, 2009).

[63] According to the 'formal and procedural ideal', the principle of the rule of law seeks to protect the judiciary and its proper functioning, as well as people's access to law, and their ability to rely upon fair and respectful procedures in the determination of their rights and claims: see J Waldron, *The Rule of Law and the Measure of Property* (Cambridge, Cambridge University Press, 2012) 77. Raz adopts a formal or thin conception, while Bingham offers a substantive view, see J Raz, 'The Rule of Law and Its Virtues' in J Raz (ed), *The Authority of Law: Essays on Law and Morality* (Oxford, Clarendon Press, 1979) 210, and T Bingham, *The Rule of Law* (London, Penguin, 2011).

[64] See 'The EU's Rule of Law Toolbox', ec.europa.eu/info/sites/info/files/rule_of_law_factsheet_1.pdf. Similarly outlined in the Commission's *2021 Rule of Law Report* (above n 7).

[65] See 'Upholding the rule of law', ec.europa.eu/info/policies/justice-and-fundamental-rights/upholding-rule-law_en.

[66] Communication from the Commission to the European Parliament and the Council, 'A New EU Framework to Strengthen the Rule of Law', COM(2014) 158 final.

[67] One of us has similarly outlined this in J Adams-Prassl and S Bogojević, *Great Debates in EU Law* (London, Bloomsbury Publishing, 2021) ch 11.

this review, is a body of judges selected by the National Council for the Judiciary, whose members are, in turn, appointed by the Polish parliament. The problem with this judicial structure is that the 'right to an effective remedy before an independent and impartial court' – as guaranteed under Article 19(1) TEU and Article 47 of the Charter of Fundamental Rights of the European Union (Charter) – is at risk, as is, too, the preliminary reference procedure that depends on politically unfettered courts for its operation.

The Commission's first step in addressing this rule-of-law crisis was to open a dialogue with the Polish government in 2016 under the Rule of Law Framework, which allows direct dialogue with a Member State on which the Commission then informs the European Parliament and the Council. As no progress was made at this stage, the Commission in 2017 activated Article 7 TEU – for the first time ever – calling on the Council to determine whether a 'clear risk of a serious breach' of the rule of law existed.[68] At the time of writing, the Council has yet to formulate an opinion on this.[69] Also noteworthy is the European Parliament's use of Article 7 TEU. In 2018, the Parliament voted in favour of action against Hungary for breaching Article 7 TEU, and similarly called on the Council to establish whether there was 'a clear risk of a serious breach' of the values on which the EU is founded.[70] The Council has not yet decided on this call either, though it has dismissed an attempt by Hungary and supported by Poland to annul the European Parliament's resolution.[71]

Clearly, Article 7 TEU allows both political and judicial action. With regard to the latter, credit is due to the national courts that have played a crucial role by issuing preliminary references, allowing the Court to develop its rule-of-law jurisprudence. The landmark case includes the Court of Justice's judgment in *Associação Sindical dos Juízes Portugueses*,[72] in which the Supreme Administrative Court of Portugal asked the European Court of Justice (ECJ) whether a reduction in the salaries of Portuguese judges was a violation of the principle of judicial independence. The Court found that it was not, but added – and this is the significant bit – that even in cases where a Member State is not 'implementing' EU law (so that it is not bound by the Charter), it may still be subject to obligations concerning its judicial structure, drawn from Article 19 TEU. This means that Article 19 TEU applies where the Charter does not,[73] giving the ECJ additional tools for supervising degradations of the rule of law, which, in contrast to Article 7 TEU, cannot be blocked by political veto. Relying on this reasoning,[74] the Court has found, in multiple actions against

[68] Proposal for a Council Decision on the determination of a clear risk of a serious breach by the Republic of Poland of the rule of law, COM(2017) 0835 final.

[69] Though interim reports have been issued, see 'Rule of Law in Poland – Article 7(1) TEU Reasoned Proposal – Report on the hearing held by the Council on 22 June 2021', Council doc. 10246/21.

[70] European Parliament resolution of 12 September 2018 on a proposal calling on the Council to determine, pursuant to Article 7(1) of the Treaty on European Union, the existence of a clear risk of a serious breach by Hungary of the values on which the Union is founded (2017/2131(INL)).

[71] C-650/18 *Hungary v European Parliament*, ECLI:EU:C:2021:426.

[72] C-64/16 *Associação Sindical dos Juízes Portugueses v Tribunal de Contas*, ECLI:EU:C:2018:117, [30].

[73] On this point see also C-824/18, *A.B. and Others v Krajowa Rada Sądownictwa and Others*, ECLI:EU:C:2021:153, [88].

[74] See M Bonelli and M Claes, 'Judicial Serendipity: how Portuguese judges came to the rescue of the Polish judiciary' (2018) 14 *EuConst* 622.

Poland concerning both the compulsory retirement[75] and the disciplinary regime for judges,[76] violations of the requirements of judicial independence. Once Poland refused to comply with interim measures to suspend the Disciplinary Chamber, the Court imposed a record fine of €1 million for each day that Poland ignores its order.[77] At the time of writing, Poland has yet to pay the accumulated fines.

Clearly, there is a great deal of both political and legal activity in this area, and rule-of-law litigation is dynamic and developing fast. According to Armin von Bogdandy, Article 2 TEU allow values to feature prominently in the Court's case law, and as such, these judicial actions can be seen as 'a veritable stepping stone towards a "Union of values" and stand on a par with the Court's constitutionalizing jurisprudence in *van Gend en Loos* and *Costa/ENEL*'.[78] But how justifiable is it for the Court to add a judicial route for supervising the rule of law in Member States under Article 19 TEU? Is the sluggish and politically torn nature of the process that Article 7 TEU establishes grounds enough? What are the risks created by this approach, and, on the flip side, are these mechanisms *enough* for safeguarding the rule of law?

V. ARE THE EU'S EFFORTS ENOUGH?

The short answer to whether the EU's efforts in arm-wrestling illiberal democracies in Europe are enough is: we do not yet know. The delivery of the *K3/21* judgment by the Polish Constitutional Tribunal is alarming, as are the findings in the Commission's annual Rule of law Reports. Moreover, the populist threat to democracy has been further fuelled by the Covid-19 pandemic.[79] As such, it is not yet time for the EU to lay down arms.

How should the EU go about responding to these crises, then? Article 7 TEU processes are painfully slow and politically fraught.[80] Indeed, on 16 January 2020, the European Parliament found that 'the situation in both Poland and Hungary has deteriorated since the triggering of Article 7(1) [TEU]' and that 'failure by the Council to make effective use of Article 7 [TEU] continues to undermine the integrity of common European values, mutual trust and the credibility of the European Union as a whole'.[81] This calls attention to the significance of constitutional drafting,[82] and

[75] See C-192/18 *Commission v Poland* ECLI:EU:C:2019:924, C-619/18 R *Commission v Poland*, ECLI:EU:C:2018:910.

[76] C-791/19 R *Commission v Poland*, ECLI:EU:C:2020:277.

[77] C-204/21 R *Commission v Poland*, ECLI:EU:C:2021:878.

[78] A von Bogdandy, 'Principles of a Systemic Deficiencies Doctrine: how to protect checks and balances in the Member States' (2020) 57 *CML Rev* 705, 712–13.

[79] The Global State of Democracy 2021: Building Resilience in a Pandemic Era (2021 International Institute for Democracy and Electoral Assistance), www.idea.int/gsod/sites/default/files/2021-11/the-global-state-of-democracy-2021_0.pdf.

[80] See eg D Kochenov, 'Article 7: A Commentary on a Much Talked-About "Dead" Provision' in von Bogdandy et al (eds), *Defending Checks and Balances in EU Member States* (above n 6) 127.

[81] European Parliament, 'Rule of law in Poland and Hungary has worsened', see 'Ongoing hearings under article 7(1) of the TEU regarding Poland and Hungary European Parliament resolution of 16 January 2020' (2020/2513(RSP)) [2021] OJ C 270/91.

[82] See eg NW Barber, M Cahill and R Ekins, *The Rise and Fall of the European Constitution* (Oxford, Hart Publishing, 2019).

invites speculation as to whether insisting on the inclusion of the primacy clause, as presented in the now failed Constitutional Treaty, might have helped avoid this crisis altogether. Perhaps also Article 7 TEU could be redrafted in future Treaty revisions to be made more effective by preventing political bottlenecks in the Council.

Yet there are more imminent legal developments worthy of our attention. These include Regulation 2020/2092 that makes funding to the Member States conditional upon their safeguarding the rule of law,[83] which would put economic pressure on Member States to comply with Article 2 TEU. Although, at the time of writing, this law is being challenged by both Poland and Hungary before the ECJ,[84] and in the interim it will not be enforced by the EU institutions, it is still a significant legislative move to highlight ways in which the rule of law might be safeguarded by pushing financial pressure points.

No less important are the Commission's multiple legislative proposals on transparency and political advertising, aimed at protecting election integrity and open democratic debate. These measures build on the Commission's *Democracy Action Plan*[85] and complement its ambitious European digital strategy, including the Digital Services Act[86] and the Digital Markets Act,[87] which seek to regulate digital platforms by addressing matters such as online advertising and disinformation. Developing so-called 'digital constitutionalism' is significant in responding to practices that have helped populist parties thwart fair democratic processes, and it shows that action on rule-of-law protection can target not only Member State measures but also the activities of businesses, in this case tech giants.[88]

Moving from legislative action, the Court has long been establishing significant legal reasoning on the rule of law,[89] which it can helpfully insist on and develop beyond the specific crises in Poland and Hungary. Here, its interpretation of Article 19 TEU, mentioned above, to include judicial independence for national courts, is noteworthy. In *Repubblika*,[90] for example, it was called on to review the compatibility of a Maltese law that permitted the Prime Minister to appoint members of the judiciary with that article. Relying on its Article 19 TEU line of cases, it found that 'In accordance with the principle of the separation of powers which characterises the operation

[83] Regulation (EU, Euratom) 2020/2092 of the European Parliament and of the Council of 16 December 2020 on a general regime of conditionality for the protection of the Union budget [2021] OJ L 433I/1.

[84] Cases C-156/21, *Hungary v European Parliament and Council*, ECLI:EU:C:2022:97; C-157/21, *Poland v European Parliament and Council*, ECLI:EU:C:2022:98.

[85] Communication from the Commission to the European Parliament, the Council, the European Economic and Social Committee and the Committee of the Regions, 'On the European democracy action plan', COM(2020) 790 final.

[86] Proposal for a Regulation of the European Parliament and of the Council on a Single Market for Digital Services (Digital Services Act) and amending Directive 2000/31/EC, COM(2020) 825 final.

[87] Proposal for a Regulation of the European Parliament and of the Council on contestable and fair markets in the digital sector (Digital Markets Act), COM(2020) 842 final, see eg preamble, recital 42.

[88] H Roberts et al, 'Safeguarding European Values with Digital Sovereignty: an analysis of statements and policies' (2021) 10 *Internet Policy Review* 1; L Floridi, 'The Fight for Digital Sovereignty: What It is; and Why It Matters, Especially for the EU' (2020) 33 *Philosophy and Technology* 369.

[89] L Pech, 'The Rule of Law in the EU: The Evolution of the Treaty Framework and the Rule of Law Toolbox', *Working Paper No 7* (March 2020 Reconnect).

[90] Case C-896/19 *Repubblika v Il-Prim Ministru*, ECLI:EU:C:2021:311.

of the rule of law, the independence of the judiciary must in particular be ensured in relation to the legislature and the executive'.[91] This shows Article 19 TEU, independently from Article 7 TEU, protecting the rule of law.

In contrast to Article 19 TEU, Article 47 of the Charter, which insists on effective judicial protection, has been given less enforceability by the ECJ. More precisely, the Court has explained that

> while Article 47 of the Charter helps to ensure respect for the right to effective judicial protection of any individual relying, in a given case, on a right which he or she derives from EU law, the second subparagraph of Article 19(1) TEU seeks to ensure that the system of legal remedies established by each Member State guarantees effective judicial protection in the fields covered by EU law.[92]

More interesting, however, is that in the same case the Court found that 'Article 47 of the Charter must be duly taken into consideration for the purposes of interpreting that provision [Article 19(1) TEU]'.[93] This gently opens the door to a more imaginative use of the Charter than has been witnessed to date in rule-of-law adjudication.

In addition to the jurisprudence on the rule of law, the Court has been developing case law on the democratic requirements for Member States in order to protect liberal democracy in Europe. In *Junqueras*,[94] for example, the Court relied on Article 10(1) TEU – which provides that the functioning of the Union is to be founded on the principle of representative democracy – in ruling on whether the composition of the European Parliament may be restricted by national legislation, concluding that:

> in the case of the European Parliament, those objectives imply not only that, in accordance with the principle of representative democracy … and with Article 14 TEU, its composition must reflect faithfully and completely the free expression of choices made by the citizens of the European Union, by direct universal suffrage, as regards the persons by whom they wish to be represented during a given term, but also that the European Parliament must be protected, in the exercise of its tasks, against hindrances or risks to its proper operation.[95]

More importantly yet, the Court also invoked Article 2 TEU in this case to rule specifically against legalism. It reasoned that

> compliance by a Member State with the values enshrined in Article 2 TEU is a condition for the enjoyment of all of the rights deriving from the application of the Treaties to that Member State. A Member State cannot therefore amend its legislation in such a way as to bring about a reduction in the protection of the value of the rule of law, a value which is given concrete expression by, inter alia, Article 19 TEU.[96]

For the legislators and the ECJ to take such action is not without risk, however. One risk is that the Union may be called out for double standards on both democracy

[91] C-585/18, C-624/18 and C-625/18, *A.K. and Others v Sąd Najwyższy*, EU:C:2019:982, para 124.
[92] Case C-896/19 *Repubblika v Il-Prim Ministru*, ECLI:EU:C:2021:311, para 52.
[93] ibid, para 46.
[94] Case C-502/19 *Oriol Junqueras Vies*, ECLI:EU:C:2019:1115.
[95] ibid, para 83.
[96] ibid [63].

and the rule of law.[97] Criticism of its alleged democratic deficit is well-known,[98] and in dealing with the 2008 economic crisis in particular, and arguably also its internal governance,[99] the EU has proven less righteous in facing rule-of-law demands of itself than it demands of its Member States today.[100] Because of this, the danger is that the EU will be left insisting on rule-of-law ideals, democratic safeguards, and human rights protection in an echo chamber. This has already been seen in the limited impact its support for the rule of law has had in legal reforms in the West Balkans.[101]

So how does 'Brussels' make sure it is not just talking to itself? The EU Regulation on climate neutrality[102] provides an example. Its Article 9 stipulates that to achieve climate neutrality by 2050, the Commission must carry out 'inclusive and accessible' dialogue at national, regional and local levels, in concert with 'social partners, academia, the business community, citizens and civil society, for the exchange of best practice'. Similarly, the 'European Climate Pact', also geared towards climate neutrality, aims to give 'everyone a voice and space to design new climate actions, share information, launch grassroots activities and showcase solutions that others can follow'. To be sure, the implementation of these objectives may well run into practical stumbling blocks.[103] How will conflicting narratives be weighed against each other? Who will be given the final say, and on what grounds? But the crucial point here is that the EU is attempting a creative and inclusive political forum required both for improving its democratic profile and establishing a joint European public debate to counteract populists.[104]

VI. FURTHER REFLECTIONS

Above we reference 'the EU' in the singular, asking what it can and should do in terms of current rule-of-law crises. This is not uncommon in EU law scholarship.

[97] See S Garben, 'The Principle of Legality and the EU's Legitimacy' in *Critical Reflections on Constitutional Democracy in the European Union* (above n 30) 395, 415.

[98] For an overview, see Adams-Prassl and Bogojević (above n 67) ch 5.

[99] This point relates to the dismissal of AG Sharpston following Brexit, see the series D Kochenov and G Butler, 'CJEU's Independence and Lawful Composition in Question', *Verfassungsblog* (19 June 2021).

[100] See eg C Kilpatrick, 'On the Rule of Law and Economic Emergency: The Degradation of Basic Legal Values in Europe's Bailouts' (2015) 35 *Oxford Journal of Legal Studies* 3. See also L Besselink, 'The Eclipse of Legality – An Assessment' in L Besselink, F Pennings, and S Prechal (eds), *The Eclipse of the Legality Principles in EU Law* (Alphen aan den Rijn, Kluwer Law International, 2011); and X Groussot and A Zemskova, 'The Rise of the Procedural Rule of Law in the European Union' in *Rule of Law in the EU: 30 Years after the Fall of the Berlin Wall* (above n 16) 269.

[101] European Court of Auditors, 'EU Support for the rule of law in the Western Balkans: despite efforts, fundamental problems persist' (Special Report January 2022), www.eca.europa.eu/en/Pages/DocItem.aspx?did=60343.

[102] Regulation (EU) 2021/1119 of the European Parliament and of the Council of 30 June 2021 establishing the framework for achieving climate neutrality and amending Regulations (EC) No 401/2009 and (EU) 2018/1999 ('European Climate Law') [2021] OJ L 243.

[103] For an empirical study of climate assemblies, see L-A Duvic-Paoli, 'Re-imagining the Making of Climate Law and Policy in Citizens' Assemblies' (2022) 11 *Transnational Environmental Law* 235.

[104] Rallying around common interests and inviting a public debate on, in this context, climate action, are suggested to be an antidote to both populism and technocracy, see W Streeck, 'In the Superstate', *London Review of Books* (27 January 2022).

EU actions are often seen as something that happens 'over there' – either 'tucked away in the fairyland Duchy of Luxembourg'[105] in the case of the ECJ, or in Brussels, 'a distant, unfamiliar, even threatening place, populated by antagonistic strangers with different interests and goals',[106] in the case of EU law-making. In fact, alienation from the EU as a public space is a key feature of Eurosceptic populism, as evidenced in both Poland and Hungary.[107] Yet any dive into the workings of the EU – whether those of law-making, the appointment of officials, or the workability of its law in practice – shows that 'the EU' is in fact a multileveled and multifaceted legal order. It is not a sole actor but a collective force. Ultimately, this means that to ensure 'eternal vigilance' of democratic values and the rule of law, collective action – by the EU institutions, the Member States, and private actors including businesses, NGOs, academics, and private individuals – will be needed.

[105] E Stein, 'Lawyers, Judges, and the Making of a Transnational Constitution' (1981) 75 American Journal of International Law 1, 1.

[106] D Kenealy and F Hayes-Renshaw, 'How Policies are Made' in D Kenealy, J Peterson and R Corbett (eds), *The European Union: How does it work?* (5th edn, OUP 2018) 124.

[107] R Csehi and E Zgut, '"We won't let Brussels dictate us": Eurosceptic populism in Hungary and Poland' (2020) Eur Politics and Society.

5

The Rule of Law and Legal Certainty

JUHA RAITIO

I. INTRODUCTION

RULE OF LAW is a highly topical issue in European legal studies and politics. The European Union has developed several institutions for the promotion of the rule of law in recent years. For example, the European Commission established an operational framework for the rule of law in 2014,[1] and the European Court of Justice has recognised its significance for its judicial practice.[2] In 2016, the European Parliament issued a statement on an EU system governing democracy, the rule of law, and fundamental rights, encouraging the Commission to establish monitoring and an annual reporting period for all Member States and the EU executive institutions and to issue recommendations for the actualisation of the rule of law.[3] Additionally, the so-called Conditionality Regulation concerning the protection of the Union's budget in situations where general shortcomings can be detected in the observation of the rule of law in the Member States is worth mentioning as well.[4] As further background, it should be noted that the development of the rule of law in Poland and Hungary in particular has been critically evaluated in both the Commission[5] and the ECJ. The ECJ has had to take a stand in defence of the rule

[1] See Communication from the Commission to the European Parliament and the Council, 'A new EU Framework to strengthen the Rule of Law', COM(2014) 158 final of 11 March 2014.

[2] See Order of the Court in Case C-619/18 R, *Commission v Poland* ECLI:EU:C:2018:1021, paras 81–84.

[3] See European Parliament Resolution of 25 October 2016 with recommendations to the Commission on the establishment of an EU mechanism on democracy, the rule of law and fundamental rights 2015/2254 (INL).

[4] See Regulation (EU, Euratom) 2020/2092 of the European Parliament and the Council of 16 December 2020 on a general regime of conditionality for the protection of the Union budget OJ L433l/1. This Regulation is legally grounded in Article 322(1)(a) TFEU, ie the financial management rules issued by the Parliament and the Council by means of regulations.

[5] See Communication from the Commission to the European Parliament, the Council, the European Economic and Social Committee and the Committee of the Regions, (*2020 Rule of Law Report*), *The rule of law situation in the European Union*, COM(2020) 580 final of 30 September 2020 and Communication from the Commission to the European Parliament, the Council, the European Economic and Social Committee and the Committee of the Regions (*2021 Rule of Law Report*), *The rule of law situation in the European Union*, COM(2021) 700 final of 20 July 2021.

of law, especially in contexts relating to the impartiality of the courts.[6] Bearing in mind this current backsliding of the rule of law in certain Member States and the attempts to enhance protection of the rule of law and the value basis of the EU, it is relevant to study the intertwined concepts of the rule of law and legal certainty.

II. THE RULE OF LAW REQUIRES LEGAL CERTAINTY

The rule of law and legal certainty are closely connected, but they have different meanings. Rule of law essentially aims at limiting the abuse of power. It implies the absence of wide discretionary powers in the government that may encroach upon the human rights of an individual citizen in a civil society. The emphasis here is on the rule of law instead of the rule by law. However, it currently seems that especially Poland and Hungary have partially returned to the old authoritarian administrative 'rule by law culture', which makes it topical to study issues such as the rule of law or mutual trust in the EU.[7] In Eastern European countries under the communist regime, the law was understood in its relation to the state. Its purpose was to discipline people and to create some kind of bureaucratic consistency in the administration of state affairs.[8] In legal literature, this recent development has been called 'illiberal democracy'.[9]

The idea of the rule of law requires a certain kind of conception of democracy, in which the government is subordinate to the legislator, or parliament. Thus, the concepts of rule of law, legality, human rights, and democracy are intertwined. At least that is what has traditionally been perceived as the main idea of the rule of law in the European context. Husa has aptly pointed out that rule of law has become a kind of legal panacea, which allegedly translates into economic and social improvement.[10] Tuori, in turn, has observed that the rule of law has been treated as an ideal of a

[6] See, eg Case C-64/16 *Associação Sindical dos Juízes Portugueses v Tribunal de Contas* ECLI:EU:C:2018:117, paras 30 and 36, and the issues concerning Poland in Case C-216/18 PPU, *Minister for Justice and Equality v LM* ECLI:EU:C:2018:586, para 48, Case C-619/18, *Commission v Poland* ECLI:EU:C:2018:910, para 21, Order of the Court in Case C-619/18 R, *Commission v Poland*, Case C-192/18 *Commission v Poland* ECLI:EU:C:2019:924, Joined Cases C-558/18 and C-563/18 *Miasto Łowicz* ECLI:EU:C:2020:234 and Case C-791/19 *Commission v Poland* ECLI:EU:C:2021:596. Even the independence of the Bar Association's Disciplinary Court has been challenged in Poland lately, which is demonstrated by Case C-55/20 *Minister Sprawiedliwości* ECLI:EU:C:2022:6.

[7] In Poland, the Law and Justice party has enacted legislative changes that questioned the independence of Poland's Constitutional Court. For this reason, the EU introduced the procedure under Article 7 TEU, on which see Commission Recommendation (EU) 2016/1374 of 27 July 2016 regarding the rule of law in Poland, [2016] OJ L 217/53. In addition, the government of Hungary has already for years weakened the independence of the Constitutional Court and the freedom of the media and the freedom of the civil society.

[8] On rule by law thought in Eastern Europe, see A Sájo, 'Rule by Law in East Central Europe' in V Gessner, A Hoeland and C Varga (eds), *European Legal Cultures* (Aldershot, Dartmouth Publishers, 1996) 471–73.

[9] See, eg B Bugarič, 'Protecting Democracy inside the EU: On Article 7 TEU and the Hungarian Turn to Authoritarianism' in C Closa and D Kochenov (eds), *Reinforcing Rule of Law Oversights in the European Union* (Cambridge, Cambridge University Press, 2016) 82–101.

[10] See J Husa, *Advanced Introduction to Law and Globalisation* (Cheltenham, Edward Elgar, 2018) 50.

good legal system as well as a legal principle of existing law.[11] So the rule of law is a context-bound legal-cultural concept, which cannot be defined by a few descriptive formulations, because of its nature as an underlying principle of law.

Also, the principle of legal certainty is such a multi-dimensional principle that it is difficult to define, and various attempts to do so have been controversial. For example, in Groussot's words, legal certainty reflects the ultimate necessity of clear, stable and intelligible law.[12] In general, legal certainty is taken to express a fundamental principle according to which the addressees of laws must know the law in order to be able to plan their actions in accordance with it. There is a division between formal and substantive legal certainty, between predictability and acceptability.[13] The attempts to define legal certainty have lately been studied from a comparative perspective in the European context. This study confirms that the formal elements of legal certainty are relatively often balanced with its more substantial ones.[14]

The principle of legal certainty has been interpreted as one sub-factor of the rule of law in the so-called Venice Commission's report.[15] According to the report, legal certainty plays a key role from the perspective of the reliability of the legal system. Achieving reliability requires legislation to be as clear and accurate as possible, easy to access and practically implementable. The application of law must be predictable and consistent, so that individual citizens are able to plan their actions in accordance with law. For example, the public must be accurately informed of the entry into force of a law.

According to the Venice Commission's report, a certain material element in law can be associated with legal certainty, because a legislator must not dismiss fundamental or human rights in legislation which offers individuals judicial protection against the executive power. On the other hand, the actions of the body applying the law may also violate legal certainty, if the higher courts' judgments internally contradict. It is therefore essential to ensure that the legal praxis is consistent and coherent. In addition, law in a material sense is also indicated by the fact that laws must be imposed in such a manner that they do not violate the general sense of justice. Individuals are also protected by the principle of legitimate expectations, wherein the government or the courts must fulfil their legal commitment in relation to the individual.[16]

In order to illuminate the intertwinement of the rule of law and legal certainty let's consider the story of an American judge as told by Bix, where the judge decided between guilt or innocence during a criminal case by the flip of a coin, when he

[11] See K Tuori, *Ratio and Voluntas, The Tension Between Reason and Will in Law* (Farnham, Ashgate, 2011) 210–11, and similarly Å Frändberg *From Rechtsstaat to Universal Law-State, An Essay in Philosophical Jurisprudence* (Dordrecht, Springer, 2014) 6, in which he states that the nucleus of his law–state thinking is that the individual enjoys legal protection against violations caused by the exercise of authority on the part of the public power.

[12] See X Groussot, *General Principles of Community Law* (Groningen, Europa Law Publishing, 2006) 189.

[13] See E Paunio, *Legal Certainty in Multilingual EU Law, Language, Discourse and Reasoning at the European Court of Justice* (Farnham, Ashgate, 2013) 51–55 and 73.

[14] See M Fenwick, M Siems, and S Wrbka (eds), *The Shifting Meaning of Legal Certainty in Comparative and Transnational Law* (Oxford, Hart Publishing, 2017) 7.

[15] See European Commission for Democracy Through Law (Venice Commission), *Report on the Rule of Law*, Adopted by the Venice Commission at its 86th plenary session, Venice 25–26 March 2011, Strasbourg, 4 April 2011, Study No. 512/2009, CDL-AD(2011)003rev., 10–11.

[16] ibid, 10–11, paras 44–51.

could not decide the case on the basis of evidence.[17] This kind of behaviour constitutes abuse of power, and it conflicts with the demands of both rule of law and legal certainty. A judge or an official making legal settlements cannot gamble with his/her decisions under the rule of law, or otherwise act in an arbitrary manner. Actions must not be based on mere chance, but instead must be based on law. The predictability in the adjudication of disputes as referred to by legal certainty is not, however, the same as predictability in probability calculus. In other words, the probability of a criminal conviction in Bix's example is 50 per cent, but this is not predictability in the context of law. Predictability is measured in relation to the relevant norms and interpretation practice, which on the other hand emphasises the significance of the coherence of judicial interpretation.

III. HOW CAN THE RULE OF LAW BE DEFINED IN THE FRAMEWORK OF EU LAW?

The rule of law is not perceived merely as a formal principle of legality or conformity required for observing law. Nowadays, the rule of law is rather often seen in EU law to have material content, which partially explains the fact that the rule of law has begun to be applied as a legal argument in EU courts. As a practical example, one can point to the legal cases concerning the independence of the judicial system, which have lately caused some debate.[18] It has been emphasised in legal praxis that the existence of effective judicial review is an inseparable part of the rule of law.[19] Each individual's right to an independent court can be justified by referring to Article 47 of the Charter of Fundamental Rights of the European Union (the Charter).[20] Judicial review and its relation to the rule of law have not very clearly been stressed in the older case law, whereas in more recent case law the connection between judicial review and the rule of law has been expressed clearly in the wording of the reasoning.[21] For example, in *Rosneft* the Court stated as follows:

> It may be added that Article 47 of the Charter, which constitutes a reaffirmation of the principle of effective judicial protection, requires, in its first paragraph, that any person

[17] See B Bix, *Language and Legal Determinacy* (Oxford, Oxford University Press, 1995) 106.

[18] See eg Case C-64/16 *Associação Sindical dos Juízes Portugueses v Tribunal de Contas* ECLI:EU:C:2018:117, paras 30 and 36, Case C-896/19 *Repubblika v Il-Prim Ministru* ECLI:EU:C:2021:311, para 53 and the issue concerning Poland, Case C-216/18 PPU, *Minister for Justice and Equality v LM* ECLI:EU:C:2018:586, para 48, as well as Case C-619/18, *Commission v Poland* ECLI:EU:C:2018:910, para 21, which states the following: 'It must be recalled that the requirement of judicial independence forms part of the essence of the fundamental right to a fair trial, a right which is of cardinal importance as a guarantee that all the rights which individuals derive from EU law will be protected and that the values common to the Member States set out in Article 2 TEU, in particular the value of the rule of law, will be safeguarded.'

[19] See Case C-72/15 *PJSC Rosneft Oil Company v HM Treasury and Others* ECLI:EU:C:2017:236, para 73 and cases cited, and Case C-64/16 *Associação Sindical dos Juízes Portugueses v Tribunal de Contas* ECLI:EU:C:2018:117, para 36.

[20] See Case C-619/18, *Commission v Poland* ECLI:EU:C:2018:910, para 20 and Case C-791/19 *Commission v Poland* ECLI:EU:C:2021:596, paras 165–67.

[21] See Case C-562/13 *Centre public d'action sociale d'Ottignies-Louvain-La-Neuve v Abdida* ECLI:EU:C:2014:2453, para 45, Case C-362/14 *Schrems v Data Protection Commissioner* ECLI:EU:C:2015:650, para 95 and Case C-72/15 *Rosneft* ECLI:EU:C:2017:236, para 73.

> whose rights and freedoms guaranteed by EU law are violated should have the right to an effective remedy before a tribunal in compliance with the conditions laid down in that article. It must be recalled that the very existence of effective judicial review designed to ensure compliance with provisions of EU law is of the essence of the rule of law.[22]

Here it is worth noting how the European Court of Justice associates the implementation of the rule of law with fundamental and human rights. In the same way as demonstrated in Article 2 TEU, it is typical for the EU concept of the rule of law to connect democracy, human rights, equality and the rule of law as part of the same ensemble, which is described well in the following quotation from the *Kadi* case:

> It is also clear from the case-law that respect for human rights is a condition of the lawfulness of Community acts (Opinion 2/94, paragraph 34) and that measures incompatible with respect for human rights are not acceptable in the Community (Case C-112/00 *Schmidberger* [2003] ECR I-5659, paragraph 73 and case-law cited).[23]

Therefore, the legal praxis of the ECJ that puts EU Member States under obligation has indications that the rule of law includes certain material prerequisites for legal decision-making in its European judicial context.[24] This is in line with the strengthened status of human rights protection, especially after the coming into force of the Lisbon Treaty and the reliance on the Charter in the case law of the European Court of Justice.[25] From the perspective of EU law, the concept of the rule of law therefore has a material element due to individuals' judicial protection and, for example, fundamental and human rights.[26]

Thus, the rule of law must be interpreted in connection with the value base of Article 2 TEU, which has been brought up in the Commission's Communication of 3 April 2019 as follows:

> The rule of law is enshrined in Article 2 [TEU] as one of the founding values of the Union. Under the rule of law, all public powers always act within the constraints set out by law, in accordance with the values of democracy and fundamental rights, and under the control of independent and impartial courts. The rule of law includes, among others, principles

[22] Case C-72/15 *Rosneft* ECLI:EU:C:2017:236, para 73. See also Case C-896/19 *Repubblika* ECLI:EU:C:2021:311, paras 43–46 and 52–54.

[23] Joined Cases C-402/05 P and C-415/05 P, *Kadi* and *Al Barakaat* ECLI:EU:C:2008:461, para 284. See, respectively, also Case C-112/00 Eugen *Schmidberger, Internationale Transporte und Planzüge v Republik Österreich* ECLI:EU:C:2003:333, para 73.

[24] See Case 8/55 *Fédération Charbonnière de Belgique v High Authority of the European Coal and Steel Community(Fédéchar)* ECLI:EU:C:1956:7, [1954–56] ECR 292, at p 299, and the cases concerning the rule of law that concern indemnity beyond EU law, see eg Case 5/71 *Aktien-Zuckerfabrik Schöppenstedt v Council* ECLI:EU:C:1971:116, Case 20/88 *Roquette frères SA v Commission* ECLI:EU:C:1989:221, Case C-152/88 *Sofrimport SARL v Commission* ECLI:EU:C:1992:21 and Case C-282/90 *Industrie- en Handelsonderneming Vreugdenhill BV v Commission* ECLI:EU:C:1992:124. See also Case C-284/16 *Slovak Republic v Achmea BV* ECLI:EU:C:2018:158, para 34, which concerns the autonomy of EU law in connection with the bilateral investment treaties.

[25] About the relationship between the Charter and the European Convention of Human Rights, see eg Case C-386/10 *Chalkor AE Epexergasias Metallon v Commission* ECLI:EU:C:2011:815, para 51 and Case C-791/19 *Commission v Poland*, para 165.

[26] See, for example, A Von Bogdandy, C Antpöhler and M Ioannidis, 'Protecting EU Values, Reverse *Solange* and the Rule of Law Framework' in A Jakab and D Kochenov (eds) *The Enforcement of EU Law and Values* (Oxford, Oxford University Press, 2017) 226.

> such as legality, implying a transparent, accountable, democratic and pluralistic process for enacting laws; legal certainty; prohibiting the arbitrary exercise of executive power; effective judicial protection by independent and impartial courts, effective judicial review including respect for fundamental rights; separation of powers; and equality before the law. These principles have been recognised by the European Court of Justice and the European Court of Human Rights.[27]

To this extent, there is reason to also refer to the so-called Venice Commission's report concerning the rule of law[28] or to the recent Conditionality Regulation,[29] wherein the rule of law is strongly connected to democracy and the requirement to implement human rights. The discourse concerning the rule of law in the EU cannot, therefore, be separated from the democracy that creates an environment for interpretation of the rule of law, the principle of the separation of powers[30] and the legal principles and human rights that legitimise the judicial system. In this context, the principle of the rule of law is not merely a 'rhetorical balloon', which can in a sense be filled up and include all that is deemed positive in law.[31] The concept of the rule of law becomes a type of value-based ideal, according to which the development of societies is measured.[32]

Bearing in mind the current backsliding of the rule of law in some Member States, one may pose the question whether the definition of the rule of law connected with Article 2 TEU is contradicted by the equality of the Member States and the respect for national identity mentioned in Article 4(2) TEU. The answer to this question is clearly negative. It may be considered important that the citizens and national authorities have trust in the actualisation of the rule of law of the Member States, in order for the EU to reach its essential objectives and act as a supranational legal system where the authorities of the Member States implement EU law.[33] The equality of the Member States requires that both small and large Member States commit to upholding and achieving the shared values and objectives of the EU. This is of course also required of countries that are seeking to become Member States, pursuant to Article 49 TEU. Equality is likewise implemented by the principle that all EU applicants are subject to the same criteria, whereby small and large countries are bound by the same rules. One should therefore note the difference between the vote and the voice of a Member State.

This is not merely a philosophical or theoretical issue, since one can observe that sometimes Member States seem to challenge the EU legal order by relying on the

[27] See Communication from the Commission to the European Parliament, the European Council and the Council, Further strengthening the rule of law within the European Union, COM(2019) 163 final of 3 April 2019, 1–2.

[28] See Venice Commission, *Report on the Rule of Law*, above n 15.

[29] See Conditionality Regulation, above n 4, recital 3.

[30] See, eg C-896/19 *Repubblika* ECLI:EU:C:2021:311, para 54.

[31] See Å Frändberg, 'Begreppet rättstat' in F Sterzel and Fredrik (eds), *Rättstaten – Rätt, Politik, Moral* (Uppsala, Rättsfondens skriftserie, 1996) 22–23.

[32] See R McCorquodale, 'Defining the International Rule of Law: Defying Gravity?' (2016) 65 *International & Comparative Law Quarterly* 284–85.

[33] See 'A new EU Framework to strengthen the Rule of Law', above n 1, para 2, 'Why the rule of law is of fundamental importance for the EU'.

national Constitution and national identity in a broad sense. For example, Tuominen has criticised the German Constitutional Court in its PSPP-judgment,[34] in which it declared the ECJ's judgment in the *Weiss* case[35] ultra vires. He points out that the German Constitutional Court's understanding of national identity seems to be detached from the holistic perspective offered by Article 4(2) TEU. He continues that while the point of Article 4(2) TEU is that the ECJ should take all the national identities of the Member States into consideration when interpreting EU law, the German Constitutional Court persistently only accords weight to its own viewpoint.[36] If this trend continues, it may lead to a situation in which other national constitutional courts or courts of final appeal adopt the same kind of nationalistic and restrictive attitude towards the principle of supremacy of EU law. This has already happened in Poland only recently.[37]

IV. HOW CAN LEGAL CERTAINTY BE DEFINED IN THE FRAMEWORK OF EU LAW?

In terms of the interpretation of the EU principle of legal certainty, it is essential to state that the ECJ interprets legal certainty, above all, in relation to EU objectives and key legal principles. In its interpretation, the Court has, for example, emphasised the special nature of EU law as follows:

> EU law is characterised by the fact that it stems from an independent source of law, the Treaties, by its primacy over the laws of the Member States, and by the direct effect of a whole series of provisions which are applicable to their nationals and to the Member States themselves.[38]

This teleological interpretation of EU law and the emphasis on objectives and principles is significant when assessing the confluences in which legal certainty has been applied in EU law.

As an underlying general principle of law, legal certainty cannot be defined accurately. However, an attempt has been made in the case law of the ECJ as follows:

> The general principle of legal certainty, which is a fundamental principle of Community law, requires, in particular, that rules should be clear and precise, so that individuals may ascertain unequivocally what their rights and obligations are and may take steps accordingly.[39]

[34] 2 BverfG 859/15, 5 May 2020.

[35] See Case C-493/17 *Weiss and Others* ECLI:EU:C:2018:1000.

[36] See T Tuominen, *The Euro Crisis and Constitutional Pluralism, Financial Stability but Constitutional Inequality* (Edward Elgar, Cheltenham, 2021) 213–14.

[37] See Judgment K 3/21 of the Polish Constitutional Tribunal, Assessment of the conformity to the Polish Constitution of selected provisions of the Treaty on European Union, 7 October 2021.

[38] *Opinion 2/13* ECLI:EU:C:2014:2454, para 166.

[39] Case C-308/06 *R (on the application of Intertanko) v Secretary of State for Transport* ECLI:EU:C:2008:312, para 69. Similarly, see eg Case C-344/04 *R (on the application of IATA and ELFAA) v Department for Transport* ECLI:EU:C:2006:10, para 68, Case C-110/03 *Belgium v Commission* ECLI:EU:C:2005:223, para 30 and Case C-143/93 *Gebroeders van Es Douane Agenten BV v Inspecteur der Invoerrechten en Accijnzen* ECLI:EU:C:1996:45, para 27.

Therefore, it seems that legal certainty in EU law refers especially to the demand for predictability in legal decision-making.[40] In the settled case law it has also been stressed that legal certainty must be observed all the more strictly in the case of rules that are liable to have financial consequences.[41]

From a more general perspective one can note that the principle of legal certainty has been utilised as an argument in the justification of legal decisions, for example, when denying retroactive legal effects, invoking the protection of legitimate expectations or the protection of acquired rights, calculating procedural deadlines and demanding understandable language from legislation or administrative decisions.[42] The confluences of legal certainty have become more comprehensive over time, and it can be stated that all the key procedural requirements, such as the justificatory reasoning of convictions and administrative decisions, promote the implementation of legal certainty.[43] The better the decisions of bodies are reasoned, the easier it will be in the future to determine whether situations are identical in relation to the relevant background of the decision. This would presumably also increase the predictability of institutions' decisions, and thus would safeguard the implementation of legal certainty. The predictability of the administration of justice is also increased by the fact that no legal action can be instituted twice for the same cause of action (*ne bis in idem*).[44]

Legal certainty has also been considered in connection with interpreting *res judicata*[45] and national procedural autonomy. The ECJ has, in many connections, highlighted the importance of the principle of *res judicata* in both national judicial systems and the EU judicial system.[46] Legal praxis that is associated with legal

[40] See, eg Case C-504/19 *Banco de Portugal and Others v VR* ECLI:EU:C:2021:335, para 51, Joined Cases C-180/18, C-286/18 and C-287/18 *Agrenergy Srl and Fusignano Due Srl v Ministero dello Sviluppo Economico* ECLI:EU:C:2019:605, paras 29–30, Case C-98/14 *Berlington Hungary Tanácsadó és Szolgáltató kft and Others v Magyar Állam* ECLI:EU:C:2015:386, para 77 as well as Case C-573/12 *Ålands Vindkraft AB v Energimyndigheten* ECLI:EU:C:2014:2037, para 128.

[41] See Case C-158/06 *Stichting ROM-projecten v Staatssecretaris van Economische Zaken* ECLI:EU:C:2007:370, para 26.

[42] See HG Schermers and DF Waelbroeck, *Judicial Protection in the European Communities*, 5th edn (Deventer, Kluwer Law and Taxation Publishers, 1992) 52–69.

[43] See ibid 53 and, for example, Case C-561/19 *Consorzio Italian Management* ECLI:EU:C:2021:799, para 51.

[44] See art 50 of the Charter and examples of legal praxis that focus and specify on the *ne bis in idem* principle, such as Case 14/68 *Wilhelm and Others v Bundeskartellamt, Berlin* ECLI:EU:C:1969:4, para 11, Case 137/85 *Maizena Gesellschaft mbH and Others v Bundesanstalt für landwirtschaftliche Marktordnung (BALM)* ECLI:EU:C:1987:493, para 23 or Case 45/69 *Boehringer Mannheim GmbH v Commission* ECLI:EU:C:1970:73, paras 60–61, Case C-17/10 *Toshiba Corp and Others v Úřad pro ochranu hospodářské soutěže* ECLI:EU:C:2012:72 and Case C-617/10 *Åklagaren v Åkerberg Fransson* ECLI:EU:C:2013:280.

[45] See Case C-529/09 *Commission v Spain* ECLI:EU:C:2013:31, paras 66–67. According to established legal praxis, *res judicata* reaches beyond the actual and legal questions which the court decision subject to review has specifically settled. The interpretation problem in terms of *res judicata* often involves whether the relevant claim and the facts and legal matters forming an integral part of a previous judgment are the same.

[46] See eg Case C-224/01 *Köbler v Republik Österreich* ECLI:EU:C:2003:513, para 38, Case C-234/04 *Kapferer v Schlank & Schick GmbH* ECLI:EU:C:2006:178, para 20; and Case C-2/08 *Amministrazione dell'Economia e delle Finanze and Agenzia delle entrate v Fallimento Olimpiclub Srl* ECLI:EU:C:2009:506, para 22.

certainty involves the prerequisites on which basis legally enforced national administrative decisions or court decisions must be reprocessed if they are deemed to conflict with EU law.[47] In accordance with this so-called *Kühne & Heitz* line of cases, a final administrative action can only be cancelled if national law allows the administrative authority to do so.[48] This legal praxis seems to balance, on one hand the efficient implementation of EU law and on the other hand the prerequisite of predictability related to legal certainty. In accordance with the principle of assimilation, all laws and regulations applicable to an appeal must be applied in the same way, regardless of whether the appeal is based on the violation of EU law or national law.[49] The ECJ has been particularly careful when intervening in the *res judicata* of national judgments.[50]

V. THE CONCEPTS OF 'THICK' RULE OF LAW AND LEGAL CERTAINTY – A MORE THEORETICAL APPROACH

I think it is important to note that the mere democratic legitimacy of legislation is not enough, since some sort of substantive acceptability of the legal rules is also a prerequisite for their legitimacy. This kind of demand for the substantive acceptability of law has an impact on both the rule of law and legal certainty as legal concepts. Fuller has succeeded in illustrating the main features of both rule of law and legal certainty by telling a fascinating allegory of King Rex, who failed to make law in eight different ways.[51] For example, laws cannot be obscure or require something that is an impossibility. They cannot be changed frequently, since the lack of stability causes many problems. They cannot be made to contradict each other, so one rule may not allow something that another one prohibits. This reference to Fuller is not as novel an idea as it may seem, since Kilpatrick, for one, has referred to Fuller in her article on the managerialism connected to the taming of the sovereign debt crisis in the EU.[52]

[47] See Case C-453/00 *Kühne & Heitz NV v Produktschap voor Pluimvee en Eieren* ECLI:EU:C:2004:17, Case C-234/04 *Kapferer* ECLI:EU:C:2006:178, Case C-2/06 *Willy Kempter KG v Hauptzollamt Hamburg-Jonas* ECLI:EU:C:2008:78, Case C-249/11 *Byankov v Glaven sekretar na Ministerstvo na vatreshnite raboti* ECLI:EU:C:2012:608, Case C-213/13 *Impresa Pizzarotti & C SpA v Comune di Bari and Others* ECLI:EU:C:2014:2067 and Case C-69/14 *Târsia v Statul român and Serviciul Public Comunitar Regim Permise de Conducere si Inmatriculare a Autovehiculelor* ECLI:EU:C:2015:662.

[48] See, eg Case C-453/00 *Kühne & Heitz* ECLI:EU:C:2004:17 and Joined Cases C-392/04 and C-422/04 *i-21 Germany GmbH and Arcor AG & Co KG v Bundesrepublik Deutschland* ECLI:EU:C:2006:586, paras 51–54. The party has had to use all possible methods of appeal to be able to challenge the final administrative decision.

[49] See eg Case C-118/08 *Transportes Urbanos y Servicios Generales SAL v Administración del Estado* ECLI:EU:C:2010:39, para 33.

[50] See eg Case C-69/14 *Târsia* ECLI:EU:C:2015:662, paras 39 and 42.

[51] See LL Fuller, *The Morality of Law* (New Haven CT and London, Yale University Press, 1969) 33–38. King Rex wanted to reform his administration of justice, which was expensive; the judges were slow and corrupted; and the language used in court was old-fashioned and clumsy. As a solution, legislator and monarch Rex stipulated that all laws were to be abolished. Thereafter, the administration of justice was based on ad hoc judgments, which in the long run were bound to form legal praxis that would guide the administration of justice. Judgments could not, however, be generalised in this way without legislation existing in the background, so the reform project was not successful. He decided to make seven other alterations, which all turned out to be failures.

[52] See C Kilpatrick, 'On the Rule of Law and Economic Emergency: The Degradation of Basic Legal Values in Europe's Bailouts' (2015) 35 *Oxford Journal of Legal Studies* 345–47.

From the perspective of European law, one may speak of the 'thick' concept of the rule of law, which emphasises not only formal legality, but also substantiality due to individual legal protections and basic human rights.[53] It must be noted here that in the broader context of international and comparative law, the concept of the rule of law is given content which deviates from this European interpretation,[54] but I have here deliberately focused on the rule-of-law concept which is based on European law. This same idea to combine the formal and substantive, even axiological, elements of law applies to legal certainty as well. In the context of EU law literature, Popelier, for one, has described how the principle of legal certainty has become a more dynamic concept that aims at securing an individual's autonomy instead of being just a conservative device for the maintenance of vested rights.[55]

The idea of 'thick' legal certainty leads us back to the Nordic legal theory of the 1980s. According to both Aarnio and Peczenik, the expectation of legal certainty *sensu largo* contains two substantial elements: the demands that arbitrariness must be avoided (formal legal certainty) and that the decision must be proper and thus acceptable (substantive legal certainty).[56] More recently, Paunio has also emphasised the division of formal and substantive legal certainty in the context of analysing the decisions of the multilingual ECJ.[57]

Formal legal certainty can be defended by stating that courts have to behave so that citizens are able to plan their activities on a rational basis, which in turn is a necessary condition for the continuity of society.[58] The need to eliminate randomness from judicial decision-making requires in turn rational legal reasoning.[59] The minimum precondition for such reasoning is that the courts support their decisions with legal norms. This precondition is connected with the principle of legality, which has

[53] See eg A Von Bogdandy, C Antpöhler and M Ioannidis, 'Protecting EU Values, Reverse *Solange* and the Rule of Law Framework' in A Jakab and D Kochenov (eds), *The Enforcement of EU Law and Values* (Oxford, Oxford University Press, 2017) 226, which states: 'This general orientation towards a "thick" concept of Rule of Law is in principle reaffirmed in the decision to submit Poland to the Framework, which notes that the Rule of Law is a constitutional principle with both formal and substantive components. Nevertheless, when it comes to the actual reprimands against Polish reforms, priority is accorded to the formal dimension'.

[54] See, eg J Husa, 'Nordic Law and Development – See No Evil, Hear No Evil?' (2015) 60 *Scandinavian Studies in Law* 16–31, and J Husa, n 10 above, at 49–63.

[55] See, eg P Popelier, 'Legal Certainty and the European Courts, Accessibility and Legitimate Expectations as Standards of Reasonableness' in M Fenwick, M Siems and S Wrbka (eds) n 14 above at 29–54. According to Popelier, the essential attributes of a dynamic concept of legal certainty are stability, simplicity and adaptability, which are operationalised in legal systems as requirements of legal expectations and accessibility.

[56] See A Aarnio, *The Rational as Reasonable, A Treatise on Legal Justification* (Dordrecht, D. Reidel Publishing Company, 1987) 3 and A Aarnio, *Reason and Authority, A Treatise on the Dynamic Paradigm of Legal Dogmatics* (Aldershot, Ashgate, 1997) 191 and A Peczenik, *On Law and Reason* (Dordrecht, Kluwer Academic Publishers, 1989) 32.

[57] See E Paunio, *Legal Certainty in Multilingual EU Law, Language, Discourse and Reasoning at the European Court of Justice* (Farnham, Ashgate, 2013) 157–97.

[58] See A Aarnio, *The Rational as Reasonable, A Treatise on Legal Justification* (Dordrecht, D. Reidel Publishing Company, 1987) 4 and A Peczenik, *Vad är rätt? Om demokrati, rättssäkerhet, etik och juridisk argumentation* (Stockholm, Fritzes Förlag, 1995) 90.

[59] See A Aarnio, *Reason and Authority, A Treatise on the Dynamic Paradigm of Legal Dogmatics* (Aldershot, Ashgate, 1997) 191.

significance especially in criminal and penal law. On the other hand, the courts must use proper interpretation methods to adapt legal norms to moral or teleological arguments and to the facts of the case.[60] The expectation of legal certainty requires also that the decision as an outcome of the court's rational legal reasoning is reasonable. Thus, the substantive aspect of legal certainty means that the judicial interpretation must be in accordance with the law and it has to meet certain minimum distinct criteria of equity and justice.[61] So, formal and substantive legal certainty are intertwined in judicial decision-making.

In European jurisprudence even more elaborated conceptions of legal certainty have been presented. Theories concerning the validity of norms and theories of legal argumentation have been especially relevant in outlining the concept of legal certainty. For example, Gustafsson has presented an idea of social acceptability and moral acceptability in the context of substantive legal certainty.[62] My contribution here, in turn, has been the threefold conception of legal certainty, namely the formal, factual and substantive legal certainty. The three elements of the conception of legal certainty may illustrate the legal positivism, legal realism and natural law theories, respectively.[63]

Factual legal certainty is a logical derivation of the Wróblewskian conception of factual validity. Wróblewski has three conceptions for the validity of norms, namely systemic, factual and axiological validity. Systemic validity can be defined with reference to a norm's formal source of origin, factual validity with reference to the operative 'law in action', and axiological validity with reference to a norm's acceptability in light of social and moral values.[64] Later in the framework of the analytical school of law, Siltala, for one, has followed this threefold conception of the validity of norms.[65] Factual legal certainty resembles the idea of social acceptability by Gustafsson. It stresses stability and efficiency in a legal system, so that the administrative practice must also be taken into consideration when evaluating predictability and acceptability in legal decision-making. The demand of stability in the context of legal certainty is not a novelty at all.[66]

[60] See A Peczenik, *On Law and Reason* (Dordrecht, Kluwer Academic Publishers, 1989) 34, and as regards the ECJ, see eg J Bengoetxea, 'Text and Telos in the European Court of Justice' (2015) 11 *European Constitutional Law Review* 184, 212. Bengoetxea studies the differences between discovery and justification in a discovery-related interpretation of the Court.

[61] See A Aarnio, *Reason and Authority, A Treatise on the Dynamic Paradigm of Legal Dogmatics* (Aldershot, Ashgate, 1997) 191–92.

[62] See H Gustafsson, *Rättens polyvalens; En rättsvetenskaplig studie av sociala rättigheter och rättssäkerhet* (Lunds universitet. Sociologiska institutionen, 2002),1 ff.

[63] See J Raitio, *The Principle of Legal Certainty in EC Law* (Dordrecht, Kluwer Academic Publishers, 2003) 347–87.

[64] See J Wróblewski, *The Judicial Application of Law* (Z Bankowski and N MacCormick eds, Dordrecht, Kluwer Academic Publishers, 1992) 75–83.

[65] See R Siltala, *A Theory of Precedent, From Analytical Positivism to a Post-Analytical Philosophy of Law* (Oxford, Hart publishing, 2000) 182.

[66] See F Bydlinski, *Juristische Methodenlehre und Rechtsbegriff* (Vienna, Springer Verlag, 1982) 325–29. Bydlinski back in the 1980s listed the following elements of legal certainty: 'Rechtsklarheit, Sicherung, der Rechtsdurchsetzung, Stabilität des Rechts, Zugänglichkeit des Rechts'.

However, one may find plausible critical arguments against the factual legal certainty for the same reason that I previously criticised the idea of the rule of law as merely a 'rhetorical balloon'. In the context of the contemporary rule-of-law backsliding in certain Member States, it might turn out to be detrimental for the rule of law understood within the framework of Article 2 TEU if both the rule of law and legal certainty may be based on mere subsequent administrative processes. This may refer to certainty based on factual behaviour instead of law, and therefore one may question whether one can refer to *legal* certainty in such circumstances. Even according to 'Hume's guillotine' one cannot derive 'ought' from 'is' – norms from facts. They belong to separate categories, which are 'knowledge of ideas' and 'knowledge of facts'.[67] However, factual legal certainty does not try to undermine Hume's guillotine. It is applicable only exceptionally, for example in the situation of obsolete invalid norms; that is, *desuetudo*. Also, Wroblewski has referred to a situation of *desuetudo* in order to illuminate the factual validity of norms.[68] So, I think that the scope of application of factual legal certainty should remain highly exceptional.

The formal, legal positivistic way to understand legal certainty is the basic mode of legal certainty for the statutory systems of law, which in turn emphasises the Wróblewskian systemic validity of norms and predictability in legal decision-making. Yet, in cases of *desuetudo* I think there is room for factual legal certainty, but at the same time I think that Wroblewski's *desuetudo* example reveals the actual problem here. One may have found the factual validity of norms relevant in Poland under the communist regime during the 1980s, but can one apply it nowadays in the Member States of the EU? If the answer were affirmative, one would need to take steps to enhance legalism and the 'thin' rule of law. For example, in the rare cases of *desuetudo* the obsolete norms should be abolished by the legislator.

Although factual legal certainty may turn out to be somewhat problematic as a logical derivation from a context-bound theory of norms, I find that the more established division between formal and substantive legal certainty will suffice to support the 'thick' concept of legal certainty. This demand of reasonableness or proportionality in legal decision-making may be illustrated by referring to the 'Judge's Rules' written by the Scandinavian Reformer Olaus Petri (1493–1552). According to one of those rules 'What is not right and equitable cannot be the law either'. This kind of emphasis on equity in Judge's Rules manifests an ideal of legal reasoning, which can be traced back to the Roman law tradition.[69]

[67] See, eg W Morrison, *Jurisprudence: From the Greeks to Post-modernism* (London, Cavendish Publishing, 1997) 108–9, in which there is an analysis of David Hume's 'A Treatise of Human Nature'(originally published in 1739). Knowledge of facts concerns statements relating to the way things actually are and thus they can be related to empirical studies. Knowledge of ideas concerns the construction of concepts and the logical relations between concepts.

[68] See J Wróblewski, *The Judicial Application of Law* (Z Bankowski and N MacCormick (eds), Dordrecht, Kluwer Academic Publishers, 1992) 75–83.

[69] See A Aarnio, *Reason and Authority, A Treatise on the Dynamic Paradigm of Legal Dogmatics* (Aldershot, Ashgate, 1997) 191.

VI. CONCLUSIONS

I have argued that both the rule of law and legal certainty are underlying principles of law so that they contain both formal and substantive elements. Therefore, I have applied the expression 'thick', borrowed from the concept of the rule of law, to legal certainty as well. Quite often the conception of thick rule of law and its substantive element can be grounded on the link between human rights and rule of law. This link becomes evident in various sources, perhaps most notably in the wording of Article 2 TEU. In practice, the rule of law seems to be typically employed as an argument in cases which are connected to the impartiality of the courts.[70] One might observe that the rule-of-law cases relate to the *Montesquieuan* separation of powers from a more general perspective.[71]

The substantive element of legal certainty and the aspiration of material fairness can also be based on human rights. Yet, the difference between rule of law and legal certainty relates to the accuracy of the scope of application. Legal certainty is connected to the principle of legitimate expectations (*Vertrauensschutz*),[72] the principle of non-retroactivity[73] and other principles, which have a relatively specific scope of application compared to the rule of law. In practice, the principle of proportionality may often come to the fore when interpreting legal certainty.[74] In England one could perhaps refer to 'reasonableness' and the so-called *Wednesbury* test in the context of proportionality analysis.[75] Thus I find that the conception of 'thick' legal certainty can be related to the conceptual scale for weighing up and balancing between predictability and acceptability, between formal justice and material fairness, in legal decision-making.[76]

[70] See, eg Case C-64/16 *Associação Sindical dos Juízes Portugueses v. Tribunal de Contas*, paras 30, 36 and the issues concerning Poland in Case C-216/18 PPU, *Minister for Justice and Equality v LM* ECLI:EU:C:2018:586, para 48 and Case C-619/18, *Commission v Poland*, para 21.

[71] See, eg Case C-477/16 PPU, *Openbaar Ministerie v Kovalkovas* ECLI:EU:C:2016:861, para 36.

[72] See, eg Case 289/81 *Mavridis v European Parliament* ECLI:EU:C:1983:142, para 21 and Case T-571/93 *Lefebvre frères et soeurs and Others v Commission* ECLI:EU:T:1995:163 and Case C-17/03 *VEMW and Others v Directeur van de Dienst uitvoering en toezicht energie* ECLI:EU:C:2005:362.

[73] See, eg Case 98/78 *Racke v Hauptzollamt Mainz* ECLI:EU:C:1979:14, paras 15 and 20.

[74] See, eg Case C-724/17 *Vantaan kaupunki v Skanska Industrial Solutions Oy and Others*, in which issues concerning legal certainty, *res judicata* and proportionality were to be interpreted by the Court.

[75] See *Associated Provincial Picture Houses, Limited v Wednesbury Corporation* [1948] 1 KB 223, especially pp 233–34. In this case Lord Greene gave unreasonableness a substantive meaning, so that a court may interfere with the exercise of discretion for unreasonableness only when the administrative authority has come to a conclusion 'so unreasonable that no reasonable authority could ever have come to it'.

[76] See eg J Raitio, *The Principle of Legal Certainty in EC Law* (Dordrecht, Kluwer Academic Publishers, 2003) 387.

6

The Primacy of the Rule of Law and Member States' Constitutional Identities

LEONARD FM BESSELINK

I. INTRODUCTION: DIVERGENCE, CONVERGENCE, AND SOLVING CONSTITUTIONAL CONFLICT

IF THE RULE of law is to have the foundational function attributed to it in European Union law, one would think this requires 'the rule of law' (*l'État de droit, der Rechtsstaat, el Estado de Derecho, rättsstaten, oikeusvaltio, o Estado de direito, de rechtsstaat*) to be a unified concept. There is reason to think this is not the case. Part of the explanation lies in the nature and reality of the European constitutional order being composed of both the EU and the national constitutional orders. It may be a better question to ask if and to what extent it *needs* to be a unified concept. After all, the Union's motto is 'united in diversity'. Academic reflection on this aspect of the rule of law (*Rechtsstaat*, etc) is urgent because, in recent years, the issues of constitutional communality and legitimate constitutional diversity have gained in prominence, leading to oversimplifications of the constitutional ins and outs of the problem of unity in diversity, legally speaking. Abusive and authoritarian constitutionalism in some Member States and 'captured courts' have created embarrassment for critical discourse about constitutional adjudication.[1] Similarly, the abusive employment of claims to diversity and national constitutional identity threatens to silence rational critical discourse about constitutional unity and diversity in the European Union. Were this to happen, it would not only be a surrender to abusive forms of constitutionalism but would ultimately also undermine the constitutional legitimacy of the Union and of the process and project of European integration.

[1] Cf M Tushnet, 'Writing While Quarantined: A Personal Interpretation of Contemporary Comparative Constitutional Law' (2021) 15 *Vienna Journal on International Constitutional Law* 53.

The ideas of unity and diversity have found expression in the Union's founding Treaties. In their present form they express constitutional unity in terms of commonality of constitutional 'values': the ideas of liberty, democracy and the rule of law are the very constitutional foundations of both the European Union and the Member States.[2] This commonality establishes a form of constitutional 'homogeneity' of the EU and the Member States.[3]

At the same time there is the constitutional norm of Article 4(2) TEU, which expresses diversity in terms not merely of value or constitutional principles, but as a legal obligation for the Union to respect the identity of the Member States' political and constitutional structures.[4] Unless this 'identity clause' is a (near) repetition of the 'homogeneity clause', it protects 'structural' constitutional identities of Member States also, and I would say precisely there, where they are mutually not fully co-extensive. This is at any rate how Member State courts tend to understand it.

Whether the rule of law in the EU is a unified concept is essentially an empirical question. Answering it would ideally require a delimitation of what the existing constitutional commonality or homogeneity in fact consists of and, in particular, of where the constitutional diversity between Member States and the Union lies. Such an exercise is far beyond the scope of this brief chapter.

Apart from the variety of understandings of what the rule of law comprises in the respective Member States, there is also a rule-of-law divergence as regards the law that applies in cases of incompatibility between legal orders. This divergence concerns the answer to the question which of the two concepts is supposed to prevail if the EU and national constitutional understandings prove to be incompatible.

So there is a twofold issue. Firstly, there is the problem that the rule of law (especially, but not only in a thick, substantive sense) has a different content in Member State law from that in Union law. Examples in the case law include the divergent interpretations of the principle of legality in criminal matters on various points – such as the prohibition of substantive retroactive effect (*lex praevia*), the principle of personal guilt (*culpa*), the *lex certa* principle, and *ne bis in idem*. Other examples are divergent interpretations of certain fundamental rights, such as the scope of the duty to respect human dignity (do laser games infringe human dignity?) or the freedom of religion (in a state based on the principle of separation of church and state, is it for the courts to determine what a specific religion does or does not require?).[5] Secondly, there is the

[2] Cf art 2 TEU: 'The Union is founded on the values of respect for human dignity, freedom, democracy, equality, the rule of law and respect for human rights … values [that] are common to the Member States'; pre-Lisbon art 6(1) EU: 'The Union is founded on the principles of liberty, democracy, respect for human rights and fundamental freedoms, and the rule of law, principles which are common to the Member States'.

[3] Art 2 TEU has been called a 'homogeneity clause', a term deriving from federal studies, eg F Schorkopf, *Homogenität in der Europäischen Union, Ausgestaltung und Gewährleistung durch Art. 6 Abs. I und Art 7 EUV* (Berlin, Duncker & Humblot, 2000); R Miccù and V Altripaldi (eds), *L'omogeneità costituzionale nell'Unione Europea* (Padua, CEDAM, 2003); G Delledonne, *L'omogeneità costituzionale negli ordinamenti composti* (Naples, Editoriale Scientifica, 2017).

[4] Art 2(4) TEU: 'The Union shall respect the equality of Member States before the Treaties as well as their national identities, inherent in their fundamental structures, political and constitutional, inclusive of regional and local self-government.'

[5] Cf. the cases leading to the *Taricco*-saga (C-105/14, *Taricco and Others*, ECLI:EU:C:2015:555, and C-42/17, *MAS and MB*, ECLI:EU:C:2017:936), as well as Cases C-399/11, *Melloni v Ministerio Fiscal*, ECLI:EU:C:2013:107; C-36/02, *Omega Spielhallen- und Automatenaufstellungs-GmbH v Oberbürgermeisterin*

related but distinct problem that the rule of law would seem to require that in case of an incompatibility of legal norms stemming from different legal orders in a concrete case, one of them will have to prevail. Uncertainty as to what law governs a specific case in practice defies the rule of law as the observance of the norms becomes uncertain. This becomes acute when there are discrepancies as to the principles on which to resolve such norm conflicts. And indeed, as a matter of empirical fact, the Union law and Member State perspectives on these diverge.

In this chapter I focus on some of the main principles governing the resolution of conflicts between legal rules pertaining to the national constitutional identities and Union law, principles I refer to as conflict rules. These rules are relevant to solving a potential or actual norm conflict in cases involving constitutional norms – and of understandings of the rule of law implicit in them – that may not be compatible with a norm of Union law.

Before I delve deeper into this matter, I first sketch the problem of reducing the meaning of the concept of the rule of law to 'thin' conceptions, as this is central to the argument I make about the primacy of the rule of law. Next, I move to look into the Union and Member State perspectives on constitutional conflict, respectively. I indicate a cause of continuous constitutional divergence and conflict, which lies in what I refer to as a 'jurisdictional gap', and sketch the various and at least seemingly contrary views of the Union and Member States on the relevant conflict rule. I subsequently make some remarks concerning ways of resolving the different approaches to constitutional conflict by bridging the various perspectives. In this context, I argue that non-abusive constitutional identity approaches by Member State courts are, paradoxical as it may seem, less problematic than is often argued from the point of view of substantive understandings of the rule of law. Ultra vires review can be more problematic, also in terms of possibilities to overcome the motive behind this form of Member State review of Union decision-making. On the part of EU law, I submit, conflict resolution requires a fundamental change in the European Court of Justice's (ECJ) understanding of primacy of Union law, one which moves from a thin and formal concept to one which focuses more clearly on substantive elements of the rule of law.

II. DIVERGENT CONCEPTIONS OF THE RULE OF LAW

Even without going into any conceptual and theoretical detail, it is useful to make the common distinction between 'thin' and 'thick' notions of the rule of law.[6] Thin notions of the rule of law focus on the subjection of the powers that be to the law, the rule of law instead of the rule of men. They focus on the inherent restraints on government broadly, including legislative power of any kind, by virtue of crucial

der Bundesstadt Bonn, ECLI:EU:C:2004:614, and C-414/16, *Egenberger v Evangelisches Werk für Diakonie und Entwicklung eV*, ECLI:EU:C:2017:851, respectively.

[6] See, *ex multis*, BZ Tamanaha, *On the Rule of Law: History, Politics, Theory* (Cambridge, Cambridge University Press, 2004), ch 7.

values such as certainty, predictability, security and the like.[7] This notion presupposes or implies values like equality before the law and the principle of legality. Otherwise, the purpose of this concept of the rule of law would largely be defeated, just as the notion would have little practical meaning in the absence of legal institutions and an independent judiciary and other institutions of law enforcement operating within a legal culture. Thinner notions of the rule of law are distinct from thicker notions in so far as the former are not dependent on any particular quality of the law's content; as a consequence, the thinner concept can apply in a greater variety of different historical, political and cultural environments. 'Thicker' notions of the rule of law incorporate the 'thin' notions, its presumed values and functions, but they go beyond them in also incorporating such principles as democracy, protection of fundamental rights, and distribution or separation of powers beyond the idea of judicial independence. More generally one can say the thicker notions of the rule of law are dependent on a particular substantive quality of the content of the law and take a broader look at state institutions than the nearly exclusively lawyerly 'thin' understanding of the rule of law. Clearly, such 'thicker' conceptions have fewer instantiations than the 'thin' ones.

Thin concepts of the rule of law are often viewed and analysed, particularly in positivist legal theory, as inherent in the concept of law; hence, lawyers and courts tend to focus on, or even equate the rule of law with, this thin concept. This lawyers' bias towards thin concepts is related to the fact that 'thick' concepts of the rule of law are determined by inherently political choices, principles and values, however fundamental these may be in the specific context of a particular political and legal order, and notwithstanding the fact that those political choices have been enshrined and reflected in specific legal rules and arrangements.

To confront the problem of unity and diversity head on, we must adopt a broad understanding of the concept which excludes neither thinner nor thicker notions.[8] This is all the more necessary because at least some articulations of the two concepts reveal that 'thin' notions presume and flow over into 'thicker' notions. This is particularly evident with the principle of legality, which is core to thin notions of the rule of law.

I would define the constitutional principle of legality, apart from everything else, as meaning that the exercise of public authority must have a basis in an act of the legislature or the Constitution itself. In democratic states under the rule of law, this principle is fundamentally geared towards two other constitutional values or principles. Its first function is to protect liberty in the classic 'liberal' sense: in that conception, the citizens are free to do as they prefer unless and in so far as the law prohibits this or otherwise tells them how they have to behave, while public

[7] See J Raitio's Chapter 5 in this volume.

[8] The Commission's and Council of Europe's concept of the rule of law strongly rely on a thin concept, which translate rule-of-law problems to legal problems or problems concerning the legal institutions for the dispensation of justice; see eg Commission Communication on A new EU Framework to strengthen the Rule of Law, COM(2014) 158 final of 19 March 2014, Annex I, and the Rule of Law Checklist, adopted by the Venice Commission at its 106th Plenary Session (Venice, 11–12 March 2016), endorsed by the Ministers' Deputies at the 1263rd Meeting (6–7 September 2016), Council of Europe, Study No 711/2013, CDL-AD(2016)007rev. This may conceal the broader political and societal dimensions of the rule-of-law problems that are presently haunting Europe.

authorities are not free to act unless and in so far as the legislature allows for this or otherwise tells them how they have to act. Secondly, at least since the introduction of the universal franchise, this principle has in essence guaranteed the democratic legitimacy of public authority as long as legislative power is essentially parliamentary, and thus directly representative of the people. Viewed in this manner, legality may in itself be a thin concept of a largely formal nature, but it involves thicker notions of the rule of law inasmuch as it incorporates the requirements of liberty and democracy. Taken in this sense, the principle of legality actually lends an important form of democratic legitimacy to government.[9]

III. THE CAUSE OF ONGOING CONSTITUTIONAL CONFLICT: THE JURISDICTIONAL GAP

Two self-evident jurisdictional truths are at the origin of much constitutional conflict: the European Court of Justice has the exclusive power to interpret European Union law authoritatively and has no power to interpret national law; national constitutional courts have the exclusive power to interpret national constitutional law and have no power to definitively interpret EU law. Each must accept the other's law as interpreted authoritatively by its competent court. The general position of constitutional courts is that if issues of incompatibility arise in the constitutional sphere, they have to refer the case to the ECJ, so that a national constitutional court can in principle, as a next step, adjudicate on the basis of an understanding of the law as authoritatively interpreted by the ECJ – just as is normally the case for the Court of Justice in preliminary rulings, where it takes national law to be what it is as authoritatively interpreted by the national court.

Yet, these various procedures may produce conflicting outcomes as to the applicable law in the concrete case. And, as we have already said, the rules that the two courts, the European and the national, employ to resolve such outcomes differ as well. Let's look at the respective European and domestic approaches.

IV. THE EU LAW PERSPECTIVE ON CONSTITUTIONAL CONFLICT: PRIMACY

At a most general level, the EU law perspective on constitutional conflict is approached with the principle of primacy – in the literature often equated with the

[9] Other aspects of legality exist independently from the substantive democratic aspect, such as the criteria of knowability and transparency, which the European Convention on Human Rights (ECHR) and the European Court of Human Rights (ECtHR) consider sufficient qualities of legality short of direct or indirect involvement of elected bodies. Thus, the ECJ has allowed 'secret' legislation, reducing the level of sufficient publicity of legislation at EU level to the relevant legislation merely being known to the person concretely affected even when the Court itself does not know it: *curia nescit iura*. Thus, European integration has eroded the scope and democratic nature of the principle of legality. Cf N Lupo and G Piccirilli, 'The Relocation of the Legality Principle by the European Courts' Case Law' (2015) 11 *EuConst* 55; M Bobek, 'Case C-345/06, *Gottfried Heinrich*, Judgment of the Court of Justice (Grand Chamber) of 10 March 2009' (2009) 46 *CML Rev* 2077; A Albi, 'From the "Banana Saga" to a Sugar Saga and beyond: Could the Post-communist Constitutional Courts Teach the EU a Lesson in the Rule of Law?' (2010) 47 *CML Rev* 791.

term 'supremacy', a term that the Court of Justice has studiously avoided in its case law – as the major rule for resolving conflicts between Union law and national constitutional law. Union law of whatever nature, either primary or secondary, either directly effective or not-directly-effective,[10] prevails over incompatible national law, including constitutional law, of whatever rank and nature.

In *Melloni* this principle was paired with 'unity and effectiveness', although the Court did not explain what precisely these two added to what primacy itself could do – and did – on its own in this case. That is not to say that 'unity and effectiveness' could not, separate or together, be a way of deciding about a conflict of norms. Other principles that can be used in EU law in situations of apparent incompatibilities are subsidiarity, procedural autonomy of the Member States, and proportionality. But primacy takes a place of honour. It is clear, simple, and uncontaminated with considerations of substantive principle: when, in a case within the scope of EU law, a conflict arises between norms, EU law prevails even if constitutional principles are involved. *Internationale Handelsgesellschaft* and *Simmenthal II* are standing case law to this day.[11] Primacy has all the characteristics of a 'thin' rule-of-law concept. It is formal and emptied out of any substantive considerations as to the quality and nature of the norms conflict that it is intended to solve: EU law *über alles*.

The 1970 judgment in *Internationale Handelsgesellschaft* was quite clear in this regard: 'the validity of a Community measure or its effect within a Member State cannot be affected by allegations that it runs counter to … the principles of a national constitutional structure'.[12] In 2009, the Lisbon Treaty chose a formulation of the national identity clause that is in striking contrast to the wording of *Internationale Handelsgesellschaft*: 'The Union shall respect the … Member States['] … national identities, inherent in their fundamental structures, political and constitutional'.[13] Below we discuss what difference this could make, also in terms of the applicability of the principle of primacy.

V. THE MEMBER STATE PERSPECTIVE ON CONSTITUTIONAL CONFLICT: CONSTITUTIONAL IDENTITY

Empirically there is little doubt that all the constitutional and supreme courts of Member States have accepted the primacy of Union law over statutory national law

[10] See Case C-399/11 *Melloni* ECLI:EU:C:2013:107 which concerned the not-directly-effective Council Framework Decision 2002/584/JHA of 13 June 2002 on the European arrest warrant and the surrender procedures between Member States [2002] OJ L190/1; differently, see Case C-579/15 *Popławski I* ECLI:EU:C:2017:503, which confirmed that the Framework Decision has no direct effect, and Case C-573/17 *Popławski II* ECLI:EU:C:2019:530, which this time took the view that, due to this lack of direct effect, EU law does not require that national law contrary to the Framework Decision be disapplied by national courts.

[11] Cases 11/70 *Internationale Handelsgesellschaft mbH v Einfuhr- und Vorratsstelle für Getreide und Futtermittel* ECLI:EU:C:1970:114, and 106/77 *Amministrazione delle Finanze dello Stato v Simmenthal SpA* ECLI:EU:C:1978:49.

[12] Case 11/70 *Internationale Handelsgesellschaft* ECLI:EU:C:1970:114, para 3.

[13] See art 4(2) TEU.

unconditionally. It is equally an empirical fact that a very large majority of Member State constitutional or supreme courts do not accept the primacy of Union law over their national constitution (Bulgaria, Malta, and Poland), or not unconditionally (which includes Belgium,[14] France,[15] Germany, Italy, and arguably now even the Netherlands[16]).[17] There are various forms of non-acceptance and some of them are more amenable to resolving potential conflict than others. I argue that non-abusive constitutional identity approaches may be among the less problematic approaches to overcoming conflict.

There are three forms of constitutional review of Union law, which are in historical order:

- fundamental rights review (of which primary examples were the Bundesverfassungsgericht's (BVerfG) *Solange I* and *II*[18] in Germany, and the Corte costituzionale in *Frontini*[19] and *Fragd*[20] in Italy);
- ultra vires review (eg Danish Højsteret in *AJOS*,[21] BVerfG in *PSPP*[22]);
- constitutional identity review (eg Conseil Constitutionnel 15 October 2021 *Société Air France*;[23] Corte costituzionale in *Taricco II/ MAS & MB*[24]).

These three forms of review can blend or overlap, if not in the overt language of the constitutional case law at least conceptually.

Fundamental rights review has often been a constitutional identity issue, although it has not always been phrased in such terms, in particular if constitutional fundamental rights protection does not find an equivalent in Union law. An early example is provided by the language used by the Italian Corte costituzionale in *Fragd*:

> It is … true that the fundamental rights guaranteed by the legal systems of the Member States constitute, according to the case law of the Court of Justice of the EEC, an essential and integral part of the Community legal order. But this does not mean that the

[14] There seems to be a divergence between the highest ordinary courts and the Constitutional Court.

[15] The Conseil constitutionnel probably has a more restricted scope of French constitutional law that prevails as compared to the Conseil d'État, although the scope of review has recently converged: see below nn 24 to 29.

[16] In *State of the Netherlands v Urgenda*, judgment of 20 December 2019, ECLI:NL:HR:2019:2007, the Hoge Raad judged the minimum greenhouse gas reductions set by the first EU Climate Package as followed by the Netherlands to be incompatible with the ECHR; the ECHR is an integral part of the Netherlands legal order and has a supra-constitutional rank within it: see L Besselink, 'Dutch and EU Targets for Greenhouse Gas Reduction Infringe the ECHR: the judicial review of general policy objectives' (2022) 18 *EuConst* 155.

[17] An overview of constitutional obstacles in the further development of Union law is contained in L Besselink, M Claes, Š Imamović, and JH Reestman, 'National Constitutional Avenues for Further EU Integration', Study, European Parliament, Constitutional Affairs Committee, PE 493.046 EN, Brussels March 2014: https://www.europarl.europa.eu/RegData/etudes/etudes/join/2014/493046/IPOL-JURI_ET(2014)493046_EN.pdf.

[18] BVerfGE 37, 271 *Solange I*, 2 BvL 52/71; BVerfGE 73, 339 *Solange II*.

[19] See n 33 below.

[20] See n 25 below.

[21] Højesteret Case 15/2014 *Dansk Industri (DI) acting for Ajos A/S v The Estate left by A*, 6 December 2016.

[22] BVerfG, Judgment of the Second Senate of 5 May 2020 (*Weiss II*), 2 BvR 859/15.

[23] Conseil Constitutionnel, *Société Air France*, Décision n° 2021-940 QPC, 15 October 2021 ECLI:FR:CEASS:2021:437125.20211217.

[24] See n 5 above.

> Constitutional Court has no competence to verify, by examining the constitutionality of the law incorporating the Treaty, whether or not a treaty norm, as interpreted and applied by the institutions and organs of the EEC, is in conflict with the fundamental principles of the Italian Constitution or violates the inalienable rights of man. Ultimately, that which is highly unlikely, could still happen. Moreover, it must be taken into account that, at least theoretically, it cannot be stated absolutely that all the fundamental principles of the Italian constitutional order are to be found amongst the principles which are common to the legal orders of the other Member States and are therefore included in the Community legal order.[25]

The fundamental principles of the Constitution here blend with inalienable human rights (which at that point in European law were only protected so far as contained in the constitutional traditions common to the Member States and the human rights treaties to which they were parties).

Ultra vires review is in general inspired by concerns to protect the powers of a Member State over fears of 'competence creep' and shifts in *Kompetenz-Kompetenz*. This sovereignty concern is clear, for instance, in the Danish Højsteret's approach in the *Maastricht* judgment, also due to the language of the constitutional provision on the transfer of competence to international organisations.[26] But in the background to its *AJOS* judgment, which on the face of it involved a mere ultra vires review, looms the constitutional principle that courts cannot review acts of parliament against unwritten general principles, which is closely linked to defining traits of the Nordic constitutional tradition.[27] Ultra vires review is, under the German approach, based on the principle of democracy, as part of the Bundesverfassungsgericht's understanding of the Federal Republic's constitutional identity. Nevertheless, ultra vires review and identity review do not substantively coincide. Although logically an infringement of the state's constitutional identity by Union law would seem to imply an ultra vires act, and not every ultra vires act would seem to be necessarily an infringement of a substantive element of constitutional identity, it is unclear to what extent this applies, if we look at for example the German *PSPP* judgment.[28] However, in Austria, for instance, ultra vires review is considered to be entirely distinct from review against constitutional provisions.[29]

An example of overlap between constitutional identity review and fundamental rights review is the Bundesverfassungsgericht's Order of 15 December 2015,[30] sometimes referred to as *Solange III*. In it the BVerfG made clear that the duty to respect

[25] N° 232/1989, *Fragd v Amministrazione delle Finanze dello Stato*, judgment of 21 April 1989 ECLI:IT:COST:1989:232, para 3.1, author's translation.

[26] The judgments of the Corte costituzionale in what is referred to as the *Taricco*-saga are a recent illustration of the same approach.

[27] H Krunke, 'Impact of the EU/EEA on the Nordic Constitutional Systems' in H Krunke and B Thorarensen (eds), *The Nordic Constitutions: a Comparative and Contextual Study* (Oxford, Hart Publishing, 2018) 194; E Smith, 'Judicial Review of Legislation' in H Krunke and B Thorarensen (eds) *The Nordic Constitutions: a Comparative and Contextual Study* (Oxford, Hart Publishing, 2018), 107–32.

[28] See n 22 above.

[29] For a presentation and discussion of further varieties as per January 2014, see Besselink and others, above n 17, 22–27.

[30] *Solange III* 2 BvR 2735/14.

human dignity under the first article of the *Grundgesetz* involves the constitutional identity of the Federal Republic as it is unamendable under the Constitution's 'eternity clause'. Consequently the Court will admit complaints of its infringement, notwithstanding the standing case law on the non-admissibility of complaints of infringements of German constitutional rights.

Let us now turn to a discussion of the conflict potential of these various ways in which national courts find themselves able to review EU law against their constitutional standards, focusing on ultra vires review and constitutional identity review respectively.

A. Ultra Vires Review

Ultra vires review by national courts concerns whether the Union has exceeded the powers conferred on it. The question whether an EU act has remained within the bounds of Union competence is itself clearly a 'rule-of-law' issue, but one which is mostly formal in nature in as much as the legal measures reviewed do not necessarily concern constitutional principles or values themselves, but thinner and more technical issues. In some respects this was the case in the *PSPP* judgment, where one problem was the relative 'incomprehensibility' for the Bundesverfassungsgericht of the Court of Justice's allegedly opaque reasoning and the European Central Bank's non-transparent decision-making. One could say that some counter-voice is useful to keep the Court of Justice sharp. This is very much in the service of the rule of law, as remaining intra vires is the most basic element of any concept of the rule of law. *Pacta sunt servanda* works both ways. This is precisely the problem of ultra vires review. As we just said, the constitutional dimension of *vires* review relates to sovereignty, understood in the European tradition as democratically legitimated government. As democratic decision-making concerns every and any legal decision or measure, the scope of *vires* review is in principle limitless, but clearly – and this is reflected in the case law of national constitutional courts that engage in this kind of review – it would defeat the purpose of entering into the constitutional compact of the European Union to engage in this review for each and every decision; doing so would raise doubts as to the *fides* that is at the basis of *pacta sunt servanda*. The question of who has the ultimate say remains sensitive because of the uncertain democratic settlement in the Union. It is historically and legally clear that the European Union is not the *locus* of constituent power in relation to the Member States. Notwithstanding the deeply enmeshed legal and political orders of Union and Member States, the opposite remains true.

This is reflected in the position of Member State constitutional courts that the national constitution is the ultimate source that determines which law can operate validly within the national legal order: without the constitution allowing for the operation of EU law, it cannot be effective in the national legal order. This argument has, of course, the conflict-prone consequence of asserting the precedence of national constitutional law in an entirely hierarchical and formal principle – it mirrors a 'thin' understanding of the rule of law.

We have seen this kind of conflict playing out in the worst possible way in the aftermath of the *Weiss/PSPP* follow-up judgment of the Bundesverfassungsgericht,[31] when presidents of European and national courts began a war of words in highly damaging press releases and interviews, in essence each asserting its supremacy, without, of course, any sensible outcome. It could only bring to mind Cassius Clay in the 1960s: 'I am the greatest!'.

B. Constitutional Identity

As pointed out above, in some Member States in case of conflicts with EU law all constitutional norms have precedence over EU law, whereas in others this precedence only exists with regard to core constitutional norms and institutions. In the latter, precedence exists only with regard to the 'constitutional identity' of that Member State, although it might of course be that in those countries where no norm of the constitution can be set aside for incompatibility with Union law, *all* constitutional norms are considered to make up the state's constitutional identity. If the latter applies, we end up again with the precedence of national constitutional law as a mere hierarchical and formal principle – which is a 'thin' understanding of the rule of law – that is prone to be more conflictual than the former understanding, as will be explained in the following.

In the doctrine it has been pointed out that two approaches to constitutional identity are discernible in the national case law. In the German case law, the scope of constitutional identity is not limited to where Germany's identity-conferring rules might be different from those of the Union or the common constitutional traditions, but is inspired by its 'eternity clause' and therefore comprises also values we find expressed in Article 2 TEU. Germany's constitutional identity may be violated when a core principle of the German Constitution is not sufficiently protected in the EU legal order, irrespective of whether or not the principle exists at the EU level (eg *nullum crimen sine culpa*,[32] or data protection). Whenever a relevant provision of Union law, as interpreted by the Court of Justice, is alleged to infringe any element of German constitutional identity in a manner that passes the threshold of seriousness in order to be admissible, the Bundesverfassungsgericht will adjudicate that claim.

The Italian approach has been likened to the German one, in as much as the Corte costituzionale will review Union law that allegedly infringes the 'supreme principles of the Constitution'.[33] In the 2018 follow-up decision in *MAS & MB*, which concerned the particularly Italian understanding of the principle of legality in criminal matters (ie that the statute of limitations touches on the prohibition of substantive retroactive effect and the *lex certa* principle) the Corte reiterates, as it had done in

[31] See n 22 above.

[32] BVerfG, 2 BvE 2/08 of 30 June 2009, *Lissabon Urteil*, 364; an application thereof in BVerfG Order of 15 December 2015 2 BvR 2735/14, which essentially rejects the ECJ judgment in *Melloni*.

[33] N° 183/1973, *Frontini*, judgment of 18 December 1973, ECLI:IT:COST:1973:183; on the concept of supreme constitutional principles M Cartabia, *Principi inviolabili e integrazione Europea* (Milan, Giuffrè, 1995), remains the standard work.

the order for referral, that 'it alone is entitled to ascertain whether EU law contrasts with the supreme principles of the constitutional system and, in particular, with the inalienable rights of the person.'[34] In this *MAS* case, the Court of Justice had for all intents and purposes reversed crucial aspects of its previous judgment in *Taricco*, thus allowing for the exceptional Italian understanding of legality. This in turn allowed the Corte costituzionale to conclude that allowing for the disapplication of the rule and interpretation formulated in *Taricco*, as a matter of EU law as interpreted by the Court of Justice, created space for accommodation under the Italian Constitution as interpreted by the Corte costituzionale.

The approach which is typical of the French Conseil d'État and Conseil constitutionnel, but arguably inspired by the German *Solange* approach, is that these courts will not adjudicate on the compatibility of Union law, as interpreted by the Court of Justice, with a norm protected by the French Constitution as such (Conseil d'État) or with a constitutional norm belonging to the French constitutional identity (Conseil constitutionnel) if that norm or its equivalent is also protected in EU law.[35] In the recent case law, this idea of 'equivalent' protection[36] is scrutinised more carefully by the Conseil d'État than the Conseil constitutionnel. The latter, in its judgment of 15 October 2021, reasserted the classic view that in the hierarchy of norms the Constitution is supreme, adopting the criterion of the Conseil d'État that it will only review the French rules and principles belonging to its constitutional identity that do not have equivalent protection in Union law, and found that the French constitutional principle that the exercise of public force cannot be privatised is not protected in Union law.[37] It found without further ado that as a consequence of this criterion the appeal on the bases of the right to personal liberty, the presumption of innocence and the *égalité devant les charges publiques* had to be dismissed. The Conseil d'État, to the contrary, scrutinised the case law of the Court of Justice on the applicability and interpretation of the Working Time Directive[38] to the armed forces – the case concerned working times of the Gendarmerie nationale (a branch of the French armed forces) – in order to conclude that the principle of the government's free disposition

[34] N° 2018/115, *MAS and MB*, judgment of 10 April 2018, ECLI:IT:COST:2018:115, 8.

[35] This approach finds its origin in *Conseil constitutionnel*, Décision n° 2006-540 DC, 27 July 2006; the *Conseil d'État* set out the framework for judicial review of the constitutionality of EU law in Conseil d'État, Assemblée, N° 393099, 21 April 2021, *France Data Network*, ECLI:FR:CEASS:2021:393099.20210421.

[36] The notion of equivalence, as traced to both the ECtHR in *Bosphorus* (n 44 below) and the BVerfG *Solange* (nn 18 and 30 above) case law, recurs in the extra-judicial speeches and writings of the previous vice-president of the Conseil d'État, Jean-Marc Sauvé, since 2012; eg *Propos introductifs* (FIDE Congress 2012, Tallinn) www.conseil-etat.fr/actualites/discours-et-interventions/la-protection-des-droits-fondamentaux-au-niveau-de-l-union-europeenne-et-des-etats-membres#1; *A l'ère du pluralisme juridique, 31 mai 2014, Intervention de Jean-Marc Sauvé* (FIDE Congress 2014, Copenhagen), www.conseil-etat.fr/actualites/discours-et-interventions/a-l-ere-du-pluralisme-juridique; *Intervention à la Faculté de droit de l'Université Humboldt de Berlin le 28 octobre 2015*, www.conseil-etat.fr/actualites/discours-et-interventions/presentation-a-berlin-d-un-ouvrage-de-droit-compare-franco-allemand; and *Intervention le 25 avril 2017 au déjeuner du Cercle des constitutionnalistes*, www.conseil-etat.fr/actualites/discours-et-interventions/le-conseil-d-etat-et-la-constitution.

[37] Conseil Constitutionnel, *Société Air France*, 15 October 2021 ECLI:FR:CEASS:2021:437125.20211217, 13.

[38] Directive 2003/88/EC of the European Parliament and of the Council of 4 November 2003 concerning certain aspects of the organisation of working time [2003] OJ L299/9.

of armed forces at all times and places was not protected in an equivalent manner by Union law.[39]

The French approach was essentially also followed by the Portuguese Constitutional Tribunal, in its judgment of 15 July 2020 on the alleged infringement of the equal protection clause of Article 13 of the Portuguese Constitution.[40] It reiterated that it exclusively is competent to adjudicate whether Union law complies with the counter-limit of the fundamental principles of the democratic state under the rule of law, as contained in Article 8(4) of the Portuguese Constitution. But it decided that it would only do so in the case of a fundamental principle which, within the scope of EU law itself, as interpreted by the Court of Justice, 'does not enjoy a parametric value that is materially equivalent' to that of the Constitution.[41]

The 'German' and 'French' approaches have distinct features and result in different judicial techniques. I submit, however, that the differences are less in terms of the substantive meaning and scope of constitutional identity. The 'French' approach essentially acknowledges that there is a body of substantively coextensive constitutional principles and norms contained in both Union and French law. The consequence is, however, only procedural in as much as it leads to a division of judicial tasks. It does not mean that EU law has superior rank over core national constitutional principles, but this becomes relevant only when they are not sufficiently protected under EU law. Moreover, one can say that also in the 'German' approach there are judicial limits in the form of admissibility requirements that have been developed both as regards fundamental rights review (*Solange II* and its progeny[42]) and as regards ultra vires review (*Honeywell*).[43] Neither of these approaches excludes a reserve power of constitutional review of Union law, nor do they diminish the importance of the Member State perspective on constitutional conflict, which is premised on the prevalence of (core) constitutional principles over Union law, no matter how absolute the latter's principle of primacy is supposed to be.

VI. RESOLVING CONFLICT

A. Convergence Between National Constitutional Law and Union Law

The hypothesis of a convergent tendency in national constitutional case law is borne out by the 'French' approach: where equivalent protection of the same constitutional rule or principle in Union law entails that there is no room or necessity for the national court to step in to protect that norm in the national context, since this is being done in the context of Union law. This means that the national constitutional

[39] Conseil d'État, 17 December 2021, ECLI:FR:CEASS:2021:437125.20211217, 16. The Conseil constitutionnel found that the constitutional identity was not infringed, and the Conseil d'État did not need to engage in identity review because there was no discrepancy between the EU Working Time Directive and the actual French rules on working times of the gendarmerie.

[40] Tribunal Constitucional, Acórdão N° 422/2020, judgment of 15 July 2020.

[41] The appeal was therefore rejected, as the Tribunal found there to be such equivalence.

[42] BVerfGE 102, 147, judgment of 7 June 2000, 2 BvL 1/97, *Bananas*.

[43] BVerfGE 126, 28, judgment of 6 July 2010, 2 BvR 2661/06, *Honeywell* (ultra vires control *Mangold*).

rules and principles are coextensive (or homogenous) with Union constitutional rules and principles. This is not only co-extensiveness or homogeneity at the abstract level of the 'value' of the rule of law, but at the level of concrete legal rules and principles.

This approach of equivalence that implies co-extensiveness of constitutional rules and principles in practice, is inspired by the German *Solange* approach, that was in a sense also adopted in the ECtHR's *Bosphorus* doctrine.[44] The same co-extensiveness occurs, for instance, in the eventual outcome of the *MAS & MB* case, where – as we saw – the Italian constitutional court observed that the principle of legality that was at stake as a matter of constitutional identity for the Italian court, was respected by the ECJ by allowing for the disapplication of the '*Taricco* rule' in its own *MAS & MB* judgment. What is striking in this particular case is that the matter of the legality principle at stake concerned a particularly Italian understanding of that principle that is shared in hardly any other Member State: Italy is one of the very few states where time limits on the ability to prosecute criminal offences is not considered to be merely a matter of procedural law that does not affect the punishability of a delict, but instead extends materially into liability to be punished at all, and therefore involves the *lex praevia* principle, the prohibition of substantive retroactive effect, and – at least under the terms of the Court of Justice's *Taricco* judgment – the *lex certa* principle. So here it was not a matter of allowing for a classic public policy exception to a free movement right, as in *Omega*, but a purely national constitutional claim that is (nearly) unique to one Member State outside the sphere of market regulation. Although the Court of Justice managed to avoid mentioning the words 'constitutional identity', it found the constitutional claim justified and legitimate in terms that concerned the constitutional substance and value of the principle of legality involved.

B. What Is the Trend in the ECJ Case Law?

The ECJ's *MAS & MB* judgment picks up where an earlier trend broke off, but it is very hard to tell whether this is incidental or not. This trend is well-known and can very briefly be summarised as one starting from a formalistic hierarchical notion of primacy that wishes to remain indifferent to national constitutional values, initially also because Community law was conceived of as administrative rather than of constitutional substance [*Stork* (1959),[45] *President Ruhrkohlen and others* (1960),[46] *Internationale Handelsgesellschaft* (1970)[47] and *Simmenthal* (1978)[48]].

[44] ECtHR, *Bosphorus Hava Yollari Turizm ve Ticaret AS v Minister for Transport, Energy and Communications and others*, judgment of 30 July 1996.See n 36 above.

[45] Case 1/58 *Friedrich Stork & Cie v High Authority of the European Coal and Steel Community* ECLI:EU:C:1959:4.

[46] Case 36/59, *Präsident Ruhrkolen-Verkaufsgesellschaft mbH, Geitling Ruhrkohlen-Verkaufsgesellschaft mbH, Mausegatt Ruhrkohlen-Verkaufsgesellschaft mbH and I. Nold KG v High Authority of the European Coal and Steel Community* ECLI:EU:C:1960:36.

[47] Case 11/70 *Internationale Handelsgesellschaft* (n 11 above).

[48] Case 106/77 *Simmenthal* (n 11 above).

This evolved into a period with judgments that were sensitive to national constitutional concerns, which corresponded with a growth of the EU into a more mature constitutional order, with an occasional early case like *Groener* (1989);[49] it was the period of roughly the first decade of the millennium with *Kadi I*,[50] *Schmidberger*,[51] *Omega*,[52] and post-Lisbon *Filipiak*[53] and *Sayn-Wittgenstein*.[54] This line was abruptly broken off in *Melloni* which aimed consciously to lower a national constitutional standard of fundamental rights protection, and subsequently *Opinion 2/13*, which can easily be considered to be the greatest disservice to the rule of law by the Court of Justice.[55] In this case law primacy was again the absolute, formal and hierarchical principle, emptied of the constitutional values of the early period, except that we were no longer dealing with more or less insignificant pieces of technical administrative law case law based on a thin rule-of-law understanding trumping the thicker rule-of-law considerations of the period of more mature constitutionalism. Given the unexpected revival of a purely formal and hierarchical understanding of primacy also after *Melloni*, it is hard to predict where the Court is going. But this does not prevent us from arguing where, normatively, the Court should be going.

VII. THE WAY FORWARDS: THE PRIMACY OF THE RULE OF LAW

Member State constitutional courts have engaged *bona fide* in forms of constitutional identity review that build on the co-extensiveness of constitutional values, principles and rules of the Union and Member States, thus limiting the area of possible conflict, emphasising the substance of the matter rather than blindly applying considerations of formal hierarchy. This is a confirmation of the earlier approach in fundamental rights review: it is the substantive importance of the matter at stake which informs the dynamics of conflict and its resolution. The *Solange* and *equivalent protection* approaches have served their purpose. In the end the reserve power of national constitutional courts in fundamental rights review has been restricted by high admissibility thresholds, which prevents abusive practices in this field. In ultra vires review cases, one can detect a similar trend: only when other substantive constitutional issues are at stake – issues similar to constitutional identity issues – does there seem to be a legitimate concern at stake. And also in such cases, admissibility thresholds should prevent abusive appeals. So all in all, I would argue that substantive rule-of-law considerations

[49] Case C-379/87 *Groener v Minister for Education and the City of Dublin Vocational Educational Committee* ECLI:EU:C:1989:599.

[50] Case C-402/05 P *Kadi and Al Barakaat International Foundation v Council and Commission* ECLI:EU:C:2008:461.

[51] Case C-112/00 *Eugen Schmidberger, Internationale Transporte und Planzüge v Republik Österreich* ECLI:EU:C:2003:333.

[52] Case C-36/02 *Omega* (n 5 above).

[53] Case C-314/08 *Filipiak v Dyrektor Izby Skarbowej w Poznaniu* ECLI:EU:C:2009:719.

[54] Case C-208/09 *Sayn-Wittgenstein v Landeshauptmann von Wien* ECLI:EU:C:2010:806.

[55] *Opinion 2/13* (Accession of the Union to the ECHR) ECLI:EU:C:2014:2454.

can or should be the only legitimate reasons for national constitutional courts to resort to these forms of review of EU law.

There are several arguments why the Court of Justice should follow suit and make a substantive rule-of-law consideration take precedence over the empty formal hierarchy that has so far characterised its primacy rule.

Firstly, the Founding Treaties have evolved. In *President Ruhrkohlen and others* the Court suggested that not only was it not its function to ensure that national constitutional rules are respected, but there were no general principles of Community law that protected relevant fundamental rights either. However, in *Internationale Handelsgesellschaft* it expressly reinterpreted Community law as containing fundamental rights that are found in the common constitutional traditions of the Member States. In *Internationale Handelsgesellschaft*, the language of the Court suggests that invocation of the principles of the constitutional structure of a Member State cannot affect the validity of European law, and precisely these constitutional structures are to be respected pursuant to the identity clause as formulated in the Lisbon Treaty.

Moreover, the national identity clause itself imposes a duty to respect Member States' constitutional identity not as a heteronomous counterbalance (*controlimite*), but as a matter of EU law itself. Primacy has, as a matter of Union law, a built-in modification of the concept as sheer hierarchical supremacy. It can no longer be a merely a 'thin' notion of the rule of law which is blind to the constitutional features of Member States as democratic states based on values such as human dignity, freedom, equality, the respect for human rights – including the rights of persons belonging to minorities – pluralism, tolerance, and solidarity. On this view, the principle of primacy must at least take into account not only the aspects of 'thin' concepts of Member States' constitutional identity, but also aspects of a 'thick' notion of the rule of law.

VIII. CONCLUSION

We can articulate the legal relation between and the consistency of Articles 2 and 4(2) TEU in this formula: the Union must respect a Member State constitutional identity that does not infringe the 'homogeneity' of constitutional values; Member States must respect the unity of EU law that does not infringe the constitutional identity.

To be constitutionally meaningful, in a democratic state under the rule of law, the rule of law must not be the hollowed out 'thin' concept we lawyers tend to embrace. To be constitutionally meaningful, EU law primacy must not be an empty shell of merely formal hierarchy that is not based on the constitutional values enunciated in Article 2 TEU.

Merely formal primacy leads at best to *aporia*. Can one require Member States to comply with the values of constitutionalism: liberty, democracy, fundamental rights, the rule of law – in short with their constitution – and simultaneously require them to accept primacy as overruling their constitution, even if it concerns liberty, democracy, fundamental rights, the rule of law?

That EU law applies in accordance with EU law and with the fundamental principles of the democratic state under the rule of law is the normative assumption of national constitutions. This is what membership of the Union rightly requires. Primacy should therefore apply with respect for the fundamental principles of the democratic state under the rule of law, lest the common foundation of the Union and Member States be undermined.

7

EU Minimum Requirements for Judicial Independence and Impartiality as Interpreted by the European Court of Justice[1]

NIILO JÄÄSKINEN

I. INTRODUCTION

Due to certain regrettable political and constitutional developments in Europe, the independence of justice and the impartiality of the judiciary and its individual members have become a topical subject since 2015 in the case law of the three European courts; that is, the European Court of Justice (ECJ or the Court), the European Court of Human Rights (ECtHR) and the EFTA Court.[2] This case law mirrors and puts into practice the voluminous international, European as well as national academic and legal policy debates relating to this aspect of the rule of law that have taken place since the end of the Cold War.[3] As a consequence, various reforms have been implemented in many European countries leading, inter alia, to the establishment of various structures supporting the independence of justice, such as authorities or bodies separate from the ministries of justice and responsible for the central administration of the court system as well as to legislative amendments protecting courts and judges from external control and influence.

This chapter describes the relevant European Union case law on judicial independence from a systemic perspective. There appears to be a rising trend in judgments

[1] The author would like to thank Mr Timothy Binham and Ms Eleonora Tuisku for their valuable comments and help. The usual disclaimer applies. For the purposes of this chapter, the case law of the Court of Justice of the European Union has been followed up to 21 December 2021.

[2] See Case E-21/16 *Pascal Nobile v DAS Rechtsschutz-Versicherungs AG*, decision of 14 February 2017. The case law of the EFTA Court is not discussed further in this chapter.

[3] For a comprehensive overview of the debate, see CEELI Institute, *Manual on Independence, Impartiality and Integrity of Justice. A Thematic Compilation of International Standards, Policies and Best Practices* (Prague, August 2022): https://ceeliinstitute.org/wp-content/uploads/2022/08/Judicial-Manual-Edition-2022.pdf.

relating to various dimensions of this subject area. These judgments, and the related Opinions of the Advocates General, form a complex web of intertwined citations and cross-references that, as a whole, express a developing and increasingly demanding Union law standard of judicial independence. Even if this legal development is a consequence of the recent rule-of-law problems in certain individual Member States, the fundaments of the case law were laid down well before. In this respect, it is necessary to remind ourselves of the close interaction of the case law of the ECtHR and that of the ECJ on judicial independence.

I will start by discussing the relevant treaty bases related to the independence of justice. I will then go on to present a short systematic exposition of the relevant case law, followed by some brief concluding remarks.

II. INDEPENDENCE OF THE JUDICIARY

A. Primary Law Bases

In the system of the founding Treaties forming the constitution of the European Union, two provisions serve as the basis of the Court's case law on judicial independence. First, Article 19(1), second subparagraph, of the Treaty on European Union (TEU) requires the Member States to provide remedies sufficient to ensure effective legal protection in the fields covered by Union law. Second, Article 47 of the Charter of Fundamental Rights of the European Union (Charter) establishes a *fundamental right to an effective remedy and to a fair trial*. The latter provision provides that '[e]veryone whose rights and freedoms guaranteed by the law of the Union are violated has the right to an effective remedy before a tribunal in compliance with the conditions laid down in this Article' (first sub-paragraph) and that '[e]veryone is entitled to a fair and public hearing within a reasonable time *by an independent and impartial tribunal previously established by law* [emphasis added]' (second sub-paragraph).

The principle of effective judicial protection, which was recognised in the 1980s by the ECJ as a general principle of then-Community law, is reflected in these two provisions. Moreover, Article 47 of the Charter establishes the *right to a fair trial* enshrined in Article 6 of the European Convention on Human Rights (ECHR). The interpretation of this human right by the ECtHR has greatly influenced and inspired the Court's case law.

As to content, there is undoubtedly a great deal of overlap between Article 19(1) TEU and Article 47 of the Charter, especially regarding the self-standing right of a person to a fair trial by '*a tribunal established by law*'. Yet, the scope of Article 19(1), second subparagraph, TEU is primarily *structural*, whereas Article 47 of the Charter is more *procedurally oriented*. The latter protects the rights of an individual, not directly the integrity of the judicial system as a whole.[4]

[4] Opinion of Advocate General Bobek in Case C-132/20 *BN and Others v Getin Noble Bank SA and Others* ECLI:EU:C:2021:557, paras 31–40, and in Joined Cases C-83/19, C-127/19, C-195/19, C-291/19 and C-355/19, *Asociația 'Forumul Judecătorilor din România' and Others v Inspecția Judiciară and Others* ECLI:EU:C:2021:746, paras 183–225.

In this respect, it is important to highlight that the material scope of application of Article 47 of the Charter is limited to situations where the Member States implement Union law, whereas this limitation does not apply to Article 19(1), second subparagraph, TEU.[5] Moreover, the applicability of Article 47 of the Charter depends on whether a right or a freedom guaranteed by the law of the Union has been violated. To my mind, one should not exaggerate the significance of these differences. In most situations, the two provisions interact as two different aspects of the broader constitutional principle of effective judicial protection.

Indeed, the Court has summed up in *WZ* that the second subparagraph of Article 19(1) TEU provides the establishment of a system of legal remedies and procedures to ensure for individuals compliance with their right to effective legal protection in the fields covered by EU law. The general principle of the effective judicial protection of individuals' rights under EU law is affirmed by Article 47 of the Charter. The latter provision must be duly taken into consideration when interpreting the second subparagraph of Article 19(1) TEU.[6]

Article 19(1) TEU establishes a division of responsibilities between the Union-level judiciary and the Member State national court systems. It functions as a cornerstone of the application of Union law in the Member States. General competence for the judicial application of Union law is vested in national courts. However, the Union courts can exercise only the strictly limited powers enumerated in Articles 256 to 279 of the Treaty on the Functioning of the European Union (TFEU). With regard to this division of responsibilities and powers between the Union and national courts, and the primordial role that the latter play in the application of Union law, it is unsurprising that Article 267 TFEU has gained much importance in the Court's case law relating to judicial independence. The preliminary rulings procedure established by Article 267 TFEU cannot function properly if the integrity of the Member State court systems is not guaranteed. In its ground-breaking judgment of March 2018 in *Associação Sindical dos Juízes Portugueses*, the Court underlined the importance of the independence of national courts and tribunals for the proper functioning of the judicial cooperation system incorporated in the preliminary ruling mechanism under Article 267 TFEU. Only an entity in charge of the application of the EU law that fulfils this criterion of independence may activate this mechanism.[7]

Unfortunately, it seems that this mechanism of judicial cooperation and dialogue is especially targeted by certain Member State measures that weaken the independence of justice.

The independence and integrity of the judicial system are one expression of the constitutional value of the rule of law, enshrined in Article 2 TEU as one of the fundamental values on which the Union is founded. The rule of law, in turn, protects other fundamental values of the Union, such as democracy, respect for human rights and equality, and, of course, the proper functioning of the internal market and the area of

[5] Case C-64/16 *Associação Sindical dos Juízes Portugueses v Tribunal de Contas* ECLI:EU:C:2018:117, para 29.

[6] Case C-487/19 *WŻ (chambre de contrôle extraordinaire et des affaires publiques de la Cour suprême – nomination)* ECLI:EU:C:2021:798, para 102, and the case law cited.

[7] Case C-64/16 (above n 5), para 43.

freedom, security and justice. The ECJ has emphasised that the Member States have freely and voluntarily adhered to the common values referred to in Article 2 TEU. They have committed themselves to respecting those values as well as to undertaking to promote them. Therefore, mutual trust between the Member States and between their courts and tribunals rests on the fundamental premise that Member States share a set of common values, on which the European Union is founded.[8]

According to the case law of the Court, Article 19 TEU embodies the value of the rule of law incorporated in Article 2 TEU. National courts and tribunals as well as the ECJ are responsible for ensuring the full application of EU law in all Member States and the judicial protection that individuals derive from EU law.[9]

In this context, Article 4(2) TEU should also be mentioned. According to this provision, the Union shall respect the equality of the national identities of the Member States that are inherent in their fundamental political and constitutional structures as well as their essential state functions, including, inter alia, maintaining law and order and safeguarding national security. There is undoubtedly a certain tension between Article 4, on the one hand, and Articles 2 and 19(1), second subparagraph, TEU, on the other. The judicial systems of the Member States belong uncontestably to their fundamental political structures and essential state functions. Hence, it is no wonder that certain Member State governments have invoked Article 4 TEU as a means to shield their judicial reforms from scrutiny as to their compatibility with Union law.

Although the organisation of justice falls within the competence of the Member States, the Court has repeatedly observed that these are required to comply with their obligations deriving from EU law when exercising that competence.[10] That may be the case, for example, as regards the substantive conditions and procedural rules of appointment procedures for judges and, where applicable, judicial review thereof,[11] and as regards disciplinary measures and civil liability applicable to judges.[12]

On the other hand, a Member State must comply with the values embodied in Article 2 TEU in order to enjoy the rights deriving from the application of the Treaties to it. Therefore, a Member State may not amend its legislation such as to reduce the protection of the EU value of the rule of law. They are thus required to prevent any regression of their laws on the organisation of justice by refraining from adopting provisions that would weaken the independence of judges.[13] Hence,

[8] Case C-791/19 *Commission v Poland (Disciplinary regime for judges)* ECLI:EU:C:2021:596, para 50; Case C-619/18 *Commission v Poland (Independence of the Supreme Court)* judgment of 24 June 2019 ECLI:EU:C:2019:531, paras 42–43 and the case law cited; and Joined Cases C-83/19, C-127/19, C-195/19, C-291/19, C-355/19 and C-397/19 (above n 4), para 160 and the case law cited.

[9] Case C-824/18 *AB and Others (Appointment of judges to the Supreme Court – Actions)* ECLI:EU:C:2021:153, para 108 and the case law cited.

[10] Case C-619/18 (above n 8), para 52 and the case law cited, Joined Cases C-558/18 and C-563/18 *Miasto Łowicz and Prokurator Generalny v Skarb Państwa – Wojewoda Łódzki and Others* ECLI:EU:C:2020:234, para 36 and the case law cited, and Case C-824/18 (above n 9), para 68 and the case law cited, Case C-791/19 (above n 8), para 56, and Case C-487/19 (above n 6), para 75.

[11] See to that effect, Case C-585/18, C-624/18 and C-625/18 *A.K. and Others (Independence of the Disciplinary Chamber of the Supreme Court)* ECLI:EU:C:2019:982, paras 134–39 and 145.

[12] Joined Cases C-558/18 and C-563/18 (above n 10), para 39.

[13] Case C-791/19 (above n 8), para 51, Case C-896/19 *Repubblika v Il-Prim Ministru* ECLI:EU:C:2021:311, paras 63 to 65 and the case law cited, and Case C-397/19 (above n 8), para 162.

within the constitutional and procedural autonomy of the Member States as to the organisation of their judiciary and the court systems, a *standstill obligation* applies, excluding any regression of the guarantees of the independence and impartiality already achieved.

B. The Concept of the Independence of the Judiciary

(i) Structural Independence of the Judiciary and Impartiality of Judges

Independence and impartiality of justice are often lumped together without any differentiation. This also applies to much of the case law of the CJEU. Nevertheless, there is a certain conceptual hierarchy between these two notions; the impartiality of the judge is understood as the *objective* that is protected by ensuring the independence of the judiciary. For example, the ECtHR observed in *Reczkowicz v Poland* that '"independence of a tribunal established by law" refers to the necessary personal and institutional independence that is required for impartial decision making, and it is thus a prerequisite for impartiality'.[14] Impartiality, in turn, goes to the very essence of the right to a *fair* trial protected by Article 6 ECHR and Article 47 of the Charter.

As I have already observed, the right to effective judicial protection, including in particular a right to a fair trial, has been recognised in the case law of the Court as a general principle of law since the 1980s. Later it was included in Article 47 of the Charter and in Article 19(1), second subparagraph, TEU. In this respect, the Court has largely followed the ECtHR case law on Article 6 ECHR, according to which the guarantees of access to an independent and impartial tribunal, and in particular those provisions which determine what constitutes a tribunal and how it is composed, represent the cornerstone of the right to a fair trial.

The Court specified in *Chronopost* that this right is to be understood as an obligation for the courts to proceed to an examination of a tribunal's composition where its independence and impartiality is disputed on a ground that does not immediately appear to be manifestly devoid of merit. This check is necessary for the confidence that the courts must inspire in those subject to their jurisdiction. In that respect, such verification is an essential procedural requirement, compliance with which is a matter of public policy. Moreover, the Court observed that the condition of impartiality has two aspects. This approach also reflects the ECtHR case law. First, the members of the tribunal themselves must be *subjectively* impartial. This means that none of its members may show bias or personal prejudice. There is a presumption of personal impartiality in the absence of evidence to the contrary. Second, the tribunal must be *objectively* impartial; that is to say, it must offer guarantees sufficient to exclude any legitimate doubt in that respect.[15] The Court repeated and elaborated further this

[14] *Reczkowicz v Poland*, judgment of 22 July 2021, Application no 43447, para 261.

[15] Case C-341/06 P and C-342/06 P *Chronopost v UFEX and Others* ECLI:EU:C:2008:375, paras 44, 46, and 54.

position in *Simpson* that concerned a procedural failure in nomination proceedings to the then European Union Civil Service Tribunal.[16]

What, then, does independence of the judiciary mean? In this case the Court has adopted a test that it repeats, with slight variations, in its various judgments relating to integrity and independence of justice. Accordingly, the concept of independence implies above all that the body in question acts *as a third party* in relation to the parties, including, in a public law context, the authority or body that made the contested decision.

This concept has two aspects. The first *external* aspect involves protection of the decision-making body and its individual members against external intervention or pressure affecting their independence. The second *internal* aspect concerns impartiality, and seeks to ensure a level playing-field for the parties to the proceedings and their respective interests in relation to the subject matter of those proceedings. This latter aspect requires objectivity as well as the absence of any interest in the outcome of the proceedings apart from the strict application of the rule of law.[17]

The rules applicable to the status of judges and the performance of their duties must prevent any *direct influence* in the form of instructions as well as more *indirect* types of influence that are liable to have an effect on the decisions of the judges concerned.[18]

Such guarantees of independence and impartiality require rules as regards the composition of the court or tribunal and the appointment, length of service and grounds for abstention, rejection and dismissal of its members. They must dispel any reasonable doubt in the minds of individuals as to *the imperviousness of that body to external factors*,[19] in particular, as to the *direct or indirect influence of the legislature and the executive*, and its neutrality with respect to the *interests before* it. Such doubts may lead to a judicial body not being conceived as independent or impartial. This is in turn likely to prejudice the trust which justice in a democratic society must inspire in those individuals.[20]

This requirement of *imperviousness* of national courts and their individual judges to external factors stems from Article 47 of the Charter[21] and equally from Article 19(1), second subparagraph, TEU.[22]

The economic resources of the courts are an aspect of the structural independence of the judiciary. The Court has emphasised that a level of remuneration of the judges

[16] Case C-542/18 RX-II and C-543/18 RX-II *Simpson and HG v Council and Commission* ECLI:EU:C:2020:232, para 56.

[17] Case C-619/18 *Commission v Poland (Independence of the Supreme Court)* judgment of 24 June 2019, ECLI:EU:C:2019:531, para 73.

[18] Case C-791/19 (above n 8), para 60 and Case C-397/19 (above n 8), para 197, and the case law cited.

[19] Case C-175/11 *HID and BA v Refugee Applications Commissioner and Others* ECLI:EU:C:2013:45, paras 95–97, Case C-64/16 (above n 5), para 44, Case C-506/04 *Wilson v Ordre des avocats du barreau de Luxembourg*, ECLI:EU:C:2006:587, para 51, Case C-503/15 *Margarit Panicello* ECLI:EU:C:2017:126, para 37 and the case law cited.

[20] Case C-791/19 (above n 8), para 86.

[21] Joined Cases C-585/18, C-624/18 and C-625/18 (above n 10), paras 118–126.

[22] Case C-824/18 (above n 9), para 150.

commensurate with the importance of the functions they carry out is a guarantee essential to judicial independence. In this sense, it is comparable to the protection of judges against removal from office, that is, the irremovability of judges.[23]

(ii) Irremovability of Judges

In national constitutional law, the irremovability of judges guarantees their independence and impartiality, and by extension, the independence and impartiality of the courts. This means that judges cannot be removed from office during their tenure, whether their mandate is limited to a fixed term or continues up to the compulsory retirement age. Exceptions to this can be made for objectively justified reasons duly set out in legislative provisions and applicable in fair disciplinary or judicial proceedings.

The Court has adopted the *principle of irremovability* of judges in its case law as a requirement stemming from Article 19(1), second subparagraph, TEU, and from the general principle of effective judicial protection. As under national constitutional law, judges' freedom from all external intervention or pressure requires appropriate protective guarantees such as guarantees against removal from office. Consequently, judges cannot be removed from their position before they reach the mandatory retirement age or their fixed-term mandate expires. Exceptions are allowed to the principle of irremovability provided they are warranted by legitimate and compelling grounds and respect the principle of proportionality. For example, judges may be dismissed if they are deemed unfit to carry out their duties due to incapacity or a serious breach of their obligations, provided the appropriate procedures are followed.[24]

The Court has found that the principle of irremovability was breached by a Polish law concerning reform of the judiciary which provided that the measure lowering the retirement age of judges of the *Sąd Najwyższy* (Supreme Court) also applied to judges already serving on that court. This resulted in the premature termination of several judges' terms of judicial office. Such an outcome did not comply with the principle of the irremovability of judges, because it was not justified by a legitimate objective.[25]

The transfer of a judge without his/her consent to another court, or between two divisions of the same court, may also weaken the principles of irremovability of judges and judicial independence. Such transfers may influence the content of judicial decisions, as they may constitute a way of exercising control over the handling of cases entrusted to judges as well as over the scope of their activities. The effects of a transfer may be similar to those of a disciplinary sanction and they may affect the career and life of the judge concerned. However, such transfers are not completely prohibited. They must be based on legitimate grounds such as the distribution of available resources to ensure the proper administration of justice and they must be capable

[23] Case C-64/16 (above n 5), para 45.
[24] Case C-619/18 (above n 8), paras 75 and 76.
[25] Case C-619/18 (above n 8), paras 78 and 96.

of being legally challenged by a procedure safeguarding the rights incorporated in Articles 47 and 48 of the Charter in order to be acceptable.[26]

(iii) Appointment Procedures and the Notion of a Tribunal Established by Law

The systems of appointments to judicial offices in the Member States of the Union vary greatly. This stems from differences in historical and constitutional experiences and developments. Internally, in most Member States, the appointments system is not unitary: the procedures may be different between supreme-level and/or constitutional courts, on the one hand, and lower-level tribunals, on the other hand, or between general, administrative and specialised courts. This said, a general tendency can be detected to shield judicial appointments from direct political influences and to increase the role of independent judicial and extra-judicial expertise in this field.[27] However, one needs to bear in mind that the judicial appointments systems of many national systems contain 'constitutional dust' in that they maintain formal prerogatives of the head of state or government even though they never personally exercise these prerogatives.

In the Court's case law, judicial appointments have been examined from various perspectives. The relevant issues can be divided into the following sub-questions:

- first, judicial independence and the notion of a tribunal established by law;
- second, participation of the executive and legislative powers in the nominations;
- third, preparatory bodies and procedures and their objectivity, including judicial review of appointments;
- fourth, observance of national constitutional requirements; and
- fifth, the effects of irregularities on the outcome in terms of the notion of a lawful judge (*juge légal*).

As to the *first sub-question*, it follows from the general EU law principle of effective judicial protection – expressed in the first sentence of the second paragraph of Article 47 of the Charter, and Article 19(1), second subparagraph, TEU – that everyone is entitled to a fair and public hearing within a reasonable time by an *independent and impartial tribunal previously established by law*.[28]

[26] Case C-487/19 (above n 6), paras 114, 115 and 118. This was not remedied by the possibility to receive an exemption of obligatory retirement, as any such exemption was based on a discretionary decision of the President of the Republic.

[27] In its Report on Judicial Appointments (CDL–AD(2007)028), adopted at its 70th Plenary Session (16–17 March 2007), the European Commission for Democracy Through Law (Venice Commission) states that 'In Europe, methods of appointment vary greatly according to different countries and their legal systems; furthermore they can differ within the same legal system according to the type of judges to be appointed.' (para 7). 'International standards in this respect are more in favour of the extensive depoliticisation of the [judicial appointment] process. However, no single non-political 'model' of appointment system exists, which could ideally comply with the principle of the separation of powers and secure full independence of the judiciary.' (para 3).

[28] Case C-487/19 (above n 6), paragraph 122.

In that regard, the Court has relied on the ECtHR case law, especially *Ástráðsson v Iceland*.[29] It has stressed the close relation between the right to trial by a 'tribunal established by law' enshrined in Article 6(1) ECHR and the guarantees of 'independence' and 'impartiality'. The process of appointing judges constitutes an inherent element of the concept of a 'tribunal established by law' in the light of its fundamental implications for the proper functioning and the legitimacy of the judiciary in a democratic state governed by the rule of law. The way the members of a tribunal are appointed may be a measure of its independence[30] and the confidence that courts must inspire in their subjects relies on the proper examination of whether, as composed, it constitutes a 'tribunal established by law' where a serious doubt arises on that point.[31]

The term 'established by law' has been introduced to prevent the executive from influencing the organisation of the judicial system and to ensure that laws emanating from the legislature regulate it. This term covers the legal basis for the very existence of a tribunal and the composition of the bench in each case, as well as domestic law provisions which, if breached, would render the participation of one or more judges in the examination of a case irregular, including provisions concerning the independence and impartiality of the members of the court in question.[32]

As to the *second sub-question*, the independence of the judiciary must be ensured in relation to the *legislature and the executive*. Thus, the principle of the separation of powers characterising the operation of the rule of law relates to the independence of the judiciary.[33] As such, the appointment of judges by the executive of a Member State, including the President or the Prime Minister, or the participation of the legislature in the appointments proceedings, neither challenges the impartiality of the judges concerned nor does it create a relationship of subordination between those judges and the executive. This holds good if, once appointed, the judges are free from influence or pressure when carrying out their judicial role.[34] Therefore, the substantive conditions and procedural rules governing the adoption of those appointment decisions must be such as to dispel any reasonable doubt as to the imperviousness of the judges concerned to external factors and their neutrality with respect to the interests before them.[35]

An example of a situation where legitimate doubts were found to exist as to the independence and impartiality of judges appointed in accordance with a particular procedure was the situation in *Prokuratura Rejonowa w Mińsku Mazowieckim and Others*,[36] concerning secondments of judges in Poland to higher-level tribunals.

[29] *Ástráðsson v. Iceland*, judgment of 1 December 2021, Application no 26374/18, paras 231 and 233.

[30] Case C-487/19 (above n 6), paras 123 and 124, citing *Ástráðsson v. Iceland* (above n 29), paras 227 and 232.

[31] Case C-487/19 (above n 6), para 126, citing Joined Cases C-542/18 RX-II and C-543/18 RX-II (above n 16), para 57 and the case law cited.

[32] Joined Cases C-542/18 RX-II and C-543/18 RX-II (above n 16), para 73.

[33] Case C-487/19 (above n 6), para 127, citing Case C-896/19 (above n 13), para 54 and the case law cited.

[34] Case C-896/19 (above n 13), paras 56 and 73 and the case law cited, Case C-272/19 *VQ v Land Hessen* ECLI:EU:C:2020:535, para 54, citing Case C-585/18 (above n 11), para 133 and the case law cited.

[35] Case C-896/19 (above n 13), para 57 and the case law cited.

[36] Joined Cases C-748/19 to C-754/19, *WB and Others v Prokuratura Rejonowa w Mińsku Mazowieckim and Others*, ECLI:EU:C:2021:931.

In Poland, the Minister for Justice has, on the basis of criteria which are not known, the power to second judges to higher courts and to terminate their secondment. He is not required to give reasons for such decisions. Thus, during the period of those judges' secondment, they are not provided with the guarantees and the independence that all judges should normally enjoy in a state governed by the rule of law. The Court considered that such a power held by the executive (the Minister of Justice) could not be considered compatible with the obligation to comply with the requirement of independence.[37]

As to the preparatory bodies and procedures and their objectivity covered by the *third sub-question*, the Court has held that the participation of a *judiciary council*[38] or a similar body in a process for the appointment of judges may, in principle, be such as to contribute to making that process more objective by circumscribing the discretion of the executive authority in making judicial appointments.[39] However, it is crucial that the procedural rules and substantive conditions regulating the making of those appointment decisions do not challenge the independence and impartiality of the judges appointed and that they are drafted in a way that meets these requirements. Therefore, the body in charge of delivering the appointment proposal must be sufficiently independent of the legislature and executive and of the authority receiving this proposal.[40] Where an appointment proposal is necessary to fill a judicial position, the degree of independence enjoyed by this body may be a relevant consideration in determining whether the selected judge complies with the requirements of independence and impartiality.[41]

As to the amenability of judicial appointments to *judicial review*, the Court has held that the impossibility to exercise a legal remedy with regard to a process of appointment to a judicial position is not, as such, incompatible with the requirements arising from the EU law. However, the assessment may be different in circumstances in which the *existing* possibilities for obtaining judicial remedies are suddenly eliminated. This may give rise to systemic doubts in the minds of individuals as to the independence and impartiality of the judges appointed at the end of that process.[42] This said, there seems to be in the case law of the Court an implicit preference for the possibility of judicial review of judicial appointment proposals and decisions, such review covering, at the very least, an examination of whether there was no ultra vires or improper exercise of authority, error of law or manifest error of assessment.[43]

As regards the *fourth sub-question* pertaining to observance of national constitutional requirements, the Court has held that an irregularity occurring during the

[37] Joined Cases C-748/19 to C-754/19 (above n 36), para 87.

[38] The case law has concerned primarily the Polish judicial council (Krajowa Rada Sądownictwa, KRS) but also Judicial Appointments Committee of Hessen (Germany) and the Judicial Appointments Committee of Malta.

[39] Case C-791/19 (above n 8), para 103.

[40] Case C-824/18 (above n 9), paras 123–25.

[41] Case C-824/18 (above n 9), paras 126–27.

[42] Case C-824/18 (above n 9), para 129.

[43] Case C-824/18 (above n 9), para 128 and case law cited. See, similarly, *Thiam v France*, judgment of 18 October 2018, Application no 80018/12, paras 25, 81.

appointment of judges constitutes an infringement of the requirement of a fair trial by a tribunal established by law. This kind of irregularity – which gives rise to a real risk that other branches of the state could exercise control over the outcome of the appointment process – is to be considered as such an infringement, because it may undermine the trust of the individuals in the independence and the impartiality of the judge or judges concerned. Indeed, the issue concerns the compliance with fundamental rules forming an integral part of the functioning and establishment of the judicial system.[44] The national courts have the power to assess whether the body including the appointed judge may be considered to be an 'independent and impartial tribunal previously established by law' in the light of any irregularities committed in the appointment process.[45]

Finally, regarding the *fifth sub-question* concerning the effects of an irregular judicial appointment procedure, the Court has drawn the conclusion that a national court must declare any decision in which a *juge illégal* took part to be null and void. This is the case if it follows, from all the conditions and circumstances in which the process of the appointment of a judge took place, that there was a clear breach of fundamental rules which form an integral part of the establishment and functioning of the judicial system concerned, and the integrity of the outcome of that procedure is undermined. The EU law standard applicable is that if the circumstances of the appointment would give rise to reasonable doubt in the minds of individuals as to the independence and impartiality of the judge concerned, it is possible to hold that the judicial decision has not been made by an independent and impartial tribunal previously established by law.[46]

(iv) Disciplinary Regimes and Civil Law Liability of Judges

The liability of judges for their wrongful acts and omissions in office entails a difficult policy trade-off between the societal need to uphold the legitimacy of the court system, on the one hand, and safeguarding the independence of justice, on the other. It is therefore no wonder that the issue of the penal, civil and disciplinary liability of members of the judiciary has received a great deal of attention in the European debate on judicial independence.

Here the Court's case law is based on the premise that the disciplinary and civil liability regimes applicable to judges fall within the organisation of justice and, therefore, within the Member States' competence. The possibility to raise the issue of the liability of judges can contribute to the accountability and effectiveness of the judicial system.[47] As always, however, the Member States must here safeguard the

[44] Case C-487/19 (above n 6), para 130 and case law cited.
[45] Case C-487/19 (above n 6), para 131.
[46] Case C-487/19 (above n 6), paras 131, 137, 153–55, and 161.
[47] When a state initiates such disciplinary proceedings, public confidence in the functioning and independence of the judiciary is at stake; in a democratic state, this confidence guarantees the very existence of the rule of law: see *Ramos Nunes de Carvalho e Sá v Portugal*, judgment of 6 November 2018, Application no 55391/13, para 196, and *Eminağaoğlu v Turkey*, judgment of 9 March 2021, Application no 76521/12 para 97, cited in Case C-791/19 (above n 8), para 83.

independence of the courts called upon to rule on questions concerning the application or interpretation of EU law so as to ensure the effective judicial protection of individuals required by the second subparagraph of Article 19(1) TEU.[48]

However, the safeguarding of the independence of justice does not totally exclude the possibility that the disciplinary liability of a judge may arise because of judicial decisions adopted by that judge in certain very exceptional cases. The same applies to civil law liability for damages caused by such decisions. Attaching such consequences to serious and totally inexcusable forms of conduct is not precluded by the principle of independence of justice. For instance, the liability of the judge can be triggered in case of a violation of national and EU law committed by the judge deliberately and in bad faith or as a result of particularly serious and gross negligence. Equally, it is possible to sanction arbitrary action or *déni de justice*.[49] However, the existence of a judicial error in a decision is not in itself sufficient to render the judge concerned personally liable.[50]

Any regime of liability of judges must provide the guarantees needed to prevent any risk of its use as a system for politically controlling the content of judicial decisions and to safeguard the independence of the judiciary. The rules defining the forms of conduct that amount to disciplinary offences and the penalties actually applicable must provide for the involvement of a body fulfilling all the requirements of independency and impartiality. The procedure must ensure the possibility to challenge the decisions made by the disciplinary bodies and compliance with the rights enshrined in Articles 47 and 48 of the Charter, including the rights of the defence.[51] The Court has pointed out that the judicial review carried out must be appropriate to the disciplinary nature of the decisions taken, because the disciplinary measures may have serious consequences for the lives and careers of the members of the judiciary.

As to civil liability, the existence of rules defining clearly and precisely the conduct triggering the judge's personal liability is essential in order to safeguard their independence and to avoid exposing them to an arbitrary application of personal liability based on the decisions they render. The principle of independence of judges does not mean that the acts performed in the exercise of their duties benefit from absolute protection. However, the personal liability of a judge can be incurred only in exceptional cases in which damage has been caused in the exercise of judicial office and serious individual culpability has been established. National legislation must guarantee precisely and clearly that neither the action for indemnity nor the investigation to determine liability is used so as to exert pressure on judicial activity.[52]

Concerning the requirement that legislative rules on the liability of judges must be clear and precise, the Court has held that even though the Romanian provisions

[48] As to civil law liability, see Joined Cases C-83/19, C-127/19, C-195/19, C-291/19, C-355/19 and C-397/19 (above n 8), paras 229 and 230. As to disciplinary liability, see Case C-791/19 (above n 8), para 61.

[49] Case C-791/19 (above n 8), para 137, and Joined Cases C-83/19, C-127/19, C-195/19, C-291/19, C-355/19 and C-397/19 (above n 8), paras 229 and 230.

[50] Case C-791/19 (above n 8), para 140, and Joined Cases C-83/19, C-127/19, C-195/19, C-291/19, C-355/19 and C-397/19 (above n 8), para 234.

[51] Case C-791/19 (above n8), para 61, and Joined Cases C-83/19, C-127/19, C-195/19, C-291/19, C-355/19 and C-397/19 (above n 8), para 198.

[52] Joined Cases C-83/19, C-127/19, C-195/19, C-291/19, C-355/19 and C-397/19 (above n 8), paras 234–35.

on civil law liability for judicial errors are worded in abstract and general terms in the national legislation, this alone does not suffice to jeopardise judicial independence. Legislation governing state liability must by its very nature lay down abstract and general criteria, for the purposes of the definition of 'judicial error', which are bound to be clarified by national case law.[53] In contrast, the generic and abstract language in the Polish provisions on disciplinary liability of judges did not prevent the liability of judges from being triggered solely on the basis of the supposedly 'incorrect' content of their decisions, while ensuring that such liability was always strictly limited to entirely exceptional situations. This was not remedied by the way these provisions were interpreted in the case law because their application was no longer entrusted exclusively to independent and impartial judicial bodies.[54]

Finally, the possibility of triggering disciplinary proceedings to restrict the right of courts and tribunals to submit requests for a preliminary ruling to the Court of Justice has been considered by the Court's case law as an infringement of the second and third paragraphs of Article 267 TFEU. For national judges, not being subject to disciplinary proceedings or measures for having brought a matter before the Court – which is a matter exclusively within their jurisdiction – also constitutes an essential guarantee of judicial independence. In particular, this independence is crucial to the proper working of the judicial cooperation system embodied by the preliminary ruling mechanism under Article 267 TFEU.[55]

III. AN EMERGING EUROPEAN UNION LAW NOTION OF JUDGESHIP UNDER THE RULE OF LAW

The case law of the Court has developed the details of a legal minimum standard regarding the independence of justice and the impartiality of judges. This standard is objective and ultimately boils down to the condition relating to the absence of any reasonable doubt in the minds of individuals as to *the imperviousness of that body to external factors*, in particular, as to the possibility of *direct or indirect influence of the legislature and the executive*, and its neutrality with respect to the *interests before* it.

Advocate General Bobek has rightly observed in his opinion in *Getin Noble Bank* that

> under EU law, there is only one principle of judicial independence. Nevertheless, in so far as the three provisions at issue (Article 267 TFEU, Article 47 of the Charter, and Article 19(1) TEU) are different in terms of their function and objective, the type of examination to be carried out in order to verify compliance with the principle of judicial independence may differ. In particular, the intensity of the Court's review with regard to compliance with that principle and the threshold for detecting an infringement thereto varies.[56]

[53] Joined Cases C-83/19, C-127/19, C-195/19, C-291/19, C-355/19 and C-397/19 (above n 8), para 228.

[54] Case C-791/19 (8), para 141, compared with paras 144, 147 and 148.

[55] Case C-824/18 (above n 9), para 95, Joined Cases C-558/18 and C-563/18 (above n 10), paras 58 and 59, Case C-791/19 (above n 8), paras 225–30.

[56] Opinion of Advocate General Bobek in Case C-132/20 (above n 3), para 36 (footnotes excluded).

This equally excludes any allegations of double standards, since the situations are objectively different in different Member States. AG Bobek continues:

> In recent years, particularly in view of the rule of law crisis in several Member States, the Court has been obliged not only to develop its case-law in order to provide guidance with regard to situations and scenarios that few would have ever imagined possible, but also to carve out exceptions to normally applicable rules due to abnormal cases.[57]

Unfortunately, the Union case law concerning rule of law in general, and judicial independence in particular, is bound to increase. This will continue as long as there are Member States' governments that are prepared to set aside their commitments regarding the values embodied in Article 2 TEU and the Copenhagen criteria as a matter of political expediency. In contrast, for the constitution of the European Union, respect for Articles 2 and 19 TEU, Article 47 of the Charter and Article 267 TFEU is of existential importance. Judicial independence is a cornerstone of a 'Union by law'.

[57] Opinion of Advocate General Bobek in Case C-132/20 (above n 3), para 71.

Part II

Protections

8

An Active EU Rule-of-Law Policy

WERNER SCHROEDER

I. THE NEED TO STRENGTHEN THE RULE OF LAW IN THE MEMBER STATES

WHEREAS SOME TIME ago there was talk of a tendency towards the rule-of-law 'backsliding' in certain Member States regarding the *acquis* of the accession,[1] it is now safe to say that 'we can no longer presume that the EU is a Union of rule-of-law-based democracies, as its Treaties presume'.[2] It has become obvious that the rule of law is under real threat in certain Member States of the Union. The current rule-of-law deficits are not coincidental but are rooted in intentional and systematic policies pursued by these Member States over a long time.

This situation threatens the Union's legitimacy[3] and identity as a common legal order,[4] which rests on its Member States' respect for the rule of law. If the rule of law systematically deteriorates in the Member States, the Union itself is also endangered. Therefore, the Union, within the framework of its competences, should be able to defend the rule of law by enforcing rule-of-law standards vis-à-vis Member States. Merely prohibiting those states from 'bringing about a reduction in the protection of the rule of law'[5] does not solve the problem.

Article 7 TEU provides for a procedure to 'penalise' Member States for severe and persistent breaches of the values contained in Article 2 TEU, in particular, to compel those states to cease breaches by ultimately depriving them of voting rights.[6] However, this instrument is also insufficient. The proceedings against Poland and Hungary have not progressed for years. The Council does not address the issues,

[1] L Pech and KL Scheppele, 'Illiberalism Within: Rule of Law Backsliding in the EU' (2017) 19 *Cambridge Yearbook of European Legal Studies* 3.

[2] KL Scheppele, D Kochenov and B Grabowska-Moroz, 'EU Values Are Law, after All: Enforcing EU Values through Systemic Infringement Actions by the European Commission and the Member States of the European Union' (2020) 39 *Yearbook of European Law* 3, 5.

[3] A Williams, 'Taking Values Seriously: Towards a Philosophy of EU Law' (2009) 29 *OJLS* 549, 563f.

[4] Case C-156/21 *Hungary v Parliament and Council* ECLI:EU:C:2022:97, para 127 ff; Case C-157/21 *Poland v Parliament and Council* ECLI:EU:C:2022:98, para 145 ff.

[5] Case C-896/19 *Repubblika v Il-Prim Ministru* ECLI:EU:C:2021:311, para 63; Joined Cases C-83/19, C-127/19, C-195-19, C-291/19, C-355/19 and C-397/19 *Asociaţia 'Forumul Judecătorilor din România' and Others v Inspecţia Judiciară and Others* ECLI:EU:C:2021:393, para 162.

[6] See Case C-156/21 *Hungary v Parliament and Council* (n 4 above), para 170.

and this situation is not expected to change in the foreseeable future. Nor have the Commission's numerous infringement proceedings brought against states such as Poland and Hungary before the European Court of Justice (ECJ) led to any significant improvement for the rule of law in those states. The ECJ always decides on individual cases, and its decisions typically lag behind the systemic strategies pursued by these states.[7]

The rule of law in the Union can only be effectively guaranteed by consistent measures aimed at defending, restoring and strengthening it. The rule of law must therefore be mainstreamed across all policy fields. In Union law there is potential for such measures, as the Union institutions and the Member States are committed to respecting the common values referred to in Article 2 TEU as well as to promoting and actively pursuing them under Articles 3(1) and (6), 4(3) and 49 TEU. Thus, the systematic realisation of the principle of the rule of law must become part of the decision-making programme for the Union's institutions.[8]

The Union had practised such an active rule-of-law policy for many years regarding candidate countries until it was provided with an explicit legal basis by the Amsterdam Treaty.[9] It mandated that accession Member States must adhere to the rule of law as part of the enlargement requirements.[10] With these requirements in mind, the Commission examined the rule-of-law situation in candidate countries, assessing which states had to adapt their laws, including, for instance, the rules on appointment of judges, and election laws. These standards were not part of the legal *acquis* but rather an expression of the Union's values.[11]

This chapter aims to strengthen the rule of law in the Union by contributing to the Union's ability to pursue an active rule-of-law policy not only in regard to non-member countries but also vis-à-vis its existing Member States. The introduction of the rule-of-law budgetary conditionality in Regulation 2020/2092,[12] under which the Union may withhold monies from Member States that do not observe the rule of law, is a first step in this direction. The Union must go further, however, systematically incorporating rule-of-law considerations into all its policies to actively promote, realise and sustain the rule of law throughout the Union.

II. CONTENT OF THE UNION RULE OF LAW

When the Union uses its regulatory competences in this regard, the question arises which kind of rule of law the Union should pursue via law-making.

[7] On the inefficiency of infringement procedures, see the contribution of J Heliskoski, Chapter 10 in this book; see also Scheppele, Kochenov and Grabowska-Moroz (n 2 above) 41f.

[8] W Schroeder, 'The Rule of Law As a Value in the Sense of Article 2 TEU: What Does It Mean and Imply?' in A von Bogdandy and others (eds), *Defending Checks and Balances in EU Member States: Taking Stock of Europe's Actions* (Berlin, Springer, 2021) 113 ff.

[9] Now, art 49 TEU.

[10] C Hillion, 'The Copenhagen Criteria and Their Progeny' in C Hillion (ed), *EU Enlargement: A Legal Approach* (Oxford, Hart Publishing, 2004) 1 ff.

[11] D Kochenov, 'Behind the Copenhagen Façade: The Meaning and Structure of the Copenhagen Political Criterion of Democracy and the Rule of Law' (2004) 8 *European Integration Online Papers* 1.

[12] Regulation (EU, Euratom) 2020/2092 of the European Parliament and of the Council on a general regime of conditionality for the protection of the Union budget [2020] OJ L433I/1.

A. Combining Formal and Material Elements

Thus far, the discussion about the content of the rule of law has been preoccupied with questions of judicial independence.[13] This focus on the judiciary is understandable given that the main rule-of-law problems in the Union concern issues of judicial backsliding in Member States. However, the rule of law cannot be reduced simply to the situation of the judiciary.[14]

In this context, one may refer to the debate over whether the Union rule of law is based on a 'thin' or 'thick' concept, that is, whether it includes only formal elements or rather consists of substantive ideas such as the principle of equality or human rights.[15] Based on the positive constitutional law of the Union and most of its Member States, the current European perception is that the rule of law must impose an obligation for fairness and a prohibition of arbitrariness in the content of legal norms.[16] This approach, based on the idea that the rule of law has not merely formal but also substantive components, has been employed by the institutions of the Union.[17] The definition of the rule of law provided in Article 2(a) of the Conditionality Regulation 2020/2092

> … includes the principles of legality implying a transparent, accountable, democratic and pluralistic law-making process; legal certainty; prohibition of arbitrariness of the executive powers; effective judicial protection, including access to justice, by independent and impartial courts, also as regards fundamental rights; separation of powers; and non-discrimination and equality before the law.

This broad understanding, which does not exceed the limits of the concept of the rule of law,[18] assumes correctly that formal aspects of the rule of law may overlap with substantive content.[19]

B. Right of the Union Legislator to Define the Rule of Law

Therefore, the issue is whether the Union legislator has the right to define the meaning of the rule of law if it pursues an active rule-of-law policy and, in this context,

[13] Case C-64/16 *Associação Sindical dos Juízes Portugueses v Tribunal de Contas* ECLI:EU:C:2018:117, para 41; Case C-619/18 *Commission v Poland* ECLI:EU:C:2019:531, para 47 ff; Case C-896/19 *Repubblika* (n 5 above), para 51.

[14] Scheppele, Kochenov and Grabowska-Moroz (n 2 above) 8 ff.

[15] See Schroeder (n 8 above) 117 ff with further references; K Lenaerts, 'Die Werte der Europäischen Union in der Rechtsprechung des Gerichtshofs der Europäischen Union: eine Annäherung' (2017) 44 *Europäische Grundrechte-Zeitschrift* 639, 641; M Krygier, 'Rule of law' in M Rosenfeld and A Sajó (eds), *The Oxford Handbook of Comparative Constitutional Law* (Oxford, Oxford University Press, 2012) 236 ff; but see E Wennerström, *The Rule of Law and the European Union* (Uppsala, Iustus Förlag, 2007) 76 ff.

[16] See T Bingham, *The Rule of Law* (London, Allen Lane, 2010) 37; P Craig, 'Formal and Substantive Conceptions of the Rule of Law: An Analytical Framework' [1997] *Public Law* 467, 470 ff.

[17] See Commission Communication on a new EU Framework to strengthen the Rule of Law, COM(2014) 158 final of 19 March 2014, 4.

[18] Case C-157/21 *Poland v Parliament and Council* (n 4 above), para 324.

[19] See W Schroeder, 'The European Union and the Rule of Law – State of Affairs and Ways of Strengthening' in W Schroeder (ed), *Strengthening the Rule of Law in Europe: From a Common Concept to Mechanisms of Implementation* (Oxford and Portland OR, Hart Publishing, 2016) 25 ff.

articulates positive legal standards for the Member States employing secondary law. If not, does the legislator have to employ the constitutional concept enshrined in Article 2 TEU and defined by the ECJ? The Union legislator may try to escape this problem by stating that its definition is exclusively applicable to the specific piece of Union legislation and not meant to be exhaustive.

However, when making the rule of law the subject of systematic legislative treatment, the Union legislator might further develop its concept.[20] The legislator is entitled to specify principles that form part of the rule of law by taking into consideration the case law of the ECJ. Such power to further develop a concept of primary law using secondary law also results from Article 3(1) and (6) TEU, which provide the Union's institutions with a mandate to promote the value of the rule of law and to pursue it within the framework of its competences. In doing so, the Union institutions have a certain degree of discretion limited by the guidelines drawn by the ECJ based on Article 2 TEU.[21] In legislative practice, this technique is commonly employed.[22]

III. THE VALUE-FUNCTION OF THE RULE OF LAW

Whether it is possible or even necessary for the Union to have an active rule-of-law policy depends not only on the content of that value but above all on the function attributed to the rule of law.[23]

A. A Functional View of the Rule of Law

A consensus of opinion regards the most basic function of the rule of law as being the institutionalised taming of the arbitrary use of public power.[24] This idea, namely that the core of the rule of law is that citizens must be safeguarded against state abuse by limiting sovereign power, also has its place in Union law.[25] Similarly to fundamental rights, the rule of law is traditionally conceived as a negative norm of competence that limits the exercise of powers by a sovereign entity.

[20] The ECJ plays down the law-making character of such a secondary law definition when it argues that it is merely declaratory, Case C-157/21 *Poland v Parliament and Council* (n 4 above), paras 224 and 323 ff.

[21] Case C-156/21 *Hungary v Parliament and Council* (n 4 above), paras 231–37; Case C-157/21 *Poland v Parliament and Council* (n 4 above), paras 324–28.

[22] The use of secondary law to develop terms of primary law can be found, for example, in Directive 2004/38/EC of the European Parliament and of the Council on the right of citizens of the Union and their family members to move and reside freely within the territory of the Member States [2004] OJ L158/77, which specifies the freedom of movement of Union citizens enshrined in art 21 TFEU.

[23] See M Krygier, 'Four Puzzles About the Rule of Law: Why, What, Where? And Who Cares?' in JE Fleming (ed), *Getting to the Rule of Law* (New York and London, New York University Press, 2011) 65.

[24] M Loughlin, *Foundations of Public Law* (Oxford, Oxford University Press, 2010) 336.

[25] See E Fuß, 'Zur Rechtsstaatlichkeit der Europäischen Gemeinschaften' (1964) 17 *Die Öffentliche Verwaltung* 577, 577f; T Holterhus, 'The History of the Rule of Law' (2017) 21 *Max Planck Yearbook of United Nations Law* 430, 463 ff; Schroeder (n 8 above) 117.

However, the rule of law also has a positive function empowering the Union's constitutional actors. The rule of law is not merely about preventing or limiting the exercise of repressive power – it also entails a programmatic function.[26] This function can be seen by examining the rule of law in the Union order, which considers its realisation to be a constitutional objective. The insight that the rule of law also has a positive dimension may inform the interpretation of this concept by the Union's institutional branches.

In that context, it should be noted that the Treaty of Lisbon rebranded the rule of law as a 'value', whereas it was formerly regarded as a 'principle'. Some scholars dismiss the relevance of this linguistic turn and take the position that nothing has changed from the point of view of the legal discipline.[27] They rely on the case law of the ECJ, which has referred to the rule of law as a 'constitutional principle' and a 'principle'.[28] However, the wording of Article 2 TEU was by no means altered accidentally. The inclusion of a canon of values in the TEU by the Treaty of Lisbon is evidence that the European integration process has deepened considerably over the years, manifesting the transformation of the Community from a single market organisation to a Union defined as a community of values.[29] The word 'value' in the context of the rule of law thus does not seem to be a meaningless formula[30] but rather indicates that the framers of the Lisbon Treaty wanted to associate the rule of law with a broader goal and strategy. Therefore, the rule-of-law notion has several potential functions. Originally, the rule of law could be understood as a constitutional principle with an ordering function for the Union's constitutional structure.[31] At the same time, it is regarded as a programme for the Union.[32]

B. A 'System-of-Values' Doctrine for the Rule of Law

Values are originally meta-legal norms that provide guidance in decision-making situations, articulating considerations based on which one state of affairs is declared preferable in relation to another state of affairs.[33] While principles are associated

[26] M Krygier, *Philip Selznick: Ideals in the World* (Stanford CA, Stanford University Press, 2012) 135 ff.

[27] See A von Bogdandy, 'Founding Principles' in A von Bogdandy and J Bast (eds), *Principles of European Constitutional Law*, 2nd edn (Oxford, Hart Publishing, 2009) 22f; M Hilf and F Schorkopf, 'Art 2 EUV' in E Grabitz, M Hilf and M Nettesheim (eds), *Das Recht der Europäischen Union*, 74th edn (Munich, CH Beck, 2021) 21.

[28] Joined Cases C-402/05 P and C-415/05 P *Kadi and Al Barakaat International Foundation v Council and Commission* ECLI:EU:C:2008:461, paras 281 and 285; Case C-355/04 P *Segi and Others v Council* ECLI:EU:C:2007:116, para 51.

[29] See Lenaerts (n 15 above) 640; J Larik, 'From Speciality to a Constitutional Sense of Purpose: On the Changing Role of the Objectives of the European Union' (2014) 63 *ICLQ* 935; on the rule of law as a 'common value', see Case C-619/18 *Commission v Poland* (n 13 above), paras 42 and 43.

[30] See LD Spieker, 'Breathing Life into the Union's Common Values: On the Judicial Application of Article 2 TEU in the EU Value Crises' (2019) 20 *German Law Journal* 1182, 1199.

[31] von Bogdandy (n 27 above) 20.

[32] Williams (n 3 above) 552 describes it as a vision.

[33] N Luhmann, *Soziale Systeme: Grundriß einer allgemeinen Theorie* (Frankfurt am Main, Suhrkamp Verlag, 1987) 433.

with a sense of obligation, a sense of purpose is connoted by values.[34] However, one cannot reduce the significance of the rule of law to 'an ideal, or at most a guiding standard, which is never fully achieved'.[35] In the Union, values have acquired legal significance through their enshrinement in Article 2 TEU. The requirement to respect those values is legally binding and constitutes an obligation that flows from membership of the Union and which no Member State may disregard.[36]

The idea that values may inform a constitutional system and, beyond that, an entire legal system stems from German constitutional theory. Developed during the Weimar period,[37] this theory later influenced post-War German constitutional jurisprudence and theory.[38] The theory indicates that a constitution provides a system of values (*Wertordnung*) that contains a material justice programme serving to identify and integrate a (state) community.[39] Fundamental rights enshrined in the constitution are a crucial expression of these values.[40] The 'system-of-values' doctrine tends to anchor the legitimacy of the polity largely in the constitution instead of seeking it in the political process. Such a reliance on the material force of a constitution appears necessary when complementary means of legitimation – particularly a supporting legitimation narrative of popular sovereignty – are unavailable.[41]

This model of immanent legitimacy also lends itself to other polities endowed with little natural legitimacy, as is the case with the Union. Indeed, against this background, the designation of the rule of law and other norms as values in Article 2 TEU might appear to be an attempt to compensate for the existing legitimacy deficits[42] of the Union. However, this attempt can only be successful if the Union's values are substantiated. Only if the rule of law, along with the other values, is endowed with a significant constitutional presence and occupies a central position within the Union's policies will it be able to contribute to the legitimacy of the Union.[43]

Recent case law seems to embrace this position and, considering the new role of values under the Treaties, to ascribe a broader significance to the rule of law

[34] J Habermas, *Between Facts and Norms* (Cambridge, Polity Press, 1996) 255.

[35] See the argument of Hungary in Case C-156/21 *Hungary v Parliament and Council* (n 4 above), para 200.

[36] Case C-156/21 *Hungary v Parliament and Council* (n 4 above), paras 231 and 232; Case C-157/21 *Poland v Parliament and Council* (n 4 above), para 282.

[37] In a reaction to the value relativism that prevailed, in particular, in Kelsen's *Pure Legal Theory*, see R Smend, *Verfassung und Verfassungsrecht* (Berlin, Duncker & Humblot reprints, 1928) 127f.

[38] See R Wahl, 'Die objektiv-rechtliche Dimension der Grundrechte im internationalen Vergleich' in D Merten and H-J Papier (eds), *Handbuch der Grundrechte in Deutschland und Europa, Band I: Entwicklungen und Grundlagen* (Heidelberg, CF Müller, 2004) § 19 10; D Rennert, 'Die verdrängte Werttheorie und ihre Historisierung' (2014) 53 *Der Staat* 31, 42.

[39] Critical, conjuring up a 'tyranny of values', is C Schmitt, *Die Tyrannei der Werte*, 4th edn (Berlin, Duncker & Humblot, 2020) 35f.

[40] Elementary to the '*Wertordnung*' (system of values), which the fundamental rights of the Basic Law establish is: BVerfG, Judgment of 15 January 1958–1 BvR 400/51; BVerfGE 7, 198, 205f – *Lüth*.

[41] As was the case in the start-up phase of the Federal Republic of Germany, see Rennert (n 38 above) 42.

[42] See U Di Fabio, 'Grundrechte als Werteordnung' (2004) 59 *JuristenZeitung* 1; P Allott, 'Epilogue: Europe and the Dream of Reason' in JHH Weiler and M Wind (eds), *European Constitutionalism beyond the State* (Cambridge, Cambridge University Press, 2003) 202.

[43] Williams (n 3 above) 552, 555 and 560 ff; critical, while referring to C Schmitt, is A von Bogdandy, 'Towards a Tyranny of Values? Principles on Defending Checks and Balances in EU Member States' in A von Bogdandy and others (eds), *Defending Checks and Balances in EU Member States: Taking Stock of Europe's Actions* (Berlin, Springer, 2021) 75.

than before. The Court of Justice perceives the values of Article 2 TEU (and above all the rule of law) as specific characteristics of the Union, forming part of its foundations[44] and defining the Union's identity.[45] These values may also support the Union's claim to autonomy.[46] Consequently, it becomes apparent that the ECJ regards the Union as a community of values, one of whose tasks is to actively protect and defend these values within the limits of its powers.[47] This objective applies at the Union level[48] as well to Member States[49] and to third countries.[50] Overall, the rule of law has become an element of the Union's identity, contributing to its substantial legitimacy. The parallels between this case law and the German system-of-values doctrine are obvious. They become even more apparent when the ECJ implicitly characterises the Union as a form of militant democracy,[51] which 'cannot be criticised for implementing in defence of its identity, which includes [its] values …, the means necessary to protect' it.[52]

C. Negative and Positive Obligations Emanating From the Rule-of-Law Value

The system-of-values theory has gained practical relevance by conceiving parts of the constitution as a positive order that sets standards for the entire legal order. This applies in particular to fundamental rights but is also true in regard to the principle of the rule of law.[53] The aim of this theory is not only to limit the sovereign's scope of action but also to derive an obligation from the constitution to protect the sphere of freedom for its citizens, including from interference by third parties.[54]

This concept also seems to be relevant for Union law and the value of the rule of law. In particular, it is based on the insight that the active protection of rights must respond to a changed situation that no longer consists only of a bipolar confrontation between citizen and state. To protect the rule of law in the Union, this idea

[44] This phrase seems to suggest that the values form a constitutional core of the Union that might be resistant to change, see also Case C-621/18 *Wightman and Others v Secretary of State for Exiting the European Union* ECLI:EU:C:2018:999, para 62; Opinion 1/91 *European Economic Area* ECLI:EU:C:1991:490, para 71.

[45] Case C-156/21, *Hungary v Parliament and Council* (n 4 above), para 127f; Case C-157/21 *Poland v Parliament and Council* (n 4 above), para 145 ff.

[46] *Opinion 1/17 (CETA)* ECLI:EU:C:2019:341, para 111; see Lenaerts (n 15 above) 640.

[47] Case C-156/21 *Hungary v Parliament and Council* (n 4 above), para 127; Case C-157/21 *Poland v Parliament and Council* (n 4 above), para 145.

[48] Case 294/83 *Les Verts v Parliament* ECLI:EU:C:1986:166, para 23.

[49] Joined Cases C-83/19 and Others *Asociația 'Forumul Judecătorilor din România and Others* (n 5 above), para 185.

[50] On international agreements of the Union, see *Opinion 1/17 (CETA)* (n 46 above), para 110 ff. See also Chapter 13 by I Govaere in this book.

[51] See JW Müller, 'Should the EU Protect Democracy and the Rule of Law inside Member States?' (2015) 21 *European Law Journal* 141; in German Constitutional theory, the doctrine of militant democracy is intertwined with the system of values doctrine, see H-J Papier and W Durner, 'Streitbare Demokratie' (2003) 128 *Archiv des öffentlichen Rechts* 340, 348.

[52] Case C-157/21 *Poland v Parliament and Council* (n 4 above), para 268.

[53] Krygier (n 26 above) 134 ff.

[54] H Jarass, 'Grundrechte als Wertentscheidungen bzw. objektivrechtliche Prinzipien in der Rechtsprechung des Bundesverfassungsgerichts' (1985) 110 *Archiv des öffentlichen Rechts* 363, 395.

holds just as it does for fundamental rights. Potential threats to the rule of law may originate from the Union itself but also from within the Member States. Against this background, it makes sense to assume that the rule of law as a fundamental value must permeate the entire Union legal order and all legal relations between the institutions, the Member States, and the citizens of the Union.[55] This objective function of the rule of law must then also give rise to an obligation on the part of the Union to actively protect by all legal means the subjects of Union law against threats to the rule of law.

The idea that substantive parts of a constitution such as the rule of law contain positive obligations, including the need to protect and enforce certain aspects of a constitution, is certainly rooted in a broader European tradition. Positive obligations have also become an important element of the European fundamental rights doctrine.[56] The European Court of Human Rights (ECtHR) has derived positive obligations from the substantive content of the human rights guarantees[57] enshrined in the European Convention on Human Rights (ECHR).[58] The ECtHR has consistently emphasised that the ECHR may demand effective legislative, administrative and judicial measures from the Member States to ensure effective freedom.

IV. THE PROMOTION OF THE RULE-OF-LAW VALUE AS AN OBJECTIVE

Values must not be confused with objectives. The Union's objectives, as mentioned in Article 3 TEU, are directives referring to policy goals of the Union and providing orientation to its action.[59] However, the reference to the values in Article 3(1) and (6) TEU, which oblige the Union 'to promote' those values as its primary objectives and to 'pursue' them 'by appropriate means', underlines that the Treaty also assigned the rule of law a functional role. A contextual reading of Articles 2 and 3 TEU reveals that values such as the rule of law may be understood not merely as constitutional principles but also as implicit work orders. This mandate to act must then be implemented regarding competence law.[60]

In practical terms, linking the rule of law with the objectives of the Union signifies that the rule of law informs the Union's institutional framework.[61] Therefore, it pertains to the legal decision-making programme of the Union's institutions.

[55] Schroeder (n 19 above) 15 ff.

[56] H Krieger, 'Positive Verpflichtungen unter der EMRK: Unentbehrliches Element einer gemeineuropäischen Grundrechtsdogmatik, leeres Versprechen oder Grenze der Justiziabilität?' (2014) 74 *Zeitschrift für ausländisches öffentliches Recht und Völkerrecht* 187, 189f.

[57] *Airey v Ireland* Series A No 32 (1979) 2 EHRR 305, 32; *Siliadin v France* ECHR 2005-VII 289 (2006) 43 EHRR 16, 89; see AR Mowbray, *The Development of Positive Obligations under the European Convention on Human Rights by the European Court of Human Rights* (Oxford, Hart Publishing, 2004) 221.

[58] Convention for the Protection of Human Rights and Fundamental Freedoms (adopted 4 November 1950, entry into force 3 September 1953).

[59] Similar provisions can be found in several Member States' constitutions of J Larik, 'Shaping the International Order as a Union Objective and the Dynamic Internationalisation of Constitutional Law' (2011) *CLEER Working Papers 2011/5*, 21f.

[60] See section V below.

[61] See art 13(1) TEU.

Like other Treaty objectives, the obligation of the Union to promote its values in Article 3(1) TEU is a legally-binding policy directive. This objective determines the handling of the Union's discretionary powers and constitutes a guideline for interpreting other provisions of the Treaties.[62]

The normative surplus stemming from the reference to the values made in Article 3(1) TEU is the apparent obligation of the Union to take positive action to fully realise the values in the process of making and enforcing Union law.[63] Therefore, the linking of Articles 2 and 3(1) TEU increases the normativity of the Union's values as a legal mandate addressed to all institutions of the Union. Article 3, paragraphs 1 and 6 TEU ensure that legal action on the part of the Union must ultimately consider the Treaties' objectives and values.

Constitutionally, the recalibration of the objectives under Article 3 TEU and their systemic linkage with the values of the Union contained in Article 2 TEU have far-reaching implications. In this way, the value orientation of the Union's constitution is interwoven with the teleology of its legal order. Article 3 TEU shows that functionalism remains relevant as a *method* for effective implementation of the objectives[64] under the Lisbon Treaty. As a factor in the output legitimacy of the Union, however, a functionalism that perceives the objectives as the raison d'être for the Union and its constitution[65] has forfeited its relevance. Under Article 2 TEU, the Union's identity and autonomy are characterised by its values.[66] This restructuring of the Union by the Lisbon Treaty reflects a 'value order functionalism', according to which the values are part of the Union's foundation and must be complied with in all areas of the Union's action.[67]

V. A SPECIFIC UNION COMPETENCE FOR PROMOTING THE RULE OF LAW?

To be sure, an invocation of values may not per se create legal competences for the Union institutions.[68] Article 3(6) TEU states that the efforts of the Union to pursue its values and other objectives must be limited to 'means commensurate with the competences which are conferred upon it in the Treaties'. Therefore, any policy aimed at

[62] See for previous objectives in art 2 EEC Treaty Case 6/72 *Europemballage Corporation and Continental Can Company v Commission* ECLI:EU:C:1973:22, paras 23 ff; *Opinion 1/91* (*European Economic Area*) (n 44 above), paras 16 ff; see K Lenaerts, *Le juge et la constitution aux États-Unis d'Amérique et dans l'ordre juridique européen* (Brussels, Bruylant, 1988) 258.

[63] J Terhechte, 'Art 3 EUV' in E Grabitz, M Hilf and M Nettesheim (eds), *Das Recht der Europäischen Union*, 74th edn (Munich, CH Beck, 2021) 21.

[64] Case 14/68 *Wilhelm and Others v Bundeskartellamt* ECLI:EU:C:1969:4, para 4 ff.

[65] According to this doctrine, the Treaties are 'only means for attaining those objectives', *Opinion 1/91* (*European Economic Area*) (n 44 above), para 18; see HP Ipsen, *Europäisches Gemeinschaftsrecht* (Tübingen, JCB Mohr (Paul Siebeck), 1972) 176 ff.

[66] Case C-156/21 *Hungary v Parliament and Council* (n 4 above), para 127 ff; Case C-157/21 *Poland v Parliament and Council* (n 4 above), para 145 ff; *Opinion 1/17* (*CETA*) (n 46 above), para 111.

[67] Case C-156/21 *Hungary v Parliament and Council* (n 4 above), paras 123–128.

[68] B de Witte, 'Conclusions: Integration clauses – a comparative epilogue' in F Ippolito, ME Bartoloni and M Condinanzi (eds), *The EU and the Proliferation of Integration Principles under the Lisbon Treaty* (London, Routledge, 2018) 182.

protecting the rule of law through legislative action presupposes that the Union acts within the limits of its powers as laid down by the Treaties.

A. No Circumvention of Other Procedures Provided by the Treaties

In general, the ECJ has accepted the policy of the Union to actively implement the rule of law using secondary law. A prominent example of Union legislation intended to protect and enhance the rule of law is the 'conditionality' Regulation (EU, Euratom) 2020/2092, which the ECJ has declared lawful.

In particular, it is now clear that the sanctioning procedure in Article 7 TEU does not constitute an exclusive legal mechanism, barring an active rule-of-law policy pursued by the Union legislator. Legislative measures aimed at promoting, assessing and protecting the rule of law differ in their aim and subject matter from the procedure laid down in Article 7 TEU, which is designed to penalise serious and persistent breaches of the values.[69] In any case, it may not be regarded as an improper 'parallel procedure' to Article 7 TEU if secondary law addresses rule-of-law issues in the Member States only to the extent that they might affect a specific policy area.[70]

B. Limited Union Competences in the Area of the Rule of Law

A starting point for determining whether the Union has the capacity to develop an internal rule-of-law policy within the framework of its law-making is the principle of conferral.[71] That said, even following the Treaty of Lisbon, neither the TEU nor the TFEU[72] ascribes a general power to the Union to enact provisions to implement the rule of law internally. This competence deficit has also been identified as a problem concerning human rights within the Union. Nor have the Treaties bestowed upon the Union the general legal competence to develop an internal human rights policy.[73] To be sure, this has not barred the Union from gradually integrating human rights concerns into many of its internal policies.[74] Similar questions and challenges arise in relation to the rule-of-law situation, characterised by the Union's recent efforts to strengthen its ability to ensure that Member States respect the rule of law.[75]

[69] Case C-156/21 *Hungary v Parliament and Council* (n 4 above), paras 168–74; Case C-157/21 *Poland v Parliament and Council* (n 4 above), paras 199 and 206 ff.

[70] Case C-157/21 *Poland v Parliament and Council* (n 4 above), para 213.

[71] TEU, art 5(2).

[72] Consolidated version of the Treaty on the Functioning of the European Union [2012] OJ L326/47.

[73] *Opinion 2/94* (*ECHR I*) ECLI:EU:C:1996:140, para 27; see the critique from P Alston and JHH Weiler, 'An 'Ever Closer Union' in Need of a Human Rights Policy: The European Union and Human Rights' (1998) 9 *European Journal of International Law* 658.

[74] See O De Schutter, 'Mainstreaming Human Rights in the European Union' in P Alston and O De Schutter (eds), *Monitoring Fundamental Rights in the EU: The Contribution of the Fundamental Rights Agency* (Oxford, Hart Publishing, 2005) 37 ff; P Craig and G de Búrca, *EU Law: Text, Cases, and Materials*, 7th edn (Oxford, Oxford University Press, 2020) 415 and 425 ff.

[75] Case C-156/21 *Hungary v Parliament and Council* ECLI:EU:C:2021:974, Opinion of AG Campos Sánchez-Bordona, para 78.

C. Implicit and Residual Union Competences Concerning the Rule of Law

In practice, the Union seems to have a limited arsenal of legal instruments available to implement and strengthen the rule of law in the Member States. The Union, however, also has at its disposal implied powers 'to attain a specific objective'.[76] In this context, it should be noted that an implicit competence may only be established to supplement an internal competence already enshrined in the Treaties.[77] In contrast, implicit internal competences may not be deduced merely by reference to the general objectives laid down in the Treaties as confirmed by Articles 3(6) and 5(2) TEU. Under these conditions, it is hardly conceivable that the Union possesses implicit law-making competences to *internally* implement its rule-of-law policy.

In principle, for pursuing an objective of the Union, such as the promotion of the rule of law by Union institutions, the 'residual powers' provision of Article 352 TFEU could be used as a legal basis. Filling a gap left by the Treaties, this provision is designed to confer powers on Union institutions to act when such powers appear necessary to enable the Union to attain one of the objectives laid out by the Treaty. The Union institutions have had recourse to the residual powers clause of Article 352 TFEU as a legal basis for some rule-of-law and human rights-related measures,[78] such as the establishment of the Union's external programme for the consolidation of democracy, the rule of law and human rights[79] and the European Union Agency for Fundamental Rights, under Regulation 168/2007.[80] Article 352 TFEU thus allows for institutional arrangements in the area of the rule of law and the adoption of substantive provisions in these areas. Expanding the tasks of the Fundamental Rights Agency according to Article 3 of Regulation 168/2007 concerning the rule of law would undoubtedly be advisable but requires a unanimous decision of the Council.

VI. MAINSTREAMING THE RULE OF LAW AS A UNION TASK

Against this background, it makes more sense for the Union institutions to implement and actively promote the rule of law in sectoral policies covered by the Treaties.

[76] *Opinion 2/94* (*ECHR I*) (n 73 above), para 26.

[77] *Opinion 1/13* (*Hague Convention 1980*) ECLI:EU:C:2014:2303, para 67 insists on this requirement under art 216(1) TFEU.

[78] *Opinion 2/94* (*ECHR I*) (n 73 above), paras 30 and 34 ff, has not ruled out the use of art 235 TEC, the predecessor provision of art 352 TFEU, for achieving a human rights policy of the Union in general.

[79] Council Regulation (EC) No 975/1999 laying down the requirements for the implementation of development cooperation operations which contribute to the general objective of developing and consolidating democracy and the rule of law and to that of respecting human rights and fundamental freedoms [1999] OJ L120/1.

[80] Council Regulation (EC) No 168/2007 establishing a European Union Agency for Fundamental Rights [2007] OJ L53/1; see A von Bogdandy and J von Bernsdorff, 'The EU Fundamental Rights Agency within the European and international human rights architecture: The legal framework and some unsettled issues in a new field of administrative law' (2009) 46 *CML Rev* 1035, 1044f.

A. Extending the Scope of Rule-of-Law Conditionality

The first step in this direction is Regulation 2020/2092 on a general regime of conditionality for the protection of the Union budget. The Regulation establishes a 'conditionality mechanism' that makes the receipt of funds from the Union budget subject to a Member State's respect for the rule of law insofar as this relates to the implementation of the Union budget.[81] The idea expressed therein – that respect for the rule of law may be required in the context of a conditionality mechanism established by secondary legislation – is compatible with the Treaties. It should be extended from budgetary policy to all other policy areas of Union law.

The Union could make active enforcement of the rule of law a cross-cutting task, drawing on existing sectoral competences. It has always been part of the integration doctrine that the effective achievement of the Union's objectives may require a broad interpretation of the existing legal competences. Where a provision of the Treaties confers a specific competence on the Union, it provides the Union, at the same time, with powers indispensable for carrying out the objectives enshrined in the Treaties. This, in turn, presupposes that the objectives and values of the Union can be integrated into the law-making process.[82] Consequently, the realisation of these objectives is a cross-sectional task that obliges all Union institutions within the scope of their activities. In this sense, the Union could streamline its actions to promote the rule of law more effectively.

The Treaties do not mention a general requirement to explicitly integrate the rule of law into the Union's sectoral policies like they do in the 'integration clauses'. These clauses include Articles 8–13 and 114(3) TFEU concerning other Treaty goals, such as the protection of social rights, consumer interests and the environment.[83] It is possible, however, to assume an implicit obligation of the Union institutions to pursue a value-driven policy when legislating in the internal market or the area of freedom, security and justice. This obligation can also extend to other areas, such as budgetary law, as seen in the 'conditionality' Regulation 2020/2092. This responsibility to implement an integrated rule-of-law policy in all sectors is precisely what Article 3, paragraphs 1 and 6 TEU aim to encourage when they express the obligation of the Union 'to promote' and 'pursue' the value as an objective.[84]

The Union's mandate to promote and pursue its values and objectives within the framework of its competences, as prescribed by Article 3(1) and (6) TEU, dispels doubts as to whether the Union legislator may pursue other objectives in addition to those set out in the specific competence norms relied upon in the law-making process. The mandate clarifies that it is legitimate as a sectoral policy measure for

[81] The definition of conditionality in Case C-157/21 *Poland v Parliament and Council* (n 4 above), paras 140 and 151; see further V Vită, 'Revisiting the Dominant Discourse on Conditionality in the EU: The Case of EU Spending Conditionality' (2017) 19 *Cambridge Yearbook of European Legal Studies* 116.

[82] See F Ippolito, ME Bartoloni and M Condinanzi, 'Introduction: Integration clauses – a prologue' in F Ippolito, ME Bartoloni and M Condinanzi (eds), *The EU and the Proliferation of Integration Principles under the Lisbon Treaty* (London, Routledge, 2018) 1.

[83] Joined Cases 281/85, 283–285/85 and 287/85 *Germany v Commission* ECLI:EU:C:1987:351, para 28.

[84] From this perspective, arts 8–13 TFEU are declaratory, see de Witte (n 68 above) 183.

the Union legislator to include requirements stemming from the general objectives or – in a broader sense – from the values of the Union.[85] Provided that the conditions for recourse to a sectoral competence norm are fulfilled, the Union may rely on that legal basis while carrying out its task of safeguarding the general interests recognised by the Treaty.[86] Against this backdrop, it is clear that secondary law aiming to enhance and realise the rule of law in specific areas of Union law is compatible with primary law.[87] A particular connection or even a genuine link between respect for the rule of law on the one hand and the efficient implementation of specific sectoral Union policies on the other is not required for such a mechanism.[88]

B. Mainstreaming the Rule of Law

However, the approach described above also allows for extending the integration of rule-of-law criteria into the sectoral activities of the Union beyond a conditionality mechanism. Under Regulation 2020/2092, conditionality aims at mere compliance with the rule of law. Integrating the rule of law into the process of Union law-making must go further and have as its goal to 'mainstream' the rule of law into all policy areas of the Union.

Mainstreaming is intended to ensure that an objective or value is fully respected across all Union policies.[89] It has been pursued in particular relation to the implementation of fundamental rights and anti-discrimination law.[90] Taking a page from these policy contexts,[91] rule-of-law mainstreaming should provide for systematic, deliberate and transparent incorporation of rule-of-law considerations into all Union policies and practices at all stages – from planning and legislation to execution and enforcement.[92]

This mainstreaming policy, which is in line with the obligation to promote and pursue the rule of law,[93] naturally involves the obligation of further realising the

[85] See de Witte (n 68 above) 184.

[86] Case C-482/17 *Czech Republic v Parliament and Council* ECLI:EU:C:2019:1035, paras 30 ff regarding internal market law.

[87] Case C-156/21 *Hungary v Parliament and Council* (n 4 above), paras 125–27; Case C-157/21 *Poland v Parliament and Council* (n 4 above), paras 148f and 165; see also *Opinion 2/94* (*ECHR I*) (n 73 above), para 32 on human rights.

[88] Unlike the mechanism of the horizontal budget-oriented conditionality regime established by Regulation (EU, Euratom) 2020/2092, see Case C-156/21 *Hungary v Parliament and Council* (n 4 above), paras 125–27; Case C-157/21 *Poland v Parliament and Council* (n 4 above), paras 142–146.

[89] Commission Communication on the 2016 Report on the Application of the Charter of Fundamental Rights, COM(2017) 239 final of 18 May 2017, 7.

[90] See De Schutter (n 74 above) 43 ff; V Kosta, 'Fundamental rights mainstreaming in the EU' in F Ippolito, ME Bartoloni and M Condinanzi (eds), *The EU and the Proliferation of Integration Principles under the Lisbon Treaty* (London, Routledge, 2018) 13 ff.

[91] De Schutter (n 74 above) 43 based on Commission Communication on Incorporating Equal Opportunities For Women and Men Into All Community Policies and Activities, COM(96) 67 final of 21 February 1996, 2.

[92] D Halberstam and W Schroeder, 'In Defense of Its Identity: A Proposal to Mainstream the Rule of Law in the EU' (*Verfassungsblog*, 17 February 2022) verfassungsblog.de/in-defense-of-its-identity/.

[93] See art 3(1) and (6) TFEU.

policy, which extends beyond merely ensuring compliance.[94] The idea that the rule of law must be systematically considered across all policy fields of the Union is of paramount importance to this approach. This view indicates that the Union's institutions need to consider rule-of-law implications for any laws they produce, not just those whose subject matter is evidently rule-of-law issues.

C. Implementing the Rule of Law Within the Framework of the Union's Competences

Several internal policy areas mainstream rule-of-law concerns and thus apply 'rule-of-law driven' policy. This is the case, in particular, with the Union's legislation in the area of freedom, security, and justice.[95] Article 67(1) TFEU makes the realisation of that area dependent on the respect for fundamental rights and the different legal systems and traditions of the Member States, including respect for the rule of law. However, systematic mainstreaming will reveal that numerous other provisions in the Treaties have untapped potential that can be exploited to allow the rule of law to influence the Union's internal policies.

First, the Union legislator can ensure that *substantive* standards set in legal harmonisation include rule-of-law elements and specify the requirements implied by the rule of law. This may apply, for instance, to the Union's provisions that have been enacted based on its competences in the areas of data protection,[96] the internal market[97] or competition policy.[98]

In addition, when harmonising the law of Member States within the framework of its competences, the Union legislator could enact *procedural* standards for the administrative and judicial enforcement of Union law that specify requirements regarding the rule of law.[99] Under the Framework Decision 2002/584,[100]

[94] Kosta (n 90 above) 21.

[95] See the examples given by KL Scheppele, 'Escaping Orbán's Constitutional Prison: How European Law Can Free a New Hungarian Parliament' (*Verfassungsblog*, 21 December 2021) verfassungsblog.de/escaping-orbans-constitutional-prison/.

[96] Art 16(2) TFEU; see for Directive (EU) 2016/681 of the European Parliament and of the Council on the use of passenger name record (PNR) data for the prevention, detection, investigation and prosecution of terrorist offences and serious crime [2016] OJ L119/132; with regard to fundamental rights, see Opinion of AG Pitruzzella in Case C-817/19 *Ligue des droits humains ASBL v Conseil des ministres* ECLI:EU:C:2022:65.

[97] Art 114 TFEU.

[98] Art 103 TFEU; on the relevance of the art 2 TEU values for the interpretation of Union competition law, see Case T-791/19 *Sped-Pro v Commission* ECLI:EU:T:2022:67, paras 84–88; see also art 4 of Directive (EU) 2019/1 of the European Parliament and of the Council to empower the competition authorities of the Member States to be more effective enforcers and to ensure the proper functioning of the internal market [2020] OJ L11/3.

[99] The Treaties refer to policy areas in which the Union may act. The Union may therefore also adopt rules on the organisation and procedure for the implementation of Union law by the Member States: see CM Kakouris, 'Do the Member States Possess Judicial Procedural "autonomy"?' (1997) 34 *CML Rev* 1389, 1389f; W Schroeder, 'Nationale Maßnahmen zur Durchführung von EG-Recht und das Gebot der einheitlichen Wirkung – Existiert ein Prinzip der "nationalen Verfahrensautonomie"?' (2004) 129 *Archiv des öffentlichen Rechts* 3, 11 ff.

[100] Council Framework Decision 2002/584/JHA on the European arrest warrant and the surrender procedures between Member States [2002] OJ L190/1.

for example, a European arrest warrant must be issued by a 'judicial authority'. Secondary law could impose requirements for the independence and institutional structure of these authorities based on rule-of-law criteria.[101]

Moreover, in areas where the principle of mutual recognition applies, such as the internal market or the area of freedom, security and justice, the Union legislator could adopt rules imposing specific requirements for the mutual recognition[102] of legal acts of Member States from the perspective of the rule of law. The mutual recognition of all legal acts, judgments, administrative decisions or documents by the Member States should be prohibited by secondary legislation if there are serious and systemic flaws in the rule of law in the issuing Member State. After all, such recognition is based on the mutual trust of Member States in their respective legal, administrative and judicial systems.[103]

The Union legislator is increasingly signalling the use of this option to integrate rule-of-law considerations into legal acts adopted in these policy areas.[104] For example, according to Article 11(1)(f) of Directive 2014/41,[105] the recognition or execution of a European Investigation Order on gathering evidence for criminal proceedings issued by the authorities of one Member State may be rejected by the authorities of other Member States where there are substantial grounds to believe this could be incompatible with Article 6 TEU and the Charter of Fundamental Rights of the European Union (the Charter).[106] Additionally, Article 3, paragraph 2, sub-paragraph 2 of Regulation 604/2013[107] obliges the Member States, when determining which Member State is responsible for examining an application for international protection, to check whether 'there are substantial grounds for believing that there are systemic flaws in the asylum procedure and in the reception conditions for applicants in [another] Member State'. This approach could be extended to the mutual recognition of civil judgments pursuant to Regulation 1215/2012.[108] Moreover, the approach could even be applied to the mutual recognition of documents in the internal market under Regulation 2019/515 on the mutual recognition of goods[109] or under Directive 2005/36 on the recognition of professional qualifications.[110] In principle,

[101] See on such requirements Joined Cases C-508/18 and C-82/19 PPU *Minister for Justice and Equality v OG and PI* ECLI:EU:C:2019:456, para 73 ff.

[102] See *Opinion 2/13 (ECHR II)* ECLI:EU:C:2014:2454, para 191 ff.

[103] Joined Cases C-187/01 and C-385/01 *Gözütok and Brügge* ECLI:EU:C:2003:87, para 33.

[104] See Schroeder (n 8 above) 115.

[105] Directive 2014/41/EU of the European Parliament and of the Council regarding the European Investigation Order in criminal matters (European Investigation Order) [2014] OJ L130/1.

[106] [2012] OJ C326/391.

[107] Regulation (EU) No 604/2013 of the European Parliament and of the Council establishing the criteria and mechanisms for determining the Member State responsible for examining an application for international protection lodged in one of the Member States by a third-country national or a stateless person (Dublin III) [2013] OJ L180/31.

[108] Regulation (EU) No 1215/2012 of the European Parliament and of the Council on jurisdiction and the recognition and enforcement of judgments in civil and commercial matters (Recast Brussels Regulation) [2012] OJ L351/1.

[109] Regulation (EU) 2019/515 of the European Parliament and of the Council on the mutual recognition of goods lawfully marketed in another Member State and repealing Regulation (EC) No 764/2008 (Mutual Recognition Regulation) [2019] OJ L91/1.

[110] Directive 2005/36/EC of the European Parliament and of the Council on the recognition of professional qualifications (Professional Qualifications Directive) [2005] OJ L255/22.

it can no longer be assumed that any decisions taken at the legislative, judicial or administrative level in a Member State facing serious rule-of-law deficiencies will have been made according to objective criteria.

D. Improving the Enforcement of the Union Rule of Law

The proactive approach advocated here, by which the rule of law is implemented and specified through secondary law and made the yardstick for legislative, administrative and judicial activity, has several advantages. Such proactive measures may help prevent the inevitable under-enforcement of rights when individuals, Union institutions and even an occasional Member State are left to challenge rule-of-law deficiencies in court.[111] This proactive approach eliminates ambiguities that may arise when courts struggle to apply the general principle of the rule of law to secondary law.[112] Additionally, it is questionable whether the rule of law as mentioned in Article 2 TEU is precise and sufficiently clear to entail a direct effect.[113] Incorporating the rule of law into secondary legislation with specific provisions might help national authorities and courts apply and enforce the rule of law in Member States.

VII. CONCLUSION

The Union's case for the rule of law cannot be won through court rulings.[114] Ultimately, court rulings only address the individual shortcomings of the Member States as they relate to the rule of law. Instead, and more structurally, adherence to the rule of law 'requires an enabling ecosystem' in the Member States.[115] Such an ecosystem can only be established and maintained if the Union takes positive action to strengthen the rule of law. The Union must systematically integrate rule-of-law issues into all its policies, specifically mobilising them to realise and promote the rule of law.

For the Union, as a community of values, there is no realistic alternative to this policy. The destruction of the rule-based international order with Russia's invasion

[111] Halberstam and Schroeder (n 92 above).

[112] See Joined Cases C-562/21 PPU and C-563/21 PPU *X and Y v Openbaar Ministerie* ECLI:EU:C:2022:100, paras 50–53 and Joined Cases C-354/20 PPU and C-412/20 PPU *L and P* ECLI:EU:C:2020:1033, para 50 ff, which require national courts to apply a two-step test when systematic or general deficiencies affect the right to a fair trial before they may refuse to execute a European arrest warrant.

[113] Case C-896/19 *Repubblika* (n 5 above), para 63 implies that it must be given more specific expression in Union law; but see Joined Cases C-83/19 and Others *Asociația 'Forumul Judecătorilor din România'* (n 5 above), para 250 regarding subprinciples which may impose 'on the Member States a clear and precise obligation'.

[114] I owe this sentence to P Nemitz, author of Chapter 9 of this volume.

[115] See Commission Communication on the 2020 Rule of Law Report: The rule of law situation in the European Union, COM(2020) 580 final of 30 September 2020, 5.

of Ukraine in February 2022 has by no means rendered the above objective obsolete. On the contrary, it illustrates how vulnerable the rule of law, democracy and human rights can be in Europe. This situation makes it all the more important to strengthen the structures that are indispensable for the identity of the Union as a common legal order and community of values. In this context, a systematic internal rule-of-law policy may contribute significantly to the Union's external resilience.

9

Acting Before it is Too Late: Promoting Democracy and the Rule of Law in the Member States of the EU

PAUL NEMITZ[1]

> Democracy is certainly a good worthy of praise, but the rule of law is like daily bread, like water to drink and like air to breathe, and the best thing about democracy is precisely this, that it alone is capable of securing the rule of law.
>
> Gustav Radbruch[2]

THE GREAT TEACHER of EU Law, the Oxford University Professor Paul Craig, concludes his comment on the judgment of the Constitutional Court of Poland in case K 3/21 of 7 October 2021 with the thought that 'the assault on judicial independence in Poland and Hungary is but part of a broader constitutional meltdown,[3] which is grounded in illiberal democracy and competitive authoritarianism.'[4]

The forceful statement by Prime Minister Mateusz Morawiecki of Poland in the European Parliament on 19 October 2021[5] indeed gives reason to believe that the judgment of the Constitutional Court of Poland of 7 October 2021 is just another piece in an effort to delegitimise all internal and external checks and balances on the power of the government of Poland. This statement, brushing away the disciplines exerted

[1] The author expresses a personal opinion and not necessarily that of the European Commission. He is the Principal Adviser on Justice Policy in the European Commission and a visiting Professor of Law at the College of Europe in Bruges.

[2] G Radbruch, 'Gesetzliches Unrecht und übergesetzliches Recht' ['Statutory Lawlessness and Superstatutory Law'] (1946)(5) *Süddeutsche Juristenzeitung*, 105, 108 (final sentence, author's translation) and in *Rechtsphilosophie*, Band III, 3rd edn (Heidelberg, CF Müller, 1990) 93.

[3] See P Craig, 'The Politics of Constitutional Meltdown' in M Tushnet and D Kochenov (eds), *Research Handbook on the Politics of Constitutional Law* (Cheltenham, Edward Elgar, forthcoming 2022), papers.ssrn.com/sol3/papers.cfm?abstract_id=3934287.

[4] Paul Craig, 'Op-Ed: The Rule of Law, Breach and Consequence', *EU Law Live* (21 October 2021), eulawlive.com/op-ed-the-rule-of-law-breach-and-consequence-by-paul-craig/.

[5] www.gov.pl/web/primeminister/statement-by-prime-minister-mateusz-morawiecki-in-the-european-parliament.

through EU law on the government of Poland, allowing it to hide behind the alleged primacy of the Polish constitution, interpreted by a constitutional court controlled by the government, stands in line with the government disabling domestic checks and balances on its power, starting with domestic courts, civil society, academia and the press. The reference to the Constitution of Poland as the highest law is a diversion, as the government has already started to disable the judicial and societal instances which could exercise the necessary checks and balances for the government to obey the rules of the Constitution and which are common in democratic societies. In Hungary, the situation is no different.

Already in 2015, referring to the case of Hungary, the Princeton University political scientist Jan-Werner Müller called a spade a spade:

> A political system with regular elections, but clear limits on media freedom, on election campaigning, and on autonomous activity by civil society is not on the road to being an illiberal democracy; it is on the road to not being a democracy at all. Unless one wants to say that having elections is *all* that is required for calling a country a democracy, one should emphasise that limits on media freedom, for instance, is not only a rule of law problem or a matter of fundamental rights violations, but a threat to democracy itself. Leaving the 'd-word' – democracy – to proto-authoritarian governments is what one might call an unforced semantic-normative error.[6]

The crisis exemplified by the latest ruling of the Constitutional Court of Poland and the speech of the Prime Minister against this background cannot be reduced simply to an issue of the independence of judges or the primacy of EU Law. It is rather a symptom of a crisis of democracy and an attempt by the government to delegitimise the law, including EU law, and to undermine its standing as the most noble expression of democracy and a classic constraint on the power of the executive. These safeguards are great European achievements following the age of enlightenment and the end of absolutism – the historic end of fascism and communism in the twentieth century.

Enlightenment also gave Europe the categorical imperative of Kant. It prescribes that the principles underlying one's actions should be able to be a general law. In contemplating democracy, the rule of law and Europe, including the relationship between domestic constitutions and EU law, one must thus ask whether putting domestic constitutions above EU law will still allow the EU to function. It is likely that this will never be the case, since, if national courts define areas of national identity reserve[7] based on their domestic constitutions, these reserves will be defined differently in the 27 Member States, and not much space will remain for Union law. *A fortiori* this is the case if the courts go as far as the Polish Constitutional Court

[6] JW Müller, 'Should the EU Protect Democracy and the Rule of Law inside Member States ?' (2015) 21(2) *ELJ* 141.

[7] The comparative analysis of Alexander Thiele of the differences between the judgment of the Constitutional Court of Poland and the jurisprudence of the German BVerfG does not touch on its line of jurisprudence on Europe which simply ignores the categoric imperative, see A Thiele, 'Wer Karlsruhe mit Warschau gleichsetzt, irrt sich gewaltig', *VerfBlog* (10 October 2021), verfassungsblog.de/wer-karlsruhe-mit-warschau-gleichsetzt-irrt-sich-gewaltig/.

and declare even rules of the EU Treaties to be unconstitutional under domestic law, 17 years after Poland expressly signed up to these rules. The Union will not be able to function in this way. It is for this simple reason that the European Court of Justice (ECJ) right from the outset identified the primacy of EU law over domestic law, including domestic constitutional law, as a key functional prerequisite of the Union. The complete system set up by the Treaties would simply not work without such a clear rule of primacy. And it is for this reason that the European Commission was right to pursue infringement procedures against Germany and to act against Poland, in order to maintain the functioning of EU law, based on the principle of primacy and, in necessary combination with that, the monopoly of the ECJ to interpret authoritatively EU law and to take decisions on the legality or illegality of the acts of EU institutions.

Incidentally, no system of public power in the world could ever function with 27 courts having the power in practice to review the decisions of the highest court on the higher level of governance. The German Constitutional Court simply forgot its Kant in this respect when introducing its own *ultra vires* control and a definition of 'preserves of national identity' based on the *Grundgesetz*. And it forgot to reflect on possible applause from corners it would not want applause from, thus not performing a key task of the constitutional court: the reflection on the consequences of its judgments. The judgment K 3/21 of the Constitutional Court of Poland may lead the German Constitutional Court to a more intense analysis of the consequences of its own judgments for the EU system as a whole, thus matching the political responsibility of the biggest Member State for the good functioning of the Union as whole. It should lead, if necessary, to the Bundestag passing legislation to oblige the German Constitutional Court to present questions of EU law to the ECJ for a preliminary ruling if a party to the dispute before it so wishes, unless this request is manifestly unfounded in light of the criteria for requests for a preliminary ruling under EU law. This obligation should also exist relating to repeated requests in the same matter, thus clarifying in German law the relation between both courts and securing the final decision of the ECJ in all cases relating to questions of EU competences.

The rule of law neither starts nor ends with the independence of the judiciary, which, however, is an essential part of a functioning rule of law.

We need to recall the essential link between democracy and the law which Jürgen Habermas identified in his seminal paper 'On the Internal Relation between the Rule of Law and Democracy'.[8]

We need to take, then, a broader look at tendencies which have delegitimised the law as the most noble instrument with which democracy shapes, and thus rules society, and at tendencies which weakened the judiciary as well as legislators over the last decades. Only a holistic approach will allow us to identify remedies which will lead to a renaissance of democracy and the rule of law, including a renaissance for the necessary respect for the crucial function of an independent and fully functional judiciary in modern democracy.

[8] J Habermas, 'On the Internal Relation between the Rule of Law and Democracy' (1995) 3(1) *European Journal of Philosophy* 12.

It is my thesis that the European Union needs to go to the roots of the 'constitutional meltdown', to cite Paul Craig, in order to ensure that the triad of well-functioning democracy, rule of law and fundamental rights is preserved and revived in the age of artificial intelligence, both at the level of the Union and in its Member States. The place to address this meltdown at the Union level is the EU budget (A), the political practices of the Commission (B), as well as a European Charter of Democracy, on which work should start as a follow up to the Conference on the Future of Europe (C). There is no doubt, however, that the Member States also have their own domestic responsibility for developing policies and processes which rejuvenate democracy and make it vibrant again, which raise citizens' understanding and support for the rule of law and fundamental rights. The rule of law is not only called into question by the practices in Hungary and Poland. Anywhere where law making fails, or is dysfunctional, due to a need to satisfy the lobby of corporate neoliberalism, and also where justice is denied in dysfunctional court systems, the rule of law and democracy are put under stress. All these challenges are now being addressed at the levels of Member States and the Union alike, so that we can hope for a renaissance of the law, which, with Habermas and Radbruch, would also be a renaissance of democracy.

I. PUT YOUR MONEY WHERE YOUR MOUTH IS: FINANCING FOR DEMOCRACY AND JUSTICE POLICIES

In this chapter, I will not address the various instruments, described in other chapters of this volume, which the Union is developing to ensure that Member State spending of EU funds which pursues other primary purposes than democracy and the rule of law – such as the Regional Development Fund and the Covid-19 Recovery Fund – takes place in an institutional setting which ensures, through the application and enforcement of law through independent courts, that that spending follows EU law and respects basic values of the EU.

Rather, the question we need to ask here is whether the Union budget has evolved in line with the Union moving from being the European Economic Community to a European Union of rights and values, endowed with a binding Charter of Fundamental Rights and the ambition of democratisation itself. Democracy and the rule of law are now in the midst of an existential fight for the future. They are being undermined worldwide by populists, autocrats, and tech absolutism, and now, in addition, in the most brutal and terrible manner by the warlord Putin and his war on Ukraine.

The increase in funding for Justice, Democracy, Fundamental Rights and Citizen Rights from €0.76 billion in the Multiannual Financial Framework (MFF) 2014–20 to €1.85 billion in the MFF 2021–27 is an important sign that all institutions have understood the challenges of the time.

But this doubling of funding starts from a very low base, which is not at all in proportion to the challenge the Union faces in regard to democracy and the rule of law. Managed directly by the Commission, even if distributed via decentralised grant-giving organisations, it also reveals an executive-centred approach which is not conducive to the plurality aimed at in democracy.

There would be great advantages of a pedagogical and conceptual nature if the Union, keeping Max Weber in mind, followed a pluralistic approach to financing democracy actions, and thus placed at arm's length from the executive the financing of a much greater part of democracy actions and provided financing directly from the European Parliament into the hands of the European political foundations representing the main world visions within the democratic spectrum. Recognising the absence of executive control over political action in society and political diversity as a key ingredient of democracy, and as the natural counter-design to autocracy, is key for EU democracy policy.

A new regulation on political parties and political foundations, adopted in 2014,[9] provides EU-level legal status for European political parties and their political foundations, aiming to increase their visibility and EU-wide recognition.[10] This legal status is a pre-condition to receiving public funding from the EU budget.

In 2018, in the first move of what could be called a 'European democracy that defends itself', these rules were further detailed, in particular sanctioning the link of EU funding to the respect for the values of the Union set out in Article 2 TEU and to the visibility of the European Party in the campaign materials of the national parties. A further reform has been proposed by the Commission.[11]

However, the European Political Parties[12] and the political foundations at EU level are severely underfunded. To illustrate that, while the two foundations of the Socialists (Foundation of European Progressive Studies – FEPS) and Conservatives (Martens Center) at EU level receive less than €10 million annually from the EU budget,[13] the similar foundations in Germany alone (Friedrich Ebert Stiftung and Konrad Adenauer Stiftung) have a budget of over €360 million annually.[14]

It is probably fair to say that the allocation of EU internal budgets for the purposes of making democracy work – that is, for education about and in support of democracy, the rule of law and fundamental rights in the EU – has clearly not

[9] Regulation (EU, Euratom) No 1141/2014 of the European Parliament and of the Council of 22 October 2014 on the statute and funding of European political parties and European political foundations [2014] OJ L317/1.

[10] The regulation sets the conditions for them to enjoy a legal status and qualify for funding from the EU budget, namely being represented in at least one-quarter of the Member States and respecting the founding principles of the EU.

[11] Proposal for a Regulation on the statute and funding of European Political Parties and European Political Foundations (recast), COM(2021) 734 final of 25 November 2021.

[12] For an extensive presentation see J Priestley, 'European Political parties: the missing link, Les partis politiques européens: le chaînon manquant' *Notre Europe policy paper No 41* (2010), https://institutdelors.eu/wp-content/uploads/2020/08/eupoliticalparties-partispolitiquesuepriestleyneoct10-3.pdf; and most recently, the study of the Research Department of the EP of March 2022 'Towards a revision of the Regulation on the statute and funding of European political parties and foundations', www.europarl.europa.eu/RegData/etudes/STUD/2022/729741/IPOL_STU(2022)729741_EN.pdf.

[13] See the report card of the European Parliament on the funding of political foundations up to 2021, available at: www.europarl.europa.eu/contracts-and-grants/files/political-parties-and-foundations/european-political-foundations/en-grant-amounts-foundations-2021.pdf;.

[14] See annual report 2017 of Konrad Adenauer Stiftung, with a total budget of €182 million in 2017, at 39, www.kas.de/c/document_library/get_file?uuid=a5ee2563–5295-af5c-fdb4-2c07f56e5240&groupId=252038, and the annual report of the Friedrich Ebert Stiftung, with a total budget of €176 million in 2017, at 71, library.fes.de/pdf-files/fes/03208/jb-2017.pdf.

been restructured in line with the development of the Union, namely its development from a Community of economic integration without its own democratic structure and with no challenges to democracy in its Member States to a Union with its own important democratic processes and a role to play in supporting and strengthening democracy within Member States. Democracy in Europe will pay a high price if European political parties and foundations remain as underfunded as they have been so far. European political parties cannot to date seriously invest in Europe-wide campaigns during election time nor indeed can the European political foundations play their most vital roles, namely to engage citizens to participate in the democratic processes on European policy making and also in domestic democracy as a vital precondition for democracy in Europe.

The European political foundations need at least 20 times the meagre funding available to them today to make an impact, particularly in those Member States which domestically need help with spreading core values such as democracy, the rule of law and fundamental rights. It is the duty of Germany to make transparent the billions of Deutsche Mark and later Euros which were invested in democracy after the Second World War through the political foundations, the federal centre for political education, and the centres for political education in each *Land*. Apart from the drafting of the *Grundgesetz* and the shaping of German institutions based on learnings from the failure of the Weimar Republic, it is probably fair to say that the other lesson from more recent German history is that billions invested in transforming a former dictatorship into a stable democracy through political education dispensed by a pluralistic structure of institutions close to, but not controlled by, the political parties in the democratic spectrum, were well invested. The hope that Europe can achieve the same result within its Member States on the cheap, without substantially resourcing the European political foundations in order to enable them to directly fund political education within Member States, and with only limited means such as legal process and discourse, or withholding funds for other purposes than political education, is overly optimistic, to say the least. 'Put your money where your mouth is' is the approach Europe needs now when it comes to ensuring that democracy and the rule of law thrive inside its Member States and are not dismantled.

II. DEMOCRACY MAINSTREAMING AS PART OF THE BETTER REGULATION TOOLBOX

In European Commission's impact assessment criteria for policy options relating to proposed new legislation, the impact on democracy of not legislating and of acting through tools alternative to legislation, is not assessed. The negative reflection on legislation, the most noble expression of democracy – when a choice is made not to go through the democratic process but to confine action, for example, to self-regulation or ethics, or simply a Commission Communication or Recommendation, thus cutting out the Parliament – is not assessed as a cost to the image of democracy but rather as a cost reduction to business by less legislation, and thus as a positive matter. Legislation in core documents of the Commission's Better legislation agenda is systematically described as a 'burden'. This reveals a bias against the democratic process of legislating, as does the 'one in one out' rule for legislation.[15] The law is presented as a problem; however, 'we need less of it' is a message not conducive to the rule of law and democracy.

If we want to address the much decried crisis of democracy, we need to change the discourse on democratic legislation in Europe. A systematic mainstreaming of democracy objectives into all decision-making processes of the Commission should do away with the bias against legislation, and the cost of not going through the democratic process for democracy should be assessed, for example, as a loss to the image of democracy and its ability to provide solutions. It is the ability to deliver laws which differentiates the democratic process of the European Union from the dysfunctional US Congress. Europe and its institutions should be proud about this and hold their head high, rather than perpetuating a misplaced bias against legislation with roots in neoliberalism which has no place anymore in the digital world of technological innovation and of business models challenging many aspects of the primacy of democracy.

In the toolbox on Better Regulation, a number of elements need to be introduced to counter the anti-legislation bias and to make it an instrument of democracy mainstreaming:

- A duty to assess the overall image the Union gives to legislation and democratic process if the Commission discards legislation as the way forward
- A duty to assess, if legislation *is* proposed, whether it maximises the scope for democratic participation and of civil society input after adoption, namely in the phase of implementation within Member States (formal rules on citizen hearings, participation in implementing decision, etc). The methodology and process for this purpose should be laid down in a Commission Strategy for 'Democracy mainstreaming' of legislative proposals.
- A duty to assess how the choice of form and content of the Commission's action may affect the overall balance of power in society between citizens, civil society, corporations, governments, etc and whether the action the Commission takes is conducive to inviting and encouraging more democratic participation by citizens and encourages citizens to make active use of their fundamental and democratic rights.

It is important not to underestimate that many rights and protections for individuals, but also institutional arrangements, which are created by secondary EU law, are key for the good functioning of democracy in Member States, in particular bearing in mind also that the rule of law and fundamental rights are core elements of democracy.[16]

[15] See, for details on the Better Regulation agenda and the related methods, which systematically describe legislation as a 'burden': ec.europa.eu/commission/presscorner/detail/it/qanda_21_1902.

[16] A prominent example is Directive (EU) 2019/1937 of the European Parliament and of the Council of 23 October 2019 on the protection of persons who report breaches of Union law [2019] OJ L305/17.

The Commission should therefore develop a policy to systematically include such 'hooks for democracy and democratic engagement' in EU secondary legislation and also develop a checklist and toolbox for such purposes, following the model of the Charter of Fundamental Rights and the Justice Scoreboard combined with the annual Rule of Law Report. For example, where EU legislation foresees domestic bodies, such as sectoral regulators, consumer protection or data protection authorities, the toolbox would require certain levels of direct citizen participation rights in the governance of these institutions, in addition to consultation rights and rights of appeal for citizens. The same rights should also be available for civil society associations in relation to such bodies, in order to create space for engagement, thus addressing the problem of the shrinking space for civil society engagement where populists gain power. The Commission needs to unleash its 'technocratic charisma' – in the words of the Commission's former Secretary-General Catherine Day – and creativity to become a driver of inspiring innovation regarding tools to activate citizens for democracy. For this purpose, it has to enter into a much more intense dialogue with academia and civil society and all actors of democracy.

A crucial question in democracy is which of the challenges on the table can be safely and with good conscience left to non-legislative action, self-regulation, voluntary codes of conduct, or simply ethics, and which challenges need to be addressed by rules which are enforceable and based on democratic process – in other words laws.

In answering this question, democracy impact assessments will have to consider the principle of essentiality which has guided legislation in constitutional democracies for so long. This principle prescribes that any matter which is essential because it either concerns fundamental rights of individuals or is important to the good functioning of the state (which includes democracy) must be dealt with by a parliamentary, democratically legitimised law.[17]

To close this section: attack is often the best defence and thus creating and extending democratic rights of engagement wherever possible in a wave of new European democratic creativity may well be the best way to go for the Commission, the other EU institutions, and Member States, as a guiding principle for policy development to avoid democracy being undermined in Europe.

[17] Jo Eric Khushal Murkens considered the judgment of the UK High Court on decisions relating to Brexit not being left alone in the hands of the government but giving Westminster a say, a case of application of the principle of essentiality, see JE Khushal Murkens, 'The High Court's Brexit Decision: A Lesson in Constitutional Law for the UK Government' *Verfassungsblog* (3 November 2016): verfassungsblog.de/the-high-courts-brexit-decision-a-lesson-in-constitutional-law-for-the-uk-government/; for the principle of essentiality in German, US and EU law, see J Saurer, 'EU Agencies 2.0: the new constitution of supranational administration beyond the EU Commission' in S Rose-Ackerman, PL Lindseth and B Emerson (eds), *Comparative Administrative Law*, 2nd edn (Cheltenham, Edward Elgar, 2017) 619; further recent examples in the jurisprudence of the ECJ are the judgments in C-355/10 *European Parliament v Council* ECLI:EU:C:2012:516 para 64 ff and Joined cases C-293/12 and C-594/12 *Digital Rights Ireland v Minister for Communication, Marine and Natural Resources and Others* ECLI:EU:C:2014:238 para 54 ff.

III. THE FUTURE OF EUROPE CONFERENCE[18] AND AN EU CHARTER ON DEMOCRACY IN MEMBER STATES

Europe has built a tradition not only of external controls over its states, but of actually protecting citizens against their state, first in the area of human rights with the European Convention on Human Rights (ECHR) and the European Court of Human Rights (ECtHR), and later with the system of directly applicable EU law in areas today going far beyond the economic rules for the internal market. There is no reason why the EU should not also develop stronger tools to support domestic democracies and democratic engagement, using the tried and tested Community methods and thus spreading resilience against autocracy.[19] Supporting democracy and constitutional resilience in the EU is an existential matter for democracy in Europe, and the misguided silence of EU institutions on existential matters, such as domestic referenda on the EU Treaties and the Brexit vote, should not be repeated in regard to democracy in Europe.

As regards fundamental rights, the ECHR and the EU Charter of Fundamental Rights are legally binding, detailed texts, interpreted in extensive jurisprudence and enforced by the respective competent courts in Strasbourg, Luxembourg and the Member States. The Commission has already in 2010 set out its policy on the application of the Charter in a strategy document.[20] Both the Commission and the independent Fundamental Rights Agency in Vienna report annually on the application of the Charter.

As regards the rule of law, there is ample jurisprudence of the Court of Justice detailing its key elements.[21] The CEPEJ[22] of the Council of Europe is a core institution reporting on and assessing the rule-of-law situation in Member States. The Commission interacts well with this institution and has adopted in 2014 for the first time a policy on how to strengthen the Rule of Law in the Member States and how to proceed under Article 7 TEU in case of non-respect for the rule of law.[23] The Union has in the meantime adopted a Regulation on the protection of the Union's budget as regards the rule of law in the Member States.[24] It also reports regularly

[18] The European Commission has not yet established its proposals for the follow up of the Conference on the Future of Europe. This chapter consists of personal proposals of the author, which are largely based on the prior publication referred to in n 27 below.

[19] In the same direction, 'The other Democratic Deficit, A Toolbox for the EU to Safeguard Democracy in Member States', Expert Group of the Friedrich-Ebert Stiftung (Berlin, 2017), library.fes.de/pdf-files/id-moe/14371–20180622.pdf.

[20] Communication of the Commission of 19 October 2010, Strategy for the effective implementation of the Charter of Fundamental Rights by the European Union, COM(2010) 573 final.

[21] Case C-64/16 *Associação Sindical dos Juízes Portugueses v Tribunal de Contas* ECLI:EU:C:2018:117; Case C-216/18 PPU *LM* ECLI:EU:C:2018:586; Order in Case C-619/18 R *Commission v Poland* ECLI:EU:C:2018:1021 Rectified by Order ECLI:EU:C:2019:615 (English not available at time of writing).

[22] Council of Europe European Commission for the Efficiency of Justice, www.coe.int/en/web/cepej.

[23] Communication from the Commission, 'A new Framework to strengthen the Rule of Law' COM(2014) 158 final of 11 March 2014; for its application see: ec.europa.eu/info/policies/justice-and-fundamental-rights/effective-justice/rule-law/rule-law-framework_en.

[24] Regulation (EU, Euratom) 2020/2092 of the European Parliament and of the Council on a general regime of conditionality for the protection of the Union budget [2020] OJ L433I/1.

on the rule of law in Member States and on the effectiveness and independence of the judiciary.

However, as for democracy, EU primary law does not contain the necessary consolidations and concretisations such as were achieved regarding fundamental rights in the Charter and the jurisprudence of the ECJ and the ECtHR. Nor is there an external mechanism which in an authoritative and obligatory manner exercises an external discipline as to democracy over Member States such as the ECtHR does as to the respect of human rights and the Fundamental Rights Agency and the ECJ do as regards the Charter.

The Commission has, importantly, presented a '*European Democracy Action Plan*',[25] an overarching policy strategy for the strengthening of democracy in Europe and for making both the EU and its Member States resilient against temptations and challenges of autocracy. It is also clear, however, that while the Union is the biggest observer of elections and democracy programmes in third countries, no similar activities have been carried out so far within the EU by the EU, this being but one symptom of a lack of instruments for democracy in Europe.

In the triangle of fundamental rights, the rule of law and democracy, democracy is still the weakest link and needs further work, building on the *European Democracy Action Plan* as an important first step. There can certainly not be democracy without either the rule of law or the protection of fundamental rights of individuals, which are constitutive of democracy. But there can be a certain rule of law and certain fundamental rights without democracy, as the history of Prussia teaches us. If we do not want Europe and its Member States to fall back into a state of Prussia, it is now time to renew the institutional and popular engagement with democracy in Europe.

With this in mind, it is now time to jump to present some sources for further work on democracy and provide a global overview of some important universal and regional democracy documents before describing possible elements of a future European Charter for Democracy (EUDC) as one part of a follow up to the Conference on the Future of Europe, to revive engagement of people in representative democracy and to equip the EU with the tools necessary to support resilience of democracies in Europe against autocracy.

Before we address the question of sources for work on a European democracy charter, let it be clear that the work on an EUDC itself will be an important source of inspiration for practical understanding and learning on democracy. This journey of discovery and comparison will, as in the case of the conventions which prepared the Treaties and the Charter of Fundamental Rights, be a key effect of work on an EUDC, first informally, then at the level of the EU institutions and eventually, upon consensus being reached, in a convention preparing a text for a possible Treaty change. It will start a broad debate and reflection and as such will serve the purpose to invigorate democracy, by involving many in the common process of discovery,

[25] Communication from the Commission to the European Parliament, the Council, the European Economic and Social Committee and the Committee of the Regions, COM(2020) 790 final of 3 December 2020 (*European Democracy Action Plan*).

learning and constitutional debate. This is the primary purpose of the first stage of work on the EUDC, leaving open for the time being the question of whether Treaty changes in the ever-more democratic European Union are necessary in the form of the EUCD (rather than in a more surgical, smaller intervention, limited for example only to the governance of the Eurozone and a few other issues, such as a legal base for election observations in Member States). One option also does not exclude the other over time.

Work on the EUDC will be the occasion to discuss questions like the advantage of representative democracy in an ever-more complex world and on the scale of the European Union (as compared to small federal polities such as Switzerland), right through to the relevance of the development of Technologies for Democracy and what impact they may have on the formulation of rules for democracy and democratic practice.

Importantly, however, many of the challenges to democracy in Europe and in the Member States, as discussed above, can be addressed at the level of secondary law and do not need a Treaty change. It is vital that the work on these challenges, as well as the general mainstreaming of all policies for democracy by the Commission, goes ahead in parallel to the preparatory work on the EUDC. And again, the debates on the EUDC will inspire discovery of such possibilities to strengthen democracy in Europe, at the EU level and in Member States, via secondary law.

Turning now to the sources of inspiration, a first step of the work would simply be to collect the information on the varied texts and practices of democracy in the EU and in the Member States. At the level of EU, there are detailed texts on democracy in the area of international relations and development aid, as well as assessments of candidate countries, and the content of Treaties and secondary law relevant to democracy is, in the case of the institutions, further detailed by inter institutional agreements and rules of procedure as well as practice. There is also an important body of jurisprudence on democratic principles by the Court of Justice, such as on the limits of delegated law making.[26] Following the methodology tried and tested in the 1999–2000 European Convention which prepared the Charter of Fundamental Rights, a consolidated overview of all elements of ECJ jurisprudence on democracy, often uttered in the context of cases of fundamental rights, will be vital.

The work on EUDC will thus first be a work of collection, codification and consolidation at the level of the EU.

Then there are the similar texts and practices as well as judgments, much richer and much more elaborate on democracy and its principles, at Member State level. The schools of comparative constitutional studies and comparative election law and parliamentary law will have important contributions to make, including on the common practices among Member States and on best practices.

There will certainly also be important learning in the comparative history of constitution making and the materials documenting the preparatory work and

[26] See Case C-355/10 *European Parliament v Council* ECLI:EU:C:2012:516, para 64 ff, with further precedents. See also Joined Cases C-293/12 and 594/12 *Digital Rights Ireland Ltd v Minister for Communications, Marine and Natural Resources and Others* ECLI:EU:C:2014:238, para 54 ff.

debates for important constitutions of the Member States and third countries with great histories of democracy, like that of the United States.

And it is possible to draw on a newer body of materials, namely universal and regional democracy documents.[27] These documents that have 'democracy' as their principal theme, address for example – mostly in separate chapters or sections – the following topics: (1) definition of democracy/the principles of democracy, (2) democratic institutions, (3) the international dimension of democracy, (4) the triangle of democracy, rule of law and human rights, (5) promotion of a democratic culture/education, (6) democratic elections, (7) election monitoring, (8) urgent measures and sanctions in case of threats or breakdown of democracy, (9) the role of the armed forces, the police and the security forces in a democracy, and (10) some final clauses.[28]

The described challenges to democracy in Europe and the mere existence of the above-mentioned democracy documents in other regions of the world are reason enough to consider the creation of an EUDC. This question is even more self-evident, when we bear in mind that the only EU document that solely addresses democracy at the highest level is the 'Declaration on democracy', adopted by the European Council in Copenhagen of 7–8 April 1978, which comprises only six paragraphs. One obvious explanation for this rather moderate result is that the field of activity of the EU is – in comparison to all other international organisations – very broad, and that, of course, the Treaties contain numerous o.perational provisions of practical relevance for a functioning democracy, which are further specified in secondary law, as discussed above. The principle of democracy is thus explicit not only in Article 2 TEU and in its 'provisions on democratic principles' (Title II, Articles 9 to 12) but also in the provisions on the institutions in the Treaties, the Charter, and in secondary law.

As I wrote with Frithjof Ehm in our Research Paper for the College of Europe in 2019:

> The EUDC could help to effectively address the many challenges to democracy on the EU level, within the Member States, and, third, in the relation between the EU and the Member States. As to the issues arising in the third group, a key question is whether, without touching the division of competences between the EU and Member States, the EUDC could add value by setting out principles and processes on how to articulate democratic process on both levels in mutual respect and within the existing competence distribution.[29]

With regard to the content of the EUDC, the starting point should be a provision that concisely defines the core elements and the common denominators of European

[27] See on the following P Nemitz and F Ehm, 'Strengthening Democracy in Europe and its Resilience against Autocracy: Daring more Democracy and a European Democracy Charter', *Research Paper in Law 1/2019* (Brugge, College of Europe, 2019), on which this contribution is largely based: http://aei.pitt.edu/97367/1/researchpaper_1_2019_paul_nemitz_frithjof_ehm_final_0.pdf (coleurope.eu). Included in S Garben, I Govaere, and P Nemitz (eds), *Critical Reflections on Constitutional Democracy in the European Union* (Oxford, Hart Publishing, 2019) 345.

[28] Democracy documents which can serve as sources are printed in F Ehm and C Walter (eds), *International Democracy Documents – A Compilation of Treaties and Other Instruments* (Leiden and Boston, Brill-Nijhoff, 2015).

[29] Above n 27.

democracy that build on Article 2 TEU. Generally speaking, the concept of 'democracy' refers to the involvement of citizens in political decision making and its core is based on consensus. A feasible *definition of democracy* is something which is often missing in many of the documents mentioned above,[30] which already shows how difficult it is to consolidate all the differing conceptions. However, a starting point for finding a European definition of democracy could be its intrinsic element, that is, the 'majority rule', which was included in the first Draft Preamble of the European Constitution, and which, at the European level, has to rely both on some majority of Member States and some majority of the population (presently set at 55 and 65 per cent respectively – see Article 16 TEU) in order to also take account of the federal nature of the EU.

Furthermore, one should take into account the international core consensus concerning this term. A comparative look at all relevant international democracy documents reveals six general principles for a democratic government: (1) human rights, (2) free and fair elections, (3) the rule of law, (4) a multi-party system, (5) the separation of powers, and (6) an independent judiciary.[31] However, the EU could never be content with such a 'skeletal structure definition' and it has to go – also due to its self-conception – beyond this. Simultaneously, it must be underlined that already these principles are extremely vague and open to different interpretations.[32] This being said, as outlined above, there is already a substantial body of concretisations through secondary law, practice and jurisprudence in these areas.

On the other hand, we also need a generally understandable definition that speaks to the people and has integrative capacity. A paradigmatic phrase for this is that democracy is safeguarded as long as there is 'a social structure open to change and novelty, and yet preserving its own basic character'.[33] By defining the minimum requirements for a functioning pluralist democracy, the definition could serve as a new legal benchmark for the Court to assess possible democracy threats, and thus strengthen the capacity of the EU to ensure, through the concept of preserving this basic character, effective and equal protection of democracy in all Member States.[34] It could be the concrete expression of the EU maturing as a democratic constitutional system, based on common EU values.[35]

As regards democracy in Member States, the EUDC could be of help even if it just were an aid to interpretation of the meaning of democracy in Article 2 TEU, and not only when it comes to Article 7 TEU procedures. It is also clear that the EUDC will not at all target any Member State and the specific situation there. It will rather be

[30] See also Ehm and Walter, above n 28, 12 ff.

[31] Ehm and Walter, above n 28, 22.

[32] For a similar conclusion see N Petersen, *Demokratie als teleologisches Prinzip* (Heidelberg, Springer 2009) 124 ff.

[33] Z Barbu, *Democracy and Dictatorship – Their Psychology and Patterns of Life* (New York, Grove Press, 1956) 4.

[34] See ideas about an analogous function of a possible 'Copenhagen Charter', cited in B Bugarič, 'Protecting Democracy and the Rule of Law in the European Union: The Hungarian Challenge' (July 2014) *LEQS Paper No. 79/2014*, 30–31.

[35] See for more details Nemitz and Ehm, 'Strengthening Democracy in Europe and its Resilience Against Autocracy: Daring More Democracy and a European Democracy Charter', above n 27.

an orientation document for all Member States and an essential element for getting the Union and its Member States ready to accept new Member States, many of which have no long history of democracy.

IV. LEARNINGS FROM THE HISTORY OF DEMOCRACY IN EUROPE AND ITS MEMBER STATES

In his famous speech before the German Bundestag in 1969, then Chancellor Willy Brandt said, 'we want to dare more democracy'.[36] The speech of Chancellor Brandt came at a time when right-wing extremism was on the rise. For the first time since the end of the war, a far-right party, the National Democratic Party of Germany (NPD), only very narrowly missed entering the German Parliament with 4.3 per cent of the votes. In conjunction with the first big economic crisis in 1966–67, the political landscape partly resembled that of today. The government introduced on the way many pro-democratic reforms in different areas of life. The voting age was reduced from 21 to 18 in 1972. More universities were created, and many reforms introduced. Students were given more participation and self-determination in university structures. Workers were given more rights of co-determination with a reform of the Works Council Constitution Act in 1972.[37] Another huge leap for workers' rights was taken with the introduction of the co-determination law in 1976,[38] which ensured that democracy does not end right at the door of the big enterprises. The policy was to create not only individual rights, but also organisational structures to empower people to jointly exercise these rights or delegate the exercise to the new bodies thus created, such as works councils or student councils. Routes of engagement for people were opened which were more than just consultation or exercise of defensive rights. These structures created a new balance of power in society and encouraged people to engage, in different ways, in democratic processes.

Europe can learn from this history of democracy as much as it can learn from the downfall of the Republic of Weimar. In this day and age, Europe needs to 'dare more democracy' and continue on its way to be a democracy that defends itself, just like at the time of Brandt '*Mehr Demokratie wagen*' and '*Wehrhafte Demokratie*', while avoiding its pitfalls.[39] As in the time of Brandt, strong political will, leadership

[36] Government Declaration of Federal Chancellor Willy Brandt in front of the German Bundestag in Bonn on 28 October 1969.

[37] Official German title Betriebsverfassungsgesetz (BetrVG).

[38] Official German title Gesetz über die Mitbestimmung der Arbeitnehmer (Mitbestimmungsgesetz – MitbestG).

[39] A key action of 'Wehrhafte Demokratie' under Willy Brandt was the much-contested order against radicals from the left and the right in public service of 28 January 1972, www.1000dokumente.de/index.html?c=dokument_de&dokument=0113_ade&object=translation&st=&l=de. On this, see Wissenschaftlicher Dienst des Deutschen Bundestages 2017, Parlamentarische und zivilgesellschaftliche Initiativen zur Aufarbeitung des sogenannten Radikalenerlasses vom 28. Januar 1972, Ausarbeitung WD 1-3000-012/17, www.bundestag.de/blob/531136/a0a150d89d4db6c2bdae0dd5b300246d/wd-1-012-17-pdf-data.pdf, and more recently the translation of 'Wehrhafte Demokratie' as 'militant democracy' in the press release of the German Constitutional Court on an order rejecting constitutional complaints against prohibitions of associations. This order recounts in part the history of '*Wehrhafte Demokratie*'

and readiness to innovate for democracy is now necessary on the part of the Commission.

The purpose of this contribution is to demonstrate that the EU can and must play an important role in avoiding a spread of the virus of autocratic populism. It can help to share among all EU Member States the historical learnings drawn from democracies sliding into dictatorship, such as it happened to the Weimar Republic.[40] And it can help to learn together today from the success of Willy Brand and '*Wehrhafte Demokratie*'. Of course, democracy and democratic engagement of people in the Member States can never be imposed from the EU level. The saying of former German constitutional judge Böckenförde[41] – that the democratic state does not command the preconditions on which its existence is predicated, and thus that law cannot secure democracy if there is no culture of tolerance and people engaging in and for democracy – is *a fortiori* true for the EU and in the relationship between the EU and its Member States. This being said, and contrary to cheap and outdated claims that the EU itself is not democratic, the EU features a success story of progressive internal democratisation and a track record as the biggest donor of democracy and election observation worldwide, that is, outside the EU.[42]

The EU will thus be able to give a new meaning to engagement in democracy in times of globalisation, based both on the history of democracy within Europe and on its experience as global actor for democracy.

and the lack of it in the Weimar Republic: German Constitutional Court, Press Release No. 69/2018 of 21 August 2018 on the Order of 13 July 2018 1 BvR 1474/12, 1 BvR 57/14, 1 BvR 57/14, 1 BvR 670/13, www.bundesverfassungsgericht.de/SharedDocs/Pressemitteilungen/EN/2018/bvg18-069.html.

[40] B Carter Hett, *The Death of Democracy: Hitler's Rise to Power and the Downfall of the Weimar Republic* (New York, St. Martin's Griffin, 2018); see also EJ Dionne Jr, 'The path to Autocracy is all too familiar', *Washington Post* (18 August 2018), www.washingtonpost.com/opinions/the-path-to-autocracy-is-all-too-familiar/2018/08/08/6f3602f8-9b25-11e8-b60b-1c897f17e185_story.html?noredirect=on&utm_term=.dbc84c6a5d36.

[41] EW Böckenförde, *Staat, Gesellschaft, Freiheit* (Frankfurt am Main, Suhrkamp Verlag, 1976) 60.

[42] It is telling that for the definition of Democracy in an opinion pool on Democracy in Europe by DG JUST of the European Commission, reference is made to the Foreign Policy Instrument (FPI), 'Special Eurobarometer 477, Democracy and Elections', November 2018, 2 (fn 1).

10

Infringement Proceedings as a Tool for Enforcing the Rule of Law in EU Member States – A Critical Review

JONI HELISKOSKI*

I. SCOPE AND PURPOSES

THE INFRINGEMENT PROCEDURE governed by Article 258 TFEU[1] is an essential instrument of the European Commission to oversee, as the Guardian of the Treaties, the application of EU law under the control of the European Court of Justice (ECJ), as provided for in Article 17(1) TEU.[2] It has been suggested that the procedure concerned also provides a useful device for addressing breaches of the rule of law in Member States of the Union.[3] This contribution aims at reviewing that suggestion in the light of the actual practice of the Commission as well as the recent case law of the Court.[4]

* The author would like to thank Christophe Hillion for valuable comments on a draft. The usual disclaimer applies.

[1] As complemented by the procedure governing the enforcement of judgments of the Court of Justice, including, where necessary, through financial sanctions (art 260 TFEU).

[2] See M Smith, 'The Evolution of Infringement and Sanction Procedures: Of Pilots, Diversions, Collisions, and Circling' in D Chalmers and A Arnull (eds), *The Oxford Handbook of European Union Law* (Oxford, Oxford University Press, 2015) 350, who, while not writing in the context of the rule of law, interestingly refers to the Commission's guardianship 'over the Union Treaties *and the rule of law*' (emphasis added).

[3] See, eg, C Hillion, 'Overseeing the rule of law in the European Union: Legal mandate and means' in C Closa and D Kochenov (eds), *Reinforcing Rule of Law Oversight in the European Union* (Cambridge, Cambridge University Press, 2016) 59, 66–74; M Blauberger and RD Keleman, 'Can courts rescue national democracy? Judicial safeguards against democratic backsliding in the EU' (2017) 24 *Journal of European Public Policy* 321, 323–26; M Schmidt and P Bogdanowicz, 'The infringement procedure in the rule of law crisis: How to make effective use of Article 258 TFEU' (2018) 55 *CML Rev* 1061, 1064–66 and 1073; and D Adamski, 'The Social Contract of Democratic Backsliding in the "New EU" Countries' (2019) 56 *CML Rev* 623, 657.

[4] Under art 259 TFEU, a Member State may also bring an infringement action before the Court. Exigencies of space preclude the treatment of such proceedings which are relatively rare in practice.

The chapter does not pretend to be a comprehensive account of a topic already extensively covered by scholarship.[5] In essence, it proposes to do two things. First, the chapter intends to look at the practice of the Commission concerning the use of infringement proceedings to enforce the rule of law in Member States, as well as the concrete results of that practice. In that context, the chapter explores some of the suggestions as to how the Commission's employment of infringement proceedings to rule-of-law matters could be improved. In particular, the chapter deals with the idea, taken up time and again by Kim Lane Scheppele and her collaborators,[6] of addressing rule-of-law problems through so-called systemic infringement proceedings, as well as certain related proposals essentially based on the notion of the rule of law as a value of the EU, as provided by Article 2 TEU (Section II). Secondly, the chapter moves on to assess the viability of those proposals in the light of the recent case law of the CJEU in general and the infringement proceedings brought in the context of the problems of judicial independence in Poland[7] in particular (Section III). Finally, there is a review and a concluding assessment (Section IV).

II. THE PRACTICE AND POLICY OF THE COMMISSION

A. A Guardian of the Treaties Enforcing the Rule of Law – The Commission's Practice and Policy

It is well established by the case law that the decision to institute infringement proceedings against a Member State, including the time and object of those proceedings, is, in principle, at the discretion of the Commission.[8] Accordingly, the decision of whether to act under Article 258 TFEU is, fundamentally, a policy choice of the Commission.[9] This begs the question as to whether there has existed, or exists, *a specific policy* of the Commission on the employment of the infringement procedure to enforce the rule of law. To find out, we need to look not only at what statements of

[5] In addition to Hillion, above n 3; Blauberger and Keleman, above n 3; and Schmidt and Bogdanowicz, above n 3, see LW Gormley, 'Infringement Proceedings' in A Jakab and D Kochenov (eds), *The Enforcement of EU Law and Values: Ensuring Member States' Compliance* (Cambridge, Cambridge University Press, 2017), 65; and P Pohjankoski, 'Rule of law with leverage: Policing structural obligations in EU law with the infringement procedure, fines, and set-off' (2021) 58 *CML Rev* 1341.

[6] See KL Scheppele, 'Enforcing the Basic Principles of EU Law trough Systemic Infringement Actions' in Closa and Kochenov, above n 3, 105, and, more recently, KL Scheppele, D Kochenov and B Grabowska-Moroz, 'EU values are law, after all: Enforcing EU values through systemic infringement actions by the European Commission and the Member States of the European Union' (2021) 39 *Yearbook of European Law* 1. See also L Pech and D Kochenov, *Respect for the Rule of Law in the Case Law of the European Court of Justice: A Casebook Overview of Key Judgments since the Portuguese Judges Case* (Swedish Institute for European Policy Studies, 2021), 50.

[7] Case C-192/18 *Commission v Poland* ECLI:EU:C:2019:924; Case C-619/18 *Commission v Poland* ECLI:EU:C:2019:531; and Case C-791/19 *Commission v Poland* ECLI:EU:C:2021:596. See also the interim orders of 14 July 2021 and 27 October 2021 in Case C-204/21 *Commission v Poland* ECLI:EU:C:2021:593 and ECLI:EU:C:2021:878 (pending).

[8] Case C-552/15 *Commission v Ireland* ECLI:EU:C:2017:698, 34.

[9] On infringement proceedings as an instrument of policy, see L Prete and B Smulders, 'The age of maturity of infringement proceedings' (2021) 58 *CML Rev* 285, 296.

policy the Commission may have made on the matter but also at the track-record of that institution of putting those statements into practice. As a preliminary point, it needs to be stressed, however, that the Commission's possession of discretion under Article 258 TFEU should of course not be regarded as a justification for its non-fulfilment of its task of overseeing, as the Guardian of the Treaties, the application of Union law under Article 17(1) TEU.[10]

While the Commission is, according to that institution itself, 'committed to make full use of its powers and continue to play its role as guardian of the Treaties to ensure the respect of EU law requirements relating to the rule of law',[11] it is apparent that that commitment needs to be qualified in several respects. First, a defining, and perhaps the most characteristic, feature of the Commission's understanding of the role of infringement proceedings in addressing rule-of-law problems in Member States has been that such proceedings 'can be launched by the Commission only where these concerns constitute … a breach of a *specific provision* of EU law' (emphasis added).[12] On the other hand, infringement proceedings are not available for addressing 'situations of concern which fall outside the scope of EU law and therefore cannot be considered as a breach of obligations under the Treaties' even when they 'pose a systemic threat to the rule of law'.[13] This approach clearly remains valid even today: in the 2021 Rule of Law Report, the Commission states that 'infringement proceedings … aim to address specific breaches of EU law',[14] as opposed to Article 7 TEU which provides the more general procedure for upholding the common values of the Union, including the rule of law.

Secondly, the Commission is conspicuously eager to underline the discretion it holds in deciding whether it is expedient to act under Article 258 TFEU: recourse to rule-of-law related infringement procedures is had 'where necessary' and 'depending on circumstances',[15] that is, on an ad hoc basis. Thirdly, the Commission's policy contains an element of subsidiarity. The Commission 'is determined to bring to the Court of Justice rule of law problems affecting the application of EU law, when these

[10] See Editorial Comments, 'Compromising (On) the General Conditionality Mechanism and the Rule of Law' (2021) 58 *CML Rev* 267, 281–22, arguing that the Commission may have an obligation under art 17(1) TEU to act in the context of Regulation (EU, Euratom) 2020/2092 of the European Parliament and of the Council of 16 December 2020 on a general regime of conditionality for the protection of the Union budget, [2020] OJ L433I/1.

[11] Commission Communication on the '2020 Rule of Law Report. The rule of law situation in the European Union', COM(2020) 580 final of 30 September 2020, 26. See also the Commission Communication on 'EU law: Better results through better application', [2017] OJ C18/10, stating that '[t]he Commission will therefore give high priority to infringements that reveal systemic weaknesses which undermine the functioning of the EU's institutional framework' (at 14).

[12] Commission Communication on 'A new EU Framework to strengthen the Rule of Law', COM(2014) 158 final of 19 March 2014, 5.

[13] Ibid. The approach is reminiscent of the one outlined in the Commission Communication on Strategy for the effective implementation of the Charter of Fundamental Rights by the European Union, COM(2010) 573 final of 19 October 2010, 10.

[14] Commission Communication on the '2021 Rule of Law Report. The rule of law situation in the European Union', COM(2021) 700 final of 20 July 2021, 28. See also Commission Communication on the '2022 Rule of Law Report. The rule of law situation in the European Union', COM(2022) 500 final of 13 July 2022, 30.

[15] Commission Communication on 'Further strengthening the rule of law in the Union: state of play and possible next steps', COM(2019) 163 of 3 April 2019, 13. See also the European Commission, 2020 Annual Report on Monitoring the Application of European Union Law, 22.

problems could not be solved through the national checks and balances.'[16] Finally, the Commission's 'strategic approach to infringement proceedings related to the rule of law' builds on its existing approach to enforcement and on the developing case law of the ECJ.[17] In sum, the Commission may, at its discretion, launch rule-of-law related infringement proceedings against a Member State when there is a breach of a specific provision of EU law that proves incapable of being solved at the national level.

Looking, next, at the Commission's track-record of applying Article 258 TFEU to rule-of-law related matters, the first thing one notices is that the Commission has not adopted an even rudimentary understanding of which cases precisely are to be labelled as falling under the notion 'rule of law'. This becomes strikingly clear in the light of the Commission's treatment of the various infringement actions brought before the ECJ against Hungary in the Commission's 2020 and 2021 reports on the rule of law[18] as well as in its annual reports on the monitoring of application of EU law.[19] Since 2017, the Commission has launched a total of three rule-of-law related infringement proceedings against Hungary before the ECJ; that is, Case C-66/18 regarding conditions for the supply of higher education services,[20] Case C-78/18 regarding transparency of foreign-funded civil society organisations,[21] and Case C-821/19 regarding the so-called 'Stop Soros law' on procedures for obtaining asylum.[22] However, only Cases C-78/18 and C-821/19 are mentioned in the 2020, 2021 and 2022 Rule of Law Reports and only the latter is taken up in the context of the rule of law in the Commission's 2018 Annual Report on the Monitoring the Application of European Union Law.[23] At the same time, there were other infringement actions against Hungary that arguably also had a rule-of-law dimension[24] but were apparently not conceived of by the Commission as falling within its policy of enforcing the rule of law under

[16] Commission Communication on 'Strengthening the rule of law within the Union: a blueprint for action', COM(2019) 343 of 17 July 2017, 14.

[17] Ibid. According to the Commission, this is in line with the more strategic approach to the Commission's enforcement actions set out in the Communication 'EU law: Better results through better application', above n 11.

[18] Above nn 11 and 14.

[19] See the European Commission's website for the Collection of Annual reports on the monitoring of the application of EU Law, ec.europa.eu/info/publications/annual-reports-monitoring-application-eu-law_en.

[20] Case C-66/18 *Commission v Hungary* ECLI:EU:C:2020:792.

[21] Case C-78/18 *Commission v Hungary* ECLI:EU:C:2020:476.

[22] Case C-821/19 *Commission v Hungary* ECLI:EU:C:2021:930. On 15 July 2022 the Commission decided to refer Hungary to the Court of Justice for breaching EU telecoms rules with the Hungarian Media Council's decision to reject, on highly questionable grounds, *Klubradio*'s application for the use of radio spectrum. European Commission, Press release IP/22/2688.

[23] See European Commission, Monitoring the application of European Union Law – 2018 Annual Report, ec.europa.eu/info/sites/default/files/report-2018-annual-report-monitoring-application-eu-law.pdf (at 24).

[24] See eg Case C-235/17 *Commission v Hungary* ECLI:EU:C:2019:432, in which the ECJ held that by adopting legislation depriving persons of their right of *usufruct* on farmland, Hungary infringed both the principle of free movement of capital and the right to property guaranteed by the Charter of Fundamental Rights. See S Mayer, 'Investment Protection in National Courts and the ECJ in Light of the Rule of Law Crisis' (2021) 1 *Europarättslig tidskrift* 17, 24–32. See also Case C-718/17 *Commission v Hungary* ECLI:EU:C:2020:257, and Case C-808/18 *Commission v Hungary* ECLI:EU:C:2020:1029, both concerning the treatment of applicants for international protection.

Article 258 TFEU. It is symptomatic of the above approach of the Commission that in the 2019 and 2020 annual reports on the monitoring of the application of EU Law, the topic of the rule of law is only mentioned in relation to Poland but not in any way in relation to Hungary.

The impression that the Commission's policy on the enforcement of the rule of law through infringement proceedings lacks design is further amplified by the fact that in none of the above actions against Hungary – labelled by the Commission as falling under the theme of the rule of law – has the Commission's reasoning, let alone the actual pleas, been based upon, or even mentioned, the value of the rule of law set out in Article 2 TEU. The Commission has rather pleaded an infringement of Treaty freedoms and/or secondary law and/or the Charter of Fundamental Rights of the European Union (the 'Charter'). This had also been the case with every previous rule-of-law related infringement procedure against Hungary.[25] While the Commission has therefore certainly been true to its conviction that the scope of application of Article 258 TFEU is limited to addressing breaches of 'specific rules' of EU law, its lack of emphasis on the rule-of-law dimension is symptomatic of the absence of a *policy* aimed at enforcing the rule of law through infringement proceedings. Admittedly, in the actions against Poland concerning judicial independence,[26] the Commission – relying on the Court's judgment of 27 February 2018 in *Associação Sindical dos Juízes Portugueses*[27] – has now employed, inter alia, the second subparagraph of Article 19(1) TEU, in conjunction with Article 47 of the Charter, thereby adopting an arguably broader approach than it did in Case C-286/12, *Commission v Hungary*, concerning the lowering of the retirement age judges, prosecutors and notaries.[28] However, in none of those actions either has the Commission pleaded an infringement of Article 2 TEU.

The above review of the Commission's practice of bringing rule-of-law related infringement proceedings also shows that that institution has certainly availed itself of its discretion to decide whether to bring proceedings and acted, as proclaimed, 'depending on circumstances'. An account of what has failed to provoke the Guardian of the Treaties to act would obviously exceed the confines of the present contribution. However, even the briefest of glances at, for example, the decisions to trigger the Article 7 TEU procedure in respect of Poland[29] and Hungary,[30] suffices to establish that the questions addressed under Article 258 TFEU concerning the state of

[25] LH Anders and S Priebus, 'Does It Help to Call a Spade a Spade? Examining the Legal Bases and Effects of Rule of Law-Related Infringement Procedures Against Hungary' in A Lorenz and LH Anders (eds), *Illiberal Trends and Anti-EU Politics in East Central Europe* (Cham, Palgrave Macmillan, 2021) 235, 240–43.

[26] Above n 7.

[27] Case C-64/16 *Associação Sindical dos Juízes Portugueses v Tribunal de Contas* ECLI:EU:C:2018:117.

[28] Case C-286/12 *Commission v Hungary* ECLI:EU:C:2012:687. The action had been based on arts 2 and 6(1) of Council Directive 2000/78/EC of 27 November 2000 establishing a general framework for equal treatment in employment and occupation, [2000] OJ L303/16.

[29] Proposal for a Council Decision on the determination of a clear risk of a serious breach by the Republic of Poland of the rule of law, COM(2017) 835 final.

[30] European Parliament resolution of 12 September 2018 on a proposal calling on the Council to determine, pursuant to art 7(1) of the Treaty on European Union, the existence of a clear risk of a serious breach by Hungary of the values on which the Union is founded, 2017/2131(INL).

the rule of law in those Member States represent but a tiny fraction of the totality of the rule-of-law problems prevailing in the countries concerned. It is telling that in the 2018 Annual Report on Monitoring the application of European Union Law the Commission 'shares the concerns expressed in the Parliament's report [on Hungary], in particular over fundamental rights, corruption, treatment of Roma and the independence of the judiciary'. This 'sharing of concerns', however, has not resulted in the Commission bringing infringement proceedings against Hungary on those issues.

What, then, of the concrete impact of the Commission's actions against Hungary and Poland? Nobody would expect infringement proceedings to make much of a change to the overall rule-of-law situation in those Member States. As Dariusz Adamski has submitted, such proceedings cannot preclude a social contract of democratic backsliding when a society concludes that an illiberal system is superior to its previously tried liberal alternatives.[31] So, the more appropriate frame of assessment would rather be whether the proceedings brought by the Commission have succeeded in ending *the alleged violations* of the rule of law as well as removing the effects created by *those violations*.

Insofar as concerns Hungary, a recent empirical study demonstrates that the 'limited cooperative stance' of the Hungarian government prevailing between 2010 and 2013 has turned into 'grim resistance' since 2017.[32] The latter stance is clearly illustrated by the Hungarian Government's reception of the three judgments labelled by the Commission as rule-of-law related infringement proceedings. Following judgment in Case C-66/18, Hungary amended the provision of the Higher Education Act declared contrary to EU law; however, the main objective of that legislation (that is, driving the Central European University out of the country) had already been achieved. The case, therefore, is an example of delayed and formal compliance.[33] In Case C-78/18, following a reasoned opinion of 18 February 2021 based on Article 260(2) TFEU,[34] the Hungarian Parliament repealed the Law on the Transparency of Organisations receiving support from abroad, adopted in 2017, and replaced it with a new law.[35] Whether the new law complies with EU law is apparently still under examination within the Commission, as the infringement procedure has not yet been closed. Finally, Hungary has signalled its intention not to comply with the judgment in Case C-821/19[36] and, accordingly, this infringement procedure remains open as well.

[31] Adamski, above n 3, 659.

[32] Anders and Priebus, above n 25, 247.

[33] For a useful account, see N Chronowski and A Vincze, 'The Hungarian Constitutional Court and the Central European University Case: Justice Delayed is Justice Denied. Decision of the Hungarian Constitutional Court of 6 July 2021 and the Judgment of the ECJ of 6 October 2020, Case C-66/18' (2021) 17 *European Constitutional Law Review* 1.

[34] European Commission, Press release INF/21/441.

[35] See 889/2017 – Hungary – Opinion on the Draft Law on the Transparency of Organisations receiving support from abroad, www.venice.coe.int/WebForms/followup/?index=1.

[36] See *bbc.com*, 'Hungary's Viktor Orban to defy EU over immigration law', 21 December 2021. www.bbc.com/news/world-europe-59748173 and Commission Staff Working Document 2022 Rule of Law Report Country Chapter on the rule-of-law situation in Hungary, SWD(2022) 517 final of 13 July 2022, 29.

Insofar as concerns the actions against Poland, it emerges from the Commission's 2020 Rule of Law Report that the Polish authorities had already amended the legislation that gave rise to Case C-192/18 concerning the lowering of the retirement regime of ordinary court judges and Case C-619/18 relating to the retirement regime for Supreme Court judges before the judgments of the ECJ,[37] in the latter case following interim measures granted by the Court.[38] That did not, however, completely remove the consequences of the infringements. While the interim measures adopted in Case C-619/18 prevented the most senior judges from being dismissed, new judges had already been appointed.[39] It seems that the situation of the ordinary court judges affected by the contested legislation has not been remedied, either.[40] On the other hand, in the two cases revolving around the Disciplinary Chamber of the Supreme Court (that is, C-791/19 and C-204/21), in both of which the Court granted the interim measures requested by the Commission,[41] no compliance has been forthcoming from the Polish authorities so far.[42] On the contrary, the disputes concerned have escalated into a major legal and political crisis between the Polish Government and the Union, a detailed description of which would clearly exceed the scope of the present analysis. Suffice it to note that, the Government having seized the Polish 'Constitutional Tribunal' for a declaration of the precedence of the Polish Constitution over EU law, that tribunal held on 14 July 2021 (that is, the day of the granting of the first interim measures in Case C-204/21) that interim orders issued by the ECJ affecting the organisation of Polish courts were not compatible with the Polish Constitution.[43] On 7 September 2021, the Commission, taking the view that the judgment in Case C-791/19 had not been fully complied with, sent a letter of formal notice under Article 260(2) TFEU to Poland.[44] In the ruling of 7 October 2021, the 'Constitutional Tribunal' held that the first and second paragraphs of Article 1 TEU, in conjunction with Article 4(3) TEU, as well as Article 19(1), second subparagraph, TEU are, in certain respects, contrary to the Constitution of Poland.[45] On 27 October 2021, the Vice-President of the ECJ ordered the Republic of Poland to pay the Commission a periodic penalty payment of €1,000,000 per day, pending non-compliance with the interim order of 14 July 2021 in Case C-204/21.[46] Finally, on 22 December 2021, the Commission decided to launch an infringement procedure pursuant to Article 258 TFEU against Poland, in view of 'serious concerns' with respect to the 'Constitutional Tribunal' and its recent case law.[47] As in the case of

[37] Country Chapter on the rule-of-law situation in Poland, SWD(2020) 320 final.

[38] C-619/18 R, *Commission v Poland (Independence of the Supreme Court)* ECLI:EU:C:2018:1021.

[39] Scheppele, Kochenov and Grabowska-Moroz, above n 6, 106. The case was closed on 2 December 2021.

[40] Pech and Kochenov, above n 6, 61. This procedure remains open at the time of writing.

[41] See C-791/19 R *Commission v Poland* ECLI:EU:C:2020:277 and Case C-204/21 R *Commission v Poland* ECLI:EU:C:2021:593 and ECLI:EU:C:2021:878, respectively.

[42] See the 2022 Rule of Law Report, above n 14, 8.

[43] P 7/20, judgment of 14 July 2021.

[44] European Commission, Press release IP/21/4587.

[45] K 3/21, judgment of 7 October 2021.

[46] Case C-204/21 R *Commission v Poland* ECLI:EU:C:2021:878.

[47] European Commission, Press release IP/21/7070. On 15 July 2022, a reasoned opinion was sent to Poland. See European Commission, Press release INF/22/3768.

Hungary, therefore, the reaction by Poland to infringement actions on the rule of law has been a combination of delayed compliance (the cases on retirement age of judges) and non-compliance (cases concerning the Disciplinary Chamber).

B. Criticisms and Suggestions for Improvement in Scholarly Literature

It emerges from the above survey of the rule-of-law related infringement proceedings concerning Hungary and Poland that the application of Article 258 (and Article 260) TFEU has not proven as effective in remedying problems relating to the rule of law in those Member States as one might have hoped for.

The scope of the Commission's actions has been as narrow as indicated by the blueprints of that institution, focusing on 'specific breaches of EU law' rather than more systemic problems concerning the rule of law. According to Agnes Batory, while such an approach allows the Commission to base its actions on 'strong legal grounds' it also 'normalizes or even trivializes the offence, limits the political scope of action and introduces predictability and formalism into the exchange that member states may abuse.'[48] At the same time, the discretion possessed by the Commission, together with the need to uphold an image of a successful Guardian of the Treaties, may, somewhat paradoxically, lead the Commission to accept what Batory calls 'symbolic and creative compliance'.[49] This seems to correspond to the analysis of the Hungarian practice between 2010 and 2013 by Lisa Anders and Sonja Priebus. Those authors also suggest that, at the same time, the Hungarian Government, whose stance has become more confrontational since 2017, has also employed a strategy of taking advantage of the length of the proceedings and delaying compliance until a moment at which the problematic practices have already reached their desired objectives.[50] As a result, the victories of the Commission have been 'pyrrhic', involving, at best, merely formal compliance with EU law. As regards Poland, such problems have in some cases been avoided thanks to the Commission requesting the use of the expedited procedure[51] or interim measures with financial penalties[52] from the Court. Even in the case of Poland, however, the increasingly confrontational stance of the Government leads to the conclusion that the Commission may hardly claim great success in terms of ending the alleged and established violations of the rule of law, let alone removing the effects of those violations.

It is therefore hardly surprising that the general view as to the role of infringement proceedings in the present context seems to be pessimistic. The conclusion reached by Anders and Priebus, for instance, is that infringement procedures as a legal instrument

[48] A Batory, 'Defying the Commission: Creative Compliance and Respect for the Rule of Law in the EU' (2016) 94 *Public Administration* 685, 696.

[49] ibid.

[50] Anders and Priebus, above n 25, 247–49.

[51] Art 23a of the Statute of the CJEU and art 133 of the Rules of Procedure of the Court of Justice.

[52] Art 279 TFEU and Case C-441/17 *Commission v Poland*, ECLI:EU:C:2018:255.

against rule-of-law backsliding are 'not only futile but even counterproductive'.[53] However, it seems that some commentators would not draw such a conclusion based on some inherent characteristics of the infringement procedure per se, but on the way the Commission *has applied* that procedure in practice. In that regard, the following criticisms in particular, alleging excessive 'circumspection'[54] in the use of infringement proceedings, have been voiced against the Commission. First, it has been argued that the Commission has construed its powers under Article 258 TFEU in an unduly narrow fashion and as being strictly confined to cases where specific provisions of the EU's acquis appear to have been breached. In the submission of Kim Lane Scheppele and her co-authors, the Commission has been unwilling to see Article 258 TFEU as something broader than 'an occasional instrument of ensuring Member States' adherence to clear-cut technical rules of secondary EU law'.[55] Secondly, the Commission has allegedly addressed only a very limited number rule-of-law related problems through infringement proceedings in respect of both Hungary[56] and Poland.[57] Thirdly, the Commission has been accused of a 'parsimonious as well as painstakingly slow use of the infringement procedure'[58] – resulting in the relevant Member State's problematic practices having already produced their desired consequences in a definitive fashion before a requirement arises to comply with the Court's judgment. Fourthly, while such a situation might in some cases be avoided through interim measures, it has been noted that the Commission has in most cases failed to request for them or, in any event, failed to do so sufficiently promptly.[59] In the light of its failure to act more decisively, it has been claimed that 'the Commission always ends up fighting yesterday's violations of the rule of law'.[60]

The above criticisms all seem to rely upon the assumption that the infringement procedure could, in principle, provide a useful tool for addressing rule-of-law questions in Member States, *if only* the Commission adopted a different understanding of the potential of Article 258 TFEU and acted more promptly and decisively once an infringement of the Treaties had been detected. The moment at which to launch the procedure, as well as that of every subsequent step of the administrative phase of the procedure, is, after all, for the Commission to decide. To speed things up at the judicial stage of the procedure, the Commission could request from the Court

[53] Anders and Priebus, above n 25, 250. But see Prete and Smulders, above n 9, 298–99, regarding the 'policy of more selective enforcement' as having marked 'significant progress in specific policy areas' such as the rule of law.

[54] Editorial Comments, above n 10, 281. See also D Kochenov, 'The Enforcement of the "Law" versus the Enforcement of "Values" in the EU' in Jakab and Kochenov, above n 5, 9, describing the approach of the Commission to art 258 TFEU as 'counterproductive and artificially narrow' (at 19–20).

[55] Scheppele, Kochenov and Grabowska-Moroz, above n 6, 61. But see I Marchioro, 'Role Models of Politics Disguised in Technique: Cases C-78/18 on Associative Transparency and C-66/18 on Academic Freedom in Hungary' (2021) 5 *Bratislava Law Review* 23.

[56] See Z Szente, 'Challenging the Basic Values – Problems in the Rule of Law in Hungary and the Failure of the EU to Tackle Them' in Jakab and Kochenov, above n 5, 458, 465–67.

[57] See L Pech, P Wachowiec and D Mazur, 'Poland's Rule of Law Breakdown: A Five-Year Assessment of EU's (In)Action' (2021) 13 *Hague Journal on the Rule of Law* 1, 22.

[58] Pech and Kochenov, above n 6, 50.

[59] ibid, 159–60.

[60] Pech, Wachowiec and Mazur, above n 57, 39.

that the case be determined under the expedited procedure. It could also request for the granting of interim measures, including financial ones. In the light of the experience from some of the actions against Poland, the ECJ is clearly showing preparedness to grant them. So, any improvement on that front, too, seems to depend on the Commission.

A much more controversial question, however, concerns the legal possibilities of broadening the reach of Article 258 TFEU beyond the addressing of 'specific violations' of EU law by Member States towards more general problems concerning the rule of law in Member States. Ideas as to how this might be accomplished have circulated amongst learned scholars and, for the purpose of assessing the true potential of Article 258 in the present context, it is appropriate to present some of those ideas in the following.

The mother of all such ideas is no doubt the proposal put forward by Kim Lane Scheppele to use Article 258 TFEU to address so-called 'systemic infringements' of EU law.[61] In a nutshell, the proposal, in a recent restatement instituted by Scheppele and her collaborators, argues that instead of specific infringements,

> [t]he Commission under Article 258 … could signal a systemic breach of EU values by an offending Member State by *bundling a group of specific alleged violations* together to argue before the ECJ that the infringement of EU law in a Member State is not minor or transient, but systemic and persistent. *Systemic* non-compliance with EU law is a different type of infringement than those typically implicated in the individual *acquis* violations taken one by one, because the *pattern* raises questions about whether the Member State is additionally violating the Rule of Law, fundamental rights, democracy, and other principles under Article 2 TEU and/or violating the principle of sincere cooperation under Article 4(3) TEU. … [A] *systemic infringement procedure* would identify a pattern of examples, possibly coming from radically different (sub-)fields of law, pointing to a persistent and coherent state practice of an assault against the values of the Union. Systemic infringement actions should argue that the pattern of activity is incompatible with values of democracy, fundamental rights, and/or the Rule of Law, extending the reach of Article 258 … TFEU to the heart of EU values.[62]

Once such a systemic infringement has been established, compliance with the specific obligations bundled together would not be enough to remedy the infringement. Instead, the ending of a systemic infringement would require 'systemic compliance' from the Member State concerned. As Scheppele et al put it:

> A Member State should be required to fix not just small technical violations in its implementation of EU law, but it should also be required to fix systemic threats to EU principles. … Simply assessing compliance with an ECJ judgment as following the motions to remove the surface violations, without touching the deeper problems of deteriorating democracy, is not enough. … [M]ore structural reforms must be required to ensure that the problem is truly solved.[63]

[61] Scheppele, above n 6.
[62] Scheppele, Kochenov and Grabowska-Moroz, above n 6, 19–20 (foonotes omitted).
[63] ibid, 103–4.

A variant of the above proposal has been put forward by Matthias Schmidt and Piotr Bogdanowicz.[64] Rather than the term 'systemic infringement', they, relying on the terminology of the 'Reverse *Solange* proposal' by Armin von Bogdandy and his collaborators,[65] speak of a 'a systemic deficiency in the rule of law'. In their submission, such a deficiency has two components. There must be, first, 'a serious impact on the Member State's legal system, institutions, in particular whole or parts of branches of government and their functioning' and, secondly a '"spill-over effect" created by that impact … which leads to a serious impact on the entire legal order of the Union and provokes reactions by other Member States and Union institutions'.[66]

As in the thinking of Scheppele et al, the cause of the deficiency 'must be rooted in *an intentional act by the Member State's government or legislature*'.[67] In Schmidt and Bogdanowicz's thesis there are, however, also important differences from Scheppele et al. According to the former, what is decisive is the *seriousness* of the impact of a deficiency on a Member State and not necessarily the duration or recurrence of the behaviour. Secondly, and perhaps more importantly, the substantive yardstick for a breach of an obligation under Article 258 TFEU would be a narrower one: while in Scheppele's construction the reference point may be any core norm of the Treaties in its constitutional function, the focus of Schmidt and Bogdanowicz would rather be on 'the rule of law as a structural and enforceable element of the legal order in all Member States'.[68] To operationalise this notion, three categories of 'building blocks for the rule of law' are then provided.[69]

A third and, it seems, more cautious proposal aimed at using Article 258 TFEU more broadly than in the context of 'specific provisions' has been put forward by Christophe Hillion.[70] Arguing, in principle, in favour of direct justiciability of the values set out in Article 2 TEU,[71] Hillion nonetheless appears to require an elaboration of the content of those values before they can be relied upon directly in the context of an Article 258 TFEU infringement procedure. In his submission, such elaboration has already taken place in an incremental fashion in the context of both the Union's enlargement policy and the case law of the ECJ. This would seem to resemble the development of 'building blocks for the rule of law' in the thinking of Schmidt and Bogdanowicz. However, recourse to Article 2 TEU is clearly not embedded in the existence of either a 'systemic infringement' or a 'systemic deficiency in the rule of law' in a Member State. According to Hillion, the Commission should be able to rely on Article 2 TEU before an infringement becomes so severe as to qualify for the application of Article 7 TEU, either alone (depending on the 'intelligibility' of the value in question) or in conjunction with a more specific infringement.

[64] Schmidt and Bogdanowicz, above n 3, 1073–1100.
[65] A von Bogdandy et al, 'Reverse Solange – Protecting the essence of fundamental rights against EU Member States' (2012) 49 *CML Rev* 489.
[66] Schmidt and Bogdanowicz, above n 3, 1073, 1083.
[67] ibid, 1087.
[68] ibid, 1088.
[69] ibid, 1090–99.
[70] Hillion, above n 3, 66 et seq.
[71] ibid, 66.

III. ENFORCEMENT UNDER ARTICLE 258 TFEU: A REVIEW IN LIGHT OF ECJ CASE LAW

Having presented the principal proposals aimed at improving the enforcement of the value of the rule of law set out in Article 2 TEU through infringement proceedings, it is now appropriate to assess whether those proposals are also legally solid in the light of the case law of the ECJ, as, for instance, Dimitry Kochenov believes to be the case with the proposal put forward by Scheppele.[72] In that regard, it has already been pointed out by others that the content of Article 2 TEU remains substantively vague, rendering it difficult to establish a breach of a sufficiently precise obligation for the purpose of activating an infringement procedure on the sole basis of Article 2 TEU, unless the more precise content of those values is further articulated.[73] Examining the proposal by Scheppele et al, Olivier De Schutter has submitted that the establishment of a systemic infringement would require the Court to treat Article 2 TEU as justiciable, something which 'still faces formidable hurdles'.[74] The same would seem to be true of the proposal by Schmidt and Bogdanowicz based on the notion of the rule of law as a structural and enforceable element of the legal order. The thinking of Hillion even seems to rest on the assumption that further elaboration of Article 2 TEU is needed as a prerequisite for the application of Article 258 TFEU.

Space precludes revisiting those past discussions at any greater length. The following remarks are none the less called for. First, the Court's case law on 'general and persistent infringements' – based on the case law springing from the judgment in the so-called *Irish Waste* case[75] and relied upon by Scheppele as supporting the idea of a systemic infringement action to enforce the rule of law – provides no assistance in turning Article 2 TEU into an independent source of obligations enforceable under Article 258 TFEU. That case law merely tells us that the Commission may seek from the Court a declaration not only that a Member State has failed to fulfil its obligations under a directive (or other source of EU law) in some specifically identified situations but also that it has failed more generally, on account of general and persistent deficiencies which characterise the application of *that directive* (or that same other source of law). Thus, it lends no support for the position that 'bundling' infringements of specific rules of law could result in one systemic infringement of some *other*, more general obligation of EU law based on, for instance,

[72] Kochenov, above n 54, 19.

[73] Editorial Comments, 'Safeguarding EU Values in the Member States – Is Something Finally Happening?' (2015) 52 *CML Rev* 619, 625. See also K Tuori, 'From Copenhagen to Venice' in Closa and Kochenov, above n 3, 225, 243; M Avbelj, 'Pluralism and Systemic Defience in the EU' in Jakab and Kochenov, above n 5, 44, 55–56; Gormley, above n 5, 76–78; and O Mader, 'Enforcement of EU Values as a Political Endeavour: Constitutional Pluralism and Value Homogeneity in Times of Persistent Challenges to the Rule of Law' (2019) 11 *The Hague Journal of the Rule of Law* 133, 159.

[74] O De Schutter, *Infringement Proceedings as a Tool for the Enforcement of Fundamental Rights in the European Union* (Open Society European Policy Institute, October 2017), 30. See also Gormley, above n 5, 76–78, and Blauberger and Keleman, above n 3, 330–31.

[75] Case C-494/01 *Commission v Ireland* ECLI:EU:C:2005:250. See P Wennerås, 'A New Dawn for Commission Enforcement Under Articles 226 and 228 EC: General and Persistent (GAP) Infringements, Lump Sums and Penalty Payments' (2006) 43 *CML Rev* 31.

Article 2 TEU, alone or in conjunction with other general provisions or principles of EU law.[76] Secondly, the significance of the *intentions* of a Member State government in committing an infringement, as suggested by the both Scheppele and Schmidt and Bogdanowicz, sits oddly with the well-established principle that the procedure governed by Article 258 TFEU is aimed at an objective assessment of the consistency of the conduct of a Member State with EU law. In other words, the reasons which prompted a certain action are usually immaterial to the establishment of an infringement.[77] Finally, the challenges resulting from the ambiguity of Article 2 TEU are arguably even greater in the context of Article 258 TFEU than in the context of a reference for a preliminary ruling. In the former case, the Court is not only required to interpret Union law but also to establish whether a given conduct of a Member State amounts to an infringement thereof.[78]

The past reactions notwithstanding, the proposals by Scheppele and others would, however, still seem to merit yet another round of legal assessment. The recent restatement of Scheppele's thesis namely rests on a conviction that the more recent case law of the ECJ following the judgment in *Associação Sindical dos Juízes Portugueses*,[79] including the recent infringement actions against Poland, has somehow fundamentally changed the legal parameters concerning the enforceability of Article 2 TEU, including in the context of Article 258 TFEU. As Scheppele et al submit,

> the ECJ's decisions are now showing how the values of Article 2 can receive concrete expression through provisions like Article 19(1) TEU. The Court now recognizes that the values of Article 2 TEU are legal and not just political requirements because they make the EU what it is, and sooner or later, the Court's insistence on the legal importance of EU values will push the Commission to fill this gap by bringing the infringement actions that the Court has clearly indicated it is ready to hear.[80]

It is therefore still appropriate to review whether such an assessment can be defended. The question concerning the enforcement of matters falling under Article 19 TEU having already largely been settled by the case law relating to judicial independence in Poland, it is appropriate to focus upon the implications of the Court's more recent case law on the rule-of-law obligations *other than those based on Article 19 TEU* being enforced under Article 258 TFEU, directly or indirectly based on Article 2 TEU.

In the submission of the present author, the actions concerning judicial independence in Poland provide no authority for the possibility of the rule of law or the other values mentioned in Article 2 TEU being enforced under Article 258 TFEU, either based on Article 2 alone or in conjunction of provisions such as Article 4(3) TEU.

[76] Scheppele herself has admitted that 'the use I propose is different from the uses we have seen thus far [in the case law]'. See Scheppele, above n 6, 114.

[77] eg, L Prete, 'Enforcement Actions' in R Schütze and T Tridimas (eds), *Oxford Principles of European Union Law: The European Union Legal Order: Volume I* (Oxford, Oxford University Press, 2018) 942, 944.

[78] On the difference between those tasks, see, eg Case C-204/21 R *Commission v Poland* ECLI:EU:C:2021:593, 105.

[79] Above n 27.

[80] Schepple, Kochenov and Grabowska-Moroz, above n 6, at 63. See also Pech and Kochenov, above n 6, 153 et seq and Schmidt and Bogdanowicz, above n 3, 1093.

That is already evident from the fact that in none of those cases did the Commission plead an infringement of those provisions and, accordingly, the Court could not have ruled on the issue without ruling *ultra petita*. As in *Associação Sindical dos Juízes Portugueses*, the reference to Article 2 TEU only served the Court's reasoning as 'a supportive argument',[81] and the same is also true with Article 47 of the Charter in matters falling outside the scope of application of the Charter as defined in Article 51(1) thereof. While Article 2 TEU is certainly part of the legal order of the Union,[82] the Court, referring to its own previous case law,[83] appears to draw a distinction between, on the one hand, the values that are 'recognised' and, on the other, 'a requirement to ensure respect of the EU law that implements those values'.[84] One such provision, deemed to implement those values, is arguably Article 19 TEU, which, as the Court has said, 'gives concrete expression to the value of the rule of law affirmed in Article 2 TEU'.[85] The above understanding of the relationship between Article 2 TEU and the provisions of EU law giving concrete expression to the value of the rule of law does not seem to have been altered by the principle of 'non-regression', laid down by the judgment in *Repubblika*,[86] to which the Court referred in Case C-791/19, *Commission v Poland* on the Disciplinary Chamber of the Supreme Court.[87] While the 'non-regression' principle may potentially open up further possibilities for the enforcement of Article 2 TEU,[88] the more specific content of that principle in the present context would still seem to require further refinement by case law. Nor should the judgments on the actions brought by Hungary[89] and Poland[90] seeking to challenge the legality of Regulation (EU, Euratom) 2020/2092 ('the Conditionality Regulation')[91] be regarded as providing authority for a suggestion that Article 2 TEU gives rise to obligations capable of being directly enforced under Article 258 TFEU. In those judgments, the Court only examined the legality, in the light of the Treaty, of the horizontal conditionality mechanism linked to Member States' respect for the value of the rule of law, set out by the regulation concerned – no

[81] Schmidt and Bogdanowicz, above n 3, 1081. But see LD Spieker, 'Breathing Life into the Union's Common Values: On the Judicial Application of Article 2 TEU in the EU Value Crisis' (2019) 20 *German Law Journal* 1182.

[82] See Case C-619/18 R *Commission v Poland*, above n 38, 68, referring to the 'serious damage to the *EU legal order and thus* to the rights which individuals derive from EU law and *to the values, set out in Article 2 TEU*, on which the European Union is founded, in particular the rule of law' (emphasis added). See also Case C-791/19 R, *Commission v Poland*, above n 41, para 92, and Case C-204/21 R *Commission v Poland*, above n 46, paras 124, 179, 207, 242.

[83] C-64/16, *Associação Sindical dos Juízes Portugueses*, above n 27, para 30 and C-216/18 PPU *Minister for Justice and Equality (Deficiencies in the system of justice)* ECLI:EU:C:2018:586, 35.

[84] eg, Case C-619/18 R *Commission v Poland*, above n 38, 43.

[85] ibid, 47. Cf, however, art 6(1) TEU providing that '[t]he Union *recognises* the rights, freedoms and principles set out in the [Charter], which shall have the same legal value as the Treaties' (emphasis added).

[86] Case C-896/19 *Repubblika v Il-Prim Ministru* ECLI:EU:C:2021:311, 63–65.

[87] Above n 7, 51.

[88] Cf Pech and Kochenov, above n 6, arguing that '[the principle of] could be very effective in allowing for a move beyond judicial independence to help countering rule of law and democracy backsliding in EU Member States through legal means' (at 154).

[89] Case C-156/21 *Commission v Hungary* ECLI:EU:C:2022:97.

[90] Case C-157/21 *Commission v Poland* ECLI:EU:C:2022:98.

[91] Above n 10.

more, no less. Indeed, the Court draws attention to the fact that numerous provisions of the Treaties (other than Article 2 TEU), including Article 19 TEU, grant the institutions the power to determine the existence of breaches of the values laid down in Article 2 committed in a Member State.[92] Arguably, it follows that no such determination may take place directly based on Article 2.

In conclusion, the more recent case law lends no additional support to any of the suggestions aimed at judicial enforcement of Article 2 TEU reviewed in the present chapter, be it directly or through the construct of a systemic infringement (Scheppele) or a systemic deficiency (Schmidt and Bogdanowicz). A provision giving 'concrete expression' to those values would be needed. This also seems to be the position put forward by Pekka Pohjankoski, who regards the rule of law as a set of 'structural obligations' of EU law.[93] In his submission, such structural obligations must be understood to 'inhere in'[94] specific EU rules and to bind the Member States even when they are not, strictly speaking, implementing EU law. Pohjankoski then puts forward an illuminating set of examples of such specific primary and secondary law obligations, covering (apart from judicial independence under Article 19 TEU) matters such as autonomy of national central banks, independence of national regulatory agencies and even the organisation of elections. In comparison to the proposals based on the idea a systemic infringement or deficiency, the suggestion by Pohjankoski is more closely linked to specific obligations of EU law and, in that sense, more firmly embedded in the traditional way of applying Article 258 TFEU.

If the judgments in infringement actions against Poland concerning judicial independence hardly add much to the potential of Article 2 TEU in terms of its enforcement, one further observation is nonetheless called for. In the case concerning the lowering of the retirement age of Polish Supreme Court judges the ECJ refers to the fact that such a major restructuring of the composition of a Supreme Court, through a reform specifically concerning that court, may itself prove to be such as to 'raise doubts as to the genuine nature of such a reform and as to the aims actually pursued by it'.[95] Here, the Court therefore seems to place some emphasis on the *intentions* of the government concerned, as suggested by both Scheppele and Schmidt and Bogdanowicz. In the proceedings concerning the Disciplinary Chamber of the Supreme Court, the Court also took account of the more general context in which that Chamber was created, referring to the creation of the Chamber, by the new Law on the Supreme Court, having taken place 'in the wider context of major reforms concerning the organisation of the judiciary in Poland'.[96] In so doing, the Court may have relied on the more general context in question for the purpose of establishing the objectives behind the creation of the Disciplinary Chamber.

[92] Eg, Case C-157/21 *Commission v Poland*, above n 90, paras 195–96. See also para 264.

[93] Pohjankoski, above n 5.

[94] ibid, 1346.

[95] Case C-619/19 *Commission v Poland*, above n 7, paras 82–86 (the quoted passage is at para 86).

[96] Case C-791/19 *Commission v Poland*, above n 7, para 88. See also Case C-791/19 R *Commission v Poland*, above n 41, para 95.

IV. CONCLUSION

There is no escape from the fact that the preceding analysis leads to a rather bleak conclusion on the potential of infringement proceedings as an instrument for enforcing the rule of law in Member States. Empirical evidence from the last 10 years reveals an essentially two-fold picture. On the one hand, in those cases deemed to have resulted in 'compliance' either before or after a judgment of the ECJ, the compliance has only followed once the governments of the Member States concerned have already accomplished (either wholly or to a significant extent) the aims of the measures contested by the Commission. This has been the case even with those cases hailed as examples of a successful employment of the infringement procedure, such as the two actions concerning the restructuring of the judiciary in Poland. On the other hand, the cases in which no compliance has been forthcoming even after a judgment of the ECJ have resulted in political disputes at the highest level, enabling the governments concerned to engage not only in 'blame games' with 'Brussels' but also in constitutional battles of the most fundamental kind, involving the authority of the ECJ being profoundly questioned by those governments. While the most illustrative example of such a development is no doubt provided by the two actions revolving around the disciplinary mechanisms created within the Polish judiciary, the same would also seem to apply to the actions against Hungary concerning, respectively, transparency of foreign-funded civil society organisations and the 'Stop Soros law'. Indeed, and regrettably so, the practice seems to know of no case having ended up before the Court that could be cited as an exemplary use of the infringement procedure in the present context. Having reached the judicial stage, the procedures have ended either in symbolic or delayed compliance, or in a political disagreement of the most profound kind between the Commission and the government concerned. Moreover, there is still no evidence of the effectiveness of eventual financial sanctions based on either Article 260 or Article 279 TFEU in so far as concerns rule-of-law matters. For a determined autocrat, a penalty of €1 million a day might not be too high a price to pay for an opportunity to blame the sinister technocrats of 'Brussels'.

It would be easy simply to blame the Commission for the ineffectiveness of Article 258 TFEU in the present context. In the opinion of the present author, that line of thinking is only partly justified. True, the Commission has often been slow in its employment of Article 258 TFEU, and there may certainly be room for improvement in that regard. The administrative stage of the procedure can be reduced to a few weeks where necessary, and the case law of the Court provides an almost open invitation to the Commission to request the use of the expedited procedure or the granting of interim measures. It is equally true that the Commission apparently lacks a coherent self-understanding of its policy on the enforcement of the rule of law and it has certainly focused its efforts solely on policing infringements of (some) 'specific provisions' of EU law. To some extent, the Commission's way of proceeding is, however, entirely natural and justifiable given that, in the current state of Union law, the Treaties lack a legal basis that is sufficiently general to capture a broader set of malpractices posing a threat to the rule of law in Member States and, at the same time, sufficiently precise to fulfil the Member States' legitimate expectations for legal certainty required under the settled case law on Article 258 TFEU. As illustrated once again by the present chapter, scholars have taken pains to identify such a legal foundation for enforcement but, regrettably, to little or no avail. Until such a foundation is created, the Commission is, in principle, justified in its current conception of obligations capable of being enforced under Article 258 TFEU and, this being the case, infringement proceedings are not likely to change much in the rule-of-law situation of any Member State.

In this author's submission, however, one should not pursue the path of seeking to turn the bare reference to the rule of law in Article 2 TEU into a magician's hat capable of suddenly curing the current impotence of Article 258 TFEU to address rule-of-law problems in Member States. While it may well be, as President Lenaerts, writing extra-judicially, has put it, 'for the Court of Justice to determine – in the fields covered by EU law – the meaning and scope of the principle of judicial independence',[97] things could easily turn much more controversial in many other areas of the rule of law. If there is one thing upon which there is agreement in the voluminous literature on the rule of law, it is surely the open-endedness of the notion.[98] Should the Court of Justice attempt to adjudicate under Article 258 TFEU solely based on that notion without a sufficient further refinement thereof by the institutions and the Member States, it would easily risk being exposed to criticism for adjudicating out of some utopian ideals that only reflect the subjective (political) preferences of the Court. True, in other areas the Court has successfully withstood such accusations many times in the past. However, would it not be somewhat ironic should the Court wish to go down that path in the name of the rule of law, the essential elements of which have traditionally included clarity and prospectivity of the norms that govern a society?[99] Such a strategy might have serious implications not only for the legitimacy of the judgments thus constructed but also for the authority of the Court more generally,[100] with no automatic guarantee of compliance by the recalcitrant Member States. It would also involve the abandonment of the well-established principles of the case law on what may constitute an infringement under Article 258 TFEU and on what kind of evidence should be required for the establishment of the infringement.

Further elaboration, by the Union's institutions and the Member States, of both the structural obligations on the rule of law, as well as their content in the context of EU law is therefore still required for more effective enforcement of the rule of law under Article 258 TFEU. Insofar as the EU institutions are concerned, one paradigm for such elaboration is provided by the Conditionality Regulation.[101] The Regulation sets out, for the sole purposes of the application of the Regulation, a definition of the concept of 'the rule of law' (Article 2(a)), an indicative list of breaches

[97] K Lenaerts, 'New Horizons for the Rule of Law Within the EU' (2020) 21 *German Law Journal* 29, 32.

[98] For a useful overview, see J Waldron, *The Rule of Law, Stanford Encyclopedia of Philosophy* (Online, 2016). One would therefore be ill-advised to subscribe to the belief of Schmidt and Bogdanowicz, above n 3, that '[i]t has been settled for the time being which principles can be found in the [ECJ's] jurisprudence that are related to the rule of law. Their use in concrete cases is a question of reasoned application for the practitioner' (at 1090).

[99] cf Mader, above n 73, 153.

[100] Cf Blauberger and Keleman, above n 3, 322, 325 and 331.

[101] Above n 10.

thereof (Article 3) as well as examples of breaches of the principles it encompasses (Article 4(2)). As noted by Advocate General Campos Sánchez-Bordona, the definition in Article 2(a) of the Regulation 'takes the concept in Article 2 TEU and develops it further by specifying the seven principles included by the legislature'.[102] Following such refinement, 'Member States are sufficiently aware of the obligations deriving from those principles'.[103] The Regulation therefore shows how the Union legislature may seek to define the parameters of the broad notion of the rule of law in Article 2 TEU more precisely for the purposes of a specific area of Union law and – that instrument having now successfully undergone legal scrutiny by the Court – there is no reason why a similar approach could not be followed in other contexts of the rule of law. Insofar as concerns further elaboration of the notion of the rule of law by the Member States, one paradigm could be provided by the Court's case law on the development of fundamental rights as general principles of Union law. In that context, it has been acknowledged long ago that international treaties 'on which the Member States have collaborated or of which they are signatories'[104] can also supply guidelines which should be followed within the framework of Union law. While an assessment of the potential of a similar strategy in matters concerning the rule of law would obviously require a detailed study in another context, there have already been indications in the Court's case law of the possibility of giving more concrete content to the rule of law through this approach.[105] Through such work of the institutions and the Member States aimed at a further articulation of the notion we may perhaps one day witness a constitutional law corpus of the idea rule of law in the European Union – a body of law capable of qualifying as an independent source of obligations that may be enforced under Article 258 TFEU. However, as hopefully demonstrated by this chapter, we are not there yet.

[102] Opinion of Campos Sánchez-Bordona AG in Case C-156/21 *Hungary v Parliament and Council* ECLI:EU:C:2021:974, para 277.

[103] ibid, 278. Cf Case C-157/21, *Poland v Commission*, above n 90, 289–91.

[104] Case 4/73 *J Nold Kohlen- und Baustoffgroßhandlung v Commission of the European Communities* ECLI:EU:C:1974:51, 13.

[105] See Opinion of Tanchev AG in Case C-192/18 *Commission v Poland* ECLI:EU:C:2019:529, 104.

11

Of Carrots and Sticks: Constitutional Limits to Rule-of-Law Conditionality

PEKKA POHJANKOSKI

I. INTRODUCTION

THE BASIC IDEA of 'rule-of-law conditionality' is easy to grasp: to benefit from European Union (EU) money, a Member State must respect the principles of the rule of law. However, making the receipt of EU funds contingent on the respect for such principles raises delicate issues. To what extent does the EU have the power to require Member States to provide systemic rule-of-law guarantees? The legal basis for financial conditionality in the EU Treaties resides primarily in the Union's budget power. Nonetheless, when such conditionality targets the 'rule of law', it has the potential to shape national constitutional systems. Additionally: what limits, if any, exist to the EU's power to condition the receipt of funds upon compliance with the rule of law? Relatedly, how should the withholding of funds from Member States be characterised: is it simple budget technique, enforcement of EU law, or a punitive sanction?[1]

Unlike mechanical budget corrections, the rule-of-law conditionality regime under the 'Conditionality Regulation'[2] is of a general nature. This instrument has so far received little sustained scholarly attention from a constitutional perspective.[3] There are multiple in-depth studies on how EU law employs conditionality as a regulatory tool.[4] Similarly, the Conditionality Regulation has been amply analysed as regards

[1] 'Withholding' EU money is used in this chapter as shorthand for the various measures to execute conditionality including, for example, suspensions, interruptions, reductions or prohibitions regarding transfers from the EU budget to Member States. On the specific measures, see eg art 5 of Regulation (EU, Euratom) 2020/2092 of the European Parliament and of the Council of 16 December 2020 on a general regime of conditionality for the protection of the Union budget [2020] OJ L433I/1.

[2] Regulation 2020/2092, above n 1.

[3] On the EU as a constitutional system, see eg K Tuori, 'European Constitutionalism' in R Masterman and R Schütze, *The Cambridge Companion to Comparative Constitutional Law* (Cambridge, Cambridge University Press, 2019). On the Commission's constitutional powers of implementation and enforcement, see S Andersen, *The enforcement of EU law: the role of the European Commission* (Oxford, Oxford University Press, 2013) 163 ff.

[4] R Bieber and F Maiani, 'Enhancing centralized enforcement of EU law: Pandora's Toolbox?' (2014) 51(4) *CML Rev* 1057; V Viţă, 'Revisiting the Dominant Discourse on Conditionality in the EU: The Case of EU Spending Conditionality' (2017) 19 *Cambridge Yearbook of European Legal Studies* 116.

both its drafting history and its substantive content.[5] Its constitutional ramifications, by contrast, have received attention mostly during the legislative process. The Regulation's legal basis, its potentially punitive nature, and the jurisdiction of the European Court of Justice (ECJ) over the instrument have been debated in the context of Hungary and Poland's judicial challenges to its validity.[6]

To assess the constitutional propriety of rule-of-law conditionality, this chapter adopts the following structure. It enquires, first, what 'rule-of-law conditionality' means in EU law and outlines the many guises under which EU money can be withheld from Member States. Second, it assesses whether such conditionality is a carrot or a stick; in other words, an incentive to promote the rule of law or a punitive sanctioning mechanism. Third, the criterion of a 'sufficiently direct' link between alleged rule-of-law breaches and the EU's money is assessed. This link is arguably a key concept for guaranteeing the appropriate implementation of the Conditionality Regulation. The concluding section recaps the findings and reflects on the utility of general rule-of-law conditionality.

II. THE MANY SHADES OF RULE-OF-LAW CONDITIONALITY

Rule-of-law conditionality permeates both the Union's internal organisation and its external action. Applicants for EU membership must meet the 'Copenhagen criteria' which refer, among other requirements, to the 'stability of institutions guaranteeing … the rule of law'.[7] The EU's enlargement and neighbourhood policies, as well as pre-accession assistance to prospective members, similarly require respect for the rule of law.[8] The EU's trade and partnership agreements with third states and international organisations contain specific clauses, according to which a failure of the other party to uphold the rule of law authorises the EU to adopt countermeasures under international law, including the withdrawal of benefits under the agreement.[9]

[5] See eg J Łacny, 'The Rule of Law Conditionality Under Regulation No 2092/2020 – Is it all About the Money?' (2021) 13 *Hague Journal on the Rule of Law* 79; T Tridimas, 'Editorial Note: Recovery Plan and Rule of Law Conditionality: A New Era Beckons?' (2020) 16 *Croatian Yearbook of European Law and Policy* vii.

[6] See Cases C-156/21 *Hungary v Parliament and Council* ECLI:EU:C:2022:97, and C-157/21 *Poland v Parliament and Council* ECLI:EU:C:2022:98.

[7] See European Council in Copenhagen 21–22 June 1993, Conclusions of the Presidency, 13. See also 'Declaration on democracy', Annex D to European Council in Copenhagen 7–8 April 1978, Conclusions of the Presidency, 12–13 (holding that safeguarding the rule of law implies 'a political system of pluralist democracy which guarantees both the free expression of opinions within the constitutional organization of powers and the procedures necessary for the protection of human rights').

[8] See eg Regulation (EU) 2021/947 of the European Parliament and of the Council of 9 June 2021 establishing the Neighbourhood, Development and International Cooperation Instrument – Global Europe, amending and repealing Decision No 466/2014/EU and repealing Regulation (EU) 2017/1601 and Council Regulation (EC, Euratom) No 480/2009 [2021] OJ L209/1, Recital 40; and Regulation (EU) 2021/1529 of the European Parliament and of the Council of 15 September 2021 establishing the Instrument for Pre-Accession assistance (IPA III) [2021] OJ L330/1, Recital 40. See also eg M Cremona, 'EU Enlargement: Solidarity and Conditionality' (2005) 30(1) *ELR* 3, and M Kmezić, *EU Rule of Law Promotion: Judiciary Reform in the Western Balkans* (New York and London, Routledge, 2017) 14–16.

[9] See eg Partnership agreement between the members of the African, Caribbean and Pacific Group of States of the one part, and the European Community and its Member States, of the other part, signed in Cotonou on 23 June 2000 [2000] OJ L317/3, arts 9 and 96(2).

Rule-of-law conditionality also manifests itself within the broader system of the Agreement on the European Economic Area (EEA).[10]

Inside the EU, the most recent Accession Treaties contain safeguard clauses enabling enhanced supervision of the rule of law in the Member States concerned and, if necessary, the suspension of membership benefits.[11] Though not explicitly about the 'rule of law', these clauses allow the Commission to take 'appropriate measures', including the suspension of treaty benefits, against a Member State defaulting on its treaty obligations. In particular, a specific rule-of-law monitoring regime, known as the Cooperation and Verification Mechanism (CVM), exists for Bulgaria and Romania.[12] The ECJ has held not only that failures to comply with the requirements of the CVM allow the Commission to act against the Member State, but also that the conditionality benchmarks in the CVM can be invoked directly by litigants before national courts against domestic laws, or even constitutional provisions, which conflict with those benchmarks.[13]

The legislative acts regarding rule-of-law conditionality are intrinsically connected to the EU budget.[14] The European Structural and Investment (ESI) Funds are governed by horizontal rules which require respect for the rule of law.[15] Among such rules features the Conditionality Regulation, which targets 'breaches of the principles of the rule of law in a Member State' that have an impact on the EU budget.[16] This conditionality is general in that it evaluates the use of all EU money against compliance with the rule of law.[17] In addition to the EU's seven-year Multiannual Financial Framework (MFF), such rule-of-law conditionality also attaches to the Covid-19

[10] The EEA/EFTA Member States Norway, Iceland, and Liechtenstein have suspended, in 2021, financial grants to Poland on grounds of its alleged rule-of-law violations. See eg R Savage, 'Norway, Iceland, Lichtenstein cancel grant to Polish "LGBT-free zone"', *Reuters* (2 February 2021), www.reuters.com/article/us-poland-lgbt-norway-trfn-idUSKBN2A22MD. See also art 1 of Protocol 38C on the EEA Financial Mechanism (2014–2021) annexed to Agreement between the EU, Iceland, Liechtenstein and Norway on an EEA Financial Mechanism 2014–2021 [2016] OJ L141/3) ('All programmes and activities funded … shall be based on the common values of … the rule of law …'). See similarly, art 2 of Agreement between Norway and the European Union on a Norwegian Financial Mechanism for the period 2014–2021 [2016] OJ L141/11.

[11] See art 4(3) of the Treaty concerning the accession of the Republic of Bulgaria and Romania to the European Union and arts 37 and 38 of the accompanying Protocol [2005] OJ L157. See also arts 38 and 39 of the Treaty of Accession of Croatia and the accompanying Act [2012] OJ L112.

[12] On the Cooperation and Verification Mechanism, see Decisions 2006/928/EC [2006] OJ L354/56, and 2006/929/EC [2006] OJ L354/58.

[13] See Joined Cases C-83/19, C-127/19, C-195/19, C-291/19, C-355/19 and C-397/19 *Asociaţia 'Forumul Judecătorilor din România' and others v Inspecţia Judiciară and others* ECLI:EU:C:2021:393, paras 249–51.

[14] For an overview of the legislation, see M Fisicaro, 'Beyond the Rule of Law Conditionality: Exploiting the EU Spending Power to Foster the Union's Values' (2022) 7(2) *European Papers* 697.

[15] See Recital 7 of Regulation (EU) 2021/1060 of the European Parliament and of the Council of 24 June 2021 laying down common provisions on the European Regional Development Fund, the European Social Fund Plus, the Cohesion Fund, the Just Transition Fund and the European Maritime, Fisheries and Aquaculture Fund and financial rules for those and for the Asylum, Migration and Integration Fund, the Internal Security Fund and the Instrument for Financial Support for Border Management and Visa Policy [2021] OJ L231/159 ('Horizontal financial rules adopted … on the basis of Article 322 TFEU apply to this Regulation … includ[ing] a general regime of conditionality for the protection of the Union budget.').

[16] Art 4(1) of Reg 2020/2092, above n 1.

[17] Recital 7 of Reg 2020/2092, above n 1. See also Recital 71 of Regulation (EU) 2021/241 of the European Parliament and of the Council of 12 February 2021 establishing the Recovery and Resilience Facility [2021] OJ L57/17 ('Horizontal financial rules adopted … on the basis of Article 322 TFEU apply to this Regulation … includ[ing] a general regime of conditionality for the protection of the Union budget.').

stimulus money disbursed through the European Union Recovery Instrument, known as 'Next Generation EU' (NGEU).[18] The withdrawal of EU funds from Hungary under the Conditionality Regulation in December 2022 constitutes the first implementation of general rule-of-law conditionality.[19]

Moreover, the Horizontal Regulation for the Common Agricultural Policy (CAP) and the ESI Funds Common Provisions Regulation establish conditions for the use of EU money.[20] The use of EU money must comply with applicable law, subject to financial corrections.[21] Not as structurally far-reaching as 'general rule-of-law conditionality', these more circumscribed conditions can be referred to as 'applicable law conditionality' and must be observed in implementing the funds. National authorities must nonetheless also observe more abstract legal rules, such as the Charter of Fundamental Rights of the European Union (the Charter), when they adopt regulations for the use of funds.[22] A Member State's failure to comply with applicable EU law can lead to forfeiture of the funds.[23]

However, the dividing line between general rule-of-law conditionality and applicable law conditionality can sometimes be fine. For example, the ESI Funds Common Provisions Regulation contains 'horizontal principles', which include respect for fundamental rights, equality between men and women, gender mainstreaming and

[18] See, respectively, Council Regulation (EU, Euratom) 2020/2093 of 17 December 2020 laying down the multiannual financial framework for the years 2021 to 2027 [2020] OJ L433I/11, and Council Regulation (EU) 2020/2094 of 14 December 2020 establishing a European Union Recovery Instrument to support the recovery in the aftermath of the COVID-19 crisis [2020] OJ L433I/23.

[19] See Council Implementing Decision (EU) 2022/2506 of 15 December 2022 on measures for the protection of the Union budget against breaches of the principles of the rule of law in Hungary [2022] OJ L325/94.

[20] See, respectively, art 54(5)(c) Regulation (EU) No 1306/2013 of the European Parliament and of the Council of 17 December 2013 on the financing, management and monitoring of the common agricultural policy and repealing Council Regulations (EEC) No 352/78, (EC) No 165/94, (EC) No 2799/98, (EC) No 814/2000, (EC) No 1290/2005 and (EC) No 485/2008 [2013] OJ L347/549 (on irregularities attributable to Member State authorities), and art 104 of Reg 2021/1060, above n 15 (financial corrections in case of Member State non-compliance).

[21] See eg art 74 of Reg 2021/1060, above n 15 ('managing authority shall … verify … that the operation complies with applicable law'). See also art 6 of Regulation (EU) No 1303/2013 of the European Parliament and of the Council of 17 December 2013 laying down common provisions on the European Regional Development Fund, the European Social Fund, the Cohesion Fund, the European Agricultural Fund for Rural Development and the European Maritime and Fisheries Fund and laying down general provisions on the European Regional Development Fund, the European Social Fund, the Cohesion Fund and the European Maritime and Fisheries Fund and repealing Council Regulation (EC) No 1083/2006 [2013] OJ L347/320 (requiring that '[o]perations supported by the ESI Funds shall comply with applicable Union law and the national law relating to its application'). This Regulation remains in force in respect of funds distributed during the previous budget cycle.

[22] See Case C-562/12, *Liivimaa Lihaveis*, ECLI:EU:C:2014:2229, para 65 (holding the Charter applicable to adoption of programme rules), and Case C-401/11, *Soukupová*, ECLI:EU:C:2013:223, paras 27–28 (holding that the definition of retirement age for purposes of early retirement support from EU funds must respect Charter). See also Commission Notice 'Guidance on ensuring the respect for the Charter of Fundamental Rights of the European Union when implementing the European Structural and Investment Funds ("ESI Funds")' [2016] OJ C269/1, 3.

[23] See esp arts 96, 97 and 104 of Reg 2021/1060, above n 15, as well as arts 142 to 147 of Reg 1303/2013, above n 21. Cf. V Viţă, 'Revisiting the Dominant Discourse on Conditionality in the EU: The Case of EU Spending Conditionality' (2017) 19 *Cambridge Yearbook of European Legal Studies* 116, 140–42 (analysing difficulties related to enforcement of conditionality against Member States and observing its increased use against private beneficiaries).

the integration of a gender perspective, prevention of discrimination, accessibility for persons with disabilities, and sustainable development.[24] Eligibility for funds is conditional on compliance with these requirements which are 'different and additional to [those] directly established by the [EU] fund from which the payment is made'.[25] Moreover, the Regulation foresees, as grounds for enforcing conditionality, not only 'irregularit[ies]', that is, 'any breach of applicable law', but also 'systemic irregularit[ies]' which are defined as

> any irregularity, which may be of a recurring nature, with a high probability of occurrence in similar types of operations, which results from a serious deficiency, including a failure to establish appropriate procedures in accordance with this Regulation and the Fund-specific rules.[26]

Another example of how rule-of-law conditionality manifests itself is provided by the individual grant programmes which may require compliance with fundamental rights, with concurrent implications for the rule of law. The Commission rejected 'town twinning' grants for certain Polish cities under the 'Europe for Citizens programme 2014–2020', which required non-discrimination on grounds of sexual orientation, after these cities had branded themselves as 'LGBT-free' zones.[27] Though based on a failure to meet specific funding terms, the Commission's decision to cut the funding to Polish cities was perceived as part of the EU's broader rule of law agenda.[28] The Commission has later commenced infringement proceedings against Poland regarding this matter and frozen additional EU funding to Polish regions.[29]

Finally, the administration of the EU's pandemic recovery fund incidentally implies very significant rule of law conditionality. By virtue of the rules on the Recovery and Resilience Facility (RRF), the grants and loans under the NGEU can only be disbursed pursuant to the Commission's proposal for a Council implementing decision, adopted on the basis of each country's national Recovery and Resilience Plan (RRP).[30] The RRPs must provide 'an explanation of how [the plan] contributes to effectively address … challenges identified in the relevant country-specific

[24] See art 9 of Reg 2021/1060, above n 15.

[25] See Opinion of AG Campos Sanchez-Bordona in Case C-156/21 *Hungary v Parliament and Council* ECLI:EU:C:2021:974, paras 108–9.

[26] See esp art 2(31) and (33) of Reg 2021/1060, above n 15.

[27] See Council Regulation (EU) No 390/2014 of 14 April 2014 establishing the 'Europe for Citizens' programme for the period 2014–2020 [2014] OJ L115/3, art 11 (requiring Commission to ensure 'coherence and the complementarity' with instruments combating discrimination). See also 'Europe For Citizens Programme Guide', eacea.ec.europa.eu/sites/eacea-site/files/COMM-2013-00367-00-00-EN-TRA-00.pdf, 6 (requiring accessibility 'without … discrimination on grounds of … sexual orientation').

[28] See eg M Pronczuk, 'Polish Towns That Declared Themselves 'L.G.B.T. Free' Are Denied E.U. Funds' *The New York Times* (30 July 2020), www.nytimes.com/2020/07/30/world/europe/LGBT-free-poland-EU-funds.html.

[29] See Press Release IP/21/3668, 'EU founding values: Commission starts legal action against Hungary and Poland for violations of fundamental rights of LGBTIQ people', 15 July 2021. See, on the freezing of 'REACT-EU programme amendments', a letter from the Commission to the marshals of five Polish voivodeships 'Responsibilities of the regional Managing Authorities to provide comprehensive answers to the letter of formal notice of 14 July 2021 and to undertake corrective measures', Ref Ares(2021)5444303, 3 September 2021.

[30] See Regulation (EU) 2021/241 of the European Parliament and of the Council of 12 February 2021 establishing the Recovery and Resilience Facility [2021] OJ L57/17, arts 18–20.

recommendations … in the context of the European Semester'.[31] In that context, the Council has recommended to Poland that it should strengthen judicial independence and noted, in the case of Hungary, that corruption remains a serious problem.[32] Based on these macroeconomic recommendations – which, incidentally, focus on the rule of law –, the Commission can wield yet another kind of rule-of-law conditionality in the administration of the Recovery and Resilience Facility. At the time of writing, no money from the NGEU has been released to Poland or Hungary.[33]

III. RULE-OF-LAW CONDITIONALITY: A CARROT OR A STICK?

Is general rule-of-law conditionality simply a carrot for Member States? Or is it, for all intents and purposes, akin to a punitive sanction? It is worth recalling that the EU Treaties do not contain an explicit authorisation for the Commission to condition payments from the budget upon compliance with EU law. By contrast, under the framework of the 1951 Treaty of Paris, the High Authority of the European Coal and Steel Community (ECSC) was empowered to 'suspend the payment of any sums which it may be liable to pay' to a state in breach of any of its obligations under the ECSC Treaty.[34] The High Authority could proceed in this way even without a determination of the breach by the Court of Justice of the ECSC, provided that the Council assented by a two-thirds majority. Although the present-day EU Treaties differ in many respects from the original treaties of the 1950s, the fact remains that no identical provision exists under the current treaty framework.[35]

Instead, Article 7 TEU establishes a process for addressing breaches of the EU's values referred to in Article 2 TEU, such as the rule of law – either pre-emptively in case of 'a clear risk of a serious breach' or after 'a serious and persistent breach'

[31] See art 19(2) and (3)(b) of Reg 2021/241, above n 30. See, on the European Semester, Regulation (EU) No 1175/2011 of the European Parliament and of the Council of 16 November 2011 amending Council Regulation (EC) No 1466/97 on the strengthening of the surveillance of budgetary positions and the surveillance and coordination of economic policies [2011] OJ 2011. See also art 18(4)(b) of Reg 2021/241, above n 30 [referring to 'recommendations made' pursuant to art 6 of Regulation (EU) No 1176/2011 of the European Parliament and of the Council of 16 November 2011 on the prevention and correction of macroeconomic imbalances [2011] OJ L306/25, or 'challenges identified in other relevant documents officially adopted by the Commission in the context of the European Semester'].

[32] See Council Recommendation of 20 July 2020 on the 2020 National Reform Programme of Poland and delivering a Council opinion on the 2020 Convergence Programme of Poland [2020] OJ C282/135, 141 (recommending that Poland 'enhance the investment climate, in particular by safeguarding judicial independence'), and Council Recommendation of 20 July 2020 on the 2020 National Reform Programme of Hungary and delivering a Council opinion on the 2020 Convergence Programme of Hungary [2020] OJ C282/107, 113 (observing that '[d]etermined systematic action to prosecute high-level corruption is lacking' and that '[s]trengthening judicial independence would also be crucial').

[33] See, on the Commission's proposal to move forward regarding Poland's RRP, P Pohjankoski, 'The rule of law takes the back seat: EU Commission greenlights "Next Generation EU" funds to Poland', *EU Law Live* (9 June 2022).

[34] See art 88(3) ECSC.

[35] The ECSC ceased to exist in 2002. The ECSC Treaty had been concluded for a period of 50 years after which it expired and its assets and liabilities were transferred to the then European Community. See Protocol no 37 on the financial consequences of the expiry of the ECSC Treaty and on the research fund for coal and steel annexed to the EU Treaties.

has occurred.[36] It enables the suspension of 'certain of the rights deriving from [membership]', including the right to receive EU money. Another way to de facto suspend the flow of money to rogue Member States is through the infringement procedure enshrined in Articles 258 to 260 TFEU. The procedure, which involves addressing individual breaches of EU law before the ECJ, covers all failures to fulfil EU obligations which undermine the rule of law, with only very narrow exceptions related to the ECJ's jurisdiction.[37] In case a Member State refuses to comply with financial penalties imposed in the Court's judgment, such penalties may be recovered, if necessary, by set-off against EU money due to the Member State concerned.[38]

Unlike these primary law mechanisms, financial rule-of-law conditionality is based on acts of the EU legislature. The legal bases for such acts include, in particular, Article 177 TFEU, which allows the Union to define the 'tasks, priority objectives and the organi[s]ation of the Structural Funds' as well as the 'general rules applicable to them and the provisions necessary to ensure their effectiveness and the coordination of the Funds with one another and with the other existing Financial Instruments'. Another key provision is Article 322(1) TFEU, which enables the enactment of 'financial rules' for determining 'the procedure to be adopted for establishing and implementing the budget and for presenting and auditing accounts', as well as 'rules' which provide for 'checks on the responsibility of financial actors, in particular authori[s]ing officers and accounting officers'. It follows that the aim of conditionality is to organise the EU's spending and to control that its money is used appropriately.

Conditionality comes in many forms. 'Simple' conditionality exists where, for example, funds granted to build a bridge over a river are forfeited if not used for that purpose. 'Cross-sectoral' conditionality, by contrast, means attaching to funds conditions which are unconnected to the funded activity, but instead linked to the achievement of a wholly different aim.[39] This incentivises and leverages compliance with rules in another regulatory sector. For example, funds meant to increase student mobility between Member States could hypothetically be made conditional upon compliance with particular EU rules on accessible digital environments for persons with disabilities; by granting the funds, the grantor achieves, ideally, not only student mobility, but also accessible digital environments. 'General' conditionality goes one step further: it requires across-the-board compliance with broad standards regarding, for example, macroeconomic indicators or the principles of the rule of law.[40]

[36] See, respectively, art 7(1) and (2) TEU. See also G Itzcovich, 'On the Legal Enforcement of Values. The Importance of the Institutional Context' in A Jakab and D Kochenov, *The Enforcement of EU Law and Values: Ensuring Member States' Compliance* (Oxford, Oxford University Press, 2017) 28–29 (noting that 'no direct enforcement of values should ever be acceptable' but arguing that art 2 TEU enumerates 'binding legal principles').

[37] The only substantive exclusion concerns the EU's foreign and security policy, see arts 24(1) TEU and 275 TFEU; art 126(10) TFEU excludes excessive budget deficits from its scope, but statutory procedures exist.

[38] On the set-off procedure, see P Pohjankoski, 'Rule of law with leverage: Policing structural obligations in EU law with the infringement procedure, fines, and set-off' (2021) 58(5) *CML Rev* 1341.

[39] See eg V Viță, 'Revisiting the Dominant Discourse on Conditionality in the EU: The Case of EU Spending Conditionality' (2017) 19 *Cambridge Yearbook of European Legal Studies* 116, 122–23 (distinguishing between 'same-sector, cross-cutting, cross-over and generic conditionality').

[40] ibid 123 (referring to requiring compliance with 'all applicable EU law and policy' as 'generic' conditionality).

The regulatory model which has inspired the EU's general rule-of-law conditionality regime is that of macroeconomic conditionality.[41] As such, the latter provides a useful comparator for conditionality measures in the field of the rule of law. Bieber and Maiani have cautioned against overly broad use of conditionality measures in the macroeconomic context, arguing that they questionably emphasise a certain subset of legal norms of 'dubious democratic legitimacy'. In their view, such measures target in reality only some Member States, which leads to diminished cohesion and legitimacy of the EU's action.[42] Can such asymmetries or legitimacy problems arise also in regard to rule-of-law conditionality?

To some extent, implementing rule-of-law conditionality shares similar challenges. At first sight, requiring compliance with principles of the rule of law in Member States may appear less controversial, since such principles can be seen as facially neutral. By contrast, different macroeconomic models based on austerity or solidarity, for example, are heavily charged politically. Nevertheless, even assuming universal acceptability of the principles of the rule of law (which may be a stretch in today's political climate in the EU), conditioning EU money upon their observance must, in any event, operate within the mandate provided by the legal basis used. If the legal basis is conceived too loosely, withholding EU funds may morph into a coercive tool to inflict punitive sanctions on Member States.

How is the line between a punitive sanction and a conditionality measure, especially a 'general' one, to be drawn? A comparative perspective illustrates the constitutional dimension of the enquiry. Under the United States (US) Constitution, the problem of constitutional limits to spending conditionality is well known. The issue has been extensively analysed by the Supreme Court of the United States (US Supreme Court) regarding the Spending Clause, which provides that '[t]he Congress shall have Power To lay and collect Taxes, Duties, Imposts and Excises, to pay the Debts and provide for the common Defence and general Welfare of the United States'.[43] Under this provision, the federal government may attach conditions to the States' receipt of federal funds, but its power is not unlimited. The conditions may constitute 'inducement', but must not be such that they become 'coercion'.[44]

The US Supreme Court has not definitively settled the question of where financial inducement becomes coercion.[45] Importantly, however, the federal government

[41] On the origins of macroeconomic conditionality in EU law, see eg J Łacny, 'The Rule of Law Conditionality Under Regulation No 2092/2020 – Is it all About the Money?' (2021) 13 *Hague Journal on the Rule of Law* 79, 82. On conditionality in the context of macroeconomic assistance to Member States in financial trouble, see Case C-370/12 *Pringle* ECLI:EU:C:2012:756, para 69. See also W Jacoby and J Hopkin 'From lever to club? Conditionality in the European Union during the financial crisis' (2020) 27(8) *Journal of European Public Policy* 1157.

[42] See R Bieber and F Maiani, 'Enhancing centralized enforcement of EU law: Pandora's Toolbox?' (2014) 51(4) *CML Rev* 1057, 1082.

[43] US Constitution Art I, §8, cl 1.

[44] See *Steward Machine Co v Davis* (1937) 301 US 548, 590 (referring to 'the point at which [financial] pressure turns into compulsion, and ceases to be inducement'); *South Dakota v Dole* (1987) 483 US 203, 211 (considering the prospect of losing 5% of highway grants as not amounting to 'coercion'); *National Federation of Independent Business v Sebelius* (2012) 567 US 519, 570 (describing the 'financial "inducement" … chosen' by Congress for States in the context of the Affordable Care Act as 'a gun to the head'). See also eg DB Thompson, '"Unmistakably Clear" Coercion: Finding a Balance Between Judicial Review of the Spending Power and Optimal Federalism' (2013) 50 *San Diego Law Review* 589.

[45] See *Steward Machine Co v Davis* (1937) 301 US 548, at 589–90 ('every rebate from a tax when conditioned upon conduct is in some measure a temptation.') Cf *National Federation of Independent Business*

may attach conditions to funds even when such conditions relate to activity which it would not have the power to regulate pursuant to its enumerated powers.[46] Thus cross-sectoral conditionality is possible. This is essentially based on the idea that conditionality is not a punitive sanction, but a transactional offer with conditions which can be freely accepted or rejected. Understood thus, the recipient of conditional spending is only encouraged to act in a certain way, but not actually forced to do so. While the line may be fluid, the starting point for analysis is clear: conditional spending is, as such, legitimate, and judges should not second-guess the States' motives for complying.[47]

In EU law, though the constitutional framework surrounding rule-of-law conditionality is different, the basic challenge is comparable. In the EU, Member States must, when using EU money, comply not only with the applicable law, but also with the broader 'principles of the rule of law'. Is withholding a benefit on these – looser – grounds tantamount to a punitive sanction? The discussion on the punitive nature of conditionality is not new in EU law either. Back in the 1970s, the Court held that the forfeiture of a deposit lodged to guarantee the obligation to export maize did not constitute a penal sanction, since the system of deposits was 'merely the guarantee that an undertaking voluntarily assumed will be carried out'.[48] Similarly, in the field of agricultural aids, the ECJ has rejected claims that the EU does not have the power to impose penalties on sheep traders guilty of irregularities, noting that exclusions from agricultural subsidies do not constitute penal sanctions.[49]

Importantly, the ECJ has held that 'the imposition of a penalty on a trader presupposes that he has just been granted a right'.[50] This implies that the Court leans towards a transactional understanding of conditionality, where the mere exclusion of a right is not equivalent to a punitive sanction. Instead, the Court has referred to such an exclusion as a 'specific administrative instrument forming an integral part of the scheme of aid and intended to ensure the sound financial management of the … public funds'.[51] For the Court, such penalties are not the key component of agricultural subsidies, but simply relate to their implementation as they 'are intended to underpin the options chosen by ensuring the proper financial management of the … funds designated for

v Sebelius (2012) 567 US 519, 574 ('The Court in *Steward Machine* did not attempt to "fix the outermost line" where persuasion gives way to coercion. … We have no need to fix a line either. It is enough for today that wherever that line may be, this statute is surely beyond it.').

[46] See *South Dakota v Dole* (1987) 483 US 203, 207 (holding that 'objectives not thought to be within Article I's "enumerated legislative fields" … may nevertheless be attained through the use of the spending power and the conditional grant of federal funds.').

[47] See *Steward Machine Co v Davis* (1937) 301 US 548, 589–90 (with Cardozo, J noting that 'to hold that … temptation is equivalent to coercion is to plunge the law in endless difficulties').

[48] Case 11/70 *Internationale Handelsgesellschaft mbH v Einfuhr- und Vorratsstelle für Getreide und Futtermittel* ECLI:EU:C:1970:114, para 18.

[49] Case C-240/90, *Federal Republic of Germany v Commission of the European Communities*, ECLI:EU:C:1992:408, para 25.

[50] ibid, para 26. See also Opinion of AG Jacobs in Case C-240/90, *Federal Republic of Germany v Commission of the European Communities*, ECLI:EU:C:1992:237, para 30 ('the producer's loss is in substance the loss of his right to retain the original benefit, which was paid in advance of his fulfilment of the conditions attached to the refund').

[51] Case C-240/90, *Federal Republic of Germany v Commission of the European Communities*, ECLI:EU:C:1992:408, para 26.

their attainment'.[52] In other words, they aim to combat irregularities in line with the objectives of the CAP.

Thus, in EU law, even far-reaching negative financial consequences appear acceptable, at least in the case of simpler forms of conditionality, on grounds of a legal basis which does not directly contemplate the imposition of penalties. This logic, applicable to individuals, can also easily apply to Member States. However, as regards *general* conditionality, it arguably requires that the EU's executive organs must not be granted a blank cheque to impose financial penalties on the Member States without clear benchmarks and limits. Rule-of-law conditionality is, of course, particularly commendable in that it relates to the fundamental preconditions of the EU legal order. Nevertheless, to guarantee that such conditionality does not constitute impermissible constitutional overreach into the Member States' retained powers, it is essential that a link between the alleged breaches of the rule of law and the EU's budget or its financial interests exists.

IV. STAYING WITHIN LIMITS: THE 'SUFFICIENTLY DIRECT' BREACH–MONEY LINK

The Conditionality Regulation's adoption in December 2020 was accompanied by a key limitation. As the European Council noted in its conclusions: 'The mere finding that a breach of the rule of law has taken place does not suffice to trigger the mechanism'.[53] A link to EU money was required. Accordingly, the adoption of measures pursuant to Article 4(1) of the Conditionality Regulation is contingent on the finding that the breaches 'affect or seriously risk affecting the sound financial management of the Union budget or the protection of the financial interests of the Union in a sufficiently direct way'. This can be referred to as the *breach–money link*. Under the Regulation, a 'sufficiently direct' link between the breaches of the rule of law, such as systemic failures in the judiciary or law enforcement, must exist to the EU's money interests which, at the very least, 'seriously risk affecting' them.

The 'sufficiently direct' breach–money link was not part of the Commission's original proposal. In fact, that proposal referred not to findings of 'breaches of the rule of law', but to a 'generalised deficiency as regards the rule of law' which 'affects or risks affecting' (without the qualifier 'seriously') the 'principles of sound financial management' (which were not specified as relating to 'the Union budget') and, above all, contained no mention that the EU's money interests must be jeopardised in a 'sufficiently direct way'.[54] Following the horse-trading between the representatives of Poland and Hungary and those of the rest of the Member States at the European Council meeting of July 2020, the final text agreed at the end of that year left considerably less latitude for the EU's executive to prosecute those rule-of-law

[52] ibid, para 37.

[53] European Council's Conclusions, 11 December 2020, EUCO 22/20, para I.2.e).

[54] See Proposal for a Regulation of the European Parliament and of the Council on the protection of the Union's budget in case of generalised deficiencies as regards the rule of law in the Member States, COM(2018) 324 final, 2 May 2018, p 8.

breaches which only have a tenuous link to the EU budget than the initially proposed legislation.[55]

The notion of a 'sufficiently direct link' was not conjured out of thin air. It has its pedigree in the EU Courts' case law concerning agriculture expenditure, regional aid, as well as other EU spending. Based on the goal of preventing Union funds from being used to finance Member State operations which are contrary to EU law, it has been consistently observed that conditionality measures do not constitute penalties but rather entail, by contrast, a 'financial correction'.[56] Such corrections to the budget operate strictly and objectively, with the Commission having, in principle, no discretion as to whether to execute them if an irregularity is found.[57] The lack of discretion is about ensuring a level playing-field: if the Commission had discretion to accept some irregularities and reject others, the intervention could distort the conditions of competition in the internal market.[58] In this respect, conditionality is fundamentally different from the infringement procedure, in which the Commission enjoys considerable discretion. Indeed, 'the two procedures are independent of each other as they serve different aims and are subject to different rules'.[59]

In the EU Courts' case law, the 'sufficiently direct' criterion originally relates to the fact that an ongoing infringement procedure may constitute grounds for a financial correction. The previously applicable Structural Funds Regulation 1260/1999 provided that interim payments applied for by Member States would be suspended if the Commission had opened an infringement procedure 'concerning the measure(s) that is or are the subject of the application in question'.[60] The logic was clear: if the Commission has reasonable grounds for suspecting that a Member State's activities are violating applicable EU law, the flow of money for those purposes should be stopped. However, in line with the principles of 'simple' conditionality, if an infringement procedure was relied on to withhold EU money, the alleged infringement had to 'concern' the funded 'measures'.[61] This relationship was judicially clarified by the General Court in proceedings brought by Italy to contest the suspension of payments from EU funds by the Commission, following the latter's decision to initiate an infringement procedure based on violations of EU law connected to the activity for which the funds were intended.[62]

[55] See European Council's Conclusions, 21 July 2020, EUCO 10/20, para A24, and annex to the conclusions, paras 22–23. See also the provisional agreement reached between European Parliament and Council of the European Union on 5 November 2020, Council doc no 12616/20, 6 November 2020, p 12.

[56] See eg Case C-332/01 *Hellenic Republic v Commission of the European Communities* ECLI:EU:C:2004:496, para 63. See also Case C-199/03 *Ireland v Commission of the European Communities* ECLI:EU:C:2005:548, paras 25 to 27.

[57] See Joined Cases 15/76 and 16/76 *France v Commission* ECLI:EU:C:1979:29, para 28.

[58] See eg, by analogy, Case C-332/00 *Kingdom of Belgium v Commission of the European Communities* ECLI:EU:C:2002:235, para 46.

[59] See Joined Cases 15/76 and 16/76 *France v Commission* ECLI:EU:C:1979:29, para 26. See also Case C-325/94 P *An Taisce – The National Trust for Ireland and WWF UK v Commission of the European Communities* ECLI:EU:C:1996:293, para 25.

[60] See art 32(3)(f) of Council Regulation (EC) No 1260/1999 of 21 June 1999 laying down general provisions on the Structural Funds [1999] OJ L161/1.

[61] ibid.

[62] See Joined Cases T-99/09 and T-308/09 *Italy v Commission* ECLI:EU:T:2013:200. For the infringement proceedings, see Case C-297/08 *Commission v Italy* ECLI:EU:C:2010:115 (finding that Italy had failed to fulfil its obligations in the field of waste recovery and disposal in Campania region).

Italy's lawsuit concerned the waste management system around Naples and, in particular, the Commission's negative decisions on its funding applications. According to Italy, the Commission had unlawfully suspended the payments due to Italy, relying on an ongoing 'generic' infringement of EU law regarding waste management, but without indicating precisely how the funded activities related to the alleged infringement. Italy protested that the suspension of payments punished the Member State before it could argue its case in court.[63] In its judgment, the General Court rejected these arguments. It noted that the Structural Funds Regulation in force at the time enabled the Commission to suspend payments in the case of an ongoing infringement procedure. Such a suspension did not presuppose that there should exist 'a specific link or a perfect coincidence' between the funded measures, on the one hand, and the matter covered by infringement procedure, on the other, but that the existence of 'a sufficiently direct link' between the two sufficed.[64] On appeal, the Court of Justice affirmed the General Court's approach.[65]

Thus, the 'sufficiently direct link' test originally relates in the EU Courts' case law to situations where the Commission suspends the payment of EU funds on grounds of a pending infringement procedure. Similarly, under the current ESI Funds Common Provisions Regulation, interim payments may be suspended based on the issuance of a reasoned opinion in an infringement procedure, provided there is a 'sufficiently direct link' between 'the matter addressed by the reasoned opinion and the expenditure at stake so as to put at risk its legality and regularity'.[66] By contrast, in the Conditionality Regulation, the expression 'in a sufficiently direct way' is employed as a test to determine whether breaches of the principles of the rule of law 'affect or seriously risk affecting' the EU's budget or financial interests. The procedures are different. The infringement procedure concerns circumscribed breaches of EU law, whereas the Conditionality Regulation conditions EU spending upon the Member States' observance of more vague 'principles of the rule of law'.[67] However, in both procedures, the Commission is invited to assess whether a breach by a Member State is 'sufficiently directly' related to another factor.

The breach–money link in the Conditionality Regulation envisages also the protection of the EU's 'financial interests'. According to the ECJ, this encompasses 'not only revenue made available to the Union budget but also expenditure covered by that budget'.[68] Administrative failures can be detrimental to the EU's financial interests: as regards financial corrections in the management of agricultural and structural funds, the EU Courts have consistently interpreted the concept of 'irregularity' broadly.[69]

[63] See Joined Cases T-99/09 and T-308/09 *Italy v Commission* ECLI:EU:T:2013:200, para 14.

[64] See ibid, paras 46 and 49.

[65] See Case C-385/13 P *Italy v Commission* ECLI:EU:C:2014:2350, paras 69–71.

[66] See Recital 70 of Reg 2021/1060, above n 15. See also ibid, art 97(1)(d) (referring to 'a reasoned opinion by the Commission in respect of an infringement procedure under Article 258 TFEU on a matter that puts at risk the legality and regularity of expenditure.').

[67] Art 3 of Reg 2020/2092, above n 1 (referring eg to endangering the independence of the judiciary, failing to maintain a functioning law enforcement system, or hindering the effectiveness of judicial protection).

[68] See Joined Cases C-357/19, C-379/19, C-547/19, C-811/19 and C-840/19 *Euro Box Promotion and Others* ECLI:EU:C:2021:1034, para 183.

[69] See Case T-265/08 *Federal Republic of Germany v European Commission* ECLI:EU:T:2012:434, para 40. See also, on appeal, the Opinion of AG Cruz Villalon in Joined Cases C-549/12 P and C-54/13 P

That concept includes not only breaches of specific provisions of EU law, but also errors which national authorities commit in the implementation of EU funds, such as shortcomings in their management and control systems.[70] Rejecting an argument that 'technical' errors in the management of funds do not rise to the level of irregularities, the Court of Justice has held that 'even irregularities which do not have a specific financial impact may be seriously prejudicial to the financial interests of the Union'.[71] Refusing to charge expenditure to an EU fund can also be justified on grounds of deficiencies in the national systems of checks and inspections.[72]

Under the Conditionality Regulation, the test of whether the EU's money is (potentially) affected 'in a sufficiently direct way' can be understood to respond to the related goals of ensuring that rule-of-law conditionality should be effective and that, at the same time, it should nevertheless provide a backstop guaranteeing that the relevant EU institutions, the Commission and the Council, do not overreach into matters which are wholly unconnected with the protection of the EU's money. That said, not only does the Regulation define the principles of the rule of law to guarantee legal certainty, but it also contains a procedure for adopting measures in its Article 6. The two-step procedure involves both the Commission and the Council, as well as affording the Member State concerned the right to be heard, encouraging dialogue with the European Parliament, and exhorting the Commission to base its assessment on reputable sources, including from relevant international bodies. The adoption of any measures pursuant to the Regulation will necessarily have been preceded by significant exchanges over the alleged breaches, protecting the Member States against excesses by the EU institutions.

What kinds of breaches are, then, related to the EU's money in a 'sufficiently direct way'? In the litigation over the suspension of the regional aid concerning the waste management around Naples, the General Court emphasised the *effet utile* of the suspension of payments. It rejected the restrictive interpretation proposed by Italy, holding essentially that in cases where there is reasonable doubt that applicable EU law is violated in connection with EU-funded activities, it is legitimate to suspend the EU money for that purpose. By analogy, the *effet utile* of the Conditionality Regulation should be borne in mind when interpreting the breach–money link in the context of that instrument. The requirement of a 'sufficiently direct' link serves to guarantee that a legitimate reason for the EU to protect its money exists, but it should not be interpreted overly restrictively to undermine safeguarding the rule of law which is part of the constitutional identity of the EU legal order. It is clear, based on an analogous interpretation of the case law, that no 'specific link or a perfect coincidence' between the breaches of the rule of law and specific EU expenditure can be required. Instead, a plausible connection, in other words a *sufficiently* direct relationship, should be enough.[73]

Federal Republic of Germany v Commission ECLI:EU:C:2014:222, paras 70–71 (arguing not only irregularities which are directly prejudicial to the EU budget are important).

[70] Case T-265/08 *Federal Republic of Germany v European Commission* ECLI:EU:T:2012:434, paras 11 and 43.

[71] Case C-199/03 *Ireland v Commission of the European Communities* ECLI:EU:C:2005:548, para 31.

[72] See Case C-346/00 *United Kingdom v Commission* ECLI:EU:C:2003:474, paras 35 to 37.

[73] See above n 66.

V. CONCLUSION

This chapter opened with the proposition that the looser framework of general rule-of-law conditionality raises questions as to the proper division of powers between the Union and the Member States. Safeguarding the rule of law is essential for the EU, but rule-of-law conditionality cannot operate without limits. The focus of this chapter has been on how to ensure that the general rule-of-law conditionality, particularly under the Conditionality Regulation, respects its legal bases in the EU Treaties. Since rule-of-law conditionality is concerned with the fundamental preconditions of the EU legal order, measures to protect it certainly enjoy a high degree of legitimacy. At the same time, it is essential, precisely because the EU is based on the rule of law, not to digress too far from the legal basis of the Conditionality Regulation. The targeted breaches of the principles of the rule of law must threaten the proper use of EU money in order to come within the Regulation's ambit.

The breach–money link is the key to the proper operation of the Conditionality Regulation. Its constitutional significance resides in the limits of the underlying legal bases it expresses. This chapter has tracked the previous use of the breach–money link in the EU Courts' case law, from which some guidance can be derived. This is particularly true regarding the *effet utile* of the regulatory context in which the breach–money link is assessed. While the 'sufficiently direct' link constitutes an essential safeguard against overreach into national constitutional systems from the EU institutions, its importance should not be overstated. The Regulation, with its validity confirmed by the Court of Justice, has been designed for use, if needed. The breach–money link should not be read so strictly as to vitiate conditionality's *effet utile*. It appears plausible that the more serious the breach of the rule of law, the less direct the threat to EU money must be to justify the adoption of corrective measures. While conditionality cannot operate without constitutional limits, the protection of the EU's financial interests becomes illusory if basic safeguards for the rule of law in its Member States fail.

12

Tackling EU Conditionality with the Hungarian Legal Manoeuvres

KATALIN MIKLÓSSY

I. INTRODUCTION: CONDITIONALITY AND LEVERAGE

THE EASTERN ENLARGEMENT of the European Union was undertaken to encourage the consolidation of democracy in the ex-communist countries. The EU, however, set strict conditions by the Copenhagen Criteria (1993), which provided a list of the required Western standards of democracy to be accomplished before the Eastern bloc countries could join the club.[1] It created the illusion that the democratic rules of the game were fully absorbed in the countries that were granted accession in 2004. And yet, after 18 years of EU membership the 'former star performers of democratic transition',[2] Hungary and Poland, are the main objects of EU criticism of states turning away from liberal democratic values.[3] According to various reports and indexes, it became obvious that EU membership in fact weakened democratic evolution in the Eastern members. Between 2010 and 2022, the decline of democracy was noticeable in all Visegrád countries, but particularly in Hungary and Poland.[4]

The new 'rule of law mechanism' (Regulation 2020/2092), introduced by the European Parliament and the Council, is an attempt to correct this situation.[5]

[1] See 'Accession Criteria (Copenhagen Criteria)', eur-lex.europa.eu/summary/glossary/accession_criteria_copenhague.html.

[2] N Lugosi and L Thorlakson, 'Theorizing democratic development after EU accession: Bringing comparative politics back in' (European Consortium for Political Research, 2014), ecpr.eu/Events/Event/PaperDetails/16351.

[3] L Cabada, 'Democracy in East-Central Europe: Consolidated, Semi-Consolidated, Hybrid, Illiberal or Other?' (2017) 13(2–3) *Politics in Central Europe* 75–87. See also The Economist, 'Illiberal Europe. Big, bad Visegrad', *The Economist* (28 January 2016), www.economist.com/news/europe/21689629-migration-crisis-has-given-unsettling-new-direction-old-alliance-big-bad-visegrad.

[4] Just to mention a few organisations that are dedicated to assessing the rule of law, see, for instance, *Freedom House*, 'Democracy in Retreat: Freedom in the World 2019', freedomhouse.org/report/freedom-world/freedom-world-2019/democracy-in-retreat; *World Justice Project*, 'WJP Rule of Law Index', worldjusticeproject.org/rule-of-law-index/global; *The Global Economy.com*, 'The Human Rights and Rule of Law Index', www.theglobaleconomy.com/rankings/human_rights_rule_law_index/Europe/; and *World Bank*, 'Worldwide Governance Indicators', info.worldbank.org/governance/wgi/Home/Reports.

[5] Regulation (EU, Euratom) 2020/2092 of the European Parliament and of the Council of 16 December 2020 on a general regime of conditionality for the protection of the Union budget [2020] OJ LI433/1.

The new Regulation returns to conditionality in dealing with the Eastern Europeans. There is a scholarly debate on how well conditionality works. What influence, for instance, did the conditionality of the accession have on Eastern European democratisation, and how did the ultimately achieved membership affect the Europeanisation process? Some argue that conditionality may have had positive impacts on governance during the accession period, that subsequently disappeared during the membership.[6]

Scholars investigating conditionality differ with regard to what drives a state to accept conditions set by an outside power. The theory of *rational bargaining* maintains that conditionality works only if the benefits it offers exceed the related domestic costs which the country in question bears. It has been also noted that the effectiveness of conditionality is determined by the credibility of threats and the size of benefits, and the clarity of the time-frame on which the transaction relies.[7] *Social constructivists*, in contrast, argue that international powers like the EU modify the international arena by the values and institutions they represent. Thus, conditionality set by such international powers can be influential only when their values, norms and rules are genuinely respected, in other words, when there is a true interest in applying those principles.[8] I argue that the question in the social constructivist approach is the temporal context: values, norms and rules change over time and their magnetism may go through a profound transformation. Reflecting on the above-mentioned theoretical approaches, Schimmelfennig and Sedelmeier pointed out, in connection to the post-communist countries' accession process, that there was an overlapping two-level conditionality: democratic conditionality based on the Copenhagen criteria and *acquis* conditionality regarding the formal adoption of rules.[9] Whereas democratic conditionality was monitored and guided for years focusing on the transition process establishing the rule of law, *acquis* conditionality was a relatively short-term assessment, emphasising the compatibility of legal framework and institutional structures.

The previous theoretical debates are important in reviewing the potential impact of the newly issued rule-of-law mechanism on the current situation. This chapter raises the question of whether bringing back conditionality will achieve its goals, or whether the evolution of illiberal regimes has already gone too far and passed the point of no return. Continuing Schimmelfennig and Sedelmeier's interpretations, I claim that Regulation 2020/2092 resembles the *acquis*-type conditionality because the EU officials monitor only a rather limited section of the democracy situation that is linked one way or another to the misuse of EU funds. It lacks the means to influence the whole system, and this gives leverage to the culprits. On the other hand, the new mechanism is finally targeting the *praxis of politics* and not only institutional

[6] See M Ugur, 'Europeanization, EU conditionality and governance quality: Empirical evidence on Central and Eastern European countries' (2012) 57(1) *International Studies Quarterly* 41. See also J Bachtler, C Mendez and H Oraze, 'From Conditionally to Europeanization in Central and Eastern Europe: Administrative Performance and Capacity in Cohesion Policy' (2014) 22 *European Planning Studies* 735; F Schimmelfennig and U Sedelmeier, 'The Europeanization of Eastern Europe: the external incentives model revisited' (2020) 27 *Journal of European Public Policy* 814.

[7] F Schimmelfennig and U Sedelmeier, 'Governance by conditionality: EU rule transfer to the candidate countries of Central and Easter Europe' (2004) 11 *Journal of European Public Policy* 661; M Vachudova, 'EU Leverage and National Interest in the Balkans: The Puzzles of Enlargement Ten Years On' (2014) 52(1) *Journal of Common Market Studies* 122.

[8] Lugosi and Thorlakson, n 2 above.

[9] Schimmelfennig and Sedelmeier, 'Governance by conditionality', n 7 above.

structures, as the previous conditionality mechanisms did. This is a huge step forward in developing a functional toolkit.

There are two challenges embedded in the new toolkit that demand attention. First, the question is how to link the stable rule-of-law principles with the fast-changing political practice. Singling out some unwanted political action on an ad hoc basis also requires a political choice on the part of the EU officials. Political will, however, can and does change in the EU decision-making bodies as well, and therefore the applicability of the new mechanism will be always dependent on the prevailing political temperature of the EU. Furthermore, the question is also about what the balance of power between central institutions is: the European Parliament, the Commission, and the Council (of the heads of Member States). Secondly, because of the fluid and transformative nature of the political modus operandi, time is of the essence to react to ever-increasing inventions of illiberal regimes – and this creates a grave problem from at least two perspectives. On the one hand, because the democratic processes take time and arriving at a majority decision can be painstakingly slow, we end up with an ironical situation where the EU, defending liberal democracy, is stuck with rigid structures and old modus operandi, whereas these illiberal regimes have an enormous capacity to adapt to new circumstances quickly and neutralise exogenous pressure. On the other hand, the question is whether the new rule-of-law mechanism is coming too late in relation to the stage of consolidation of un-democracy, relying on a 'deep state', out of reach of the EU.

This chapter will elaborate the Hungarian case for two main reasons. First, it is the Hungarian governance that launched the EU discussions about the rule of law back in 2011 and has accelerated the debate ever since. Secondly, the Hungarian administration displays a peculiar legal flexibility and fluid administrative practices that have served the powerholders in their conflicts with the EU during the past decade. The analysis concentrates on three central aspects of these practices: (1) the institutional re-arrangements, strengthening the central grip on the incoming funds; (2) competition regulations regarding EU tendering procedures; and (3) restrictions on the elbow-room of regional and local self-government bodies, which are the end-users of EU funds. The chapter is structured around these three themes, starting, however, with an overview of EU–Hungarian relations that highlights how profoundly the Hungarian case influenced the evolution of the discussion about the rule-of-law instruments and why arriving at a dead-end with Hungary was, in fact, inevitable. Finally, I will briefly deliberate what kind of impact the Covid-19 pandemic has had on the rule-of-law issue. The analysis relies on legal and media sources, speeches, and writings of political actors.

II. 'LIMITS OF OUR INSTITUTIONAL ARRANGEMENTS':[10] THE EU'S DILEMMA OVER HUNGARY

Regimes with authoritarian tendencies place a distinct stress on legality that serves both as an argument against international criticism and a justification in domestic

[10] Jose Manuel D Barroso, President of the European Commission, 'State of the Union 2012 Address' Plenary Session of the European Parliament, Strasbourg 12 September 2012, ec.europa.eu/commission/presscorner/detail/en/SPEECH_12_596.

debates for restricting the social sphere. The rule-of-law debate hence is easy to divert by moving the emphasis towards the narrow meaning of the concept, as if it were just a legal-technical issue. From the Hungarian point of view, this approach is supported by over 200 years of political thought. According to the historical understanding, state politics are best handled by legal experts. This need for exact arguments of law developed during the long struggles for independence: first against the Habsburg overlords, then safeguarding the integrity of the polity in the interwar years, and later in the opposition's strategies challenging the communist powerholders from the 1980s onward.[11]

After a decade of an EU-compatible democratic phase between the late 1990s and 2010, the re-activation of this old tradition began in 2010, due to the frequent criticism targeting the consecutive national-conservative Fidesz governments. The first warnings were raised already in January 2011 by the plenary session of the European Parliament (EP) about a new Hungarian media law (issued in December 2010), restricting the freedom of the media.[12] After the two-thirds Fidesz majority decided to introduce a new constitution, called the Basic Law of Hungary, adopted on 18 April 2011, the Venice Commission took a stand in defining the rule of law, which seemingly was needed for standardising the diverse national interpretations.[13] Hungary gain attention by consistent attacks against the freedom of its Constitutional Court, Supreme Court, Chief Prosecutor's Office and judges. Hence, in January 2012 the Commission started an infringement procedure, which the European Parliament supported, first raising the dilemma of whether to activate Article 7(1) of the Treaty on the European Union (TEU).[14] The President of the Commission, Jose Manuel Barroso, however, noted in his yearly State of the Union speech, in 2012 that 'We need a better developed set of instruments – not just the alternative between the "soft power" of political persuasion and the "nuclear option" of article 7 of the Treaty'.[15] The turning point was in March 2013: in a letter to Barroso, the ministers of foreign affairs of Denmark, Finland, Germany and the Netherlands envisioned novel elements in dealing with rule-of-law matters, which have formed the basis for new conceptions ever since.[16] The ministers suggested a consistent rule-of-law mechanism based on continuing and comparative monitoring, structured dialogue, and more efficient instruments, such as the suspension of EU funds. From Finnish documents it becomes obvious that the parties wanted to avoid earmarking the initiative to Hungary, since the reforms were intended to safeguard fundamental values in general.[17]

[11] K Miklóssy, 'Lacking rule of law in the lawyers' regime: Hungary' (2018) 26(3) *Journal of Contemporary European Studies* 270.

[12] European parliament Strasbourg Plenary Session, 17–20 January 2011, multimedia.europarl.europa.eu/en/the-news-presidential-aims-more-choice-for-europes-patients_N001-110119_ev.

[13] Report on the Rule of Law, Adopted by the Venice Commission at its 86th Plenary Session (25–26 March 2011) CDL-AD(2011)003rev.

[14] European Parliament resolution of 16 February 2012 on the recent political developments in Hungary (2012/2511 (RSP)) P7_TA(2012)0053.

[15] JMD Barroso, President of the European Commission, 'State of the Union 2012 Address', n 10 above.

[16] ÁB Gát, 'Az Európai Unió és a jogállamiság: az elmúlt évtized trendje' (30 March 2020) *Nemzeti Közszolgálati Egyetem, Európa Stratégia Kutatóintézet*, eustrat.uni-nke.hu/document/eski-uni-nke-hu/03_30_G%C3%A1t%20%C3%81kos%20Bence.docx.pdf.

[17] Letter to Mr José Manuel Barroso, President of the European Commission, from Dr Guido Westerwelle, Frans Timmermans, Villy Søvndal and Erkki Tuomioja. Archive of the Finnish Ministry of

Meanwhile, the EP commissioned monitoring reports. In 2013, the rapporteur Rui Tavares found all the key elements already in place that are still mentioned repeatedly today. The erosion of the rule of law and weakening checks and balances were well under way, including problematic legislative procedures and electoral practices, restrictions on the freedom of civil society and media, and threats against the integrity of the judiciary and the rights of minorities. Tavares also mentioned that these constituted a 'systematic and general trend' and recommended that if the Hungarian authorities did not comply with the EU requirements, Article 7 TEU should be activated.[18] This process led eventually to the creation of a new framework in March 2014 by the Commission, designed especially for those cases where systematic activity could be detected. The framework now outlined a detailed three-stage procedure on how to assess and negotiate, follow up and, if necessary, discipline the culprit countries.[19] The problem was that the ultimate punishment was still the implementation of Article 7 TEU, which – as the 'nuclear option' – was to be avoided by all costs, and there was no other correcting instrument available. However, after five years and the new report of Judit Sargentini, reaffirming further worsening conditions, the European parliament voted with a majority of 448 to 197 votes against to begin the Article 7 procedure against Hungary.[20] Finally, the Commission launched, in July 2019, an annual rule-of-law review to monitor every Member State consistently on an equal basis.[21]

Simultaneously with the legal-political evolution of the rule-of-law thinking on the EU level, the Hungarian government learned to deal with the increasingly awkward situation. The Orbán administration implemented offensive tactics right from the start. It developed three types of response. First, it invented a *double language* with the purpose of differentiating between rhetoric targeted at the EU arena and at domestic audiences. By cultivating the required EU liturgy the country was seeking leverage vis-à-vis the EU and, at the same time, the national interpretations of the EU's intentions ensured domestic popularity.[22] Accordingly, the government refused to take into consideration any criticism, discredited all recommendations, blamed the rapporteurs' individually and their party fractions in the European Parliament, and questioned the contents of the reports, alleging that they consciously falsified the situation in Hungary. The Orbán administration played all the rhetorical cards, from historical victimhood, the right to self-determination, legitimacy of power, to

Foreign Affairs, file UH 289; see also www.eerstekamer.nl/eu/documenteu/_brief_nederland_duitsland/f=/vji8oh6slx9o.pdf.

[18] R Tavares, 'Report on the situation of fundamental rights: standards and practices in Hungary' (24 June 2013), website of the European Parliament, www.europarl.europa.eu/doceo/document/A-7-2013-0229_EN.pdf.

[19] Communication from the Commission to the European Parliament and the Council, A New EU Framework to Strengthen the Rule of Law, COM(2014) 158 final of 11 March 2014.

[20] European parliament, News: 'Rule of law in Hungary: Parliament calls on the EU to act' 12 September 2018. Available at: www.europarl.europa.eu/news/en/press-room/20180906IPR12104/rule-of-law-in-hungary-parliament-calls-on-the-eu-to-act.

[21] Communication from the Commission to the European Parliament, the European Council, the European Economic and Social Committee and the Committee of the Regions, Strengthening the rule of law within the Union, A blueprint for action', COM(2019) 343 of 17 July 2019.

[22] G Török, 'ha Habony Árpád lennék … A kettös beszédröl' (19 March 2012) *HVG*, hvg.hu/napi_merites/20120319_torok_gabor_kettos_beszed_habony.

the demand for equal treatment and objectivity.[23] One of the latest innovations in this field is playing with *semantics*. This practically means that central concepts such as the rule of law and democracy are used frequently with a different connotation, moving the focus from the vertical dimension of the rule of law (regarding the people–power relations) to the horizontal dimension (of the people–people nexus), without making the diverging content transparent. This creates a fuzzy and complex web of misunderstandings where the opponent, coming from a different political culture, does not realise the logic of the game.[24] For domestic use, the government's freedom fighter image has been utilised repeatedly with the message that the administration courageously resisted the EU-empire which bullied the Hungarian People.

Secondly, to accentuate its legitimacy towards the EU the government held consecutive referenda on questions that stirred particular criticism at the Union level. In the past decade, national consultations have been organised in 2011 concerning the one-party manufactured new Constitution, in 2016 about the refugee quota, in 2017 on the 'Stop Brussels' campaign, in 2021 regarding the post-pandemic socially sensitive economic policy, in 2022 on 'saving our children' from LGBTQ propaganda, and against the EU sanctions against Russia.[25] The results of these consultations are not verifiable because the data about how many people replied and how is not public. The questions are designed in such a leading way that responses can be predictable. Since the referenda are only consultative – in other words not binding on the decision-making bodies – it is hard to see what else their role would be than to show the EU the infallibility of national decisions. As the Minister of Foreign Affairs, Péter Szíjjártó, explained in January 2022, there is no other EU country where the administration would ask people's opinion so many times, which makes all democracy-related accusations against Hungary invalid.[26]

Thirdly, the administration took every opportunity to seek out legal loopholes in EU procedures in order to claim that the recommendations and warnings were illegal. The most important argument relied on the thin line between matters belonging to domestic decision-making and matters on which the EU could make demands from its Member States. The rule-of-law debate was particularly burdened by the effort to divert the discussion to legal technicalities, where the 'lawyers' regime'[27] was strong. By steering the deliberations exclusively toward the legal domain, the Hungarian politicians tried to blur the distinction between rule of law and rule by law. This tactic was, however, very effective for playing for time, particularly because the EU was rather hesitant to start serious disciplinary procedures against Hungary, anyway.

[23] See eg PM Orbán's speech at the European Parliament Plenary, www.facebook.com/watch/?extid=SEO----&v=10151681612279836, in response to the Tavares report on 2 July 2013 or the Fidesz MPs' letter to the Hungarian Parliament: Országgyûlés Hivatala, H/11729 (4 July 2013), www.parlament.hu/irom39/11729/11729.pdf.

[24] S Turtiainen, 'Unkari pitää Suomen tavoittetta sitoa EU-rahat oikeusvaltioperiaatteeseen turhana.' *YLE Uutiset* (1 October 2019), yle.fi/uutiset/3-10998236.

[25] See PM Viktor Orbán's announcement of the necessity to organise a new referendum, 'Orbán Viktor: Nemzeti kozultációt inditunk + video.' *Magyar Nemzet*, 28 September 2022, magyarnemzet.hu/belfold/2022/09/orban-viktor-nemzeti-konzultaciot-inditunk-video.

[26] Magyar Hírlap, A kormány a legfontosabb kérdésekben konzultációt hirdet, 17 January 2022, www.magyarhirlap.hu/belfold/20220117-a-kormany-a-legfontosabb-kerdesekben-konzultaciot-hirdet.

[27] Miklóssy, 'Lacking rule of law in the lawyers' regime: Hungary', n 11 above.

The watershed regarding Hungarian–EU relations can be dated to 2015 for two reasons. The refugee crisis was a game-changer for the modus operandi of the Orbán administration. Whereas between 2010 and 2015 it was only Hungary that stubbornly refused to respond to EU requirements – now, Hungary has found a wider understanding. Criticism of the EU spread in the Eastern Members States concerning the EU's suggestions of obligatory quota, to share the burden of accommodating refugees, leading later to general dissent and rising EU-scepticism all over Europe.[28] On the other hand, in the Polish Parliamentary elections in October 2015, Jaroslav Kaczynski's Law and Justice party (PiS) gained a majority. Kaczynski had made public already in 2011 that he admired Viktor Orbán's model of governance and that he intended to implement it eventually in Poland.[29] These two events had tremendous influence on the transformation of behaviour of the Hungarian administration.

The first sign of change was when Hungary and Poland began to cooperate more closely, and the Visegrad alliance started to drive the common agenda of opposing the migrant quotas. The affinity between the V4, and ensuing criticism of the EU, evolved because similar national conservative elites acquired power in these countries, almost simultaneously.[30] PM Orbán could now count on group pressure and hence became more and more proactive and increasingly offensive. The government's threshold for turning to the European Court of Justice to dispute EU-level criticism became lower, as when, after the Sargentini report on the deteriorating situation, the EP voted for the implementation of Article 7 TEU.[31] The aforementioned double language also began to converge into a pattern of outspokenness and even arrogance. From 2016 onwards, Hungary gradually started to challenge the EU consistently in different matters, gaining increasing popularity also in Western conservative circles. PM Orbán became the lead figure of a new political trend openly questioning the EU's liberal principles.[32] This had a very practical effect: to activate Article 7 TEU became completely impossible, due to the required

[28] E Maurice, 'Refugee quotas unacceptable for Visegrad states', *euobserver* (4 September 2015), euobserver.com/migration/130122; see also IP Karolewski and R Benedikter, 'Europe's Migration Predicament: The European Union's Refugees' Relocation Scheme versus the Defiant Central Eastern European *Visegrad Group*' (2018) 1 *Journal of Inter-Regional Studies: Regional and Global Perspectives* 40, www.waseda.jp/inst/oris/assets/uploads/2018/03/JIRS-Vol.1_Invited-Article_Karolewski-and-Benedikter.pdf; E Heldt, 'Disintegration Dynamics during the Refugee Crisis: partial Empowerment, Reluctant Agents, Cacophony of Voices, and Unilateral Actions' *EUI Conference* 22–23 June 2017, www.eui.eu/Documents/RSCAS/JMF-25-Presentation/Heldt-Disintegration-Dynamics-150617.pdf.

[29] Kaczynski claimed 'Viktor Orban gave us an example of how we can win. The day will come when we will succeed, and we will have Budapest in Warsaw.' N Buckley and H Foy, 'Poland's new government finds a model in Orban's Hungary', *Financial Times* (6 January 2016), www.ft.com/content/0a3c7d44-b48e-11e5-8358-9a82b43f6b2f.

[30] K Miklóssy, 'Subregional Integration in East Central Europe: Strategies in the In-Between Sphere' in M Broad and S Kansikas (eds), *European Integration Beyond Brussels* (London, Palgrave Macmillan, 2020) 269.

[31] Ministerium of Justice, 'A Sargentini-jelentés miatt az Európai Unió Bíróságához fordult a kormány' (18 October 2018), 2015-2019.kormany.hu/hu/igazsagugyi-miniszterium/hirek/a-sargentini-jelentes-miatt-az-europai-unio-birosagahoz-fordult-a-kormany.

[32] PM Orbán made a serious effort to construct a new party group including 16 like-minded national-conservative, EU-skeptic parties, see eg M De La Baume, 'Orbán, Le Pen, Salvini join forces to blast EU integration', *Politico* (2 July 2021), www.politico.eu/article/viktor-orban-marine-le-pen-matteo-salvini-eu-integration-european-superstate-radical-forces/.

consensus. Between a rock and a hard place, the Commission in 2018 suggested introducing conditionality regarding the Union's budget.[33]

III. INSTITUTIONAL RECALIBRATION

The Hungarian government became increasingly alert to the gradually multiplying EU warnings. The administration has never admitted its fears of the possibility that the EU would finally act on these cautions. The political elite kept repeating that Hungary was entitled to its 'fair share' of the EU budget. Yet, the government launched an administrative restructuration of the incoming European funds – arguably as a safety measure. The government regulation was issued in December 2020 when it became eventually obvious that there was a wide consensus of most of the Member States about the rule-of-law mechanism introducing conditionality to receiving EU-support. This new EU instrument was planned to be activated in the beginning of January 2021, and so the Hungarian administrative rearrangement occurred on the same date.

According to the regulation, all incoming EU funding was now coordinated by the aegis of the Prime Minister's Office. The Minister without portfolio, running the PM's Office, would now be coordinating all resources arriving from the European Structural and Investment Funds to the wide range of different sectors. The current Minister, Gergely Gulyás, a loyal politician trusted by PM Orbán, also put forward proposals on who would benefit from the funding as an end-user of EU support. Furthermore, he was entitled to prepare the national plan for the next programme period of EU budget 2021–27.[34]

The change in the structure of decision-making regarding the use of EU funding was dramatic also in the Hungarian context. Back in February 2019, the government issued a regulation about the preparation for the new EU programme period and at that time the sectoral ministers and the minister of innovation and technology, on an equal basis, were together responsible for managing and allocating the EU funds.[35] The organisational reform in December 2020 relocated the entire EU resources openly under the authority of the Prime Minister.[36] The concentration of EU funds was consistent with the centralisation of power. It can be argued that transferring the control of these funds to the Prime Minister's Office reflects the ever-growing power of the PM himself. Confining the decision-making about the use of the funds to a small circle undermines the chances of public monitoring and transparency.[37]

[33] Proposal for a Regulation of the European Parliament and of the Council on the protection of the Union's budget in case of generalized deficiencies as regards the rule of law in the Member States, COM(2018) 324 final of 2 May 2018.

[34] 535/2020. (XII.1) Korm. Rendelet, Nemzeti Jogszabálytár, *Magyar Közlöny*, njt.hu/jogszabaly/2020-536-20-22.0.

[35] 1064/2019. (II.25.) Korm. Határozat, Nemzeti Jogszabálytár, *Magyar Közlöny*, njt.hu/jogszabaly/2019-1064-30-22.1.

[36] *Portfolio* (2 December 2020), www.portfolio.hu/unios-forrasok/20201202/gulyas-gergelynel-lesznek-januartol-az-eu-s-penzek-460002.

[37] KL Scheppele, RD Kelemen and J Morijn, *The EU Commission has to Cut Funding to Hungary: The Legal Case* (Greens/EFA group, European Parliament, July 2021), www.greens-efa.eu/en/article/document/the-eu-commission-has-to-cut-funding-to-hungary-the-legal-case.

IV. COMPETITION STRATEGIES

The EU supports Hungary with six major European Structural and Investment Funds, including the *Cohesion Fund*, the *Regional Development Fund, European Social Fund, Agriculture Fund for Rural Development, European maritime and Fisheries Fund*, and the *Youth Employment Initiative*. The country received €25.4 billion in the programme period 2014–20.[38] These special instruments promoted among other goals competitiveness, economic development, productivity, employment, and public administration. The EU prioritised small and medium-sized enterprises, special sectors such as tourism industry, infrastructure projects, public administration, expansion of public services, urban transport, and local communities.[39]

Competition rules are one of the key instruments affecting the flow of economic assets and changing the balance on the domestic market. We can find a typology in the ways of conduct, developed over the last decade of Fidesz rule. There are direct and indirect means including *technical tuning* of the rules of competition; *institutional restructuring* and more *drastic ad hoc state interventions*, like issuing extra-taxation, sudden audits, objecting to international loans, influencing customers, and launching business consortiums. The fundamental problem with this practice is that there is a broad palette of colourful means that can be taken advantage of. In addition, the regime seems innovative in coming up with yet another new trick.

The most obvious breach concerning the European competition law is where the call for tenders is written with an eye for a particular firm or institution that is intended to benefit from it. In July 2020, the EU Council addressed the systemic problems of Hungarian public procurement and tendering processes. It was noted that 'nearly half of all public tenders result in a single-bid procedure'. These were projects co-funded by the EU.[40] I argue that the ever-changing *technical tuning* of calls for tenders is the most difficult to detect from the outside because the single-bid procedures are only the tip of the iceberg. A more generic practice is when discrimination is not so obvious because a wide range of applicants can participate in a competition. In addition, the true ownership of the applicant firms can be hidden behind dummy companies. Among the numerous examples, one that can be presented as the 'veterinarian's horse' which displays all the possible problems, is the EU's financial support for tourism in 2020.[41] In addition to the standard practice that government-loyal businessmen operating hotels naturally benefitted from the call,[42] this time the professional tourist guides were also allowed to run for a subsidy – except those that worked in Budapest.[43] The call prioritised tourist regions, but the small companies of Budapest, the most vibrant tourist place in Hungary, were not selected without

[38] European Commission, European Structural and Investment Funds, Country Data for Hungary, cohesiondata.ec.europa.eu/countries/HU#.

[39] European Commission, EU Regional and Urban Development, ec.europa.eu/regional_policy/en/atlas/programmes/.

[40] Council Recommendation of 20 July 2020 on the 2020 National Reform Programme of Hungary and Delivering a Council opinion on the 2020 Convergence Programme of Hungary (2020/C 282/17).

[41] 1099/2020 (III.12.) Kormányhatározat.

[42] K-Monitor, *K-Blog*, 27 July 2020, k.blog.hu/2020/07/27/morzsanak_tunnek_a_panziotamogatasok_meszaros_ner_hoteljeihez_kepest.

[43] 24.hu/belfold/2020/09/11/koronavirus-idegenvezetok-segitseg/.

any explanation. The main reason – as will be discussed below – was that in the 2019 local elections the opposition won the national capital. In addition, timing is always a significant factor in the toolkit of tricks. The call in this case was opened during Christmas 2019 and suddenly disrupted on January 7, because of the number of applications exceeded the available funding.[44]

The concentration of power can be seen also in the *institutional arrangements*, as mentioned earlier. In September 2020, the government established the National Concession Agency, which administratively was under the Prime Minister's Office where the decisions on which enterprise would get a concession to operate would now be decided.[45] The authority to regulate concessions covered five broad economic fields, including the operation and maintenance of public transport and public roads, waste management, gambling, public electric services and mobile connections.[46] These are considered as operators of vital public services and thus requiring extra official attention. Except for the casino and gambling business, all other fields are the subjects of EU funding instruments. The new Agency enables the government to circumvent competition requirements and favour loyal businessmen.

But there are also other more subtle means to improve loyal enterprises' competitive advantages over their unwanted counterparts on the market, namely by *ad hoc interventions*. The central idea is that the government takes actions against businesses and weakens their positions by administrative or legal methods. One of the latest examples is the case of the Liszt Ferenc Airport in Budapest – a business that is central to the tourism industry, and hence an important source of EU funds. The airport was privatised between 2005–11 and has been run very successfully by a German company, while the majority owner is a Canadian pension fund. The Hungarian administration tried to acquire the airport back into Hungarian possession for years, but the owners refused to sell. The Covid-19 pandemic, however, hit the travel business worldwide and flying decreased considerably – so the airport operation suffered significant financial losses. The company turned to the European Bank for Reconstruction and Development (EBRD) for loans. The Hungarian government saw the opportunity and made an offer on the behalf of a brand-new consortium, specifically established by the state to carry out the take-over.[47] In addition, it vetoed the company's loan application at the EBRD,[48] by which it undermined an independent international firm's liquidity and debilitated its value. According to the news in October 2021, the owner was considering selling because of the fear of government retaliation.[49]

The cases mentioned above reveal the broad toolkit employed in the competition procedures. It means that the power-elite is confident that it can always switch from

[44] Korrupciófigyelö, Elsö jelentés. *K-Monitor – TASZ*, Budapest 2020, 20–21.

[45] 424/2020. (IX. 4.) Korm. Rendelet a Nemzeti Koncessziós Irodáról, njt.hu/cgi_bin/njt_doc.cgi?docid=221689.388897.

[46] 495/2020. (XI.11) Korm. Rendelet egyes koncesszióköteles tevékenységel tekintetében az illetékes ágazati miniszteri feladatok ellátásáról, njt.hu/jogszabaly/2020-495-20-22.

[47] hvg.hu/kkv/20201009_budapest_airport_mol_orban_viktor_magyar_kormany.

[48] nepszava.hu/3098495_meg-nem-tudtak-foldre-vinni-a-repteret.

[49] A Nardelli, 'Hungary said to offer $4.6 billion for Budapest Airport control', *Bloomberg* (15 October 2021), www.bloomberg.com/news/articles/2021-10-15/hungary-said-to-offer-4-6-billion-for-budapest-airport-control; see also *Korrupciófigyelö: második jelentés* (Second Corruption Monitoring Report), https://tasz.hu/a/img/corruption_monitor2.pdf.

one instrument to another if the circumstances so require. I argue that especially because the formal and informal regulations of competition are fluid and very flexible, this characteristic endows the administration with the potential to resist EU pressures.

V. REGIONAL CENTRALISATION

The original aim of the European Regional Development Fund (ERDF) was to strengthen territorial cohesion by boosting regional economic and social progress, and to support underdeveloped areas. One of the five funding priorities of the budget period of 2021–27 was to transfer money closer to the end-user citizens, in other words, to locally-led decision-making bodies.[50] As in so many cases, the idealistic goals and priorities clashed with the spatial and temporal context and were thus in the end compromised. The temporal factor is significant in two ways. On the one hand, in October 2019 there was a local election where the opposition won several areas from the government party.[51] The power shifted in Budapest, in 10 major cities out of 23, and in 50 towns out of 100. Some political scientists remarked that local elections would predict a forthcoming profound change, especially in authoritarian regimes, because power can be challenged only from the grass-roots level.[52]

Seemingly one could argue that regional structures and revisions in their autonomous positions do not matter when we talk about effectiveness of the rule-of-law mechanism. In fact, however, the leverage of municipal autonomy has an enormous impact on who the actual end-users of EU funds are. That is why the gradual but consistent centralisation of power over local governments has considerable relevance not only for who are entitled to EU supports but also to the overall public assessment of the role and significance of the EU in the local population's life. And, even more importantly, it affects the public's perceptions about what party must be voted for in local elections if the existing local services are at stake.

Regional funds are distributed according to the evidenced needs of underdeveloped rural areas, based on an application procedure. The plain truth is that the Hungarian authorities have a free hand on how to prioritise the numerous poverty-stricken municipalities. This is a strategy that has been applied since 2019 and it puts the European Union into an awkward position. The EU officials cannot argue that the chosen regions do not need the funding. Furthermore, the EU 'outsiders' lack also the necessary fine-tuned local knowledge about the different shades of destitution in the Hungarian countryside. The selection procedure, in addition, has been sending a powerful political message particularly to the most vulnerable localities about how loyalty will be rewarded.

[50] European Commission, *European Regional Development Fund*, ec.europa.eu/regional_policy/hu/funding/erdf/.

[51] *Nemzeti Választási Iroda* (National Election Office), *Municipal Elections*, 13 October 2019, www.valasztas.hu/helyi-onkormanyzati-valasztasok-2019.

[52] C Carothers, 'The Surprising Instability of Competitive Authoritarianism' (2018) 29(4) *Journal of Democracy* 129; A Lucardi, 'Building Support From Below? Subnational Elections, Diffusion Effects, and the Growth of the Opposition in Mexico, 1984–2000' (2016) 49(14) *Comparative Political Studies* 1855.

The agrarian countryside is also the governing Fidesz party's core area of support. Many top-politicians' and oligarchs' families have considerable land property. The running programme of regional development 2014–20 did not distinguish between genuine farmers and politicians with an agrarian hobby. The tender procedures where there are several competitors running, are hard to find.[53]

A few months after the local elections, the Covid-19 pandemic broke out. The administration decided to take advantage of the extra opportunity to accelerate the centralisation of power, in parallel with and behind the scenes of the Covid crisis management. Since also Western democracies introduced restrictions on civil liberties and increased executive power with shortcuts in parliamentary decision-making, not to mention economic shutdowns – these policies offered an unexpected point of reference. Covid-19 was not only a 'godsend', presenting strong arguments that crisis-legislation was 'inevitable', but also because the attention of Western countries turned away from the rule-of-law matters and focused on their national strategies fighting the virus.

The pandemic measures struck against the opposition-led municipalities. One of the most efficient policies was to drain resources from local governments by taking away their core income sources. In April 2020 the government established a Fund for Protecting the Economy (*Gazdaságvédelmi Alap*) that was justified by the urgency to minimise the damage caused by the pandemic for the Hungarian economy and its actors.[54] This new decree gave free rein for the government to redirect key tax-areas from the municipalities to the central budget. For example, losing the power of taxation of motorcars hit hard both small villages, where this was the only income, and big cities, where the number of vehicles was significant. Similarly, parking in public areas became prescribed as free of charge – to prevent people spreading infection by using public transport.[55] Parking had been a considerable source of income for local administrations, and this intervention was particularly targeted against Budapest, which was led by a non-Fidesz Mayor and predominantly opposition forces. In addition, the government withheld already budgeted resources for regional development from opposition-led Budapest. The money was, allegedly, just spent on fighting the disease and the local administrations, it was said, would have to make sacrifices.[56] The most drastic decision, decreasing immensely the income of the municipalities, was restricting their right to revenues of local enterprises, which made up about 32 per cent of their budget; 90 per cent of the municipalities had access to this type of taxation.[57]

[53] *Agrárszektor*, 3 February 2021, www.agrarszektor.hu/agrarpenzek/ok-most-a-leggazdagabb-agrarvallalkozok-magyarorszagon-itt-a-lista.27732.html.

[54] Decree 92/2020 (IV.6) *Magyar Közlöny* 6 April 2020, 1814–19.

[55] Pandemic communique of the government, 6 April 2020, available on the government website: koronavirus.gov.hu/cikkek/orszagos-tisztifoorvos-az-ingyenes-parkolas-jarvany-lassitasat-szolgalja.

[56] Undersecretary Tibor Pogácsás' speech in the Parliament 18 May 2020, available on the website of the Parliament: www.parlament.hu/web/guest/aktiv-kepviseloi-nevsor?p_p_id=hu_parlament_cms_pair_portlet_PairProxy_INSTANCE_9xd2Wc9jP4z8&p_p_lifecycle=1&p_p_state=normal&p_p_mode=view&p_auth=2YdkryMy&_hu_parlament_cms_pair_portlet_PairProxy_INSTANCE_9xd2Wc9jP4z8_pairAction=%2Finternet%2Fcplsql%2Fogy_naplo.naplo_fadat%3Fp_ckl%3D41%26p_uln%3D129%26p_felsz%3D113%26p_szoveg%3D%26p_felszig%3D113.

[57] Németh Tamás, 'Jelentös bevételt képeznek – mindent az iparűzési adóról', *Pénzügyi Szemle* (6 August 2020), www.penzugyiszemle.hu/tanulmanyok-eloadasok/jelentos-bevetelt-kepeznek-mindent-az-iparuzesi-adorol.

Establishing a centrally-led 'special economic belt' was originally a Chinese model that, under the pretext of the pandemic, the Hungarian administration introduced. The purpose here was to cut off lucrative economic areas from local opposition-run self-governance and manage them centrally, taking advantage particularly of the revenues. The first such special region was Göd where a huge Samsung factory had its site. After Göd the government established two other similar territories where profitable economic assets could be found.[58]

The gradual opening of Hungary in the summer of 2021 did not cure the economic situation of opposition-led local administrations but accelerated their distress. The government started to compensate for the budgetary losses of loyal municipalities and left others unattended.

Covid-19 gave the opportunity to fine-tune the discursive strategy, already in use in communication with the EU since 2012 – but now with a new purpose: to channel attention away from one crisis to another, that is, from the rule-of-law mechanism endangering the country's budgetary interests in EU funds, to Covid, which hit all countries around the world. The new waves and new mutations of the virus were capitalised on by magnifying both the ad hoc crises at hand and the pandemic's character that required extreme measures also in the West.

VI. BUILDING A DEEP STATE WITH PANDEMIC POWER

The pandemic offered a unique opportunity to build a 'deep state' that would be resistant to the results of parliamentary elections in April 2022. The idea of cementing power was obviously linked to the previously mentioned local elections in 2019 where it became evident that the governing party might lose power. The actions which took place targeted thematically two areas: institutional position and property. The means were provided by the state of emergency, which constitutes a special mandate and extraordinary legal order whereby the government is entitled to suspend laws and accelerate the decision-making processes by statute.[59]

The state of emergency was declared on 11 March 2020.[60] But because of the ardent Western criticism, the government decided, relying on a supermajority in the Parliament, to preserve the smoke-screen of democratic image and emphasised in quarterly parliamentary debates the pandemic necessity of continuing the emergency measures – covering practically the whole year in 2021.[61] On 30 November 2021, the

[58] About establishing 'special economic belt' in Göd Government Decree 136/2020 (IV.17) *Magyar Közlöny* 17 April 2020, 2075–76; in Mosónmagyaróvár Government Decree 44/2021 (II.5) *Magyar Közlöny* 5 February 2021, 484–85; in Dunaújváros Government Decree 362/2021 (VI. 28) *Magyar Közlöny* 28 June 2021, 5620.

[59] Z. Lomnici, 'A veszélyhelyzet meghosszabbítása a kormány gyorsreagálású képességét erôsíti.' *Alaptörvény* (29 September 2021), alaptorvenyblog.hu/a_veszelyhelyzet_meghosszabbitasa_a_kormany_gyorsreaglasu_kepesseget_erositi.html.

[60] 40/2020. (III.11) Kormányrendelet veszélyhelyzet kihírdetéséröl. *Magyar Közlöny* 11 March 2020, magyarkozlony.hu/dokumentumok/af0a665e93020a1bb69193ed9a8379f516854bf7/megtekintes.

[61] *2021. évi XCIX. törvény a veszélyhelyzettel összefüggő átmeneti szabályokról.* Hatályos Jogszabályok, *Wolters Kluwer*: net.jogtar.hu/jogszabaly?docid=a2100099.tv; *2021. évi I. törvény* a koronavírus-vilagjárvány

government ordered another extension until 1 June 2022.[62] The parliamentary elections were scheduled to be organised on 3 April 2022. While the government ended compulsory mask-use and vaccination policy in early March 2022, still the 'emergency situation' was not lifted[63] because the government needed time to ensure its grip on deep structures of power before the election.

Securing key political and legal positions that can be changed only by a two-thirds supermajority in the Parliament has been a complex and multilevel government operation. The President of Hungary, Katalin Novák, was elected just three weeks before the parliamentary elections by the Fidesz majority. The President can exercise a veto on parliamentary legislation.[64] Similarly, a new law was issued regarding the election procedure for the role of Chief Prosecutor – here too, a parliamentary supermajority is required.[65] The Fidesz-loyal Chief Prosecutor, Péter Polt, has been in office since 2010 and can actively hinder investigations of corruption or criminal cases against the elite. The Chief Prosecutor can be changed only at the suggestion of the President. In addition, the presidents of the Supreme Court, András Varga, and of the National Office for the Judiciary, György Barna Senyei, will stay in office until 2028. Whereas the former has the authority to assign cases to judges and determine the composition of judicial courts, the latter can influence the appointment of judges and assess their performance. As for the Constitutional Court, the president's position is secured until 2026, four of its members until 2023, two until 2025, two til 2026, four til 2028, two til 2031 and one til 2033. The purposes of maintaining power can be served efficiently by occupying the media, and the minds and hearts of the people. The president of the Media Council, András Koltay, who oversees the media market and governmental advertisements, remains in position until 2030.[66] This position can be viewed in the context of the massive concentration of over 400 media enterprises into a media holdings company, Central European Media Foundation (KESMA), which the administration carried out in 2018, thus establishing an 85 per cent share of the media landscape. The Fidesz-run media empire was declared to belong to the area of *national strategic importance* and thus not subject to national or EU competition legislation.[67] The European Commission investigated the case, but the Commissioner for Values and Transparency, Vera Jourova, admitted in May 2021 that there was nothing the EU can do about it.[68]

elleni védekezésröl. Hatályos Jogszabályok, *Wolters Kluwer*: https://net.jogtar.hu/jogszabaly?docid=a2100001.tv and see also Jogászvilág, 'Meghosszabbították januárig a veszélyhelyzetet', *Wolters Kluwer*, 28 September 2021. https://jogaszvilag.hu/napi/meghosszabbitottak-januarig-a-veszelyhelyzetet/.

[62] Miniszterelnökség, Törvényjavaslat, 23 November 2021, www.parlament.hu/irom41/17671/17671.pdf.

[63] Adó Online: 'A maszkoknak búcsút inthetünk, de a veszélyhelyzet velünk marad.' 3 March 2022, ado.hu/ado/a-maszkoknak-bucsut-intunk-de-a-veszelyhelyzet-velunk-marad/.

[64] On the rights of the President, see the website of Office of the President of the Republic, www.keh.hu/about_the_institution_of_the_president_of_the_republic/1586-About_the_institution_of_the_President_of_the_Republic&pnr=1.

[65] The new initiative clarifying the election of the Chief Prosecutor, see the Parliament's website: www.parlament.hu/irom41/17282/17282.pdf.

[66] The Hungarian Helsinki Committee's website: cementezettek.helsinki.hu/en/.

[67] 229/2018. (XII.5.) Korm. Rendelet a Közép-Európai Sajtó és Média Alapítvány nemzetstratégiai jelentöségüvé minösítéséröl. *Magyar Közlöny* 2018/192, 5 December 2018, www.kozlonyok.hu/nkonline/MKPDF/hiteles/MK18192.pdf.

[68] Z Sándor, 'Jourová: a bizottság tehetetlen a KESMA ügyében' *Euronews* (3 May 2021), hu.euronews.com/my-europe/2021/05/03/jourova-a-bizottsag-tehetetlen-a-kesma-ugyeben.

Accelerating property transfers to loyal supporters was another key function in this process. The continuous 'emergency situation' prolonged the temporal window of opportunities to seize new economic assets. The assets acquired under the emergency measures encompassed companies that were considered *vital for crisis-management*.[69] The fight against the epidemic necessitated special attention to *strategically important enterprises*, some of which, like a carton-firm (an unlikely suspect), were simply taken over.[70] There were over 100 businesses on the same list to be nationalised.[71] These production areas, including for example information technology, construction, transport, logistics, food, agriculture, tourism, and others, are listed in a government statute in April 2021.[72] Furthermore, the party-loyal oligarchs were able to expand economic control over new enterprises.[73] They possess the banking sector, insurance companies, agricultural land, media firms, and energy enterprises. While the 'emergency situation' officially ended in June 2022, the acquired economic assets would, nevertheless, not be transferred back to their original owners. In addition, there is a problem: how to use the rule-of-law mechanism to change the property ownership structure on political grounds?

The emergence of the deep state strongly indicates the Fidesz' fears that it might lose power. For them it was necessary to ensure that if the liberal and pro-EU opposition were to win the 2022 parliamentary elections, the new government would have only limited power in state matters. As it turned out, the Fidesz won for the fourth time a two-thirds majority of the votes; thus it became rather obvious that Hungary has passed the *point of no easy return* and a new systemic transformation would be necessary to change the political course – in the same fashion as in 1989. The European Parliament adopted with a huge majority (433 votes for – 123 against) a report in September 2022 declaring that Hungary is a 'hybrid regime of electoral autocracy'.[74]

VII. TRIGGERING THE RULE-OF-LAW MECHANISM

The European Union warned Hungary but did not launch the conditionality mechanism during the electoral campaign period to avoid influencing, in any way, the election

[69] 128/2020. (IV. 17.) Korm. Rendelet a veszélyhelyzet során teendő intézkedések keretében gazdálkodó szervezet működésének a magyar állam felügyelete alá vonásáról.

[70] A Domány, 'Azonnali hatállyal állami felügyelet alá vonták a Kartonpackot' *HVG* (17 April 2020), hvg.hu/gazdasag/20200417_Azonnali_hatallyal_allami_felugyelet_ala_vontak_a_Kartonpackot?fbclid=IwAR0ZLXAAsv9qfkpT7TIvA6fNfeyJ4AQGG68GtQUL6hYina5VWw4z8GHhFZY.

[71] 'Coronavirus: Military Taskforces to Oversee More Strategic Companies' *Hungary Today* (17 April 2020), hungarytoday.hu/coronavirus-hungary-companies-military-taskforces/.

[72] 289/2020. (VI. 17.) Korm. Rendelet a magyarországi székhelyű gazdasági társaságok gazdasági célú védelméhez szükséges tevékenységi körök meghatározásáró, Nemzeti Jogszabálytár, njt.hu/jogszabaly/2020-289-20-22.

[73] Y Szabó and Á Gyenis, 'A fülkeforradalom felfalja sajátjait: bevált receptek alapján viszik Fidesz-közeliek cégeit is' *HVG* (25 November 2021), hvg.hu/360/20211125_fulkeforradalom_Fidesz_uzlet_felvasarlas_kleptokracia_Vitezy_Tamas_Meszaros_Lorinc_Garancsi_Istvan_Orban_Viktor.

[74] 'MEPs: Hungary can no longer be considered a full democracy' European Parliament Press Release, 15 September 2022, www.europarl.europa.eu/news/en/press-room/20220909IPR40137/meps-hungary-can-no-longer-be-considered-a-full-democracy.

outcome. The renewal of the supermajority has provided the Fidesz regime with a strong argument vis-à-vis the EU: it not only showed the people's unquestionable support but also the temporal endurance of legitimacy. After the election was over in April, the Commission triggered the mechanism but the Hungarian administration – overconfident from its landslide victory – denied corruption allegations and refused to take any actions to change the political line.[75] The government was also counting on the fact that the ongoing war in Ukraine would distract attention away from the rule-of-law agenda. When the EU pressure increased in July, the powerholders became scared because the election campaign was financed by massive public expenditure. Budgetary problems were compounded by growing inflation and the dropping standard of living of the Fidesz-constituency, with possible consequences for the stability of power. So, when the European Commission proposed to suspend payment of €7.5 billion, which is one-third of the cohesion funds allocated to Hungary, and in parallel with the conditionality mechanism, €5.8 billion of grants from the EU's Recovery and Resilience Fund became at stake too[76] – the government started to bend.

Perhaps the extraordinary legitimacy of the Hungarian regime had an impact on the European rule-of-law deliberations because the EU seemingly restricted its attention to fighting corruption. In her 2022 speech on the State of the European Union, Commission President, Ursula von der Leyen, emphasised the link between the rule of law – mentioning solely judicial independence – and protecting the budget through the conditionality mechanism.[77]

The Hungarian Parliament produced a new legislative package, containing four laws and three government statutes, in a fortnight.[78] Interestingly, the legal attention concentrated mostly on old tricks, already mentioned above, that is, *institutional rearrangements* and *re-regulating competition procedures*. To protect the EU funds, the administration established a supposedly independent state agency called Integrity Authority, assisted by a consultative Anti-Corruption Task Force, both of whose members are carefully selected by the government interest. The task is defined as monitoring, analysing, and recommending further actions but has no 'authority' to act independently without state-controlled institutions such as the Prosecutor's Office, Competition Agency, and Public Procurement Authority.[79] New regulation

[75] European Commission, Communication from Commissioner Hahn to the Commission, 20 July 2022, www.politico.eu/wp-content/uploads/2022/09/14/C20225313_0.pdf.

[76] European Commission, COM(2022) 485, Proposal for a Council Implementing Decision on Measures for the Protection of the Union Budget against Breaches of the Principles of the Rule of Law in Hungary, 18 September 2022, www.europeansources.info/record/proposal-for-a-council-implementing-decision-on-measures-for-the-protection-of-the-union-budget-against-breaches-of-the-principles-of-the-rule-of-law-in-hungary/.

[77] EU, '2022 State of the Union Address by President von der Leyen', 14 September 2022, Strasbourg, https://ec.europa.eu/commission/presscorner/detail/ov/speech_22_5493.

[78] *Magyar Közlöny* 163/2022, 10 October 2022, 6678–6714, magyarkozlony.hu/hivatalos-lapok/7HHUHszy9D8szM3wNgwF633740d7b5b24/dokumentumok/144170049decdef153ae913a69b5521fcadc0590/letoltes and Magyar Közlöny 166/2022, 14 October 2022, 6808–9, magyarkozlony.hu/hivatalos-lapok/mLwUjLNteQR73wsMUviP633ed4f522d1e/dokumentumok/26c5689c018f684c6c87f1439768845a0fce1598/letoltes.

[79] 2022. évi XXVII. Törvény az európai uniós költségvetési források felhasználásának ellenőrzéséről. See also the assessment of the new measures by Transparency International; Hungarian Helsinki Committee and K-Monitor, *Half-hearted promises, disappointing delivery*, https://transparency.hu/wp-content/uploads/2022/10/Assessment-of-measures-to-protect-EU-budget.pdf#page=1&zoom=auto,-206,622.

on competition is focused primarily on remedying the single-bid tendering practices, which the government promised to minimise to 15 per cent (from over 50 per cent) by the end of 2022. While the new bill is to control the conflict of interest in public procurements, there is no in-built transparent monitoring mechanism to identify 'false' applicants. Furthermore, there are grave doubts whether the Public Procurement Agency can be assumed to be independent from the reigning power elite.[80]

These are steps taken by a desperate government in need of money – and not because of its true will to revisit the course of undemocratic development. If the EU accepts these 'window-dressing' actions, it means that the European authorities admit that Hungary is beyond cure. Compromise with illiberal EU members like the Orbán regime will, however, bear long-term consequences for the future of the European Union.

VIII. CONCLUSION

In this chapter I investigated the warehouse of available means that has enabled the Hungarian government over the past 12 years to resist the EU's requirements, rather successfully. I discussed three sectors (institutional restructuring, competition strategies and regional centralisation) that have been particularly useful for the administration because of their non-transparent and changing nature. Therefore, these are extremely difficult to monitor from the outside. In addition, these sectors contain instruments that can be represented as EU-compatible variants, working as counterarguments in the rule-of-law debates.

The rule-of-law mechanism is a new means to restore EU unity based on shared principles and values. The toolkit of conditionality is powerful only when the timing is right. The EU's long hesitation and underestimation of the emerging democracy problems for years led to an erosion of credibility and prestige of the community itself. This can be seen in the ways in which the repeated warnings had no impact on Hungary or Poland, and seemingly Slovenia, Bulgaria and others are joining the group. It can be argued that the EU's reluctance to use proper instruments against these dubious developments strengthened and even consolidated the illiberal trend in Hungary and Poland.

Timing has another equally important consequence. The current semi-authoritarian regimes are learning organisms. This endows these regimes with an enormous capacity to adapt to new circumstances and neutralise pressure, coming either from the EU or from below. The long-lasting warning rhetoric and the constant delays in taking advantage of and using the EU instruments offer time to these administrations to adjust and reinvent their strategies in tackling the intended measures.

[80] A közbeszerzésekről szóló 2015. évi CXLIII. törvény módosítása. *Magyar Közlöny* 163/2022, 6697–6700.

13

Promoting the Rule of Law in EU External Relations: A Conceptual Framework

INGE GOVAERE

I. INTRODUCTION

ARTICLE 3(5) OF the Treaty on the European Union (TEU) unequivocally states the firm objective for the Union 'to uphold and promote its values and interests' in its relations with the wider world.[1] Those values, which are common to the Member States and on which the Union is founded, are listed in Article 2 TEU and include respect for the rule of law but also human dignity, freedom, democracy, equality and human rights. The Treaty thus solidly underpins the global positioning of the EU as a soft power, which was on the whole rather successful until the large-scale Russian invasion of Ukraine in 2022 exposed its limits. Policy-wise, a corresponding ambition clearly transpires in the 2016 EU Global Strategy which asserts:

> [o]ur interests and values go hand in hand. We have an interest in promoting our values in the world. At the same time, our fundamental values are embedded in our interests. Peace and security, prosperity, democracy and a rules-based global order are the vital interests underpinning our external action.[2]

Proclaiming that the EU shall promote such a rules-based global order based on 'principled pragmatism',[3] however, sounds like an oxymoron. If the stated Treaty objective

[1] The use of the word 'shall' (meaning must) is telling in this respect: article 3(5) TEU reads: 'In its relations with the wider world, the Union *shall* uphold and promote its values and interests and contribute to the protection of its citizens. It *shall* contribute to peace, security, the sustainable development of the Earth, solidarity and mutual respect among peoples, free and fair trade, eradication of poverty and the protection of human rights, in particular the rights of the child, as well as to the strict observance and the development of international law, including respect for the principles of the United Nations Charter' (emphasis added). Similarly, the French version states unequivocally: 'Dans ses relations avec le reste du monde, l'Union *affirme et promeut* ses valeurs et ses intérêts' (emphasis added).

[2] HR F Mogherini, 'A Global Strategy for the European Union's Foreign And Security Policy', June 2016, 13–14, see www.eeas.europa.eu/sites/default/files/eugs_review_web_0.pdf.

[3] See ibid, 8, 16.

and the corresponding EU Global Strategy ambition may be declared openly in this way, a major difficulty lies in their interpretation as well as their translation into a forceful, coherent and consistent practice in line with Articles 21(3) TEU and 7 of the Treaty on the Functioning of the European Union (TFEU).

The key question addressed in this chapter is whether promoting the rule of law whilst ensuring consistency of the EU's policies and activities necessarily implies a 'one-size-fits-all' approach or rather calls for differentiation between states based on objective criteria. Not only will the distinction between the EU and its Member States as compared to third states be scrutinised, but also, and especially, objective factors calling for a categorisation among third states. Correspondingly this chapter will consider whether the use of diversified instruments to promote the rule of law may be warranted to meet the single objective expressed in Article 3(5) TEU.

The proposed conceptual framework uses a five-sided prism to deconstruct the Article 3(5) TEU objective with a focus specifically on the rule of law. A first part builds on how both the 'EU rule-of-law' framework and concept translate in a broader and international setting, based on two questions. Why and to what extent is the internal EU rule-of-law framework at all relevant for EU external relations (section II)? Is the internal 'EU' rule-of-law concept sufficiently distinct to propel the EU as a normative actor and what is the possible external impact of flanking concepts underlying thick constitutional democracy (section III)? What emerges, secondly, is a three-pronged meaning of the rule of law according to the actors involved, which is then systematically dissected in the subsequent sections on the basis of, at first sight, simple questions. Should a distinction be drawn between third countries according to whether they qualify as functioning democracies or not? Superimposed on that issue is the question whether there is a need for further differentiation between those third countries that are candidates for EU accession and others, in particular when EU 'values' and EU 'interests' may not always and necessarily align (section IV)? And should a distinction be drawn in terms of the respect for the rule of law between the EU as an international actor, on the one hand, and third countries, on the other hand (section V)? The latter question reveals its full importance when one considers that, of all the international actors, only the EU and its Member States are bound to comply externally too with the rules of the 'Autonomous EU Legal Order', such as the primacy of EU law and the principle of mutual trust. Finally, the last part turns briefly to the often invoked quest for consistency and coherence in EU external relations and the avoidance of double standards, by examining possibly differentiated uses of the EU's soft power and hard law instruments in relation to differentiated rule of law concepts (section VI).

II. INTERNAL VERSUS EXTERNAL EU RULE OF LAW REFERENCE FRAMEWORK

Internally, the EU faces major difficulties in systematically upholding, let alone promoting its values in all of the Member States, in accordance with its stated ambition in Article 3(1) TEU. The long treasured presumption that all Member States automatically and fully endorse the EU's values was shattered over the past few years by blatant rule-of-law backsliding, most notably in Hungary and Poland in relation to the independence of the judiciary.[4] In the rule-of-law financial conditionality judgments of 16 February 2022,[5] the European Court of Justice (ECJ) forcefully ruled that the common values expressed in Article 2 TEU, and in particular respect for the rule of law, were not only identified and shared by all the Member States but furthermore constitute the 'very identity of the European Union as a common legal order'.[6] As a logical consequence, it expressly held for the very first time that compliance with those values is not merely an accession requirement but instead stringently linked to continuing EU membership.[7] Respect for the rule of law can thus be labelled as an 'inherent constitutional condition' of EU membership, which triggers existential questions of political and legal rule-of-law enforcement within the EU in case of breach.[8]

Externally the setting is totally different. In relation to third countries there is no similar offhand presumption of commonly shared values or constitutional 'rule-of-law' conditionality, nor can there reasonably be one. The external dimension thus necessarily presents extra challenges compared to an already complex internal situation with which it cannot simply be assimilated. This is apparent also from Article 3(5) TEU which states that the EU should uphold and promote 'its' values and interests in its relations with the wider world, not the values and interests which the EU has in common with third states. The internal EU values expressed in Article 2 TEU are thus seemingly projected extraterritorially as the ultimate benchmark for all EU external action.

A complicating factor lies in the fact that, internally, discussion is still ongoing about what precisely the rule-of-law concept entails as a value 'common' to the Member States,[9] considering the scope of EU competence conferred by the Treaties.[10] For instance, in his contribution to this book, Leonard FM Besselink questions whether, constitutionally, there really exists such a unified concept of the rule of law, having regard not only to the constitutional homogeneity expressed in Article 2 TEU but also the underlying constitutional diversity expressed through the national identity clause in Article 4(2) TEU.[11] In the rule-of-law conditionality judgments, the ECJ for its part firmly underlines the existence of an obligation of

[4] See especially the chapters in Part I of this book dealing with the intra-EU dimension.

[5] For a discussion of the rule-of-law financial conditionality, including these judgments, see Chapter 11 by P Pohjankoski in this book.

[6] Case C-157/21 *Poland v Parliament and Council* ECLI:EU:C:2022:98, para 145; Case C-156/21 *Hungary v Parliament and Council* ECLI:EU:C:2022:97, para 127.

[7] Case C-156/21 *Hungary v Parliament and Council* ECLI:EU:C:2022:97, para 126.

[8] See Helsinki Rule of Law Forum, 'A Declaration on the Rule of Law in the European Union' (2022) 27 *ELJ* 306.

[9] Art 2 TEU stipulates that '[t]hese values are common to the Member States in a society in which pluralism, non-discrimination, tolerance, justice, solidarity and equality between women and men prevail'.

[10] The principle of conferral is laid down in art 5(2) TEU. It was argued elsewhere that the principle of conferral is the very first structural principle of EU law, see I Govaere, 'To Give or to Grab: The Principle of Full, Crippled and Split Conferral of Powers Post-Lisbon' in M Cremona (ed), *Structural Principles in EU External Relations Law* (Oxford, Hart Publishing, 2018) 71. On this principle, see also S Garben and I Govaere (eds), *The Division of Competences between the European Union and its Member States: Reflections on the Past, Present and Future* (Oxford, Hart Publishing, 2017; paperback 2020).

[11] See Chapter 6 by LFM Besselink in this book.

result, but not necessarily one of means, for the Member States to respect the rule of law. It held that

> [e]ven though, as is apparent from Article 4(2) TEU, the European Union respects the national identities of the Member States, inherent in their fundamental structures, political and constitutional, such that those States enjoy a certain degree of discretion in implementing the principles of the rule of law, it in no way follows that that obligation as to the result to be achieved may vary from one Member State to another.[12]

Such internal discussions do not facilitate the framing of the rule-of-law concept to be upheld and promoted by the EU in its relations with the wider world pursuant to Article 3(5) TEU.

Expressly and stringently linking the internal and external objectives to uphold and promote EU values can thus easily backfire. The current actions undertaken by the EU (institutions) against backsliding Member States can be said (and demonstrated) to be fully in compliance with precisely those founding EU principles. The EU's international position is nonetheless undermined by being exposed to an easy 'get your own house in order before you start telling us what to do' response. The apparent paradox of holding third countries to standards and values that are openly challenged and breached by EU Member States may perhaps be accommodated by highlighting the somewhat 'softer' wording of the first subparagraph of Article 21(1) TEU. Here it is more realistically stated that

> [t]he Union's action on the international scene *shall be guided by* the principles which have inspired its own creation, development and enlargement, and which *it seeks to advance* in the wider world: democracy, the rule of law, the universality and indivisibility of human rights and fundamental freedoms, respect for human dignity, the principles of equality and solidarity, and respect for the principles of the United Nations Charter and international law (emphasis added).[13]

Whereas the internal EU values are also here put forward as the reference frame for EU external action, the crucial differentiating factor lies in an (external) obligation as to means as opposed to the (internal) obligation as to result. This distinction is of fundamental significance in assessing the consistency of EU external action.

III. THE 'RULE-OF-LAW' CONCEPT REVISITED FOR EXTERNAL USE

Related to but also distinct from the above issue of the rule-of-law reference frame is the question of the formulation or definition of the very EU rule-of-law concept in its interaction with international law. At least three fundamental questions emerge which will be addressed in turn. Firstly, how does the EU internal definition of 'rule of law' relate to the international understanding thereof and how does this reflect on

[12] Case C-156/21 *Hungary v Parliament and Council* ECLI:EU:C:2022:97, para 233.

[13] On the use of the word 'principles' instead of 'values' in this context, see Chapter 8 by W Schroeder in this book, as well as W Schroeder, 'The Rule of Law as a Value in the Sense of Article 2 TEU: What Does It Mean and Imply?' in von Bogdandy et al (eds), *Defending Checks and Balances in EU Member States: Taking Stock of Europe's Actions* (Springer, 2021) 105.

the EU as a global normative actor (A)? Secondly, what can it possibly mean for the EU to promote and thus to 'export' the EU rule-of-law concept in terms of principled pragmatism (B)? And lastly, is there consensus and consistency in the formulation of the rule-of-law concept? A related question is whether the rule of law is a stand-alone concept or whether it should rather be linked to the flanking and interrelated trinity concepts of respect for democracy and fundamental rights (C).

A. Scope for the EU as a Global Normative Actor?

It would be not only shortsighted but also counterproductive to present the necessity to uphold respect for the rule of law as a matter of concern only for the EU and its Member States. Other contributions in this book have already pointed to the crucial importance of the broader international context to (help) uphold the rule of law in the EU Member States, most notably in the framework of the Council of Europe.[14] Not surprisingly, therefore, EU legislation as well as the ECJ openly refer to such external benchmarks, and in particular the Venice Commission Rule of Law Checklist,[15] inter alia in order to reject attempts by Poland and Hungary to limit the concept of the rule of law adopted by the EU in relation to its Member States in terms of references to the protection of fundamental rights and non-discrimination.[16]

The elaboration of an active internal rule-of-law approach[17] is thus systematically and necessarily accompanied by integrating international law elements, including, where relevant, reference to the European Convention on Human Rights (ECHR),[18] within the EU's autonomous legal order balloon.[19] This is consonant not only with the EU Treaty requirement to contribute to 'the strict observance and the development of international law, including respect for the principles of the United Nations Charter',[20] but also with the international commitments undertaken by the EU.

[14] See in particular the chapters in this book by P Craig (Chapter 3), A Rosas (Chapter 2), and S Bogojević and X Groussot (Chapter 4). See also J Polakiewicz and JK Kirchmayr, 'Sounding the Alarm: The Council of Europe As the Guardian of the Rule of Law in Contemporary Europe' in von Bogdandy et al (eds), *Defending Checks and Balances in EU Member States: Taking Stock of Europe's Actions* (Springer, 2021) 361.

[15] Rule of Law Checklist, adopted by the Venice Commission at its 106th Plenary Session (Venice, 11–12 March 2016), endorsed by the Ministers' Deputies at the 1263rd Meeting (6–7 September 2016), Council of Europe, Study No 711/2013, CDL-AD(2016)007rev.

[16] Reference to the Venice Commission Rule of Law Checklist is made both in recital 16 of the Rule-of-Law 'Conditionality Regulation', Regulation (EU, Euratom) 2020/2092 of the European Parliament and of the Council of 16 December 2020 on a general regime of conditionality for the protection of the Union budget [2020] OJ L433I/1, and in the Court's related judgment (Case C-156/21 *Hungary v Parliament and Council* ECLI:EU:C:2022:97 paras 229–30, where the ECJ links the protection of fundamental rights and non-discrimination to the principle of effective judicial protection, 'which is also guaranteed in Article 19 TEU', which refers to the EU rule of law.

[17] See the Chapter 8 by W Schroeder in this book.

[18] Art 6(3) TEU and art 53 of the Charter of Fundamental Rights of the European Union (the Charter).

[19] On the reasons why (and how) interaction between EU and international law is indispensable for the survival of the EU autonomous legal order, see I Govaere, 'Interconnecting Legal Systems and the Autonomous EU Legal Order: a Balloon Dynamic' in I Govaere and S Garben (eds), *The Interface Between EU and International Law: Contemporary Reflections* (Oxford, Hart Publishing, 2019) 19–43.

[20] See arts 3(5) and 21(1) TEU, as well as Declaration no 13 concerning the common foreign and security policy [2016] OJ C 202/343.

For instance, the 2007 Memorandum of Understanding with the Council of Europe expressly states that '[t]he Council of Europe will remain the benchmark for human rights, the rule of law and democracy in Europe'.[21] On a larger and global scale, the United Nations (UN) has framed the rule of law as

> a principle of governance in which all persons, institutions and entities, public and private, including the State itself, are accountable to laws that are publicly promulgated, equally enforced and independently adjudicated, and which are consistent with international human rights norms and standards. It requires measures to ensure adherence to the principles of supremacy of the law, equality before the law, accountability to the law, fairness in the application of the law, separation of powers, participation in decision-making, legal certainty, avoidance of arbitrariness, and procedural and legal transparency.[22]

In recent years various international initiatives have, furthermore, been deployed inter alia by the UN to enhance respect for the rule of law worldwide, such as the creation of the Global Focal Point for the Rule of Law (GFP)[23] and the Rule of Law Coordination and Resource Group (RoLCRG).[24]

Considering the international attention already given to respect for the rule of law, it was pointedly argued by Laurent Pech that in this field 'there has always been … extremely limited room for normative leadership by the EU'.[25] Added to this the dual backdrop of lack of internal consensus on the rule-of-law concept among the EU Member States and reliance on already existing international rule-of-law benchmarks to settle EU internal disputes, it seems rather illusory and futile to try to discern a sufficiently precise, distinct, and forceful 'EU-specific' rule-of-law concept that could serve the ambitions of a global normative actor.[26] It may thus legitimately be questioned what margin as well as what role is left for the EU to effectively uphold and promote the rule of law in its relations with the wider world as prescribed by Article 3(5) TEU.

B. Scope for Principled Pragmatism in 'Exporting' the EU Rule of Law?

Reverting back to the wording of Article 3(5) TEU, it is noteworthy that the EU should not simply 'export' its values but rather it should uphold and promote both its values and interests in its relations with the wider world. Considering the complexity underlying EU external relations it is illusory to hold that EU values and interests will always and necessarily fully coincide. Furthermore, as mentioned above,[27] the 'softer'

[21] MoU EU-Council of Europe (2007), at para 10, available at: rm.coe.int/16804e437b.

[22] See 'What is the Rule of Law', www.un.org/ruleoflaw/what-is-the-rule-of-law/.

[23] Created in 2012, see www.un.org/ruleoflaw/globalfocalpoint/.

[24] 'Strengthening and Coordinating Rule of Law Activities', www.un.org/ruleoflaw/blog/2019/10/strengthening-and-coordinating-rule-of-law-activities/.

[25] L Pech, 'Rule of Law as a guiding principle of the EU's external action', *CLEER Working Papers 2021/3*, 28.

[26] This is in strong contrast to the worldwide normative role played by the EU in other fields such as data and environmental protection: see inter alia, A Bradford, *The Brussels Effect: How the European Union Rules the World* (Oxford, Oxford University Press, 2020).

[27] See above n 13.

wording of Article 21(1) TEU suggests an obligation as to means, not one of result, in upholding and promoting its values abroad.

It could thus be argued that the Treaties do leave a certain margin of flexibility for the EU as an international actor to adopt or negotiate a rule-of-law approach targeted to a specific international context. Instead of a rigid parallelism between internal and external rule-of-law approaches, there thus seems to be scope for principled pragmatism in practice. As the wording suggests, principled pragmatism does not, however, imply complete and total political expediency in any given case but rather points to the systematic pursuit of coherent principles underlying policy decisions.

The important question addressed here is whether, from a conceptual point of view, flexibility can or should relate to the concept of the rule of law as such, or rather to the *approach* to the rule of law to be adopted (or not) towards a specific country, or to a combination of both. In search of coherent principles to underpin such pragmatism, it is necessary to first turn to the possible different readings of the rule-of-law concept before pinpointing essential third-country specificities that may warrant conceptual differentiation on the basis of superimposed criteria, such as whether or not third states purport to be functioning democracies and/or seek to closely align themselves with the EU.

C. Conceptual Ambiguity and Flanking Concepts

Although it is commonly understood what the rule-of-law concept stands for in a general manner – for instance equality before the law and independence of the judiciary – when pressed for more precision, it reveals highly chameleonic features which may cause conceptual ambiguity.[28] The rule-of-law concept can be understood in a thin (minimalist, largely procedural), or in a thick (maximalist, more substantive) sense,[29] and can either be expressly linked to important flanking concepts such as democracy and fundamental rights or be considered in isolation. There are thus numerous possible variations which allow for underlying differentiation in the use of one and the same concept on the surface.

Even in the intra-EU context, where the rule of law is a common value, what precisely constitutes this concept is increasingly the topic of discussion and fundamental disagreement. In the financial rule-of-law conditionality judgments of 2022, a thin concept of the rule-of-law argument was openly deployed by Poland and Hungary but expressly and firmly rejected by the ECJ.[30] Instead the ECJ embraced

[28] Robert Stein has pointedly remarked: 'Everyone, it seems, is in favor of the rule of law. The phrase has become chameleon-like, taking on whatever shade of meaning best fits the author's purpose': see R Stein, 'Rule of Law: What Does It Mean' (2009) 18 *Minnesota Journal of International Law* 250, 296. Brian Tamanaha also observed that 'the rule of law … stands in the peculiar state of being the pre-eminent legitimating political ideal in the world today, without agreement upon precisely what it means': B Tamanaha, *On the Rule of Law: History, Politics, Theory* (Cambridge, Cambridge University Press, 2004) 4.

[29] J Møller and SE Skaaning, *The Rule of Law: Definitions, Measures, Patterns and Cause* (London, Palgrave Macmillan, 2014) 13–27 (chapter on 'Systematizing Thin and Thick Rule of Law Definitions'). See also P Craig, 'Formal and Substantive Conceptions of the Rule of Law: An Analytical Framework' [1997] *Public Law* 467.

[30] Case C-157/21 *Poland v Parliament and Council* ECLI:EU:C:2022:98, at para 145; Case C-156/21 *Hungary v Parliament and Council* ECLI:EU:C:2022:97.

a thick concept of the rule of law, expressly including fundamental rights and non-discrimination, by reference in particular to the Venice Commission Rule of Law Checklist as the (supporting) external benchmark.[31]

It is apparent from both Articles 2 and 49 TEU, as well as the Copenhagen Accession criteria,[32] that the rule of law as an EU value common to the Member States is, furthermore, stringently linked to respect for democratic values and protection of fundamental rights. Also this is consonant with the Council of Europe approach which equally presents the rule of law, democracy and fundamental rights as a trinity.[33]

It has already been argued elsewhere[34] that within the EU and its Member States this trinity or triptych is to be upheld without compromise as they form indissociable concepts crucial to upholding liberal democracy. Safeguarding the rule of law essentially implies that disputes will be settled on the basis of a predetermined set of rules and by independent judges who have, as a primary task, to balance both individual and societal interests. As such it stands in sharp contrast to enforcing the will of the majority or to settling disputes by leveraging financial, economic or political power, or by plain force. Constitutional democracy, which is not to be equated simply with democratic elections, guards against backsliding on the rule of law. It provides procedural constitutional safeguards to ensure that envisaged changes in rule-setting which entail a fundamental or lasting societal impact may not be subject to an 'accidental' majority at a given point in time, for instance a one-off referendum, but, to the contrary, raise a sufficiently large and lasting public debate and support. As such, constitutional democracy also guards against the occurrence of a democratic paradox, whereby democracy is undermined from within by democratically elected leaders systematically undermining democratic checks and balances such as judicial and parliamentary control. Constitutional democracies lay down not only important procedural safeguards but also key constitutional principles such as the protection of rights of minorities and individuals in society. This triggers the last element of the triptych, respect for fundamental rights, which embraces the protection of human rights and minority rights ensured by independent judges, furthermore based on the premises that all are equal before the law[35] and that all benefit from equal protection of the law. The 'given' that under the rule *of* law no one is above the law, including the

[31] See above n 15, at point 3 (a).

[32] The Copenhagen accession criteria were first established by the Copenhagen European Council in 1993 and later on strengthened by the Madrid European Council in 1995. The first criterion expressly mentions 'stability of institutions guaranteeing democracy, the rule of law, human rights and respect for and protection of minorities'. The other two criteria relate to 'a functioning market economy and the ability to cope with competitive pressure and market forces within the EU' and 'the ability to take on the obligations of membership, including the capacity to effectively implement the rules, standards and policies that make up the body of EU law (the "*acquis*"), and adherence to the aims of political, economic and monetary union'. For an assessment, see C Hillion, 'The Copenhagen Criteria and their Progeny' in C Hillion (ed), *EU Enlargement: A Legal Approach* (London, Hart Publishing, 2004) 1.

[33] See also Chapters 2 and 3 by A Rosas and P Craig respectively, in this book.

[34] S Garben, I Govaere and P Nemitz, 'Critical Reflections on Constitutional Democracy in the European Union and its Member States' in S Garben, I Govaere and P Nemitz (eds), *Critical Reflections on Constitutional Democracy in the European Union* (Oxford, Hart Publishing, 2019) 1, esp at 2–3.

[35] Art 20 of the Charter.

state (authorities), is an important factor distinguishing it from a system based on the rule *by* law,[36] whereby the law is instrumentalised by power.

The concept of the rule of law, in particular such a thick understanding of the rule of law, intertwined with fundamental rights and democracy, is not universally shared. Not all states profess to be democratic in nature. Even among democratic states there is not necessarily agreement about what precisely is covered by fundamental rights protection (suffice it to think of abortion or capital punishment), or to what extent such rights are enforceable before the courts.[37] This raises questions as to the extent to which the EU can realistically aspire to export liberal democracy beyond its borders in a rigid manner. Against this backdrop the following sections will consider what differentiating factors among third countries may call for a differentiated rule-of-law concept, in search of consistency underlying principled pragmatism.

IV. CONCEPTUAL DIFFERENTIATION BETWEEN THIRD COUNTRIES

Whilst proclaiming that the EU strategy to promote a rules-based global order should be based on 'principled pragmatism', little guidance was offered in the 2016 EU Global Strategy as to how to understand and apply this new guiding principle of EU foreign policy in practice in a consistent manner.[38] Interestingly, in the 2019 follow-up assessment, 'Principled Pragmatism' was first labelled as the 'philosophy',[39] later as 'the leitmotif'[40] of the EU Global Strategy. The question as to whether in particular the EU values expressed in Articles 2 and 3(5) TEU would benefit from a more 'principled' or more 'pragmatic' approach was rather enigmatically addressed as follows: 'The EU can act pragmatically on the grounds of a lucid assessment of reality, while being unwavering in its commitment to the principles, values and rules enshrined in our Treaties'.[41] In spite of this assertion, the EU strategy based on principled pragmatism has already been strongly criticised for its inconsistencies in relation to a given country, such as Russia after the invasion of Crimea,[42] which can only be aggravated when comparing the EU's response to different countries.

Given the great variety in political, economic and legal models applicable in the various countries across continents, but also within regions, it appears futile to try to

[36] See B Tamanaha, *On The Rule of Law: History, Politics, Theory* (Cambridge, Cambridge University Press, 2004) 91.

[37] Australia, for instance, does not have a Bill of Rights: see M Groves, J Boughey, D Meagher (eds), *The Legal Protection of Rights in Australia* (London, Hart Publishing, 2019).

[38] See HR F Mogherini, 'A Global Strategy for the European Union's Foreign And Security Policy', June 2016, 13–14, see www.eeas.europa.eu/sites/default/files/eugs_review_web_0.pdf., 16: 'We will be guided by clear principles. These stem as much from a realistic assessment of the strategic environment as from an idealistic aspiration to advance a better world. In charting the way between the Scylla of isolationism and the Charybdis of rash interventionism, the EU will engage the world manifesting responsibility towards others and sensitivity to contingency. Principled pragmatism will guide our external action in the years ahead.'

[39] F Mogherini (High Representative), 'The European Union's Global Strategy Three Years On, Looking Forward', 2019, 22, www.eeas.europa.eu/sites/default/files/eu_global_strategy_2019.pdf.

[40] ibid 31.

[41] ibid.

[42] F Bossuyt and P van Elsuwege (eds), *Principled Pragmatism in Practice The EU's Policy towards Russia after Crimea*, vol 19 *Studies in EU External Relations* (Leiden, Brill, 2021).

measure the consistency and coherence of the EU approach against a single yardstick of the internal EU rule-of-law concept.[43] Instead the best course of action would seem to be to conceptually differentiate the concept of rule of law between third countries on the basis of two distinctive yet superimposed criteria, namely whether or not they are functioning democracies (A) and whether or not they are seeking accession to the EU (B). How this impacts on the rule-of-law concept to be flexibly understood externally will be considered in turn.

A. Functioning Democracy as a Conceptual Differentiation Criterion

Within the EU the concept of the rule of law is stringently linked to that of a functioning democracy and respect for human rights. Democracies are, however, fragile and not to be taken for granted, whether in the EU or globally. According to the latest figures of the Economist Intelligence Unit's 2021 Democracy Index, which measures democracy in a thick sense on the basis of five measures (electoral process and pluralism, the functioning of government, political participation, democratic political culture, and civil liberties),[44] only 21 out of 167 countries worldwide currently qualify as 'full' democracies.[45] Of those, 12 are countries in Western Europe albeit not all of them EU Member States.[46] The report points out that 'full democracy' currently benefits only 6.4 per cent of the world population, whilst 'less than half (45.7%) of the world's population now live in a democracy of some sort'.[47] This includes the other EU Member States (as well as, for instance, the USA) which are currently

[43] The combination of those contextual elements has led to the identification of four 'ideal types' of relationship between the EU and its counterpart in trade negotiations by Maryna Rabinovych: Type 1: undemocratic state (or group of states), yet economically oriented on trade with the EU and dependent on the EU aid (eg MENA region); Type 2: economically powerful yet undemocratic countries that hold a prominent role in regional economic integration projects other than the EU (eg Russia, China, the Gulf Cooperation Countries); Type 3: high-income democracies marked by convergence of regulatory rules (eg Canada, Japan, South Korea); Type 4: 'combination of a counterpart's democratic aspirations and its ambitions pertaining to the EU membership or close association relations, coupled with its dependence on the exports/imports to the EU and development aid' (eg Albania, Montenegro, Macedonia, Serbia, Turkey, the 'associated' Eastern Neighbourhood (Ukraine, Moldova and Georgia) and the Organisation of African, Caribbean and Pacific States (ACP) group of countries); M Rabinovych, *EU Regional Trade Agreements: An Instrument of Promoting the Rule of Law to Third States* (London and New York, Routledge, 2021) 55.

[44] Economist Intelligence Unit, 'Democracy Index 2021' (the report may be requested via *The Economist*, 'A new low for global democracy: More pandemic restrictions damaged democratic freedoms in 2021', 9 February 2022, www.economist.com/graphic-detail/2022/02/09/a-new-low-for-global-democracy). Except for political participation which shows an upward trend, the other four indicators show worrying signs of decline over the period 2008–2021, see ibid, the figure at 25. On the choice for a 'thick' concept of democracy, including protection of basic human rights and the methodology used, see the Appendix to the report, at 66.

[45] ibid, Table 1 at 4. The concept of 'Full democracies' refers to '[c]ountries in which not only basic political freedoms and civil liberties are respected, but which also tend to be underpinned by a political culture conducive to the flourishing of democracy. The functioning of government is satisfactory. Media are independent and diverse. There is an effective system of checks and balances. The judiciary is independent and judicial decisions are enforced. There are only limited problems in the functioning of democracies.' See ibid at 68.

[46] For instance, the Scandinavian countries, in particular Norway (best country) and Iceland, together with Finland, Sweden and Denmark, rank highly as full democracies.

[47] Economist Intelligence Unit, 'Democracy Index 2021', above n 44, at 4.

labelled as 'flawed' democracies, although they may still qualify as 'functioning' democracies.[48] Importantly, 59 countries, or more than one-third of the world population, live under authoritarian rule,[49] with the remaining 34 countries (amounting to a further 17 per cent of the world population) having some but not all of the required democratic elements and therefore being labelled as 'hybrid' regimes.[50] Quite worryingly, over the past years democracy seems to be in decline in all parts of the world, with the number of democratic states going down, not up.

The World Justice Project, for its part, annually measures respect for the rule of law in a thick sense worldwide.[51] It does so in 139 countries, based on the following eight factors: constraints on government powers, absence of corruption, open government, fundamental rights, order and security, regulatory enforcement, civil justice, and criminal justice.[52] When comparing the above '2021 Global Democracy Index' map[53] with the World Justice Project (WJP) 'Rule of Law Index 2021' global map,[54] the resemblances in outcome are striking. Full democracies consistently have a high rule-of-law ranking whereas declining democratic features correspond to a decrease in rule-of-law score. If this finding may not be surprising as such, it does raise questions about the proper interpretation to be given to the EU objective to promote and

[48] See Table 7 for the qualification of Eastern European countries and Table 12 for the Western European countries, above n 44, at 44 and 62 respectively. The concept of 'Flawed democracies' refers to '[t]hese countries also have free and fair elections and, even if there are problems (such as infringements on media freedom), basic civil liberties are respected. However, there are significant weaknesses in other aspects of democracy, including problems in governance, an underdeveloped political culture and low levels of political participation' (ibid at 68).

[49] The report (above n 44, at 68) states that 'Authoritarian regimes' refers to the following: 'In these states, state political pluralism is absent or heavily circumscribed. Many countries in this category are outright dictatorships. Some formal institutions of democracy may exist, but these have little substance. Elections, if they do occur, are not free and fair. There is disregard for abuses and infringements of civil liberties. Media are typically state-owned or controlled by groups connected to the ruling regime. There is repression of criticism of the government and pervasive censorship. There is no independent judiciary'.

[50] See the report (above n 44 at 68) which describes them thus: 'Hybrid regimes: Elections have substantial irregularities that often prevent them from being both free and fair. Government pressure on opposition parties and candidates may be common. Serious weaknesses are more prevalent than in flawed democracies – in political culture, functioning of government and political participation. Corruption tends to be widespread and the rule of law is weak. Civil society is weak. Typically, there is harassment of and pressure on journalists, and the judiciary is not independent.'

[51] See The World Justice Project (WJP) Rule of Law Index 2021, 14 (accessed via worldjusticeproject.org/our-work/research-and-data/wjp-rule-law-index-2021), where it is explained that the WJP definition of the rule of law is based on four Universal Principles. 'The rule of law is a durable system of laws, institutions, norms, and community commitment that delivers:

- Accountability: The government as well as private actors are accountable under the law.
- Just Law: The law is clear, publicized, and stable and is applied evenly. It ensures human rights as well as contract and property rights.
- Open Government: The processes by which the law is adopted, administered, adjudicated, and enforced are accessible, fair, and efficient.
- Accessible and Impartial Justice: Justice is delivered timely by competent, ethical, and independent representatives and neutrals who are accessible, have adequate resources, and reflect the makeup of the communities they serve'.

[52] The World Justice Project (WJP) Rule of Law Index 2021, 9. It is stated (at 12) that 'The World Justice Project (WJP) developed the WJP Rule of Law Index to serve as a quantitative tool for measuring the rule of law in practice'. For the methodology used, see 180 ff.

[53] To be consulted at: www.economist.com/graphic-detail/2022/02/09/a-new-low-for-global-democracy.

[54] For the interactive (WJP) Rule of Law Index 2021 map, see worldjusticeproject.org/rule-of-law-index/.

uphold its values in its relations with the wider world, in particular the rule of law, according to whether it is faced with functioning democracies or not.

The challenges to externally uphold and promote the rule of law in functioning (and to a large extent like-minded Western) democracies are more aligned with the internal situation in the EU Member States and the EU should thus aim at upholding the rule of law in a thick sense. If anything, the internal EU rule-of-law issues (as well as the USA surge on the capitol on 6 January 2021) show that due attention should be paid to established liberal democracies quasi imperceptibly sliding into illiberal democracy.[55] Also in its relations with functioning democracies the EU should therefore be wary against complacency, which dangerously facilitates rule-of-law backsliding. A better option would seem to be to (pro)actively formulate common answers to the potential impact of digitalisation on the democratic processes and, importantly, to maintain in force democratic checks and balances not just in theory but also in practice.[56] This may necessitate revisiting and strengthening the role and function of institutions to ensure effective judicial control by independent courts and democratic control by parliaments, but also the role and functions of media and social media.

A more difficult exercise, conceptually, is to pinpoint what it can possibly mean to uphold and promote the rule of law in EU relations with the majority of countries worldwide, which openly or in practice clearly do not share democratic aspirations. Other chapters in this book have pointed to the close link between the concepts of 'rule of law' and 'democracy' and have reflected on the existence of a sequential interaction between the two.[57] It is hardly an option, realistically, for the EU to refuse to interact economically and politically with more than half the countries of the globe solely because they do not share liberal democracy as a preferred or sustained model. Policywise, the emphasis is instead put on the strategic interest for the EU to advance its 'global leadership' with respect to human rights and democracy.[58] A crucial policy feature for the EU to emphasise is that it remains 'steadfast as a strong defender of human rights and democracy', which translates into 'maximising the EU's role on the global stage by expanding the human rights toolbox, its key instruments and policies'.[59] The very notion of a toolbox[60] indicates that a differentiated approach may need to be taken, and different instruments employed, depending on the assessment

[55] See F Zakaria, 'The Rise of Illiberal Democracy' (1997) 76(6) *Foreign Affairs* 22.

[56] On the importance of the practical impact, see Chapter 12 by K Miklóssy in this book.

[57] See in particular Chapter 2 by A Rosas in this book.

[58] Joint Communication to the European Parliament and the Council, 'EU Action Plan on Human Rights and Democracy 2020–2024', JOIN(2020) 5 final of 25 March 2020, 1. This builds on the 'EU Strategic Framework and Action Plan on Human Rights and Democracy', Council of the European Union, 25 June 2012: see www.consilium.europa.eu/uedocs/cms_data/docs/pressdata/EN/foraff/131181.pdf.

[59] As indicated (ibid, at 4) the Action Plan 'will set out EU ambitions and identify priorities for action around five interlinked and mutually reinforcing lines of action:

- I Protecting and empowering individuals
- II Building resilient, inclusive and democratic societies
- III Promoting a global system for human rights and democracy
- IV New technologies: Harnessing opportunities and addressing challenges
- V Delivering by working together'.

[60] On the expanding Human Rights toolbox, see also Chapter 14 by S Blockmans in this book.

of the actual situation in the third country concerned.[61] Seen from this perspective, it would be counterproductive for the EU then to steadfastly not engage in relations with third countries which do not share the last part of the triptych, namely a (thick) rule-of-law concept. The main challenge for the EU as a global leader in this respect does not lie in preaching to the choir. For the sake of consistently pursuing the EU Treaty objective of promoting and upholding the rule of law in relations with the wider world, a gradual step-by-step approach may instead be called for, targeted to the specific external context and interlocutor. Such a finding is also in line with the external reference frame discussed above.[62]

B. Pre-accession Conditionality (Or Not) as a Conceptual Differentiation Criterion

Superimposed onto the above distinction between third countries based on their democratic status, a further conceptual differentiation is called for according to whether or not the third country concerned aspires to EU membership. It is only with respect to the latter that the 'values' and 'interests' of the EU, as referred to in Article 3(5) TEU, always and necessarily coincide. It is clearly in the interest of the EU to ascertain that candidate countries fully share all the EU values expressed in Article 2 TEU, at least by the time of their accession. The pre-accession conditionality requires full compliance with the 'thick' rule-of-law concept and triggers the full intra-EU reference frame as applies to the EU Member States.[63] Candidate countries are thus under a firm obligation as to result to duly respect the rule of law, democracy and human rights, subject to control by the European Commission. The fact that the leverage exerted by the prospect of EU membership status is lost immediately upon EU accession, qualifies the pre-accession conditionality truly as the most powerful rule-of-law enforcement instrument at the disposal of the EU, all internal and external situations taken together.

A similar presumption that promoting and upholding the EU's 'values' and its 'interests' always and necessarily coincides, appears more problematic with respect to all other third countries, regardless of whether they are functioning democracies. It would also simply be wrong to assume that the closer the geographical proximity of a third country to the EU the more likely that, for the EU, promoting its values will ultimately prevail over its interest. It has been suggested that instead of geographical proximity, it is rather the third country's ambition of integration with the EU that is the crucial factor, pointing out that the EU leverage to export the rule of law would then logically be more important in respect of associated countries.[64] Some level of policy coherence may thus be explained depending on the differentiated nature of the bilateral relations with those countries.

[61] See also section VI below.

[62] See section III above.

[63] See section II above.

[64] P Van Elsuwege and O Burlyuk, 'Exporting the Rule of Law to the EU's Eastern Neighbourhood: Reconciling Coherence and Differentiation' in S Poli, (ed), *The European Neighbourhood Policy – Values and Principles* (London and New York, Routledge, 2018) 176.

In theory the EU's leverage to promote the rule of law may indeed be stronger the more closely a country wishes to integrate with the EU, so that the EU instruments to enforce the rule of law thus become more effective. Yet other studies have shown that in practice there are important inconsistencies in the EU's approach to promoting its values under its neighbourhood policy, in spite of the express mention of the Union's 'values' in Article 8 TEU,[65] which can mostly be explained by reference to more immediate and narrow interests that the EU has sought to protect.[66]

It thus appears that whereas pursuant to Article 3(5) TEU the EU should consistently endeavour to promote its values and its interests, in practice it systematically pursues its interests whereas it promotes its values to the extent possible. Except for countries under pre-accession conditionality, where the EU has an existential interest in fully upholding its rule-of-law concept in a thick sense, the third country concerned may simply not at all share a similar concept or concern for the rule of law, thereby inducing a pragmatic compartmentalisation approach by the EU. Yet all too often it is simply the pursuit of more immediate EU interests, whether economic, or geopolitical, but also for instance related to migration or the fight against terrorism, that take the upper hand.

V. CONCEPTUAL DIFFERENTIATION BETWEEN THE EU AND THIRD COUNTRIES

A last important differentiation relates to the rule-of-law concept as applicable to the EU itself, in its external action, compared to the third countries with which it interacts. Whereas the rule of law may be understood and enforced differently externally depending on the above-mentioned specificities of the third country concerned,[67] it is undisputed that the EU and its institutions of course always and systematically need to respect the EU values expressed in Article 2 TEU, including the rule of law, pursuant to Article 13(1) TEU[68] both in the EU's internal and external action.[69]

[65] Art 8(1) TEU stipulates: 'The Union shall develop a special relationship with neighbouring countries, aiming to establish an area of prosperity and good neighbourliness, founded on the values of the Union and characterised by close and peaceful relations based on cooperation.'

[66] See also the conclusion by Nathalie Tocci that 'in practice, the pursuit of narrow interests has often hindered the EU's potential to advance those long-term goals that reflect the values on which the Union is founded': N Tocci, 'Comparing the EU's role in neighbourhood conflicts' in M Cremona (ed), *Developments in EU external relations law* (Oxford, Oxford University Press, 2008) 216, 243.

[67] See section IV above.

[68] Art 13(1) TEU: 'The Union shall have an institutional framework which shall aim to promote its values, advance its objectives, serve its interests, those of its citizens and those of the Member States, and ensure the consistency, effectiveness and continuity of its policies and actions.'

[69] Ilaria Vianello makes the following distinction: 'The rule of law as a structural principle in EU external relations law requires the Union to abide by certain principles in its relations with those countries outside the Union's legal structure. This obligation has nothing to do with the actual content of the Union policies, it is rather concerned with the action targeted at their development and implementation': see I Vianello, 'The rule of law as relational principle structuring the Union's action towards its external partners' in M Cremona (ed), *Structural Principles in EU External Relations Law* (Oxford, Hart Publishing, 2018) 225, 239–40.

When looking at the external action of the EU there is, however, an extra layer to the rule of law concept to consider – here called the rule of 'EU' law – which may not immediately be apparent in relations with third countries. It has been argued elsewhere that EU external action and instruments, too, come squarely within the autonomous EU legal order and thus unequivocally need to comply specifically with the rule of 'EU' law in the sense of Article 19 TEU.[70] The rule of 'EU' law thus comprises the EU values as expressed in Article 2 TEU as well as all other 'intra-balloon' characteristics, not least primacy, direct effect and uniform interpretation by the ECJ. Cases such as the *Mauritius Agreement*[71] and *Rosneft*[72] illustrate how the horizontal scope of Article 19 TEU has also been instrumental to reduce the practical impact of the express carve-out for the Common Foreign and Security Policy (CFSP) in Articles 24(1) TEU and 275(1) TFEU. At the same time, this case law triggered a shift from CFSP measures needing to respect solely a domestic or internationally formulated and enforced rule-of-law concept towards safeguarding respect for specifically the 'EU' rule of law under the control of the ECJ.[73]

Going a step further by externalising the effects of the EU autonomous legal order in terms of requiring respect for the rule of 'EU' law by international bodies or under dispute settlement in international agreements to which the EU is a party is, however, highly unlikely. On the one hand it could theoretically be argued that since such international agreements 'form an integral part of EU law from their coming into force',[74] full respect for Article 19 TEU, or at least the EU values as expressed in Article 2 TEU, is warranted by all international bodies set up (or acceded to) by the EU. On the other hand, and more importantly, the ECJ has clarified that the international legal personality of the EU necessarily implies that the EU institutions, including the ECJ itself, are bound by decisions of such bodies,[75] adopted in compliance with international, not EU, law. Apart from the fact that third countries would of course hardly accept being (in)directly bound by EU law in such a construction, also some crucial elements seem to be lacking from the side of the EU itself.

[70] See I Govaere, 'Interconnecting Legal Systems and the Autonomous EU Legal Order: a Balloon Dynamic' in I Govaere and S Garben (eds), *The Interface Between EU and International Law: Contemporary Reflections* (Oxford, Hart Publishing, 2019) 19.

[71] Case C-658/11 *Parliament v Council* (*Mauritius Agreement*) ECLI:EU:C:2014:2025. For a comment, see P Van Elsuwege, 'Securing the Institutional Balance in the Procedure for Concluding International Agreements: European Parliament v. Council (Pirate Transfer Agreement with Mauritius)' (2015) 52 *CML Rev* 1379.

[72] Case C-72/15 *PJSC Rosneft Oil Company v HM Treasury and Others* ECLI:EU:C:2017:236. See inter alia S Poli, 'The Common Foreign and Security Policy after Rosneft: Still Imperfect but Gradually Subject to the Rule of Law' (2017) 54(6) *CML Rev* 1799.

[73] For a discussion of this development, see also G Butler, 'The Coming to Age of the Court's Jurisdiction in the Common Foreign and Security Policy' (2017) 13(4) *EuConst* 673; I Govaere, 'To Give or to Grab: The Principle of Full, Crippled and Split Conferral of Powers Post-Lisbon' in M Cremona (ed), *Structural Principles in EU External Relations Law* (Oxford, Hart Publishing, 2018) 71, esp at 83–84; C Hillion and R Wessel, '"The Good, the Bad and the Ugly": three levels of judicial control over the CFSP' in S Blockmans and P Koutrakos (eds), *Research Handbook on the EU's Common Foreign and Security Policy* (Cheltenham, Edward Elgar, 2018) 65; P Van Elsuwege and F Gremmelprez, 'Protecting the rule of law in the EU legal order: a constitutional role for the Court of Justice' (2020) 16(1) *EuConst* 8.

[74] Case 181/73 *Haegeman v Belgian State* ECLI:EU:C:1974:41, para 5.

[75] *Opinion 1/76* (*Draft Agreement establishing a European laying-up fund for inland waterway vessels*) ECLI:EU:C:1977:63 and *Opinion 1/91* (*Draft EEA Agreement*) ECLI:EU:C:1991:490, paras 39–40.

The strongest arguments in favour of EU competence to enforce the rule of 'EU' law internally, instead of international or domestic law, are stringently linked to the necessity to maintain mutual trust between the national courts of the Member States as EU courts under Article 267 TFEU.[76] To the contrary, in *Opinion 1/17* the CJEU has forcefully underlined that in relation to third countries no such presumption of mutual trust in an independent and functioning judiciary may be taken to exist,[77] not even in relation to a functioning democracy such as Canada. If from an EU law perspective internally so much emphasis is placed on the link between mutual trust and respect for the rule of 'EU' law, then it would appear to be difficult, if not impossible, to externalise the rule of 'EU' law without the anchorage of mutual trust.

VI. CONSISTENCY AND INSTRUMENTS TO PROMOTE THE RULE OF LAW

The one consistent factor in the external action of the EU is that it openly seeks to 'leverage the broad range of policies and tools at its disposal to promote and defend human rights, democracy and the rule of law'.[78] This does not mean that the EU will always use the same instruments for all countries, or that it will always adopt a similar and standardised response, but rather that the various EU instruments may be put into effect depending on the specific circumstances and context. The question is whether the instruments are currently used consistently and systematically with regard to the above-mentioned factors which call for a conceptual differentiation between third countries in terms of functioning democracy and membership aspirations. A complicating factor is that the degree of leverage to be expected from EU trade policy, in particular, and the prospect of market access may play out very

[76] In an external relations setting, see in particular Case C-284/16 *Slowakische Republik v Achmea BV* ECLI:EU:C:2018:158, paras 34: 'EU law is thus based on the fundamental premiss that each Member State shares with all the other Member States, and recognises that they share with it, a set of common values on which the EU is founded, as stated in Article 2 TEU. That premiss implies and justifies the existence of mutual trust between the Member States that those values will be recognised, and therefore that the law of the EU that implements them will be respected. It is precisely in that context that the Member States are obliged, by reason inter alia of the principle of sincere cooperation set out in the first subparagraph of Article 4(3) TEU, to ensure in their respective territories the application of and respect for EU law, and to take for those purposes any appropriate measure, whether general or particular, to ensure fulfilment of the obligations arising out of the Treaties or resulting from the acts of the institutions of the EU (Opinion 2/13 (Accession of the EU to the ECHR) of 18 December 2014, EU:C:2014:2454, paragraphs 168 and 173 and the case-law cited)'. In an internal setting, see in particular the so-called 'Independence of judges cases', see eg C-64/16, *Associação Sindical dos Juízes Portugueses v Tribunal de Contas* ECLI:EU:C:2018:117, para 30: 'According to Article 2 TEU, the European Union is founded on values, such as the rule of law, which are common to the Member States in a society in which, inter alia, justice prevails. In that regard, it should be noted that mutual trust between the Member States and, in particular, their courts and tribunals is based on the fundamental premiss that Member States share a set of common values on which the European Union is founded, as stated in Article 2 TEU (see, to that effect, Opinion 2/13 (Accession of the European Union to the ECHR), of 18 December 2014, EU:C:2014:2454, paragraph 168)'.

[77] *Opinion 1/17 (CETA)* ECLI:EU:C:2019:341, para 129: 'However, that principle of mutual trust, with respect to, inter alia, compliance with the right to an effective remedy before an independent tribunal, is not applicable in relations between the Union and a non-Member State'.

[78] EU Action Plan on Human Rights and Democracy 2020–2024, JOIN(2020) 5 final, 4, www.eeas.europa.eu/sites/default/files/eu_action_plan_on_human_rights_and_democracy_2020-2024.pdf.

differently depending on the counterpart and the counter leverage the latter can exert in terms of economic or geopolitical weight.

The EU toolbox to promote the rule of law consists of both legally binding instruments and soft power tools, possibly used in combination to increase the effectiveness in any given case. What is most crucial, however, is for the EU to lead by example, so as not to undermine the external credibility of the EU and to spark the criticism of double standards.

The legally binding instruments at the disposal of the EU to promote the rule of law in its relations with the wider world are manifold. The EU may leverage and apply longstanding unilateral measures such as the Generalised Scheme of Preferences Plus (GSP+)[79] but also the recently elaborated EU Global Human Rights Sanctions Regime 2020.[80] Since the mid-nineties, at the instigation of the European Parliament, most bilateral agreements concluded by the EU contain a human rights or conditionality clause,[81] which allows for a carrot-and-stick approach and should, if need be, also facilitate the adoption of sanctions and suspension of the agreement. But also content-wise the agreements can aim to promote EU values and in particular human rights and the rule of law. There may be provisions calling for either compliance with, or accession to, international agreements (external benchmarking) or approximation and direct alignment to EU values so as to secure market access (trade leveraging). Rule-of-law issues may also be addressed in Political Dialogue Chapters of agreements.[82]

Among the soft power instruments it is noteworthy to mention state-to-state initiatives such as not only classical diplomacy, dialogues with indication of priority areas (HR dialogue;[83] Policy dialogue) and Financial and Technical Financial Assistance, but also for instance engagement with civil society and people-to-people contacts.[84] Although in practice such soft instruments may help to overcome the deadlock otherwise posed by the reluctance or plain refusal of third countries to undertake obligations in relation to rule of law and human rights, it should be used with caution. The efficiency of those soft instruments in also overcoming sometimes difficult internal discussions on issues of competence cannot hide the fact that in so doing EU external action may be withdrawn from direct judicial and democratic control by the ECJ and European Parliament. It would be paradoxical to weaken the respect for the thick intra-EU rule-of-law concept by the EU institutions by sidestepping democratic checks and balances at EU level, in order to promote an often only 'thin' rule-of-law concept, if any, in those third countries concerned by such measures.

[79] Regulation (EU) No 978/2012 of the European Parliament and of the Council of 25 October 2012 applying a scheme of generalised tariff preferences [2012] OJ L303/1.

[80] Council Regulation (EU) 2020/1998 of 7 December 2020 concerning restrictive measures against serious human rights violations and abuses [2020] OJ L410/1. See also Chapter 14 by S Blockmans in this book.

[81] See eg the study made by Dr Lorand Bartels for the EP, 'The European Parliament's Role in Relation to Human Rights in Trade and Investment Agreements', February 2014, www.europarl.europa.eu/cmsdata/86031/Study.pdf.

[82] On the discussion on whether this necessarily implies CFSP is a legal basis and mixity, see Case C-180/20 *Commission v Council* (*Accord avec l'Arménie*) ECLI:EU:C:2021:658.

[83] See Council of the EU, 'EU guidelines on human rights dialogues with third countries_update', PESC 1591, 22 December 2008, data.consilium.europa.eu/doc/document/ST-16526-2008-INIT/en/pdf.

[84] See eg Commission and High Representative, 'EU-Russia relations: Push back, constrain and engage', JOIN(2021) 20 final of 16 June 2021.

VII. CONCLUSION

It is of paramount importance for the credibility of the EU worldwide to be seen to be consistent, for it to lead by example, and in particular not to be accused of double standards when it comes to the rule of law. Nonetheless, to a large extent abstraction was made in this chapter of the highly unwarranted effects of the currently defaulting intra-EU rule-of-law implementation and enforcement. Instead the focus was to elaborate a conceptual framework for the external promotion of the rule of law by the EU, specifically tailored to meet identified external challenges and stakes. Consistency in promoting the rule of law should not be measured against one single yardstick in terms of outcome or instrument. Instead, upholding and promoting the rule of law in relations with the wider world implies a deliberate and flexible process with policy choices based on conceptually distinctive factors. It was argued that even the very concept of the rule of law as used by the EU in different settings cannot be steadfast. Both the meaning and the reference frame of the rule of law are distinct when dealing with the EU and its Member States or with third countries. It was argued that the rule of law should be further conceptually differentiated between third countries, based on objective criteria in terms of functioning democracy and membership aspirations. All too often the external practice of the EU, based on 'principled pragmatism', is perceived as favouring narrow and pointed EU interest over the systematic promotion of EU values. The adoption of an underlying conceptual framework, allowing for objective grounds for differentiation and sufficient flexibility, could only enhance the coherence and credibility of the EU and strengthen its position as a global soft power.

14

The EU's Magnitsky Act: An Innovative Tool Fit for the Enforcement of Human Rights and Rule of Law Worldwide?

STEVEN BLOCKMANS

I. INTRODUCTION

RUSSIA'S FULL-SCALE INVASION of Ukraine on 24 February 2022 has been almost universally condemned as a blatant violation of the canons of international law enshrined in the Charter of the United Nations.[1] It led the International Court of Justice to order Russia to immediately suspend its military operations.[2] *Quod non.* In the face of fierce resistance mounted by the Ukrainian armed forces, the invaders resorted to systematic and indiscriminate missile strikes and shelling of civilian areas in Kyiv and other major cities (notably Mariupol and Kharkhiv), as well as small towns and villages.[3]

In response, the West unleashed its own kind of 'shock and awe' on Russia and its Belarusian accomplice. With commendable unity among its Member States and in partnership with G7 allies, the EU weaponised its trade and finance instruments to punish Russia for its leadership's war of choice. In the weeks and months after the invasion, the EU adopted a series of crippling sanctions, rapidly widening the net cast over growing numbers of targeted individuals and institutions, and limiting the Russian state's access to multilateral financial institutions, investments – particularly in the energy, transport and other strategic sectors, and trade (including suspending Russia's 'most-favoured nation' treatment at the WTO).[4]

[1] More than 90 countries united for peace (cf UNGA Res 377) led a total of 141 countries (ie more than a two-thirds majority) in an emergency session to adopt UN General Assembly Resolution ES-11/1, 2 March 2022. Five countries – Belarus, DPRK, Eritrea, Russia and Syria – voted against it, while 35 (including China) abstained.

[2] See ICJ Order delivered on the request for the indication of provisional measures submitted by Ukraine in the case concerning 'Allegations of Genocide under the Convention on the Prevention and Punishment of the Crime of Genocide (Ukraine v. Russian Federation)', 16 March 2022.

[3] According to estimates from the Kyiv School of Economics, Mariupol was already 90% destroyed after one month of the war, with other cities such as Kharkhiv and Chernihiv around 20 to 30% destroyed: kse.ua/about-the-school/news/zbitki-naneseni-infrastrukturi-ukrayini-v-hodi-viyni-skladayut-mayzhe-63-mlrd/.

[4] See European Commission, 'EU sanctions against Russia following the invasion of Ukraine', ec.europa.eu/info/strategy/priorities-2019-2024/stronger-europe-world/eu-solidarity-ukraine/eu-sanctions-against-russia-following-invasion-ukraine_en.

While the Russian invasion may not have started with clear genocidal intent,[5] the evidence of such practices has (literally) been piling up.[6] Following the massacre in Bucha and atrocities committed in other places under effective Russian control, and thus subject to the international law of occupation,[7] the EU Council agreed its fifth package 'intended to reinforce pressure on the Russian government economy' and aimed at stopping 'the reckless, inhuman and aggressive behaviour of the Russian troops and mak[ing] clear to the decision-makers in the Kremlin that their illegal aggression comes at a heavy cost'.[8] The sanctions included an embargo of Russian coal and other solid fossil fuels; a harbinger of EU bans on oil and gas imports, the main pillars on which the Russian economy rests. As such, Russia's 'dumb' bombs were met with increasingly 'dumb' EU sanctions.

Diverging from the blanket economic embargoes that dominated the international landscape up until the mid-1990s, the European Union has preferred to employ smart(er) sanctions targeted against natural and legal persons in order to change their policy or conduct and align them with the EU's Common Foreign and Security Policy (CFSP) objectives. Over the past 25 years, the EU's use of 'restrictive measures' (in French: '*mesures restrictives*') has increased exponentially. On 1 January 2023, 47 EU sanctions regimes were in force.[9] On the EU sanctions map, the online tool developed under the Estonian Presidency of the Council of 2017 and managed since

[5] In his televised address marking the launch of the invasion, President Putin invoked the objectives of demilitarisation and 'de-Nazification' of Ukraine, which he holds responsible for genocidal attacks on the Russian people in Eastern Ukraine. A transcript of the speech is available on the website of Bloomberg: www.bloomberg.com/news/articles/2022-02-24/full-transcript-vladimir-putin-s-televised-address-to-russia-on-ukraine-feb-24. See, further, V Putin, 'On the Historical Unity of Russians and Ukrainians', 12 July 2021, available at en.kremlin.ru/events/president/news/66181.

[6] T Sergeytsev, 'Что Россия должна сделать с Украиной' (What Russia should do with Ukraine?), *RIA Novosti* 3 April 2022. An English translation of this despicable text is available at ccl.org.ua/en/news/ria-novosti-has-clarified-russias-plans-vis-a-vis-ukraine-and-the-rest-of-the-free-world-in-a-program-like-article-what-russia-should-do-with-ukraine-2/. For an authoritative analysis, see T Snyder, 'Russia's Genocide Handbook: The evidence of atrocity and intent mounts', 8 April 2022, available at snyder.substack.com/p/russias-genocide-handbook?s=r. For further indications of genocidal 'intent', the deportation of Ukrainian children for assimilation in Russian families and institutions was 'legalised' by President Putin in May 2022 with a decree simplifying the procedure for obtaining Russian citizenship for Ukrainian orphans and children left without parental care. See https://t.me/rian_ru/165351, 30 May 2022. Despite the patriotic fanfare about Russia's humanitarian mission in Ukraine, the forced displacement amounts to a violation of Article 2(e) of the 1948 Genocide Convention. According to its own figures, Russia has seized some 200,000 Ukrainian children in the first two months of this war. Report by Interfax, www.interfax.ru/world/839058. See OHCHR, 'Human rights concerns related to forced displacement in Ukraine', 7 September 2022.

[7] See 'Ukraine: Declaration by the High Representative on behalf of the EU on Russian atrocities committed in Bucha and other Ukrainian towns', Council of the EU, Press release No 355/22, 4 April 2022: 'The Russian authorities are responsible for these atrocities, committed while they had effective control of the area. They are subject to the international law of occupation. The perpetrators of war crimes and other serious violations as well as the responsible government officials and military leaders will be held accountable. The European Union supports all measures to ensure accountability for human rights violations and violations of international humanitarian law in Ukraine by Russian Armed forces. In particular, we fully support the investigation launched by the ICC Prosecutor into war crimes and crimes against humanity as well as the work of the OHCHR Commission of Inquiry. The EU is assisting the Ukrainian Prosecutor General and Civil Society focused on collection and preservation of the evidences of the war crimes.'

[8] Dixit J Borrell, 'EU adopts fifth round of sanctions against Russia over its military aggression against Ukraine', Council of the EU, Press release No 365/22, 8 April 2022.

[9] See EU Sanctions Map, available at www.sanctionsmap.eu/#/main.

by the European Commission, these regimes are mostly presented in a 'vertical' – ie a country-specific – fashion (eg Russia and Belarus). Of those regimes, a majority of the EU's country-based sanctions are concerned with human rights.[10]

Facilitated by a revision of Article 215 of the Treaty on the Functioning of the EU (TFEU) in 2009 to provide for sanctions against non-state actors,[11] the Union used the precedent of the counter-terrorism regime[12] to respond to a worsening security environment with the introduction of new thematic sanctions. An increasing use of hybrid threats, disinformation, space and cyber warfare[13] led the EU institutions to adopt targeted sanctions mechanisms for 'horizontal' purposes, like the fight against cyber[14] and chemical warfare.[15]

Adding to the EU's sanctions toolbox, the Foreign Affairs Council on 7 December 2020 adopted the EU's 'Global Human Rights Sanctions Regime' (GHRSR).[16] The objective of the horizontal GHRSR is to give the EU a framework instrument to address serious human rights violations and abuses worldwide.[17] It follows the examples of the US,[18] Canada[19] and UK,[20] and is also known as the EU's 'Magnitsky Act' – after Sergei Magnitsky, a Ukrainian-born Russian lawyer and tax auditor whose untimely death in a Moscow prison in 2009 led to the adoption of the original

[10] See C Beaucillon, 'Opening Up the Horizon: The ECJ's new take on country sanctions' (2018) 55 *CML Rev* 387–415.

[11] Previously, only individuals closely connected to the targeted regime could be listed in country-based sanctions. Without such a link, as in the *Kadi* case, what is now art 352 TFEU was required as an additional legal basis. See Joined Cases C-402/05 and C-415/05 P *Kadi and Al Barakaat International Foundation v Council and Commission* ECLI:EU:C:2008:461, para 166.

[12] Compare with the original Council Common Position 2001/931/CFSP of 27 December 2001 on the application of specific measures to combat terrorism, [2001] OJ L344/93; Council Regulation 2580/2001/EC of 27 December 2001 on specific restrictive measures directed against certain persons and entities with a view to combating terrorism, [2001] OJ L344/70.

[13] See Communication from the Commission to the European Parliament, the European Council, the Council, the European Economic and Social Committee and the Committee of the Regions on the EU Security Union Strategy, COM(2020) 605 final, Brussels, 24 July 2020.

[14] Council Decision 2019/797/CFSP of 17 May 2019 concerning restrictive measures against cyber-attacks threatening the Union or its Member States, [2019] OJ L129I/13; and Council Regulation 2019/796/EU of 17 May 2019 concerning restrictive measures against cyber-attacks threatening the Union or its Member States, [2019] OJ L129I/1.

[15] Council Decision 2018/1544/CFSP of 15 October 2018 concerning restrictive measures against the proliferation and use of chemical weapons, [2018] OJ L259/25; Council Regulation 2018/1542/EU of 15 October 2018 concerning restrictive measures against the proliferation and use of chemical weapons, [2018] OJ L259/12.

[16] Council Decision 2020/1999/CFSP of 7 December 2020 concerning restrictive measures against serious human rights violations and abuses, [2020] OJ L410I/13; Council Regulation 2020/1998/EU of 7 December 2020 concerning restrictive measures against serious human rights violations and abuses, [2020] OJ L410I/1.

[17] Art 1(1) of Council Decision 2020/1999/CFSP.

[18] Global Magnitsky Human Rights Accountability Act, Public Law 114-328 ('Global Magnitsky Act'), www.govinfo.gov/content/pkg/PLAW-114publ328/pdf/PLAW-114publ328.pdf; Executive Order 13818 titled 'Blocking the Property of Persons Involved in Serious Human Rights Abuses or Corruption', www.treasury.gov/resource-center/sanctions/Programs/Documents/glomag_eo.pdf.

[19] Justice for Victims of Corrupt Foreign Officials Act (Sergei Magnitsky Law) S.C. 2017, c. 21, full text available at laws.justice.gc.ca/eng/acts/J-2.3/FullText.html.

[20] Proceeds of Crime Act 2002 (POCA) and the Sanctions and Anti-Money Laundering Act 2018 (SAMLA). In July 2020, the UK imposed the first sanctions under the SAMLA: www.legislation.gov.uk/uksi/2020/680/introduction/made?view=plain; see also: www.gov.uk/government/publications/financial-sanctions-global-human-rights.

US Magnitsky Act of 2012.[21] This Act was directed at the persons who were responsible for his detention and demise and who did not face legal consequences in Russia for their human rights and rule-of-law violations. In 2016, the US gave the original act worldwide reach by the Global Magnitsky Human Rights Accountability Act.[22]

Initiated by the Netherlands[23] and pushed by the European Parliament,[24] the EU's 'Magnitsky Act' was supposed to fill a gap by providing a legal basis for targeted individual sanctions without the need for a country-based regime, thereby supplementing existing restrictive measures and reinforcing collective action on human rights to ensure – rather bombastically – that 'perpetrators of human rights violations and abuses have nowhere to hide.'[25] Like the preceding horizontal sanction regimes, the restrictive measures available under the GHRSR combine entry and transit restrictions (visa bans) with freezing of targeted persons' and entities' assets.[26] Although seventeen individuals and five legal entities from six countries were blacklisted in its first year of operation,[27] those Russians deemed politically or operationally responsible for grave human rights violations in Ukraine were, at the time of writing, only added to the country-specific list.[28] This raises the question whether the GHRSR is fit for purpose.

This chapter will examine the GHRSR's aims and material scope (section II), choice of legal basis, process of adoption, as well as the blacklisting and de-listing procedures of individuals (section III). As such, this investigation goes beyond the question about the usefulness of the GHRSR in a particular case such as that of Russia's human rights violations in Ukraine. It asks whether the EU's new thematic sanctions instrument itself is 'rule of law-proof' and, if so, whether the required evidentiary standards inhibit listings under the top category of the new instrument: genocide and crimes against humanity. Taken together, these aspects raise further questions about the EU's supposed 'global leadership'[29] role on human rights and the claim that the GHRSR will pursue CFSP objectives in this regard.[30] Such legitimacy concerns (section IV) are, indeed, reasons to be cautious about whether the GHRSR

[21] The Russia and Moldova Jackson–Vanik Repeal and Sergei Magnitsky Rule of Law Accountability Act, Public Law No 112-208.

[22] Unlike the current EU regime, it targets corruption as well as human rights violations.

[23] Remarks by the Dutch Minister of Foreign Affairs Stef Blok, 20 November 2018, www.government.nl/documents/speeches/2018/11/20/blok-on-eu-global-human-rights-sanction-regime.

[24] See eg European Parliament resolution 2019/2580(RSP) of 14 March 2019 on a European human rights violations sanctions regime, P8_TA(2019)0215.

[25] Keynote address by the EU Special Representative for Human Rights, Eamon Gilmore at the launch of the EU Action Plan on Human Rights and Democracy 2020–2024, 23 November 2020.

[26] Arts 2 and 3 of Council Decision 2020/1999/CFSP.

[27] They included natural and legal persons from Belarus, China, Eritrea, Libya, North Korea, Russia (including the mercenary Wagner Group). See Council Decision 2021/372/CFSP, [2021] OJ L71I/6; Council Implementing Regulation 2021/371/EU, [2021] OJ L71I/1; Council Decision 2021/481/CFSP, [2021] OJ L99I/25; Council Implementing Regulation 2021/478/EU, [2021] OJ L99I/1; Council Decision 2021/2160/CFSP, [2021] OJ L436/40; Council Implementing Regulation 2021/2151/EU, [2021] OJ L436/1; Council Decision 2021/2197/CFSP, [2021] OJ L445I/17; and Council Implementing Regulation 2021/2195/EU, [2021] OJ L445I/10.

[28] Research for this chapter was closed on 1 January 2023.

[29] Council Conclusions on the EU Action Plan on Human Rights and Democracy 2020–2024, Council doc 12848/20, 18 November 2020, para 6.

[30] Art 1(1)(d) of Council Decision 2020/1999/CFSP; art 2(1)(d) of Council Regulation 2020/1998/EU.

can meet the expectations that have been raised by the roaring rhetoric with which it has been launched.

II. AIMS AND SCOPE

Sanctions have been widely understood to be imposed in reaction to behaviour that the senders, be they individual states or international organisations, consider objectionable, even if this has not been codified as illegal.[31] It is recognised by scholarship that compliance is often not the only, or not even the primary, aim of sanctions but that they fulfil other functions. These include the desire to demonstrate the sender's willingness and capacity to act, to anticipate or deflect criticism, to maintain certain patterns of behaviour in international affairs, to deter further engagement in the objectionable actions by the target and third parties, to support international institutions, to promote subversion within the target state or entity, and to assuage domestic audiences.[32] While each situation may see a combination of two or more of these objectives, the central aim of restrictions imposed in reaction to undesirable acts is mostly geared toward exercising pressure to alter the political behaviour of the targeted parties.[33]

A. A Taxonomy of Violations

The Council Decision and Regulation introducing the GHRSR refer to 'serious human rights violations and abuses worldwide', falling into three categories. Genocide and crimes against humanity are singled out as the most serious ones.[34] These violations qualify without further conditions. The second category of violations and abuses of human rights regarded as sufficiently serious in themselves lists five types of crimes: 'torture and other cruel, inhuman or degrading treatment or punishment; slavery; extrajudicial, summary or arbitrary executions and killings; enforced disappearance of persons; and arbitrary arrests or detentions'.[35] Here too, no further specific conditions apply to violations. A third category refers to 'other human rights violations or abuses' which are 'widespread, systematic or … otherwise of serious concern as regards the objectives of the common foreign and security policy set out in Article 21 TEU.'[36] This category includes but is not limited to: 'trafficking in human beings,

[31] See P Koutrakos, *Trade, Foreign Policy and Defence in EU Constitutional Law: The Legal Regulation of Sanctions, Exports of Dual-use Goods and Armaments* (Oxford, Hart Publishing, 2001) 49: 'Sanctions are measures that connote the exercise of pressure by one state or coalition of states to produce a change in the political behaviour of another state or group of states'.

[32] See eg J Barber, 'Economic Sanctions as a Policy Instrument' (1979) 55(3) *International Affairs* 367; and JM Lindsay, 'Trade Sanctions as Policy Instruments: A re-examination' (1986) 30(2) *International Studies Quarterly* 153.

[33] See C Portela, 'The EU's Use of 'Targeted' Sanctions: Evaluating Effectiveness', *CEPS Working Document No 391*, March 2014.

[34] Art 1(1)(a) and (b) of Council Decision 2020/1999/CFSP; art 2(1)(a) and (b) of Council Regulation 2020/1998/EU.

[35] Art 1(1)(c) of Council Decision 2020/1999/CFSP; art 2(1)(c) of Council Regulation 2020/1998/EU.

[36] Art 1(1)(d) of Council Decision 2020/1999/CFSP; art 2(1)(d) of Council Regulation 2020/1998/EU.

as well as abuses of human rights by migrant smugglers'; 'sexual and gender-based violence; violations or abuses of freedom of peaceful assembly and of association; violations or abuses of freedom of opinion and expression; violations or abuses of freedom of religion or belief'.[37]

By directly targeting grave human rights violations, the EU's GHRSR is first and foremost a supranational response to a security environment whereby certain threats and crimes exceed domestic jurisdiction and require a more flexible framework to deal with them.[38] As an interpretative guide, the GHRSR refers to 'customary international law and widely accepted instruments of international law' such as the Genocide Convention, the 1966 UN human rights covenants, the Rome Statute of the International Criminal Court, and the European Convention for the Protection of Human Rights and Fundamental Freedoms.

The fact that only the third category of 'other human rights violations or abuses' is conditioned on being either widespread, systematic or otherwise of serious concern raises the question whether the GHRSR is supposed to only target transnational violations. After all, the distinguishing feature of this open-ended category does not lie in the gravity of the violations but primarily in their geographical coverage or sustained character. Such a narrow reading should be dismissed though. The human rights violations could, as the first year of practice shows, well be contained within the borders of a single state, as long as they cover an extensive part of the territory or otherwise reveal a regular and organised pattern. Regardless of the level of gravity traditionally (and internationally) attributed to human rights violations, the Council of the EU could still motivate the blacklisting of natural and legal persons on grounds that their breaches are of 'serious concern as regards the objectives of the common foreign and security policy set out in Article 21 TEU'. It has rightly been pointed out that the phrasing of this political conditionality is puzzling:

> the objectives set out in Article 21 TEU apply to all EU external action, including but certainly not limited to, the CFSP. While the reference to 'the objectives of the common foreign and security policy set out in Article 21 TEU' may perhaps be acceptable in the CFSP decision, it is a solecism to have carried it over into the Regulation, perpetuating the pre-Lisbon, Kadi-era understanding of the relation between CFSP and other external powers.[39]

That said, the third factor justifying the use of the GHRSR certainly introduces a level of flexibility in the choice between several of the Union's sanctions cudgels. Indeed, it may serve as a safety valve to overcome political objections about the adoption of vertical sanctions for (relatively) minor human rights violations that are more isolated and incidental. On the other hand, the political justification is expected to mirror the lowest common denominator reached between Member States to adopt

[37] ibid.

[38] See C Eckes, 'EU Global Human Rights Sanctions Regime: Is the genie out of the bottle?' (2021) 30(2) *Journal of Contemporary European Studies* 255.

[39] See Editorial Comments, (2021) 58(3) *CML Rev* 621, 628–29. The second preambular paragraph of Council Decision 2020/1999/CFSP does get it right though: 'Such acts violate the principles and threaten the objectives of the Union's external action as set out in Article 21(1) and (2) of the Treaty on European Union (TEU).'

a CFSP decision. In situations where EU countries do manage to agree to adopt thematic sanctions, the political nature of the justification carries the risk of debasing the level of gravity of the third category of human rights violations which was intended to be reserved for the most serious kinds. The vaguely formulated foreign and security policy objectives in Article 21 TEU are unlikely to be a constraining factor in this respect.

This illustrates the inherently political character of the new sanctions regime. Whereas the EU is fond of presenting its human rights and democracy agenda as that of a virtuous global citizen altruistically defending a higher order of human dignity, the definition and adoption of restrictive measures, whether country-based or thematic, is a formal acknowledgement of EU values, as much as it reflects the political choices made in deciding which persons (not) to target and what level of pain to inflict, and thus a European 'sovereign' interest. By openly stating that designations 'shall take into account' of the objectives of the CFSP,

> another step (is taken) towards the politici[s]ation of the human rights discourse that may also undermine its success as a seemingly neutral tool urging international actors to commit at least formally and rhetorically to the value of protecting human rights.[40]

In terms of the material scope of the human rights violations listed in the Council Decision and Regulation, a question to be entertained in the context of this book is whether key elements of the rule-of-law concept are covered by the GHRSR. The answer leans towards the affirmative. Just like 'genocide' and 'crimes against humanity', the notions of 'extrajudicial' killings and 'arbitrary' arrests or detentions in the second category point in that direction. These belong to the most serious of internationally recognised human rights violations and are among the most egregious expressions of a complete breakdown of checks and balances as a result of a concentration of the *trias politica* into a power vertical, ie a situation in which the rule of law has been turned upside down into the law of the ruler.

The European Parliament has nevertheless argued that the inclusion of other crimes undermining the rule of law should be considered by the Commission when proposing an amendment to the current EU GHRSR legislation.[41] The reference here is notably to acts of corruption beyond bribery, ie offences such as illicit enrichment, trafficking in influence, and abuse of power, which often undermine the functioning and legitimacy of institutions and can have a devastating impact on the state of human rights. The suggestion to include corruption in a revised GHRSR was taken up by Commission President, Ursula von der Leyen, in her State of the Union address of 14 September 2022. It remains to be seen if Member States will endorse the Commission's impending proposal. If acts of corruption were not to be included in the revision of the existing regime, then the EP would expect the Commission and the Member States to

> draw on the UK legislative proposal for Global Anti-Corruption Sanctions Regulations or the US Global Magnitsky Act or the Canadian Justice for Victims of Corrupt Foreign

[40] See C Eckes, 'EU Human Rights Sanctions Regime: Striving for Utopia Backed by Sovereign Power?' (2021) 26(2) *European Foreign Affairs Review* 219, 240.

[41] European Parliament, Resolution on the EU Global Human Rights Sanctions Regime (EU Magnitsky Act), EP doc 2021/2563(RSP), 8 July 2021.

> Officials Act, or other similar regimes, and adopt an EU anti-corruption sanctions regime in order to complement the EU GHRSR,[42]

ie a fifth thematic sanctions regime.

Yet, as argued above, the non-exhaustive list of violations in the third category opens the door to including other elements of the rule-of-law concept,[43] including anti-corruption. Article 21 TEU in particular, which is mentioned as the legal backstop to the political conditionality attached to this grouping of human rights violations, refers to the rule of law. Moreover, in the context of sanctions, the European Court of Justice (ECJ) has linked the respect for the rule of law to Article 47 of the Charter of Fundamental Rights of the European Union (the Charter) and the right to an effective remedy (see section II.B, below).[44]

That said, a tension nevertheless lies in the inclusion of more 'regular' rule-of-law violations among the breaches covered by the GHRSR. After all, if the subjects targeted by the new thematic instrument are primarily non-state actors, then early practice with the instrument shows that in a power vertical it is hard to get away from the state and its governance structures. If this pattern is confirmed by the EU's future sanctions practice, then this would rob the GHRSR of one of its supposedly innovative traits,[45] ie the ability to target non-state actors.

In terms of evidentiary standard, a further tension lies in the broad listing criteria for the new sanctions and the 'clear and distinct' conditions required under EU law.[46] Indeed, for the GHRSR to comply with the Union's own rule-of-law standards, much depends on the listing and delisting criteria and the information on which Council decisions are based.[47]

B. Targets and Due Process

Like the violations, the targets of the GHRSR are also distinguished in three categories. At the centre, natural or legal persons, entities or bodies, who are directly 'responsible' for the kinds of violations or abuses mentioned above, are targeted.[48] Then those 'who provide financial, technical, or material support for or are otherwise involved in [violations or abuses], including by planning, directing, ordering, assisting, preparing, facilitating, or encouraging such acts', are included.[49] And in a third concentric circle feature those who are 'associated' with those in the first two categories.[50] By extending

[42] ibid, point 4.

[43] For a conceptual clarification and material deconstruction of the principle of rule of law, see the chapters in Part I of this volume.

[44] Case C-72/15 *PJSC Rosneft Oil Company v HM Treasury and Others* ECLI:EU:C:2017:236, para 73.

[45] On the supposed value added of the GHRSR, see section IV below.

[46] Declaration no 25 on Articles 75 and 215 of the Treaty on the Functioning of the European Union [2016] OJ C202/346.

[47] Based on a detailed analysis of ECJ sanctions case law, Eckes has set out the requirements with which the GHRSR has to comply. See C Eckes, 'EU Human Rights Sanctions Regime: Striving for Utopia Backed by Sovereign Power?' (2021) 26(2) *European Foreign Affairs Review* 219.

[48] Art 3(3)(a) of Council Regulation 2020/1998/EU.

[49] Art 3(3)(b) of Council Regulation 2020/1998/EU.

[50] Art 3(3)(c) of Council Regulation 2020/1998/EU.

sanctions to the latter category, the GHRSR casts a wider net so as to also catch the bigger fish, in other words those political, spiritual, economic and financial enablers of crimes, 'encouraging', aiding and abetting the ones who are directly and physically involved in human rights violations or abuses. Yet, as under conventional criminal law, the more tenuous the link to the actual crimes, the heavier the burden of proof imposed.

Recalling that 'the respect for fundamental rights and freedoms implies, in particular, that proper attention is given to the protection and observance of the due process rights of the individuals or entities concerned', the drafters of the Treaty of Lisbon declared that, 'for this purpose and in order to guarantee a thorough judicial review of decisions subjecting an individual or entity to restrictive measures, such decisions must be based on clear and distinct criteria.'[51] In other words, these conditions should be tailored to the specifics of each sanctions measure.

During the drafting phase of the GHRSR, the European Parliament also stressed the importance of due process rights for the legitimacy and legality of the GHRSR. It called for transparent criteria 'directly linked with the crime committed' and 'the systematic inclusion of clear and specific benchmarks.'[52] Despite this appeal, and Declaration No 25 attached to the Treaty of Lisbon, Decision 2020/1998/CFSP contains neither criteria nor references to benchmarks. It only prescribes that when listing '*other non-State actors* under point (c) of paragraph 3, the Council *shall take into account* in particular … the objectives of the common foreign and security policy as set out in Article 21 TEU; and the gravity and/or impact of the abuses' (emphasis added).[53] That is not to say that no causality is established at all: the annexes to the implementing decisions do provide details of the specific conduct of the blacklisted individuals and the types of violations or abuses they committed.[54] However, even at this level of implementing acts no reference is made to breaches of specific human rights instruments. Contrary to conventional criminal law, it would appear that 'no subjective element of knowledge or at least acceptance of the risk that the violation might occur is necessary for a person to be sanctioned'[55] under the GHRSR.

[51] Declaration no 25 on Articles 75 and 215 TFEU (n 46 above).

[52] European Parliament resolution of 14 March 2019 on a European human rights violations sanctions regime, P8_TA(2019)0215, para 11.

[53] Decision 2020/1999/CFSP, art 1(4).

[54] See eg Council Decision 2021/2160/CFSP, Annex, point 2, at 5: 'As Secretary of the Political and Legal Affairs Committee of the Xinjiang Uyghur Autonomous Region (XUAR) (2016 to 2019), Zhu Hailun was responsible for maintaining internal security and law enforcement in the XUAR. As such, he held a key political position in charge of overseeing and implementing a large-scale surveillance, detention and indoctrination programme targeting Uyghurs and people from other Muslim ethnic minorities. Zhu Hailun has been described as the "architect" of this programme. He is therefore responsible for serious human rights violations in China, in particular large-scale arbitrary detentions inflicted upon Uyghurs and people from other Muslim ethnic minorities'; and Council Decision 2021/2197/CFSP, Annex, point 1, at 18: 'Valery Zakharov, a former member of the Russian state security (FSB), is the security counsellor to the President of the Central African Republic (CAR). He is a key figure in the Wagner Group's command structure and keeps close links with the Russian authorities. Given his influential position in CAR and his leading role in the Wagner Group, he is responsible for serious human rights abuses committed by the Wagner Group in CAR, which include extrajudicial, summary or arbitrary executions and killings.'

[55] C Eckes, 'EU Restrictive Measures against Natural and Legal Persons: From counter-terrorist to third country sanctions' (2014) 51(3) *CML Rev* 869.

What's more, as with pre-existing EU sanction procedures, no trial or any process of adjudication is foreseen under the EU's latest thematic sanctions regime.

This raises the question of whether, in the implementation of the GHRSR, the highest possible standards in terms of judicial review are kept up. Arguably, proper scrutiny of the implementation of the regime ought to be integral to ensuring the legitimacy of the EU's horizontal sanctions instrument. This would require not just clearly defined and transparent criteria and a methodology for the listing and de-listing of sanctioned individuals or entities, but also a regular review of listings and appropriate legal procedures through which a listing can be challenged in order to guarantee a thorough judicial review and rights of redress.[56]

In cases of counter-terrorism sanctions, the ECJ has accepted that their aim is primarily preventive (that is, blocking access to funds that might be used for terrorist purposes), rather than punitive.[57] And since targeted sanctions are thus not considered criminal measures, the presumption of innocence protected by Article 48(1) of the Charter is not infringed,[58] and Article 49 of the Charter does not apply.[59] The preamble to Regulation 2020/1998 affirms respect for the Charter and in particular 'the right to an effective remedy, the right to defence, and the right to the protection of personal data', but in the case of the GHRSR it will be harder to argue that the nature of the measures, while temporary and subject to regular review, is purely preventive. After all, they clearly do 'imply an accusation of a criminal nature',[60] though not in the context of criminal proceedings.

Under the counter-terrorism sanctions regime, there is a requirement of a finding by a competent authority (judicial or equivalent);[61] and where persons are 'identified as responsible' for misappropriation of state funds in the context of country-based sanctions, this requires at least the commencement of criminal proceedings or a pre-trial investigation in the country in question.[62] In both situations the Council, in relying on such decisions taken by the authorities of a third country, must verify whether that decision was adopted in accordance with the rights of the defence and the right to effective judicial protection.[63] It is hardly surprising, given the different

[56] European Parliament, Resolution on the EU Global Human Rights Sanctions Regime (EU Magnitsky Act), EP doc 2021/2563(RSP), 8 July 2021, point 7.

[57] Of course, the consequences for the listed individual may be severe. See Joined Cases C-584/10, C-593/10 and C-595/10 P *Commission and Others v Kadi* ECLI:EU:C:2013:518, para 132.

[58] Case T-49/07 *Fahas v Council* ECLI:EU:T:2010:499, para 67: 'the restrictive measures in question adopted by the Council with a view to combating terrorism do not entail confiscation of the assets of the persons concerned as the proceeds of crime but a freezing of such assets as a precautionary measure. Such measures do not therefore constitute criminal sanctions and, what is more, do not imply any accusation of a criminal nature.'

[59] Case T-256/11 *Ahmed Abdelaziz Ezz and Others v Council* ECLI:EU:T:2014:93, paras 77–80, confirmed on appeal in Case C-220/14 P, ECLI:EU:C:2015:147.

[60] Case T-49/07 *Fahas v Council* ECLI:EU:T:2010:499, para 67.

[61] Common Position 2001/931/CFSP on the application of specific measures to combat terrorism [2001] OJ L344/93, art 1(4).

[62] Case T-256/11, *Ahmed Abdelaziz Ezz and Others v Council* ECLI:EU:T:2014:93, para 67.

[63] On counter-terrorism sanctions, see Case C-599/14 P *Council v Liberation Tigers of Tamil Eelam (LTTE)* ECLI:EU:C:2017:583, paras 22–27. On misappropriation of state funds the Court has recently strengthened its position: compare Case C-598/16 P *Yanukovych v Council* ECLI:EU:C:2017:786, paras 71–75 with Joined Cases C-72 & 145/19 P *Suzanne Saleh Thabet and Others v Council* ECLI:EU:C:2020:992, paras 34–40 and 46.

context, that the GHRSR does not require any prior decision of a judicial or otherwise competent authority; but since it is does not explicitly require any specific evidence that listed persons or entities are 'responsible', it is difficult to see how the 'solid factual basis' for the decision can be tested.[64] This is, no doubt, one reason why most of the listings so far have targeted persons and entities with clear links to the state, where official lines of responsibility can be more easily identified.[65]

III. LEGAL BASIS AND ADOPTION PROCEDURE

The GHRSR equips the EU with a new sanctions regime that not only has global reach but that also promises flexibility and speed. As with other horizontal regimes, the GHRSR provides a legal framework which can be triggered in specific cases. The Framework Decision 2020/1999/CFSP and Regulation 2020/1998/EU define the targeted (natural and legal) persons, their human rights violations, the kinds of restrictive measures to be imposed, and the procedures for listing and exemption. For the activation of the regime, all that should then be required is to graft implementing decisions and regulations onto the trunk of the GHRSR, thereby personalising the targets in the Annexes to the Framework Decision and Regulation. Yet, despite attempts to distinguish the decision-making procedures between the two phases,[66] the listing measures rest on the same legal basis and follow the same heavy procedure as for any other EU sanctions, thus requiring a Council Decision adopted by unanimity under CFSP powers (Article 29 TEU) and a Council Regulation adopted by a qualified majority vote (QMV) under Article 215 TFEU. The activation of the GHRSR may thus not be as easy as anticipated.

As for the alleged efficiency in getting thematic sanctions through the EU's authorising environment by decoupling the definition of restrictive measures from the EU's relations with the third country concerned, it is true that horizontal regimes like the GHRSR raise the bar for individual Member States to veto proposed listings, for reasons not directly related to the targeted persons and their objectionable conduct. This is important given the need for unanimity in adopting implementing decisions. Proposals by the Commission and others to make consistent use of the opening given by the third indent of Article 31(2) TEU to move to QMV for such CFSP decisions have so far not been accepted,[67] even if precedents exist for amending

[64] See eg Joined Cases C-584/10, C-593/10 and C-595/10 P (n 57 above), para 119.

[65] See Editorial Comments, (2021) 58(3) *CML Rev* 621–34.

[66] ibid.

[67] See eg Communication from the Commission to the European Council, the European Parliament and the Council, 'A stronger global actor: a more efficient decision-making for EU Common Foreign and Security Policy', COM(2018) 647 final, Brussels, 12 September 2018, 11; Proposal of the High Representative, HR (2020) 113, Council doc 12102/20, 19 October 2020, art 5(1); and a Commission declaration included in minutes of Council doc 12329/20, 30 November 2020. The latter's insistence on the use of unanimity was regretted by Belgium in a declaration in subsequent Council minutes: 'This requirement will hamper the impact of the sanctions regime as part of our human rights toolbox and as a CFSP policy instrument.' See Council doc 12329/20 ADD 1, 4 December 2020. In a similar vein, see European Parliament resolution of 8 July 2021 on the EU Global Human Rights Sanctions Regime (EU Magnitsky Act) (2021/2563(RSP)) P9_TA(2021)0349, point 1. C Eckes, 'EU Human Rights Sanctions Regime: Striving for Utopia Backed by Sovereign Power?' (2021) 26(2) *European Foreign Affairs Review* 219, section 4, discusses why adopting

listings.[68] Pursuant to Article 5(1) of Decision 2020/1999/CFSP, amendments to the list set out in the Annex will, upon a proposal from a Member State or from the High Representative, be adopted by unanimity in the Council.

IV. LEGITIMACY CONCERNS

Country-based sanctions inevitably put in question the whole relationship of the EU (and its Member States) to that country. While that may be exactly the point, as the adoption of a series of sanctions packages 'against Russia' over the war in Ukraine shows,[69] the EU's GHRSR was launched in an attempt to bolster the role of 'normative power Europe' by decoupling the protection of human rights from country-specific situations. The presumption was that by severing the link to the country where violations occur, horizontal regimes would make it easier to dissociate restrictive measures from the EU's diplomatic relations with the third country concerned. Yet, this presumption of depoliticising the EU's overall relations with a third country is flawed. This is not just because – as shown above – the proper implementation of the GHRSR impels the EU institutions to bring the state into the centre of analysis,[70] thus blurring the boundaries between the new thematic regime and country-specific sanctions and raising questions about consistency and complementary.[71] It is also because the back-listing of individuals and entities under the GHRSR does not prevent third countries from objecting and/or retaliating, thereby severely impacting bilateral relations, as famously shown in the case of China: on 22 March 2021, the same day when the EU listed under the GHRSR four persons and one entity deemed responsible for the reported mass detention and persecution of the Uyghur ethnic minority in Xinjiang Province,[72] China adopted countersanctions against 10 individuals and four entities in the EU, including a handful of Members of the European Parliament from across the political spectrum, the EP's Sub-committee on Human Rights and the Council's Political and Security Committee, think tankers and academics that it claimed 'severely harm China's sovereignty and interests and maliciously spread lies and disinformation'.[73]

sanctions under the GHRSR by QMV is one bridge too far. She engages with the move towards centralisation under EU sanctions regimes and addresses the legality of national alternatives to the GHRSR.

[68] Eg Council Implementing Decision 2018/1086/CFSP concerning restrictive measures in view of the situation in Libya [2018] OJ L194/150.

[69] See www.consilium.europa.eu/en/policies/sanctions/restrictive-measures-against-russia-over-ukraine/.

[70] See n 54 above and the accompanying text.

[71] Why were the first three individuals deemed responsible for their role in the detention and prosecution of Alexei Navalny (a Category 2 breach of human rights) not listed under the country-specific measures instead? Did the Commission and the Member States perhaps want to use the emblematic leader of the *Russian* opposition as a poster child to brand the new EU Magnitsky Act? Was the dispersion of restrictive measures (which extended to those held responsible for Navalny's poisoning, who were added to the EU's chemical sanctions list) intended to de-politicise the EU's relations with Russia over the attempted murder, arrest, fake trial and detention of President Putin's most important dissident (and subsequent recipient of the EP's Sakharov Prize)?

[72] See Council Decision 2021/2160/CFSP.

[73] See M Perry, 'China's Counter Sanctions on EU Targets', *EPRS At a Glance* No PE 690.617, May 2021. Shortly afterwards, the Swedish retailer H&M was all but dropped from China's digital platforms and Chinese consumers launched a boycott against other Western brands which announced that they would stop procuring cotton from Xinjiang.

These sweeping countermeasures led the European Parliament to effectively put the ratification procedure of the draft EU–China Comprehensive Agreement on Investment in the freezer, an agreement that the Commission and German Presidency of the Council had sought hard to conclude ('in principle') before the US administration of President Joe Biden took office.[74]

There exist several other arguments that militate against the rationale that underpins the GHRSR. Firstly, even if the GHRSR were to shift the target focus away from states and zoom into the culpability of the actual perpetrators, one might ask whether it is desirable for state-sponsored human rights abuses targeted by the EU to be obscured in this way.[75]

Secondly, the successful deployment of the GHRSR requires that its implementing measures fit into an integrated approach to the EU's external action. To that end, the Council needs to ensure that the designation of targets aligns with both the EU's overall foreign policy strategies[76] *and* those vis-à-vis individual countries like China[77] and Russia.[78] Furthermore, the High Representative, supported by the EEAS and in coordination with the Commission and the Council, needs to ensure the coherence between the GHRSR and the EU's other external policies (Articles 18(4) and 21(3) TEU), in particular those concerning human rights and democracy support, as well as coherence with the CFSP and the CSDP (Article 26(2) TEU). In the same vein, the GHRSR would need to be consistent with international efforts at cracking-down on grave human rights violations. This would require the Commission, the EEAS and the EU's missions and operations launched under the Common Security and Defence Policy (CSDP) to cooperate with external judicial institutions such as the International Criminal Court, the European Court of Human Rights, the Inter-American Court of Human Rights, the African Court on Human and Peoples' Rights, UN-assisted tribunals and other bodies, including the Office of the United Nations High Commissioner for Human Rights and international supervisory and monitoring bodies, the OSCE and the Council of Europe, all with the aim of gaining evidence for imposing sanctions and deterring serious human rights violations.[79] The challenge for the EU is to cohere the implementation of its horizontal sanctions regime, which presupposes a

[74] ibid. See also W Hu, 'The EU-China Comprehensive Agreement on Investment: An in-depth reading', *CEPS Policy Insights* No 7, May 2021.

[75] See Editorial Comments, (2021) 58(3) *CML Rev* 621.

[76] 'Shared Vision, Common Action: A Stronger Europe. A Global Strategy for the European Union's Foreign and Security Policy', EEAS, June 2016.

[77] European Commission and HR/VP contribution to the European Council, 'EU-China – A strategic outlook', JOIN(2019) 5 final, Strasbourg, 12 March 2019.

[78] Before Russia's full-blown invasion of Ukraine on 24 February 2022, the reference here would have been to the five guiding principles developed by HR/VP Federica Mogherini and endorsed by the Foreign Affairs Council in April 2016. A proper EU strategy for Russia will have to be developed for the post-war period.

[79] See eg Council Decision (CFSP) 2022/638 of 13 April 2022 amending decision 2014/486/CFSP on the European Union Advisory Mission for Civilian Security Sector Reform Ukraine (EUAM Ukraine) [2022] OJ L117/38, which provides support to Ukrainian authorities to facilitate the investigation and prosecution of any international crimes committed in the context of Russia's unprovoked and unjustified military aggression against Ukraine. The mission will ensure close cooperation with the International Criminal Court and with *Eurojust*, as well as with Member States acting in direct support of the investigation and prosecution of international crimes in Ukraine.

removal of the country link to serious human rights abuses, with the country-specific target focus of most of the external judicial, monitoring and supervisory mechanisms. Indeed, it is difficult to imagine how the EU would motivate the activation of GHRSR based on joint actions and investigations that lead like-minded states with similar Magnitsky Acts to adopt country-specific sanctions.

Finally, in the latter context, it does not suffice to argue that the GHRSR offers alternative punitive measures and operates differently in the autonomous EU legal order from the international conventions, courts and tribunals which it refers to.[80] If, indeed, the GHRSR is supposed to be an instrument of the European Union's global leadership[81] that encourages third countries to ratify universal human rights treaties and adopt similar restrictive measures,[82] then the EU should do better in showing exactly how its new thematic sanctions regime increases the effectiveness in terms of targets' behavioural change and human rights compliance.[83]

V. CONCLUSIONS

Setting up the GHRSR served a noble objective, that is, to create a tool specifically designed to confront those that commit serious human rights violations with punitive measures adopted by the EU, without further disrupting diplomatic relations with the third countries from which the targeted individuals and entities hail. The first year of practice with the regime showed the EU's commitment to make good use of the new instrument. In year two, however, the instrument lay dormant. The supposed innovative character of the GHRSR is doubtful. Even if the novelty of the thematic sanctions instrument lies in the grave nature of the human rights abuses it covers, the targets of such violations might as well be blacklisted under (existing) vertical sanction regimes, especially if a case-centric approach appears necessary to meet the high evidentiary standards set in the ECJ's case law. The blacklisting of those held responsible for the arbitrary arrest, trial and detention (GHRSR Category 2 abuses) of Russia's main political opposition figure, Alexei Navalny, is a case in point. In the absence of a threat of veto by one or more Member States, the adoption of restrictive measures under the country-specific sanctions regime would have been preferable to signal the EU's dismay at the evolution of Russian politics. Conversely, in the case of restrictive measures adopted against individuals held responsible for the mass suppression of the Uyghur population in Xinjiang Province, the unintended effect of the use of the GHRSR was immediately felt by the adoption of sweeping countermeasures by the

[80] See Editorial Comments, (2021) 58(3) *CML Rev* 632.

[81] See Council Conclusions on the EU Action Plan on Human Rights and Democracy 2020–2024, Council doc 12848/20, 18 November 2020, para 6.

[82] A number of candidate and other neighbouring countries have aligned themselves to the High Representative's declaration on the new instrument: Albania, Bosnia and Herzegovina, Montenegro, North Macedonia, Norway, Serbia and Ukraine.

[83] See eg NN Bapat and TC Morgan, 'Multilateral Versus Unilateral Sanctions Reconsidered: A Test Using New Data' (2009) 53 *International Studies Quarterly* 1075; F Giumelli, *The Success of Sanctions: Lessons Learned from the EU Experience* (Surrey/Burlington VT, Ashgate, 2013); and C Portela, P Pospieszna, J Skrzypczynska and D Walentek, 'Against All Odds: Explaining the persistence of EU sanctions on Russia' (2020) 43(6) *Journal of European Integration* 683.

People's Republic of China. It is noteworthy that, in taking aim at Beijing's – independently verified[84] – genocidal practices in Xinjiang, the EU refrained from branding the malign behaviour of the targets as GHRSR Category 1 abuses. This raises the question whether targets guilty of genocide and crimes against humanity will ever be hit under the GHRSR. If so, then probably only long after the occurrence of the events, when sufficient evidence has been gathered to hold up in court. Hence, no doubt, the absence – for now – of Mr Putin and his henchmen from the GHRSR list, whereas they *do* appear on the blacklist under the EU's sanctions against Russia. This amplifies the question about the value added of the horizontal human rights sanctions regime. The answer supposedly lies in the reduction of reasons for individual Member States to veto the adoption of restrictive measures against (former) incumbents deemed responsible for grave human rights violations. Absent reform of CFSP decision-making procedures in the Council that might not be such a bad thing. Indeed, seen from that perspective, the Council deserves an encouragement to make better use of the instrument and to strengthen its impact.

[84] For evidence materials and further references, see Judgment of the Uyghur Tribunal, led by Sir Geoffrey Nice QC (lead prosecutor of Slobodan Milosevic in front of the International Criminal Tribunal for the former Yugoslavia), 9 December 2021, uyghurtribunal.com/wp-content/uploads/2022/01/Uyghur-Tribunal-Judgment-9th-Dec-21.pdf. This judgment and other authoritative sources are referred to in the United Nations' 'OHCHR Assessment of human rights concerns in the Xinjiang Uyghur Autonomous Region, People's Republic of China', 31 August 2022, available at: www.ohchr.org/sites/default/files/documents/countries/2022-08-31/22-08-31-final-assesment.pdf.

Annex

A Declaration on the Rule of Law in the European Union – Helsinki Rule of Law Forum

SINCE THE SECOND World War, Europe has witnessed the benefits of rule-based order. Peace, prosperity, and progress have grown out of a shared commitment to the rule of law, both between individuals and states. As of late, these unprecedented achievements are increasingly under threat, as the basics of the rule of law, including the need for an independent judiciary, are questioned both at the heart of Europe and in countries beyond our borders. Time is of the essence. If backsliding on the rule of law occurs faster than corrective action, the passage of time will inevitably erode the rule-based order. We, the signatories of this declaration, urgently call on all leaders, in Member States and the EU Institutions, to uncompromisingly safeguard the rule of law in Europe. Our reasons are as follows:

1. The EU is built upon the rule of law. As the foundation of European integration, the rule of law reflects a specific vision for establishing a union among the peoples of Europe. This vision is intrinsically connected to the EU's values, listed in its founding treaty and drawn from the historic inheritance of Europe. These values include – besides the rule of law – respect for human dignity, freedom, democracy, equality, and respect for human rights, including the rights of persons belonging to minorities. Without the rule of law, these values are illusory. They are observed in a society in which pluralism, tolerance, justice and equality prevail. The rule of law is more than legality; it transcends the letter of the law. It is indissociable from the Union's values.
2. In joining the EU, the Member States have bound themselves, voluntarily and following their own constitutional requirements, to respect the key principles of liberal constitutional democracy. These principles informed the drafting of the original Treaties and have been reaffirmed upon each accession. In the course of membership, the Member States are obligated to continue respecting these structural principles, which underpin the Union's legal order and are articulated in the Treaty as founding values. These principles cannot flourish in the EU if they are not observed at the national level. In fact, the interdependence between the political and legal orders of the Union and its constituent members is such that breaches in Member States will inevitably put into question the EU's compliance with them, both internally and towards the wider world.

3. In the EU, as everywhere, liberal democracy, human rights, and the rule of law are interconnected at their root. There can be no real democracy without the guarantees of free and fair elections, individual liberty, and active civil society; there can be no effective protection of individual rights, nor of democracy, without independent courts, and there can be no rule of law without the democratic legitimacy of government and substantive fundamental rights. Under the EU Treaties, the rule of law's concept is premised on the respect of liberal democracy: freedom, consent of the governed, and equality before the law. Its antitheses, for which there is no room in the EU, are authoritarianism, the rule of the few, and arbitrary use of power. The principles of the rule of law are well known and enshrined in the EU's legal order, developed over seven decades by the Court of Justice and inspired by the national constitutional traditions. They entail requirements for the independence of the judiciary, the democratic character of law-making processes, checks and balances for the separation of powers, the freedom of the media, and the protection of minorities.
4. Not simply an aspiration, the rule of law is a set of legal principles essential for the practical realization of the rights of European citizens. The rule of law preserves the democratic state through legal certainty, which enhances the predictability of official decisions and allows people to plan their lives. Without the rule of law, the EU inevitably fails to function adequately and to deliver the public goods it is expected to guarantee. Moreover, it ceases to command moral legitimacy in the eyes of people in Europe and beyond. That the Union and its constituent Member States share a commitment to the rule of law is, moreover, the basis for their mutual trust. This trust can only exist under conditions guaranteeing that people and businesses are treated according to the law in all Member States, including when they appeal to courts in a State other than their own, and that their rights are protected.
5. The primacy of EU law is a core element of our common legal order. While the EU must respect the specific national constitutional identities of its Member States, this does not detract from the obligation of the latter to grant EU law its full effect in their national legal orders. Constitutional identity cannot serve as a pretext for departing from the fundamental principles of the rule of law. To ensure trust in the EU's legal order, the rule of law must be vigilantly protected at the Union level. Resilience against threats to the rule of law requires positive action on the part of the EU legislative and executive branches. The EU's values bind the EU's institutions, bodies, offices, and agencies, which must constantly strive to be exemplary in observing them. Adherence to the rule of law, in particular, safeguards the EU's decision-making processes and ultimately guarantees that all Member States are treated equally in the Union.
6. The Union and its Member States must be held up to equivalent standards as regards compliance with the rule of law. There is a need to understand the rule of law coherently. To this end, the EU should consistently have regard to the rule of law standards developed by the relevant Council of Europe bodies and mechanisms, such as the European Court of Human Rights, the European Commission for Democracy through Law (Venice Commission), the European Commission for the efficiency of justice (CEPEJ) and the Group of States

against Corruption (GRECO). In due time and form, the EU should accede to the European Convention on Human Rights to further safeguard the consistent application of the principles of the rule of law throughout Europe.

The EU cannot survive without the rule of law. Protecting it requires immediate action. Because of the overriding importance for sustaining liberal democracy and considering the magnitude of the task, its resolution cannot be left to the Court of Justice alone. Under threat, the rule of law cannot be guaranteed solely by the judiciary, but its preservation requires comprehensive legal and political action. The leaders of Member States, acting through the EU institutions in accordance with the procedures foreseen in the EU Treaties, as well as individually, must step up with urgency. The causes of Europe's rule of law malaise must be remedied decisively. Time is of the essence. Even as the EU confronts profound global challenges, the time for action to uphold the rule of law within the Union is now.

18 March 2022

Tiina Astola
Leonard Besselink
Steven Blockmans
Carlos Closa
Paul Craig
Inge Govaere
Xavier Groussot
Daniel Halberstam
Joni Heliskoski
Katalin Miklóssy
Paul Nemitz
Pekka Pohjankoski
Miguel Poiares Maduro
Juha Raitio
Allan Rosas
Werner Schroeder
Mirosław Wyrzykowski

Members of the Helsinki Rule of Law Forum

Index

www.ingramcontent.com/pod-product-compliance
Ingram Content Group UK Ltd.
Pitfield, Milton Keynes, MK11 3LW, UK
UKHW020809290926
15470UKWH00003B/1051

9 781509 955077